HEATH MATHEMATICS
CONNECTIONS

Edward Manfre

James M. Moser

Joanne E. Lobato

Lorna Morrow

HEATH

D.C. Heath and Company
Lexington, Massachusetts / Toronto, Ontario

HEATH MATHEMATICS CONNECTIONS

Authors

Edward Manfre is a former elementary, intermediate, and secondary school-teacher who has for over twenty years created classroom materials that encourage thinking. He has also conducted workshops on instructional methods and problem solving.

James Moser has been a teacher of mathematics at several levels, a teacher educator, a researcher, and curriculum developer. He is the author of mathematics textbooks for elementary, secondary, and college students. Currently, he is a mathematics consultant for the Wisconsin Department of Public Instruction.

Joanne Lobato has taught at the secondary level and has worked as a designer of mathematics software for grades K-8. She conducts research on elementary schoolchildren and frequently presents teacher workshops.

Lorna Morrow has taught at the elementary, secondary, and college levels, and has written numerous books, articles, and curriculum materials on topics in mathematics.

Contributing Authors

B. Joan Goodman, Puesta del Sol Elementary School, Rio Rancho, New Mexico
Lee V. Stiff, North Carolina State University, Raleigh, North Carolina
William F. Tate, University of Wisconsin, Madison, Wisconsin

ACKNOWLEDGMENTS

Editorial: Rita Campanella, Yoma Ingraham, Jane M. Melick, Susan D. Rogalski
Design: Robert H. Botsford, Victor Curran, Carmen Johnson
Production: Stonegate Associates, Inc.
Marketing: Jean Banks, Mary I. Connolly
Permissions: Dorothy Burns McLeod
Cover: Cover design, art direction, and electronic imaging by
Sheldon Cotler + Associates
Front cover photography by Arie deZanger, © D.C. Heath
Back cover photography by Ken O'Donoghue, © D.C. Heath

CONTENTS

● Cooperative Learning   ✳ Readiness for Algebra

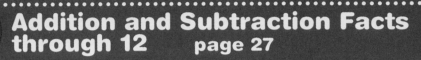

2 Addition and Subtraction Facts through 12 page 27

🐾 Cooperative Learning ✳ Readiness for Algebra

 Cooperative Learning   ✳ Readiness for Algebra

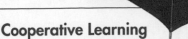

Cooperative Learning ✳ Readiness for Algebra

● Cooperative Learning   ✳ Readiness for Algebra

Cooperative Learning   ✳ Readiness for Algebra

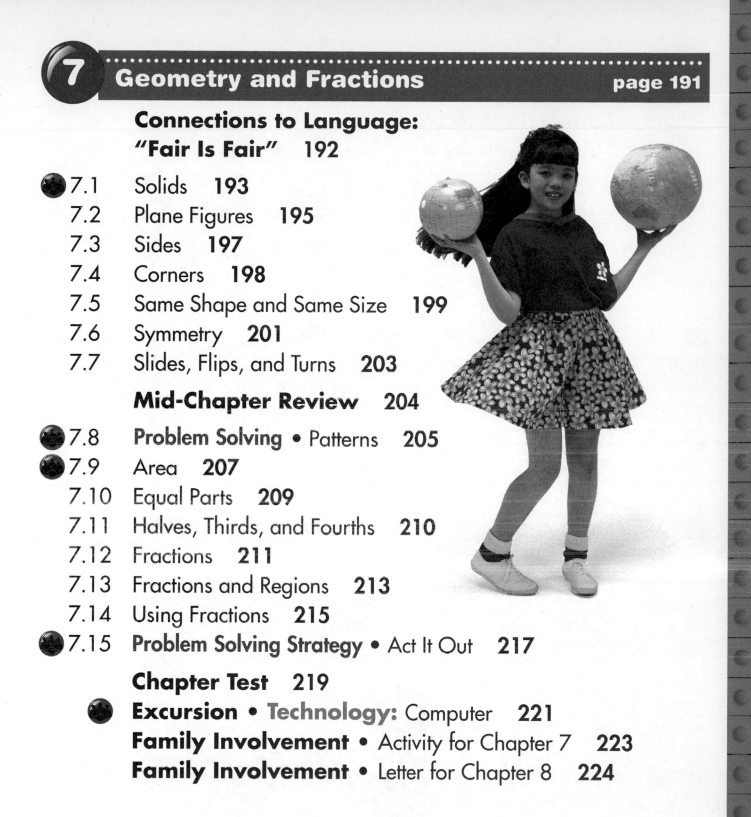

7 Geometry and Fractions

**Connections to Language:
"Fair Is Fair"** 192

7.1 Solids **193**
7.2 Plane Figures **195**
7.3 Sides **197**
7.4 Corners **198**
7.5 Same Shape and Same Size **199**
7.6 Symmetry **201**
7.7 Slides, Flips, and Turns **203**

Mid-Chapter Review 204

7.8 **Problem Solving** • Patterns **205**
7.9 Area **207**
7.10 Equal Parts **209**
7.11 Halves, Thirds, and Fourths **210**
7.12 Fractions **211**
7.13 Fractions and Regions **213**
7.14 Using Fractions **215**
7.15 **Problem Solving Strategy** • Act It Out **217**

Chapter Test 219
Excursion • Technology: Computer **221**
Family Involvement • Activity for Chapter 7 **223**
Family Involvement • Letter for Chapter 8 **224**

 Cooperative Learning   ✳ Readiness for Algebra

8 Subtraction of 2-Digit Numbers

● Cooperative Learning   ✳ Readiness for Algebra

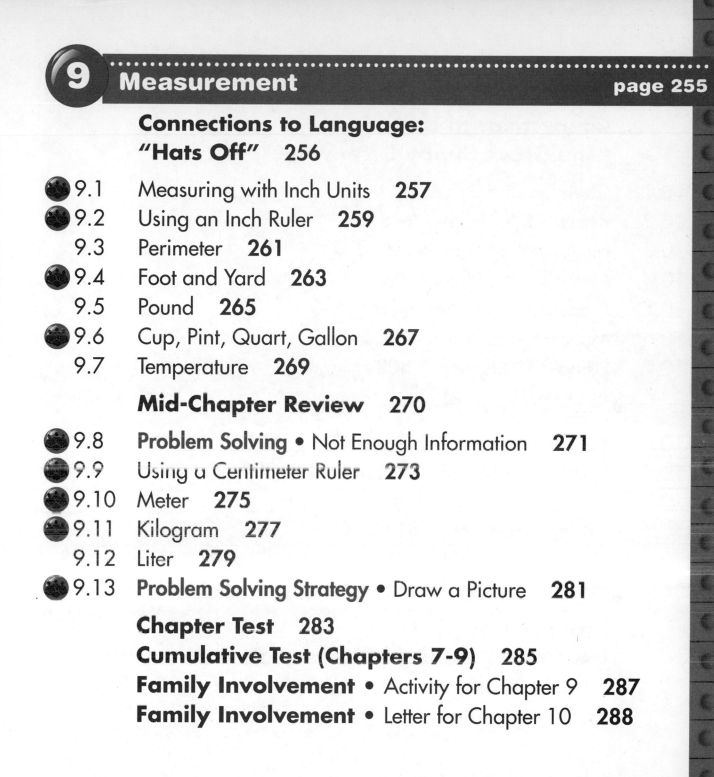
Cooperative Learning ✳ Readiness for Algebra

10 Multiplication and Division Readiness page 289

Cooperative Learning   ✳ Readiness for Algebra

11 Place Value through 1000 — page 323

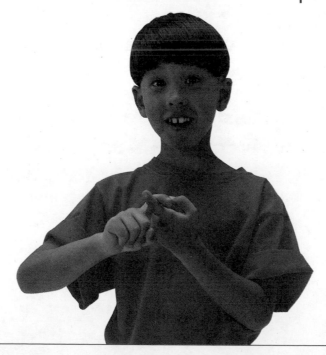

 Cooperative Learning   ✳ Readiness for Algebra

Cooperative Learning   * Readiness for Algebra

Note to the Family

Dear Family,

Welcome to the exciting experience of helping your child make connections in math with the *Heath Mathematics CONNECTIONS* program. By being a math model, you can set the example your child needs to be math motivated.

Over the school year, your second-grader will practice adding and subtracting, manipulating with time and money, and place value with increasingly larger numbers. Your child will also become familiar with measurement, as well as simple geometry and fraction concepts. We will also be gearing up for the more complicated functions of multiplication and division.

During the school day, your child will work with other children to solve problems, and they will discuss their findings in class. You can help your child build competence and confidence with newly acquired skills by practicing them at home. Throughout the year, we will be sending home enjoyable activities for you and your child to do together. These will help introduce or review mathematical concepts in a very applicable setting—everyday living.

Heath Mathematics CONNECTIONS stresses the fact that math plays a big part in everyday activities. Together, we can help your child relate mathematics to real life by bringing these concepts home. We hope you and your child both enjoy the *Heath Mathematics CONNECTIONS* program.

Sincerely,

In the next few weeks, your child will be reviewing counting and writing the numbers 0–10 and 11–20. Some of the skills your child will practice will include sorting objects into groups (sets); learning how to make a graph; and using the terms *more than, fewer than,* or *about the same as* in talking about sets of objects.

It is important for your child to see these number ideas being used outside of school. Have your child talk about and count objects while doing household chores, such as straightening up his or her bedroom (for example, number of beds, windows, books, shelves, drawers, and so on) or living room (chairs, magazines, tables, and so on). You could ask questions such as "Do you think that there are more drawers in the kitchen or in your bedroom?" You and your child could check the answer by counting.

Thank you for helping us review the numbers 0 through 20 with your child.

Your child might enjoy doing the following activity with you.

MIX AND SORT

You will need up to ten beans, buttons, toothpicks, pieces of macaroni, crayons, or any other small, available household objects. (Try to collect sets of at least three different kinds of objects.) You will also need a paper bag, a pencil, and small pieces of paper or index cards.

1. Put some of the objects into a paper bag and shake to mix them. Then spill the contents onto the table or the floor.

2. Have your child sort the objects into separate groups. (Your child might sort by kind first, then by color, then by size.)

3. Ask your child how many there are in each group and have your child write the number on a small piece of paper or on an index card.

4. Do the activity again. This time, take from or add to the objects so there is a different number of objects in the bag. You may also wish to switch roles and let your child put the objects in the bag while you sort and count them.

NUMBERS THROUGH 20

Listen to the story.

Name _____

You need crayons.

Color to show the pattern.

Numbers through 10

0	1	2	3	4	5	6	7	8	9	10
zero	one	two	three	four	five	six	seven	eight	nine	ten

Look at the picture.
Count each animal.
Write how many.

There are **fewer than** 4 ◯ .

There are **more than** 4 🥛 .

1. Draw fewer than four 🥛 .

2. Draw more than eight ◯ .

3. Draw more than five but fewer than ten 🍎 .

4. Draw fewer than nine but more than six 🥛 .

5. Draw more than three but fewer than seven ◯ .

Critical Thinking
Talk with a friend. Did you both draw the same numbers?

4 (four)

Graphing

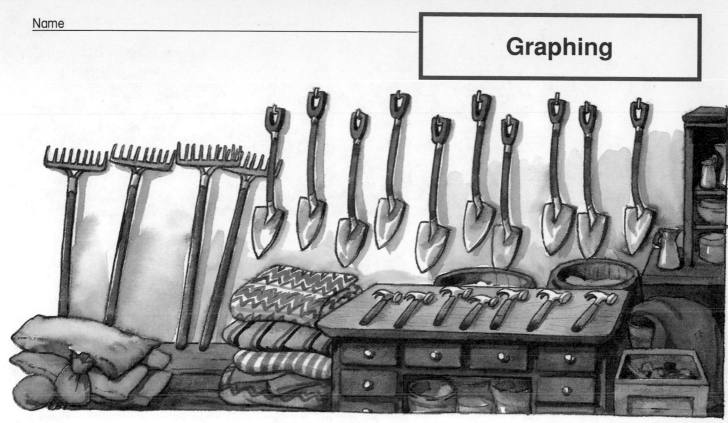

Draw the tools. Finish the **graph.**

Tools

	rake								
rake									
shovel									
hammer									

Use the graph. Loop the answer.

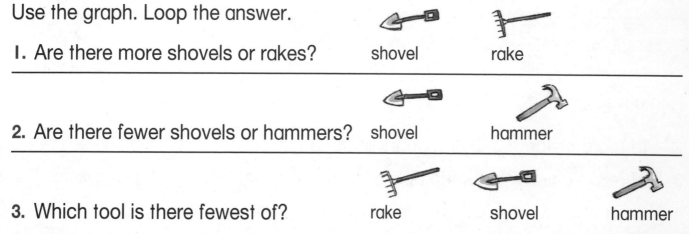

1. Are there more shovels or rakes?   shovel   rake

2. Are there fewer shovels or hammers?   shovel   hammer

3. Which tool is there fewest of?   rake   shovel   hammer

You need a crayon.

Work in groups.

You can pick I toy.

Loop the toy you would pick.

Ask 10 children which toy they would pick.

Color I square each time a child picks that toy.

Toys Picked

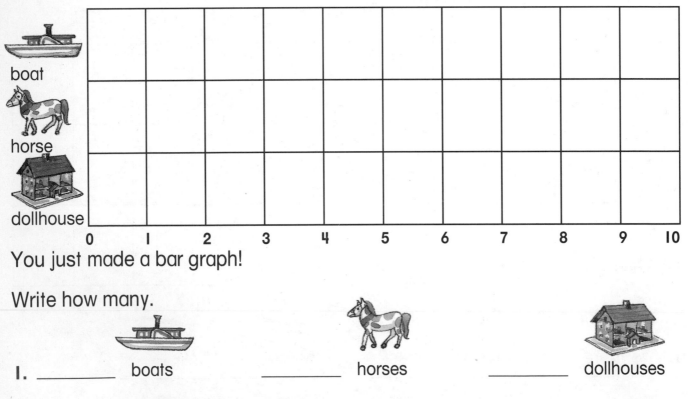

You just made a bar graph!

Write how many.

1. _____ boats   _____ horses   _____ dollhouses

Use the graph. Loop the answer.

2. Did more children pick the horse or the boat?   boat   horse

3. Did fewer children pick the dollhouse or the boat?   boat   dollhouse

4. Which toy did most children pick?   boat   horse   dollhouse

More Practice Set 1.2, page 387

Ordering Numbers through 10

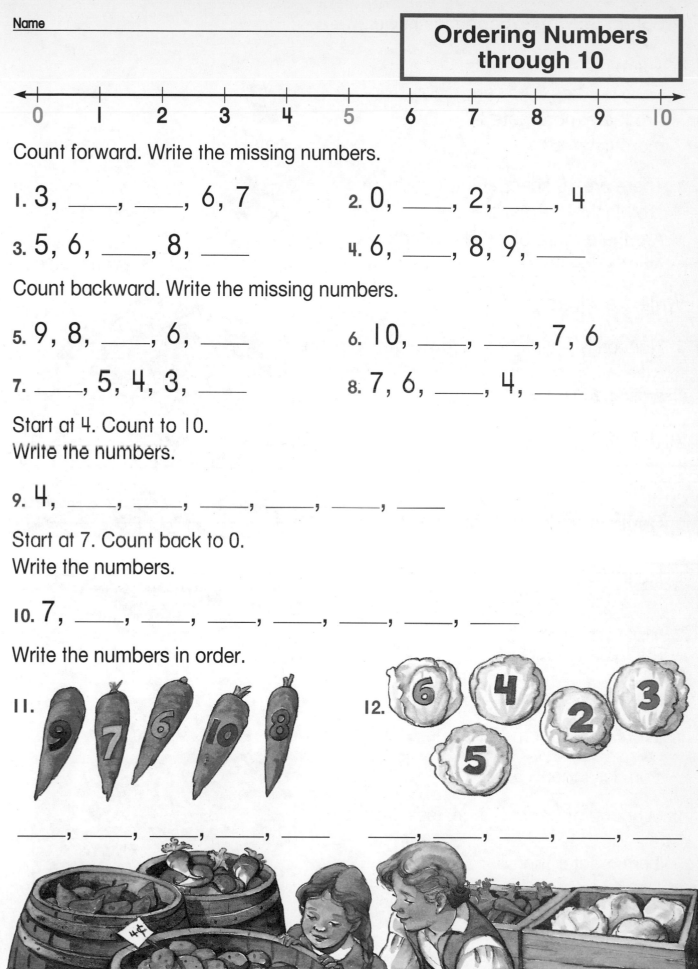

0 1 2 3 4 5 6 7 8 9 10

Count forward. Write the missing numbers.

1. 3, ___, ___, 6, 7

2. 0, ___, 2, ___, 4

3. 5, 6, ___, 8, ___

4. 6, ___, 8, 9, ___

Count backward. Write the missing numbers.

5. 9, 8, ___, 6, ___

6. 10, ___, ___, 7, 6

7. ___, 5, 4, 3, ___

8. 7, 6, ___, 4, ___

Start at 4. Count to 10.
Write the numbers.

9. 4, ___, ___, ___, ___, ___, ___

Start at 7. Count back to 0.
Write the numbers.

10. 7, ___, ___, ___, ___, ___, ___, ___

Write the numbers in order.

11.

12.

___, ___, ___, ___, ___   ___, ___, ___, ___, ___

Problem Solving   Loop the answer.

1. There are 4 flower pots.
   Each pot has 2 flowers.
   Are there more pots or
   more flowers?

pots   flowers

2. There are 10 sheep. Only 6 of them
   are black. The rest are white.
   Are there more black sheep or
   white sheep?

black sheep   white sheep

Write the answer.

3. Hannah is 4 years old. How old

   was she last year? _____

4. How old will Hannah be next

   year? _____

5. Cousin Tom is younger than
   Hannah. Samuel is older than
   Hannah. Who is the oldest?

   _____

....

CHALLENGE •Number Sense

1. What number am I? I come after 8.

   I am less than 10. _____

2. What number am I? I am less than 7.

   I am greater than 5. _____

3. What number am I? I am between

   3 and 6. I am 1 more than 4. _____

8 (eight)

More Practice Set 1.3, page 388

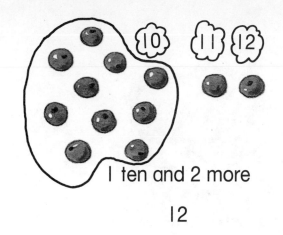

1 ten and 2 more

12

There are
12 in all.

Loop 10. Write how many in all.

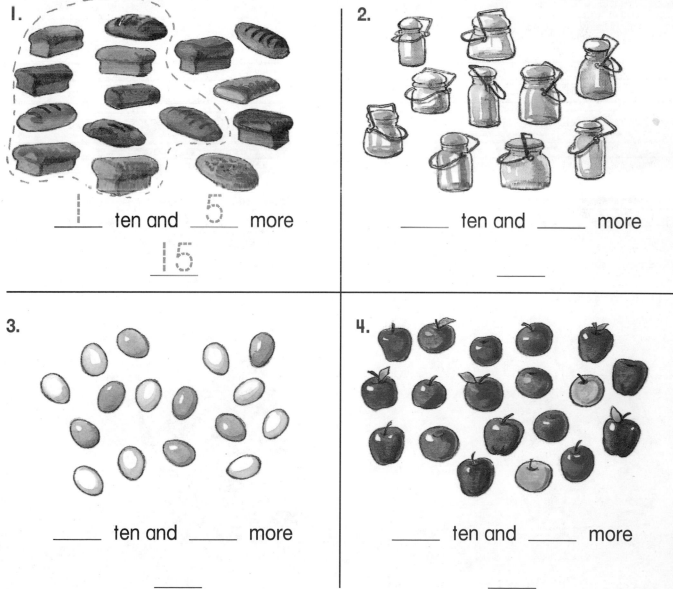

1.

___ ten and ___5 more

15

2.

_____ ten and _____ more

_____

3.

_____ ten and _____ more

_____

4.

_____ ten and _____ more

_____

Draw more to show the number.
Write how many tens and how many more.

1. 17

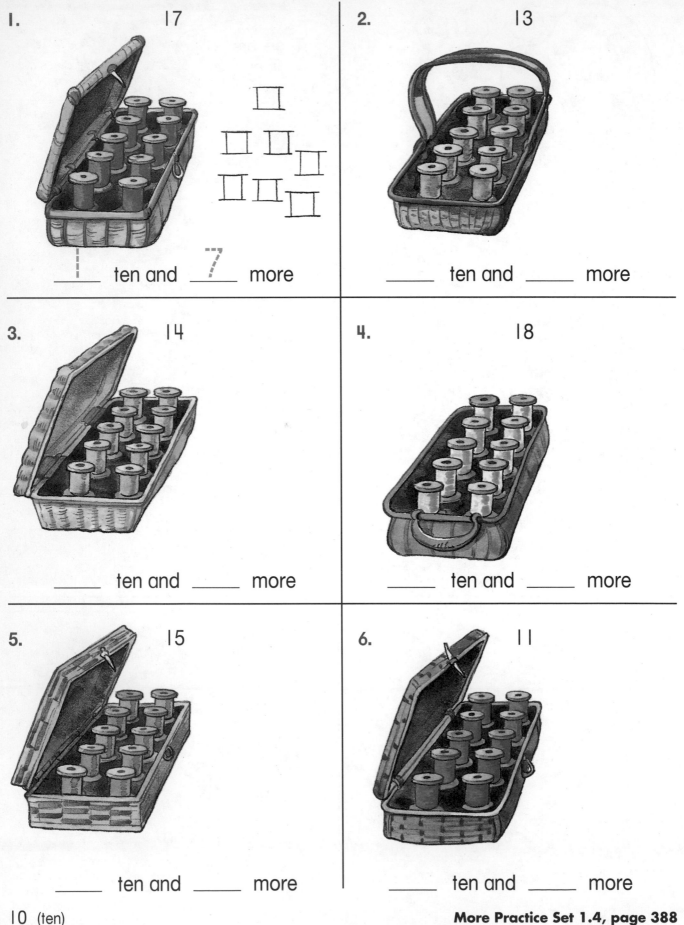

____ ten and __7__ more

2. 13

____ ten and ____ more

3. 14

____ ten and ____ more

4. 18

____ ten and ____ more

5. 15

____ ten and ____ more

6. 11

____ ten and ____ more

Estimating 10

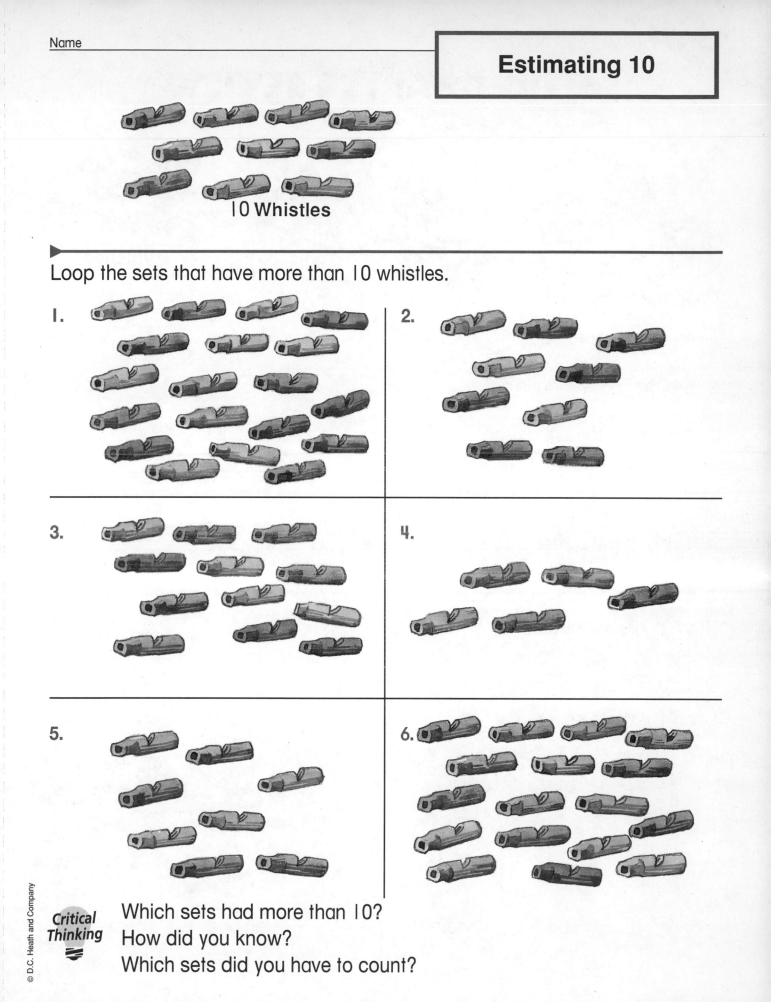

10 Whistles

Loop the sets that have more than 10 whistles.

1.

2.

3.

4.

5.

6.

Critical Thinking

Which sets had more than 10?
How did you know?
Which sets did you have to count?

MID-CHAPTER REVIEW

for pages 3–10

Buckles　　　　**Dolls**　　　　**Whistles**

Loop the answer.

1. Are there more buckles or whistles?　　　　buckles　　　　whistles

2. Are there fewer dolls or buckles?　　　　buckles　　　　dolls

3. Which are there most of?　　　　buckles　　　dolls　　　whistles

Write the numbers.
Start at 2. Count to 8.

4. 2, ＿＿, ＿＿, ＿＿, ＿＿, ＿＿, ＿＿

Start at 10. Count back to 4.

5. 10, ＿＿, ＿＿, ＿＿, ＿＿, ＿＿, ＿＿

Loop 10. Write how many.

6.

＿＿ ten and ＿＿ more

＿＿

7.

＿＿ ten and ＿＿ more

＿＿

Patterns

Name _____

Work with a partner.
You may use cubes
to find the pattern.

Draw the next picture.
Write how many.

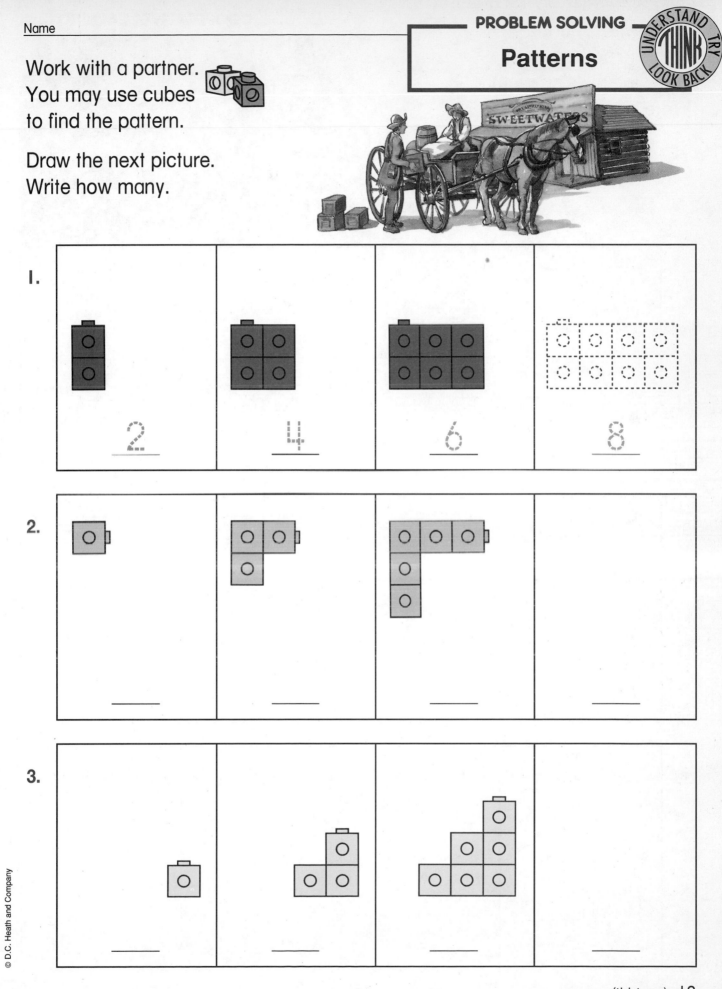

1.

2
4
6
8

2.

___ ___ ___ ___

3.

___ ___ ___ ___

(thirteen) 13

Work with a partner.
Find the pattern.
Draw the missing picture.
Write how many.

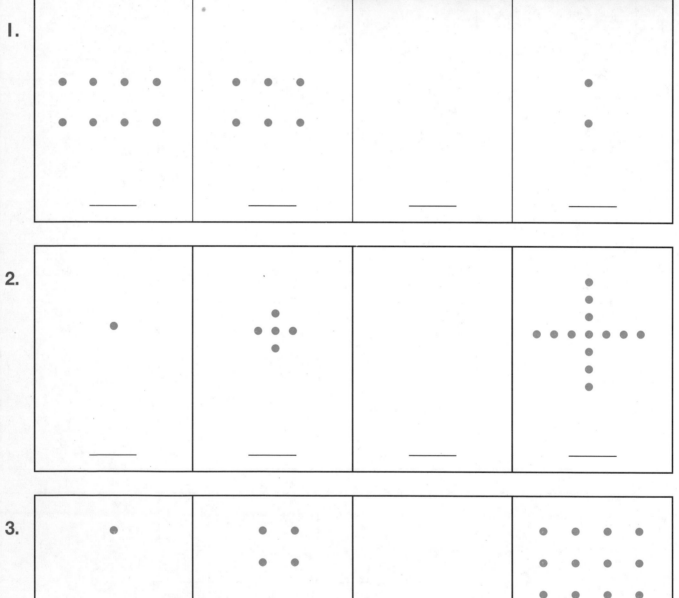

1.

2.

3.

Comparing Numbers through 20

1. Write how many.
Loop each number that is
greater than 13.

 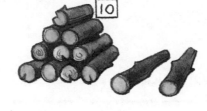 

14

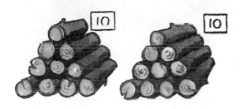  

 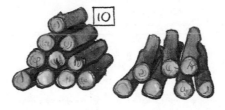 

2. Write how many.
Loop each number that is
less than 15.

Write how many.

1.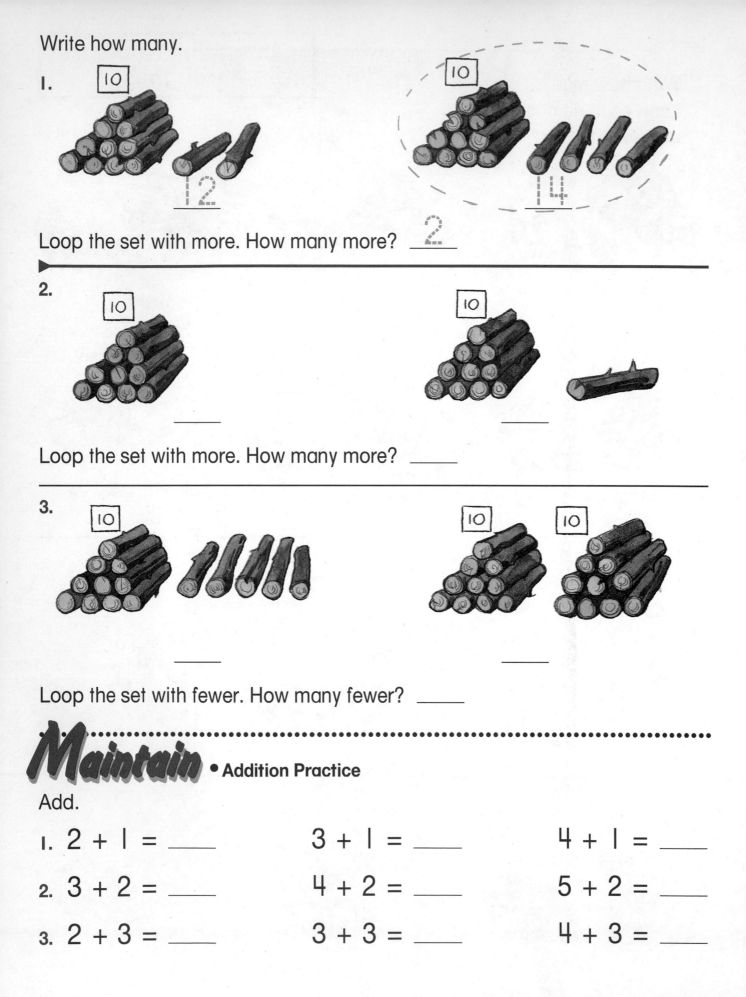

10

12

10

14

Loop the set with more. How many more? ___2___

2.

10

10

___

___

Loop the set with more. How many more? ___

3.

10

10   10

___

___

Loop the set with fewer. How many fewer? ___

Maintain •Addition Practice

Add.

1. 2 + 1 = ___   3 + 1 = ___   4 + 1 = ___

2. 3 + 2 = ___   4 + 2 = ___   5 + 2 = ___

3. 2 + 3 = ___   3 + 3 = ___   4 + 3 = ___

Ordering Numbers through 20

Answer each question.

1. The bird is on what number? _____

2. The flower is on what number? _____

3. The sheep is behind what 2 numbers? _____ and _____

4. What number is between the flower and 15? _____

5. What number is between the bird and 5? _____

6. What 2 numbers are between the ball and the bunny? _____ and _____

Loop the answer.

7. What is the ball closer to?

8. What is the ball closer to?

9. What is the flower closer to?

10. What is the bunny closer to?

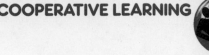

You need number cards for 0–20 and a paper bag.

0 1 2 3 4 5 6 7 8 9 10 11 12 13 14 15 16 17 18 19 20

Work with a partner.
Put the cards in the bag.

Numbers Picked

1. Pick 5 cards. Write the numbers here. Put the cards back in the bag. →

First Pick				
Second Pick				
Third Pick				

2. Pick 5 cards. Write the numbers here. Put the cards back in the bag. →

3. Pick 5 cards. Write the numbers here. Put the cards back in the bag. →

4. Look at your table.
Loop all the numbers that are less than 15.

5. If you pick five cards again, what do you think you will pick? Loop your guess.

   a. more numbers greater than 15
   b. more numbers less than 15

6. Try again. Pick 5 more cards. Write the numbers in order here. →

Fourth Pick				

 MATH LOG
Talk with your partner.
Was your guess right?
How did you make your guess?

More Practice Set 1.8, page 389

Name _____

PROBLEM SOLVING
Shapes and Numbers

THINK
UNDERSTAND
TRY
LOOK BACK

Work in pairs.
Here are some rectangles.

red

orange

yellow

green

blue

Write the color of the rectangle.

1. The longest rectangle is _____.

2. The tallest rectangle is _____.

3. The rectangle with the most

   squares is _____.

4. The rectangle with the fewest

   squares is _____.

Work in pairs.

You need a crayon.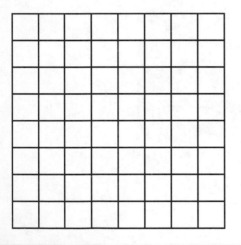

Write how many.

1.

2.

How many red squares? _____   How many blue squares? _____

---

3. Color 13 squares to show a T.   **4.** Color 12 squares to show an F.

5. Color 10 squares to show an L.   **6.** Color 17 squares to show an H.

CHAPTER TEST

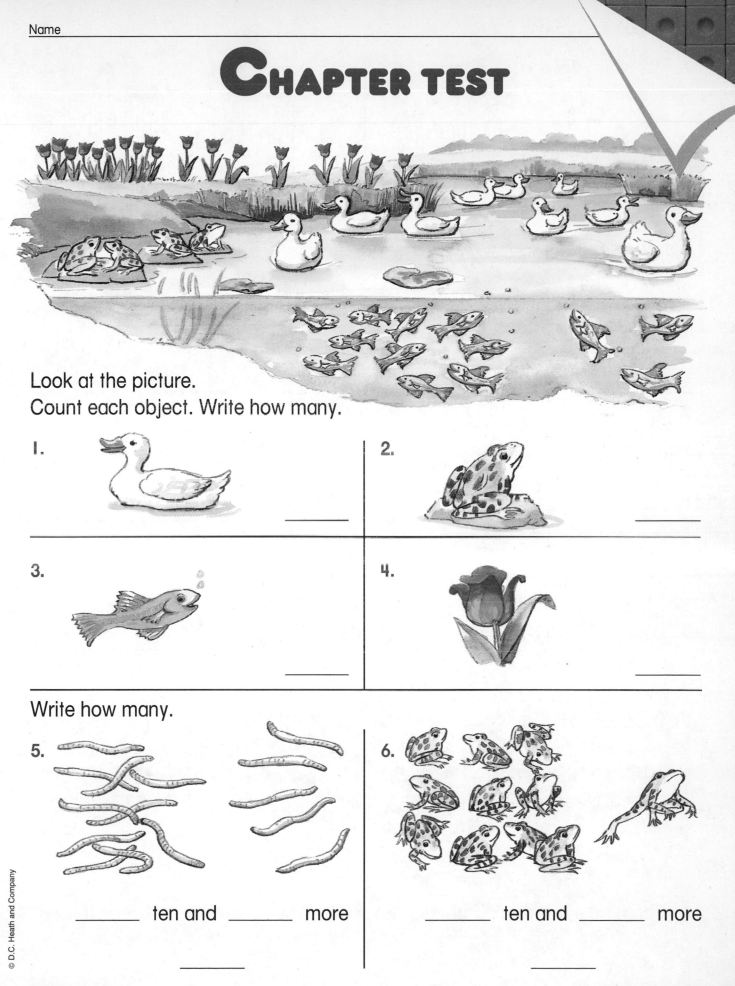

Look at the picture.
Count each object. Write how many.

1. _____

2. _____

3. _____

4. _____

Write how many.

5. _____ ten and _____ more

_____

6. _____ ten and _____ more

_____

Loop the set that has more.

7.

8.

Loop the set that has fewer.

9.

10.

Count forward.
Write the missing number.

11. ___, 2, 3, 4

12. 15, ___, 17, 18

Count backward.
Write the missing number.

13. 5, 4, ___, 2

14. 20, 19, 18, ___

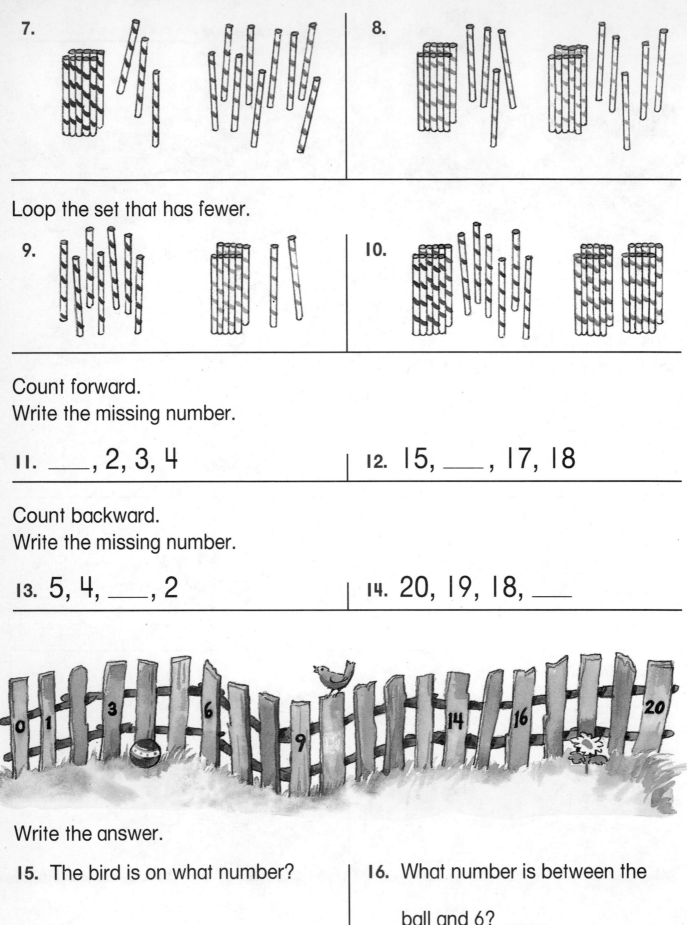

Write the answer.

15. The bird is on what number?

___

16. What number is between the

ball and 6? ___

Chapter Test

Excursion

TECHNOLOGY

Use tape and a piece of paper.
Work with a partner.

You can make the Logo turtle move.

To make the turtle:	You can type:
move forward 10 steps	F D 1 0 RETURN
move back 5 steps	B K 5 RETURN
turn right	R T 9 0 RETURN
turn left	L T 9 0 RETURN

Tape the paper onto the screen.
Move the turtle under the paper.
Write each step you type.

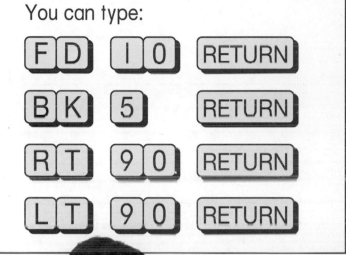

_____

_____

_____

_____

_____

_____

Computer

I. Tape the paper onto a different place. Move the turtle under the paper. Write each step you typed.

_____

_____

_____

_____

_____

_____

_____

_____

_____

_____

2. Look at the steps you typed.

Type  .

Move the turtle under the paper again, using fewer steps. Write each step you typed.

_____

_____

_____

_____

_____

_____

_____

_____

_____

_____

MATH LOG

Did you use fewer steps the second time? What did you do?

Note to the Family

Your child has been learning about numbers 0 through 20. This activity sheet gives your child an opportunity to share new skills with you.

KITCHEN COUNT

You will need a pencil and the chart on this page.

1. Take an inventory of specific food items in your kitchen with your child.

2. Help your child to complete the inventory sheet and make a shopping list.

3. You can substitute items listed here with other items, such as fruits or vegetables.

Our Family Kitchen

Item	How Many?
cans of soup	_____
cans of fruit	_____
cans of juice	_____
cans of vegetables	_____
boxes of cereal	_____
loaves of bread	_____

What things do you think you need more of?

_____

_____

What would you buy from the store? Write a shopping list.

_____   _____

_____   _____

_____   _____

Note to the Family

In the next few weeks, your child will be learning about addition and subtraction facts through 12. He or she will be introduced to different strategies which will help your child use these facts more easily. Some of these strategies include the order property (If you know 2 + 3 = 5, you know 3 + 2 = 5.); counting on by 1, 2, and 3 mentally; doubles plus 1 (If you know 4 + 4 = 8, you know 4 + 5 = 8 + 1, or 9.); counting back by 1, 2, and 3 mentally; and using a number line.

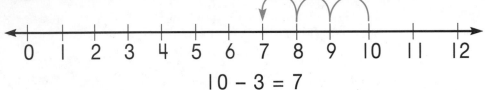

$$10 - 3 = 7$$

It is important for children to see addition and subtraction used outside of school. Your child can practice these skillls by participating in daily activities, such as determining the total number of family members attending a family dinner or the total number of friends attending a birthday party.

Thank you for helping us teach your child addition and subtraction facts through 12!

It might be fun to play the following game with your child.

EGG FACTS

You will need 1 empty egg carton and 2 different types of buttons or other small objects.

1. Put one of the same type of button in each of 3 compartments.

2. Ask your child to put some of the other type of buttons in other compartments.

3. Encourage your child to talk about the number of each type of button and the total number of buttons (the sum).

4. Vary the game by having your child put in buttons, and then you take some away. Ask your child to talk about the number of buttons taken away and the number of buttons left (the difference).

ADDITION AND SUBTRACTION FACTS THROUGH 12

Listen to the story.

Adventure at Bear Mountain

Name

List the ways out of Bear Mountain.
Write how many bears are along each path.

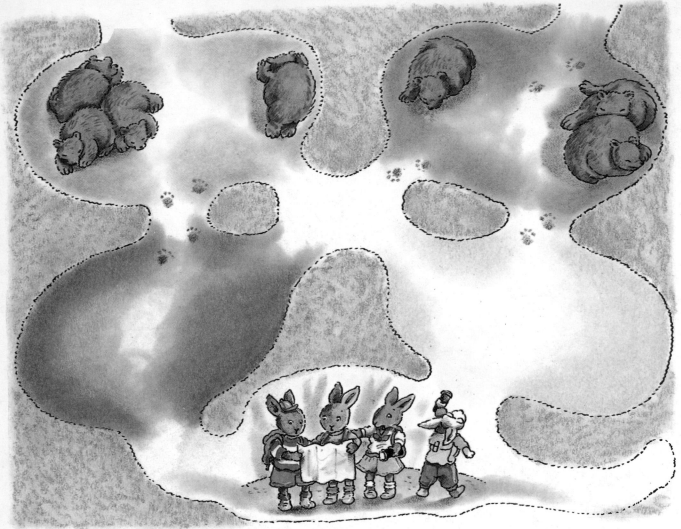

	Path	Number of Bears
1.	red ⟶ brown	
2.	red ⟶ blue	
3.	_____ ⟶ _____	
4.	_____ ⟶ _____	

5.   Which path should the rabbits take? _____

28 (twenty-eight)

You need number cards for 0–6, 12 cubes, and crayons.

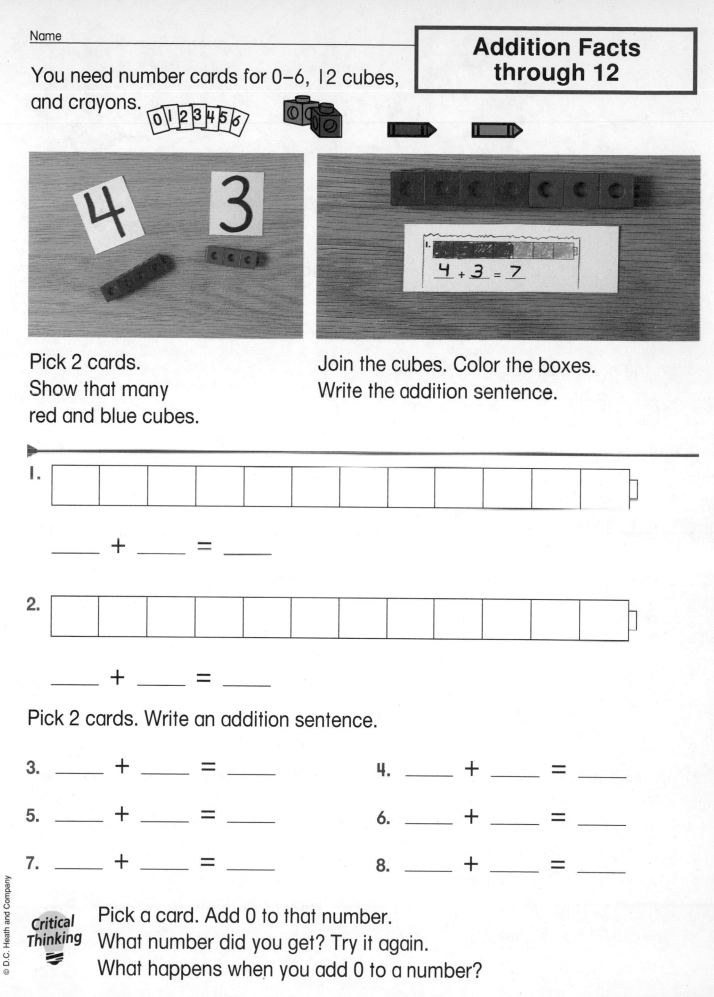

Pick 2 cards.
Show that many
red and blue cubes.

Join the cubes. Color the boxes.
Write the addition sentence.

$4 + 3 = 7$

1.

____ + ____ = ____

2.

____ + ____ = ____

Pick 2 cards. Write an addition sentence.

3. ____ + ____ = ____   4. ____ + ____ = ____

5. ____ + ____ = ____   6. ____ + ____ = ____

7. ____ + ____ = ____   8. ____ + ____ = ____

Critical Thinking Pick a card. Add 0 to that number.
What number did you get? Try it again.
What happens when you add 0 to a number?

You may use cubes.

You can write an addition fact 2 ways.

$$3 + 5 = 8$$

addend addend sum

$$\begin{array}{r} 3 \text{ addend} \\ +5 \text{ addend} \\ \hline 8 \text{ sum} \end{array}$$

Write the sum. Use cubes if you like.

1. $3 + 6 = \underline{9}$ $2 + 7 = \underline{}$ $5 + 7 = \underline{}$

2. $8 + 0 = \underline{}$ $5 + 5 = \underline{}$ $6 + 3 = \underline{}$

3.
$$\begin{array}{r} 9 \\ +3 \\ \hline \end{array} \qquad \begin{array}{r} 7 \\ +0 \\ \hline \end{array} \qquad \begin{array}{r} 3 \\ +5 \\ \hline \end{array} \qquad \begin{array}{r} 8 \\ +4 \\ \hline \end{array} \qquad \begin{array}{r} 7 \\ +5 \\ \hline \end{array} \qquad \begin{array}{r} 10 \\ +1 \\ \hline \end{array}$$

4.
$$\begin{array}{r} 4 \\ +4 \\ \hline \end{array} \qquad \begin{array}{r} 5 \\ +5 \\ \hline \end{array} \qquad \begin{array}{r} 6 \\ +6 \\ \hline \end{array} \qquad \begin{array}{r} 7 \\ +4 \\ \hline \end{array} \qquad \begin{array}{r} 8 \\ +3 \\ \hline \end{array} \qquad \begin{array}{r} 2 \\ +9 \\ \hline \end{array}$$

Problem Solving   Write a number sentence for each story.

5. There were 5 rabbits playing tag. Then 3 more rabbits joined them. They all played 2 more games of tag. How many rabbits played tag?

_____

6. The rabbits played for 2 hours on Monday. They did not play at all on Tuesday. How many hours did they play?

_____

Name _____

You need 10 cubes of one color and 10 cubes of another color.

Read the story. Act it out with cubes.
Write the addition sentence.

1.
> I see 3 red rocks and 2 blue rocks.

> I see 2 blue rocks and 3 red rocks.

___ + ___ = ___   ___ + ___ = ___

2.
> I pick 1 red flower and 7 blue flowers.

> I pick 7 blue flowers and 1 red flower.

___ + ___ = ___   ___ + ___ = ___

Critical Thinking Look at each pair of addition sentences.
What can you say about each pair?

Write the sum. You may use cubes.

3. 6 + 4 = ___   2 + 8 = ___   9 + 0 = ___

   4 + 6 = ___   8 + 2 = ___   0 + 9 = ___

4. 9 + 2 = ___   7 + 3 = ___   8 + 3 = ___

   2 + 9 = ___   3 + 7 = ___   3 + 8 = ___

© D.C. Heath and Company

(thirty-one) 31

Add. You may use cubes.

1. $7 + 4 =$ ___ $5 + 2 =$ ___ $2 + 4 =$ ___

   $4 + 7 =$ ___ $2 + 5 =$ ___ $4 + 2 =$ ___

2. $6 + 0 =$ ___ $4 + 5 =$ ___ $10 + 1 =$ ___

   $0 + 6 =$ ___ $5 + 4 =$ ___ $1 + 10 =$ ___

First add. Then write the number sentence in another order.

3. $6 + 5 = 11$ $8 + 2 =$ ___ $2 + 7 =$ ___

   $5 + 6 =$ ___   ___ + ___ = ___   ___ + ___ = ___

4. $5 + 3 =$ ___ $9 + 3 =$ ___ $10 + 2 =$ ___

   ___ + ___ = ___   ___ + ___ = ___   ___ + ___ = ___

CHALLENGE • Technology

You need a calculator. Add.

1. $25 + 8 =$ ___ $14 + 7 =$ ___ $32 + 8 =$ ___

   $8 + 25 =$ ___ $7 + 14 =$ ___ $8 + 32 =$ ___

2. $41 + 4 =$ ___

3. What do you think the sum of $4 + 41$ is? ___

   Add to check your answer.

You can **count on** when you add.

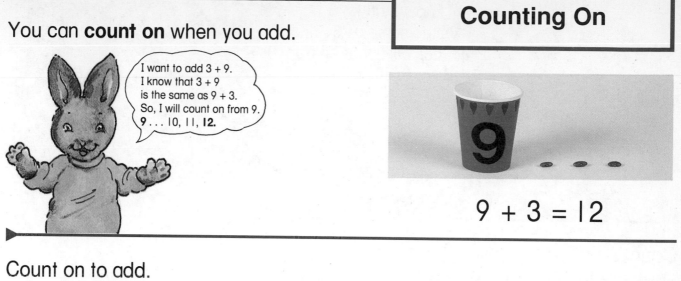

> I want to add 3 + 9.
> I know that 3 + 9
> is the same as 9 + 3.
> So, I will count on from 9.
> 9 . . . 10, 11, **12.**

$9 + 3 = 12$

Count on to add.

1. $7 + 2 = \underline{9}$

2. $6 + 3 = \underline{}$

3. $4 + 1 = \underline{}$

4. $8 + 2 = \underline{}$

Count on to add.

5.

9	3	6	8	7	10
+1	+2	+2	+3	+1	+ 2

6.

10	5	9	7	4	5
+ 1	+3	+2	+3	+2	+1

I want to add 4 + 8.
I know that 4 + 8
is the same as 8 + 4.
So, I will count on from 8.
8 . . . 9, 10, 11, **12.**

$$\begin{array}{r} 4 \\ +8 \\ \hline 12 \end{array}$$

Count on to add.

Remember, you can add numbers in any order.

1.
$$\begin{array}{r} 2 \\ +6 \\ \hline \end{array}$$
$$\begin{array}{r} 7 \\ +1 \\ \hline \end{array}$$
$$\begin{array}{r} 2 \\ +5 \\ \hline \end{array}$$
$$\begin{array}{r} 10 \\ +2 \\ \hline \end{array}$$
$$\begin{array}{r} 4 \\ +2 \\ \hline \end{array}$$
$$\begin{array}{r} 3 \\ +5 \\ \hline \end{array}$$

2.
$$\begin{array}{r} 1 \\ +10 \\ \hline \end{array}$$
$$\begin{array}{r} 3 \\ +7 \\ \hline \end{array}$$
$$\begin{array}{r} 6 \\ +2 \\ \hline \end{array}$$
$$\begin{array}{r} 8 \\ +1 \\ \hline \end{array}$$
$$\begin{array}{r} 2 \\ +9 \\ \hline \end{array}$$
$$\begin{array}{r} 7 \\ +2 \\ \hline \end{array}$$

3.
$$\begin{array}{r} 4 \\ +3 \\ \hline \end{array}$$
$$\begin{array}{r} 10 \\ +1 \\ \hline \end{array}$$
$$\begin{array}{r} 8 \\ +3 \\ \hline \end{array}$$
$$\begin{array}{r} 8 \\ +4 \\ \hline \end{array}$$
$$\begin{array}{r} 7 \\ +3 \\ \hline \end{array}$$
$$\begin{array}{r} 7 \\ +4 \\ \hline \end{array}$$

CHALLENGE • Problem Solving

Solve each problem.

1. There are 22 rabbits at a party. Later, another rabbit comes to the party. How many rabbits are at the party now?

_____ rabbits

2. Jake blows up 2 balloons before lunch. After lunch, he blows up 17 more. How many balloons does Jake blow up?

_____ balloons

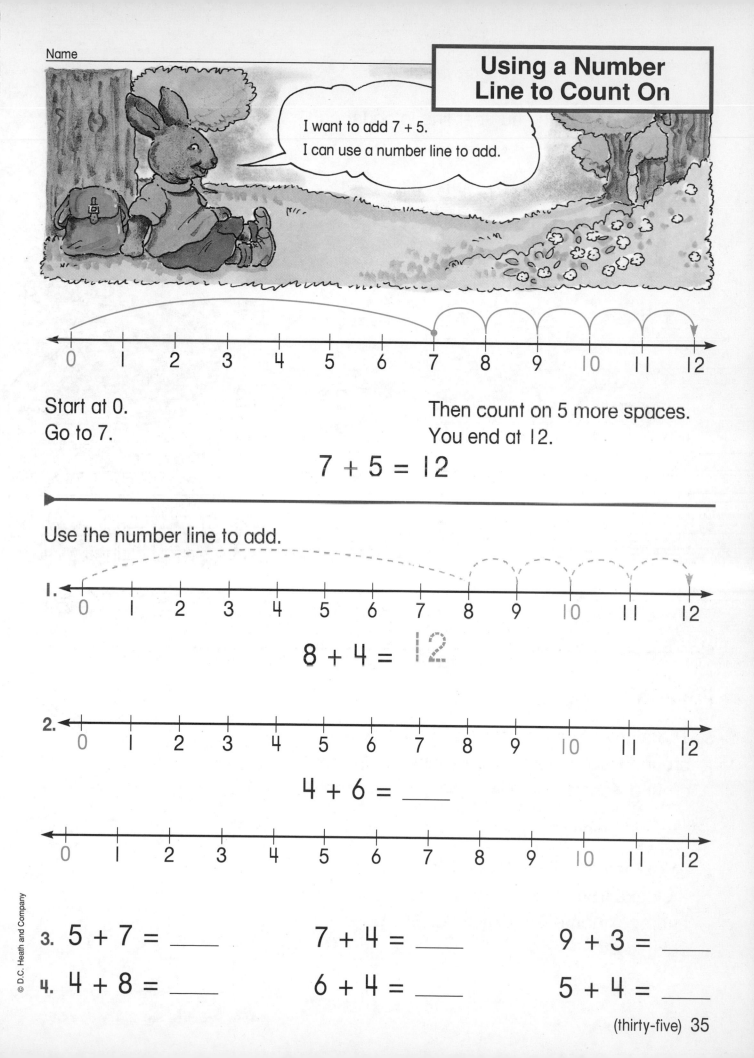

I want to add 7 + 5.
I can use a number line to add.

Start at 0.
Go to 7.

Then count on 5 more spaces.
You end at 12.

$$7 + 5 = 12$$

Use the number line to add.

1.

$$8 + 4 = 12$$

2.

$$4 + 6 = \underline{}$$

3. $5 + 7 = \underline{}$ $7 + 4 = \underline{}$ $9 + 3 = \underline{}$

4. $4 + 8 = \underline{}$ $6 + 4 = \underline{}$ $5 + 4 = \underline{}$

```
◄──┼────┼────┼────┼────┼────┼────┼────┼────┼────┼────┼────┼──►
   0    1    2    3    4    5    6    7    8    9   10   11   12
```

Add. You may use the number line to count on.

1.
$$\begin{array}{r} 7 \\ +3 \\ \hline \end{array}$$
$$\begin{array}{r} 5 \\ +7 \\ \hline \end{array}$$
$$\begin{array}{r} 4 \\ +8 \\ \hline \end{array}$$
$$\begin{array}{r} 10 \\ +1 \\ \hline \end{array}$$
$$\begin{array}{r} 4 \\ +7 \\ \hline \end{array}$$
$$\begin{array}{r} 5 \\ +4 \\ \hline \end{array}$$

2.
$$\begin{array}{r} 6 \\ +4 \\ \hline \end{array}$$
$$\begin{array}{r} 9 \\ +0 \\ \hline \end{array}$$
$$\begin{array}{r} 6 \\ +6 \\ \hline \end{array}$$
$$\begin{array}{r} 6 \\ +2 \\ \hline \end{array}$$
$$\begin{array}{r} 8 \\ +4 \\ \hline \end{array}$$

3.
$$\begin{array}{r} 2 \\ +7 \\ \hline \end{array}$$
$$\begin{array}{r} 3 \\ +4 \\ \hline \end{array}$$
$$\begin{array}{r} 8 \\ +0 \\ \hline \end{array}$$
$$\begin{array}{r} 3 \\ +2 \\ \hline \end{array}$$
$$\begin{array}{r} 3 \\ +3 \\ \hline \end{array}$$

4.
$$\begin{array}{r} 7 \\ +1 \\ \hline \end{array}$$
$$\begin{array}{r} 7 \\ +2 \\ \hline \end{array}$$
$$\begin{array}{r} 8 \\ +1 \\ \hline \end{array}$$
$$\begin{array}{r} 8 \\ +2 \\ \hline \end{array}$$
$$\begin{array}{r} 8 \\ +3 \\ \hline \end{array}$$

Problem Solving

5. There are 7 blue flowers and 4 red flowers around Karla's home. How many flowers are around Karla's home?

_____ flowers

6. Jake lives at 3 Pine Street. His home is 4 blocks from school. He walks to school and back home. How many blocks does Jake walk?

_____ blocks

36 (thirty-six)

More Practice Set 2.4, page 390

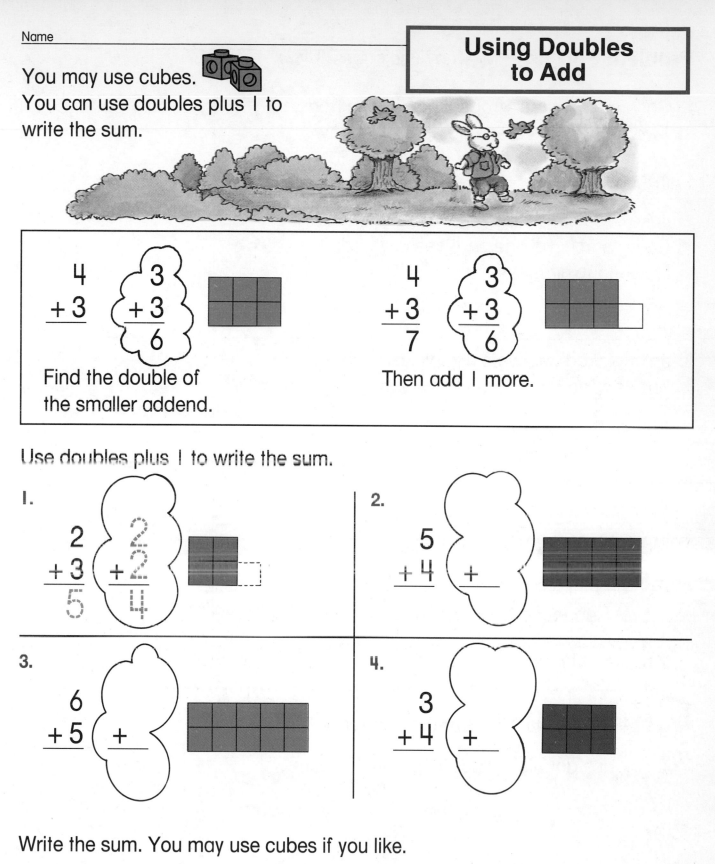

Name _____

You may use cubes.
You can use doubles plus 1 to write the sum.

$$\begin{array}{r} 4 \\ +3 \\ \hline \end{array}$$ $$\begin{array}{r} 3 \\ +3 \\ \hline 6 \end{array}$$

Find the double of the smaller addend.

$$\begin{array}{r} 4 \\ +3 \\ \hline 7 \end{array}$$ $$\begin{array}{r} 3 \\ +3 \\ \hline 6 \end{array}$$

Then add 1 more.

Use doubles plus 1 to write the sum.

1.
$$\begin{array}{r} 2 \\ +3 \\ \hline 5 \end{array}$$ $$\begin{array}{r} 2 \\ +2 \\ \hline 4 \end{array}$$

2.
$$\begin{array}{r} 5 \\ +4 \\ \hline \end{array}$$ $$\begin{array}{r} \\ + \\ \hline \end{array}$$

3.
$$\begin{array}{r} 6 \\ +5 \\ \hline \end{array}$$ $$\begin{array}{r} \\ + \\ \hline \end{array}$$

4.
$$\begin{array}{r} 3 \\ +4 \\ \hline \end{array}$$ $$\begin{array}{r} \\ + \\ \hline \end{array}$$

Write the sum. You may use cubes if you like.

$$\begin{array}{r} 4 \\ +5 \\ \hline \end{array} \qquad \begin{array}{r} 6 \\ +5 \\ \hline \end{array} \qquad \begin{array}{r} 4 \\ +3 \\ \hline \end{array} \qquad \begin{array}{r} 3 \\ +2 \\ \hline \end{array} \qquad \begin{array}{r} 1 \\ +2 \\ \hline \end{array} \qquad \begin{array}{r} 5 \\ +6 \\ \hline \end{array} \qquad \begin{array}{r} 5 \\ +4 \\ \hline \end{array}$$

Problem Solving You may use cubes.

1. Carla sees 5 green frogs and 6 brown frogs. Two of the frogs are jumping. How many

   frogs does Carla see? _____ frogs

2. Jake sees 4 birds on the way to the pond. Going home, he does not see any birds. How many birds does Jake see?

   _____ birds

3. Jake picked 6 flowers. He picked 2 more, but he gave them to Carla. How many

   flowers does he have now? _____ flowers

4. Rob found 5 rocks at the pond. Jody found the same number of rocks as Rob. How

   many rocks did they find in all? _____ rocks

5. Rob and Jody had the same number of rocks. Rob found 2 more rocks. Jody lost

   2 rocks. Who has more rocks now? _____

CHALLENGE • Number Patterns

You can use doubles minus 1 to write the sum.

$4 + 3 = ?$ →
Think:
$4 + 4 = 8$
3 is 1 less than 4.
So, $4 + 3$ is 1 less than $4 + 4$.
→ $4 + 3 = 7$

Write the sum.

$5 + 4 =$ _____

$2 + 3 =$ _____

$5 + 6 =$ _____

$8 + 7 =$ _____

$7 + 6 =$ _____

$8 + 9 =$ _____

More Practice Set 2.5, page 390

You need a crayon.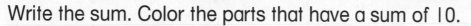

Write the sum. Color the parts that have a sum of 10.

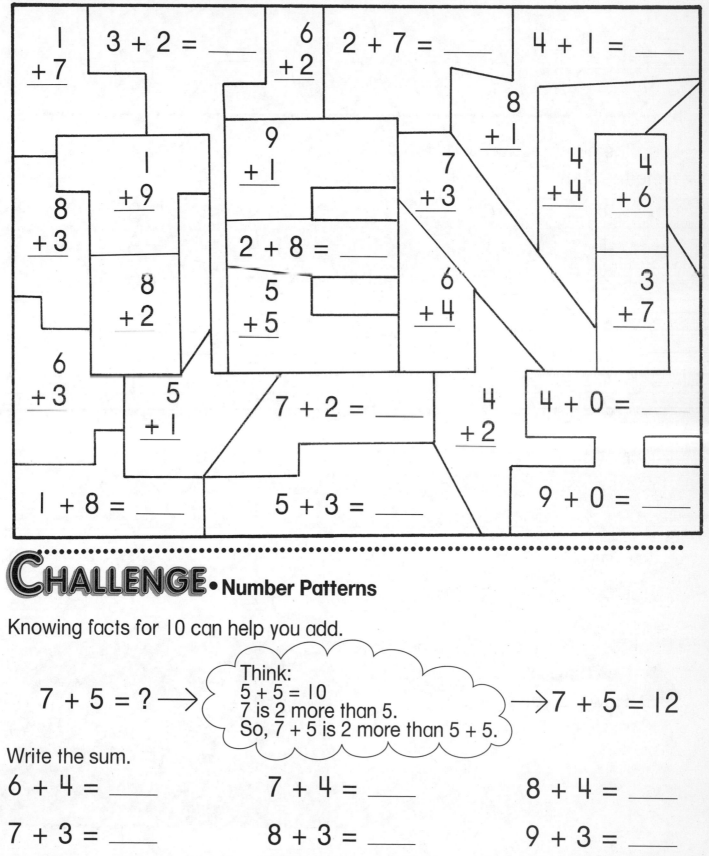

$$\begin{array}{c} 1 \\ +7 \\ \hline \end{array}$$

$$3 + 2 = \underline{}$$

$$\begin{array}{c} 6 \\ +2 \\ \hline \end{array}$$

$$2 + 7 = \underline{}$$

$$4 + 1 = \underline{}$$

$$\begin{array}{c} 1 \\ +9 \\ \hline \end{array}$$

$$\begin{array}{c} 9 \\ +1 \\ \hline \end{array}$$

$$\begin{array}{c} 8 \\ +1 \\ \hline \end{array}$$

$$\begin{array}{c} 7 \\ +3 \\ \hline \end{array}$$

$$\begin{array}{c} 4 \\ +4 \\ \hline \end{array}$$

$$\begin{array}{c} 4 \\ +6 \\ \hline \end{array}$$

$$\begin{array}{c} 8 \\ +3 \\ \hline \end{array}$$

$$2 + 8 = \underline{}$$

$$\begin{array}{c} 8 \\ +2 \\ \hline \end{array}$$

$$\begin{array}{c} 5 \\ +5 \\ \hline \end{array}$$

$$\begin{array}{c} 6 \\ +4 \\ \hline \end{array}$$

$$\begin{array}{c} 3 \\ +7 \\ \hline \end{array}$$

$$\begin{array}{c} 6 \\ +3 \\ \hline \end{array}$$

$$\begin{array}{c} 5 \\ +1 \\ \hline \end{array}$$

$$7 + 2 = \underline{}$$

$$\begin{array}{c} 4 \\ +2 \\ \hline \end{array}$$

$$4 + 0 = \underline{}$$

$$1 + 8 = \underline{}$$

$$5 + 3 = \underline{}$$

$$9 + 0 = \underline{}$$

CHALLENGE • Number Patterns

Knowing facts for 10 can help you add.

$$7 + 5 = ? \rightarrow$$

Think:
5 + 5 = 10
7 is 2 more than 5.
So, 7 + 5 is 2 more than 5 + 5.

$$\rightarrow 7 + 5 = 12$$

Write the sum.

$$6 + 4 = \underline{} \qquad 7 + 4 = \underline{} \qquad 8 + 4 = \underline{}$$

$$7 + 3 = \underline{} \qquad 8 + 3 = \underline{} \qquad 9 + 3 = \underline{}$$

You can add these numbers in any order.

```
  3        3         3         3         3         4
  1      + 3         1       + 1         1       + 2
+ 2        6       + 2         6       + 2         6
  6                  6                   6
```

▶ Loop the numbers you add first.
Write the sum.

1.
```
  3        5        2        4        3        5
  4        1        2        4        3        4
+ 2      + 3      + 1      + 3      + 6      + 2
  9
```

2.
```
  7        3        2        9        1        3
  2        4        4        0        6        4
+ 1      + 0      + 3      + 1      + 3      + 3
```

3.
```
  2        3        4        6        7        8
  2        3        4        4        3        2
+ 2      + 3      + 4      + 2      + 1      + 0
```

MATH LOG
How did you pick the numbers to add first?

More Practice Set 2.7, page 391

Name

You may use coins.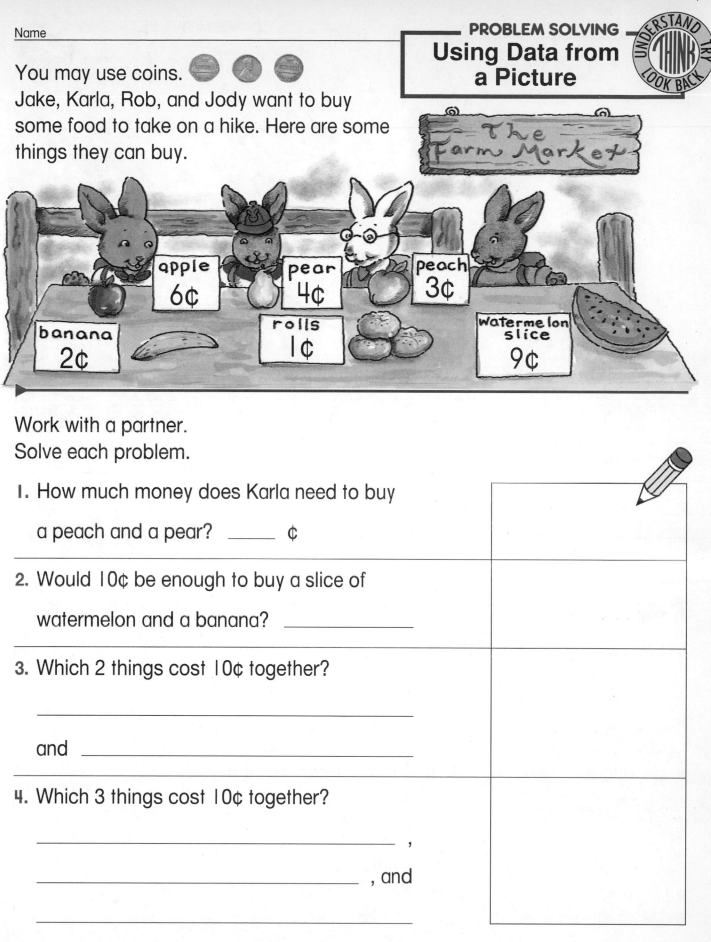
Jake, Karla, Rob, and Jody want to buy
some food to take on a hike. Here are some
things they can buy.

The Farm Market

apple 6¢

pear 4¢

peach 3¢

banana 2¢

rolls 1¢

watermelon slice 9¢

Work with a partner.
Solve each problem.

1. How much money does Karla need to buy

   a peach and a pear? _____ ¢

2. Would 10¢ be enough to buy a slice of

   watermelon and a banana? _____

3. Which 2 things cost 10¢ together?

   _____

   and _____

4. Which 3 things cost 10¢ together?

   _____ ,

   _____ , and

   _____

© D.C. Heath and Company

(forty-one) 41

Jody, Karla, Jake, and Rob have this much ── **COOPERATIVE LEARNING**
money left to spend.

Jody	Karla	Jake	Rob
11¢	7¢	5¢	9¢

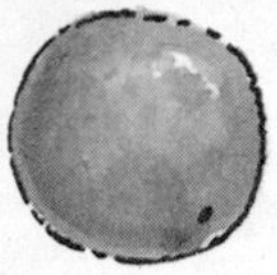

orange
3¢

tomato
2¢

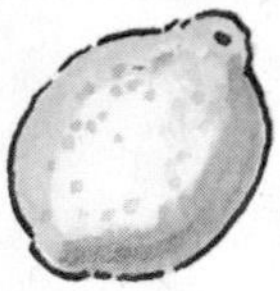

lemon
1¢

plum
4¢

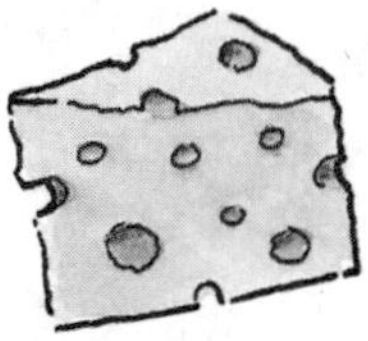

cheese
9¢

Work with a partner. Solve each problem.

1. Karla wants to buy a plum and an orange. Does she have enough money? _____

2. Does Jody have enough money to buy an orange and cheese? _____

3. If Karla and Jake put their money together, can they buy cheese and a tomato? _____

4. Can Jake buy a plum and a tomato? _____

5. What would you buy if you had 10¢?

_____

Making an Addition Table

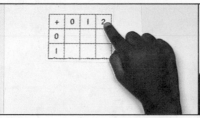 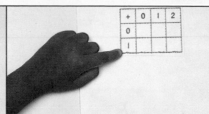 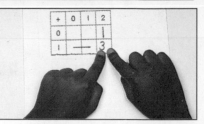

Put a finger on a number in the top row.

Put a finger on a number in the side row.

Move your fingers across and down until they meet. Write the sum. 2 + 1 = 3

Complete the addition table.

+	0	1	2	3	4	5	6
0							
1			3				
2						7	
3							
4			6				
5							
6							

What pattern do you see in the blue boxes?
What pattern do you see in the red boxes?

MID-CHAPTER REVIEW

for pages 29–42

Write the sum.

1. $7 + 5 =$ _____ $0 + 9 =$ _____ $8 + 2 =$ _____

2. $5 + 5 =$ _____ $3 + 8 =$ _____ $10 + 1 =$ _____

3.
$$\begin{array}{cc} 4 \\ +7 \\ \hline \end{array} \quad \begin{array}{cc} 5 \\ +6 \\ \hline \end{array} \quad \begin{array}{cc} 6 \\ +6 \\ \hline \end{array} \quad \begin{array}{cc} 4 \\ +2 \\ \hline \end{array} \quad \begin{array}{cc} 1 \\ +9 \\ \hline \end{array} \quad \begin{array}{cc} 10 \\ +\ 2 \\ \hline \end{array}$$

4.
$$\begin{array}{cc} 9 \\ +3 \\ \hline \end{array} \quad \begin{array}{cc} 2 \\ +2 \\ \hline \end{array} \quad \begin{array}{cc} 5 \\ +4 \\ \hline \end{array} \quad \begin{array}{cc} 3 \\ +1 \\ \hline \end{array} \quad \begin{array}{cc} 6 \\ +2 \\ \hline \end{array} \quad \begin{array}{cc} 3 \\ +3 \\ \hline \end{array}$$

5.
$$\begin{array}{cc} 3 \\ 4 \\ +3 \\ \hline \end{array} \quad \begin{array}{cc} 5 \\ 4 \\ +2 \\ \hline \end{array} \quad \begin{array}{cc} 9 \\ 0 \\ +3 \\ \hline \end{array} \quad \begin{array}{cc} 4 \\ 2 \\ +4 \\ \hline \end{array} \quad \begin{array}{cc} 2 \\ 3 \\ +5 \\ \hline \end{array} \quad \begin{array}{cc} 1 \\ 2 \\ +6 \\ \hline \end{array}$$

Problem Solving

6. Jake, Rob, and Jody bring chairs for the play. Jake brings 2 chairs. So does Jody. Rob brings 3 chairs. How many chairs do

   they bring? _____ chairs

7. The rabbits need flowers for the play. Jody brings 6 tulips. Rob brings 4 roses. How many flowers do Rob and Jody bring?

   _____ flowers

Name _____

Making Both Sides the Same

You can make both pots the same.

$$4 = 3 + 1$$

An **equal sign** means both sides are the same.
4 is the same as 3 plus 1.

▶

Draw flowers to make the pots the same.
Write a number sentence.

1. ___7___ = ___5___ + ___2___

2. _____ = _____ + _____

3. _____ = _____ + _____

4. _____ = _____ + _____

© D.C. Heath and Company

(forty-five) 45

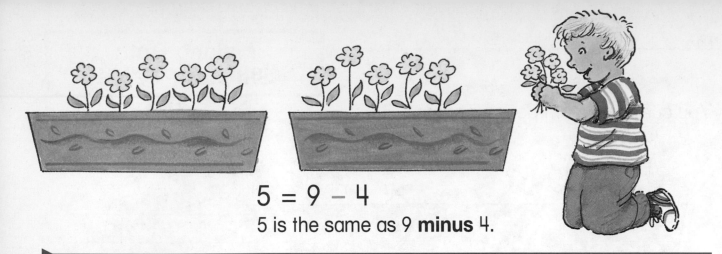

$$5 = 9 - 4$$
5 is the same as 9 **minus** 4.

Cross out flowers to make the pots the same.
Write a number sentence.

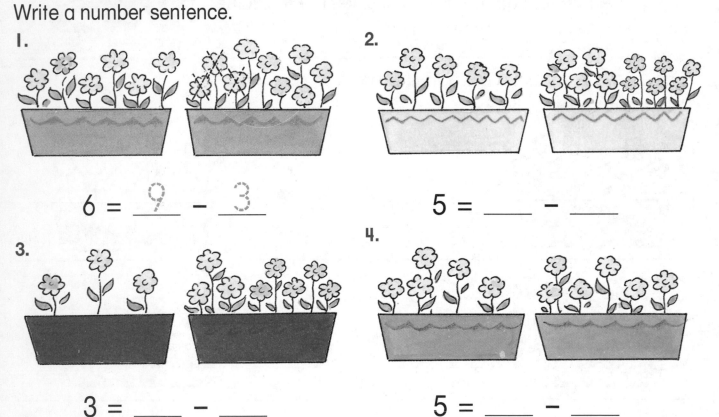

1.

$6 = \underline{9} - \underline{3}$

2.

$5 = \underline{} - \underline{}$

3.

$3 = \underline{} - \underline{}$

4.

$5 = \underline{} - \underline{}$

Problem Solving

5. Jody picks 7 cards. Karla picks 5 cards.
They need the same number of cards to play
the game. What can they do?

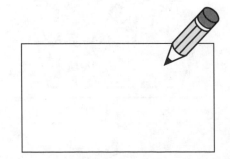

_____

MATH LOG
What does an equal sign mean?

Name _____

You need beans. 🫘🫘

Work with a partner.
Take turns.

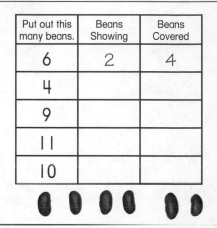

Put out this many beans.	Beans Showing	Beans Covered
6		
4		
9		
11		
10		

Put out this many beans.	Beans Showing	Beans Covered
6	2	
4		
9		
11		
10		

Put out this many beans.	Beans Showing	Beans Covered
6	2	4
4		
9		
11		
10		

Put out this many beans. Tell your partner to look away.

Cover some beans. Write how many are still showing. Your partner looks and guesses how many are covered.

Uncover the beans to check. Write how many.

▶

	Put out this many beans.	Beans Showing	Beans Covered
1.	6	2	4
2.	4		
3.	9		
4.	11		
5.	10		

Critical Thinking How did you know how many beans were covered?

3 plus how many more equals 5?

$3 + \underline{\ 2\ } = 5$

Draw the counters.
Complete the number sentence.

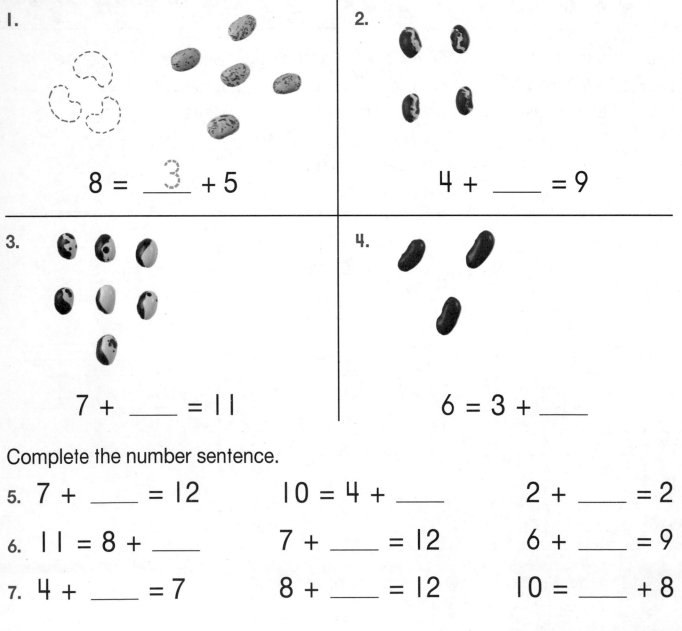

1.

$8 = \underline{\ 3\ } + 5$

2.

$4 + \underline{\quad} = 9$

3.

$7 + \underline{\quad} = 11$

4.

$6 = 3 + \underline{\quad}$

Complete the number sentence.

5. $7 + \underline{\quad} = 12$ $\qquad 10 = 4 + \underline{\quad}$ $\qquad 2 + \underline{\quad} = 2$

6. $11 = 8 + \underline{\quad}$ $\qquad 7 + \underline{\quad} = 12$ $\qquad 6 + \underline{\quad} = 9$

7. $4 + \underline{\quad} = 7$ $\qquad 8 + \underline{\quad} = 12$ $\qquad 10 = \underline{\quad} + 8$

More Practice Set 2.11, page 391

You need number cards for 0–6 and 12 cubes.

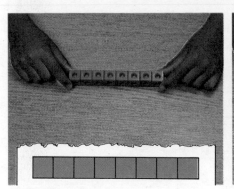

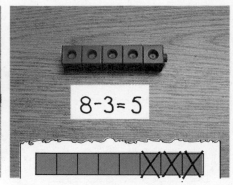

Count how many boxes. Put that many cubes together.

Pick a card. Take away that many cubes.

8-3=5

Cross out that many boxes. Count the boxes left. Write a subtraction sentence.

I.

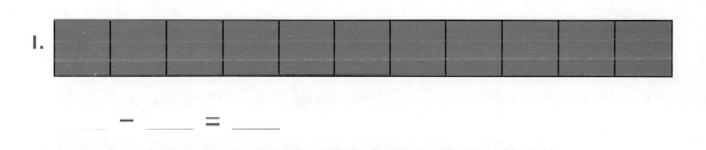

___ – ___ = ___

2.

___ – ___ = ___

Pick a card. Complete the subtraction sentence.

3. 7 – ___ = ___   4. 12 – ___ = ___

5. 10 – ___ = ___   6. 8 – ___ = ___

7. 11 – ___ = ___   8. 9 – ___ = ___

Critical Thinking Start with 8 cubes. Take away 0 cubes.
Start with 6 cubes. Take away 0 cubes.
What happened?

You know how to write an addition fact 2 ways.	You can also write a subtraction fact 2 ways.

$$3 + 4 = 7 \qquad \begin{array}{r} 3 \\ + 4 \\ \hline 7 \end{array}$$

sum   sum

$$5 - 2 = 3 \qquad \begin{array}{r} 5 \\ - 2 \\ \hline 3 \end{array}$$

difference   difference

Write the sum or difference. You may use cubes.

watch the signs

1. $5 - 4 = \underline{1}$ $8 - 1 = \underline{\hspace{1cm}}$ $6 + 3 = \underline{\hspace{1cm}}$

2. $7 + 5 = \underline{\hspace{1cm}}$ $2 + 8 = \underline{\hspace{1cm}}$ $10 - 4 = \underline{\hspace{1cm}}$

3.
$$\begin{array}{r} 2 \\ - 2 \\ \hline \end{array} \quad \begin{array}{r} 12 \\ + 0 \\ \hline \end{array} \quad \begin{array}{r} 8 \\ - 5 \\ \hline \end{array} \quad \begin{array}{r} 12 \\ - 10 \\ \hline \end{array} \quad \begin{array}{r} 9 \\ + 3 \\ \hline \end{array} \quad \begin{array}{r} 7 \\ - 5 \\ \hline \end{array}$$

4.
$$\begin{array}{r} 11 \\ - 6 \\ \hline \end{array} \quad \begin{array}{r} 9 \\ - 3 \\ \hline \end{array} \quad \begin{array}{r} 4 \\ + 5 \\ \hline \end{array} \quad \begin{array}{r} 4 \\ - 0 \\ \hline \end{array} \quad \begin{array}{r} 11 \\ - 8 \\ \hline \end{array} \quad \begin{array}{r} 5 \\ + 6 \\ \hline \end{array}$$

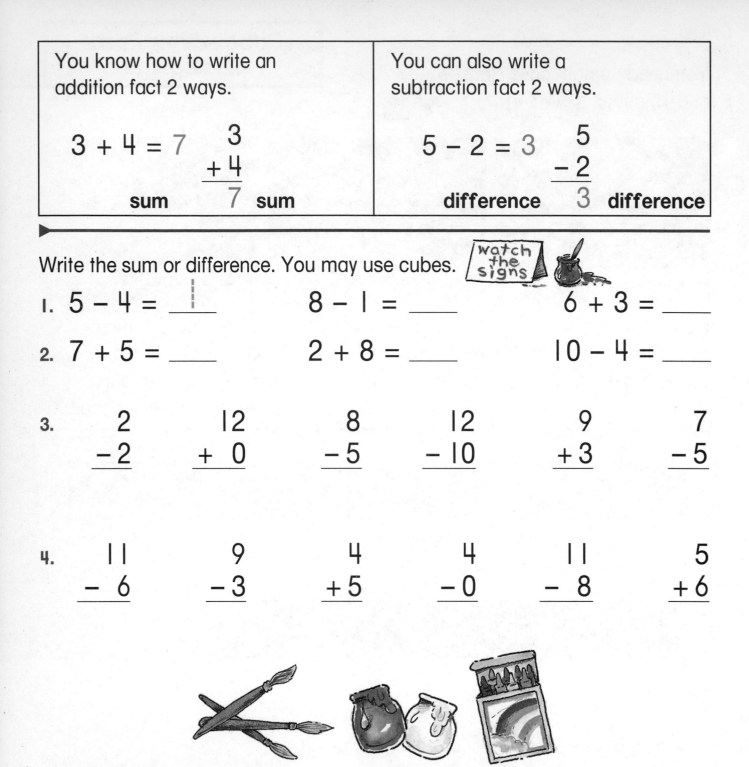

Problem Solving   Write a number sentence for each story.

5. Rob takes 3 brushes from the shelf. There were 11 brushes. How many brushes are on the shelf now?

6. Jody paints 4 trees. Jake paints 7 trees and 2 houses. How many trees do they paint?

_____   _____

Comparing with Subtraction

How many more chairs are needed?

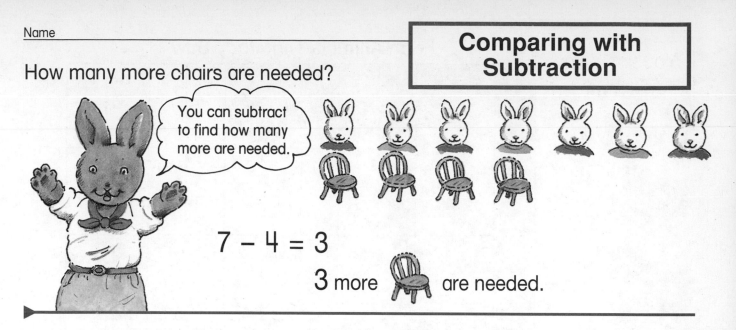

You can subtract to find how many more are needed.

$7 - 4 = 3$

3 more are needed.

Write a number sentence.
Write how many more are needed.

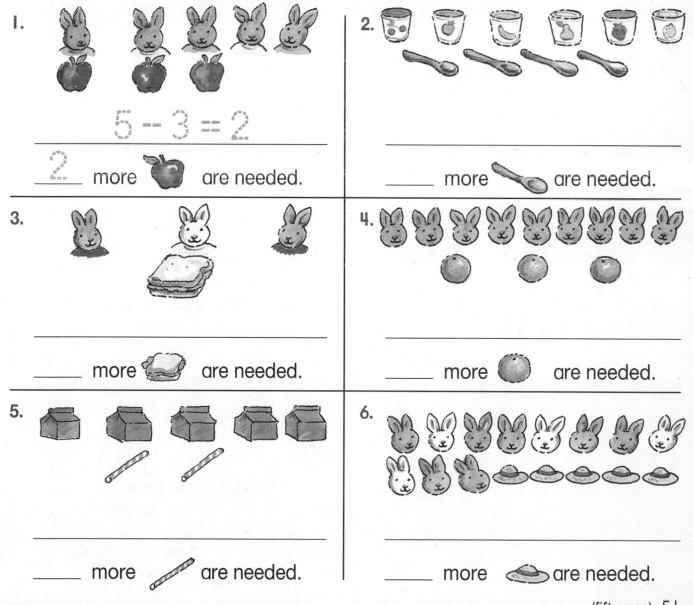

1. $5 - 3 = 2$

_2_ more are needed.

2. _____ more are needed.

3. _____ more are needed.

4. _____ more are needed.

5. _____ more are needed.

6. _____ more are needed.

Farm Animals That Jody Saw

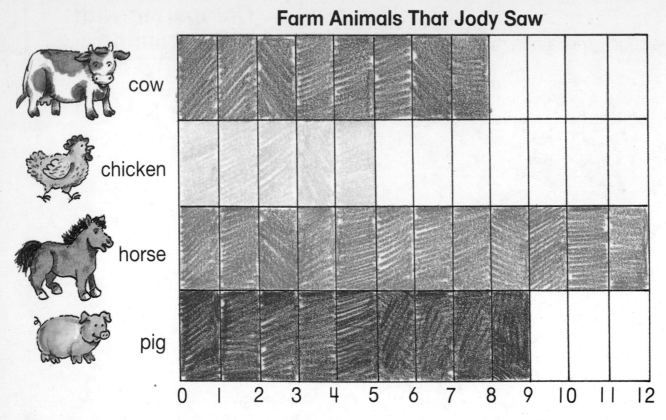

cow

chicken

horse

pig

0 1 2 3 4 5 6 7 8 9 10 11 12

Problem Solving   Use the graph.

Write a number sentence.

1. How many more cows are there than chickens?

   _____

   _____ more cows

2. How many fewer pigs are there than horses?

   _____

   _____ fewer pigs

3. How many more horses are there than cows?

   _____

   _____ more horses

4. How many fewer chickens are there than pigs?

   _____

   _____ fewer chickens

5. How many more pigs are there than cows?

   _____

   _____ more pig

6. How many fewer chickens are there than horses?

   _____

   _____ fewer chickens

52 (fifty-two)

Using a Number Line to Count Back

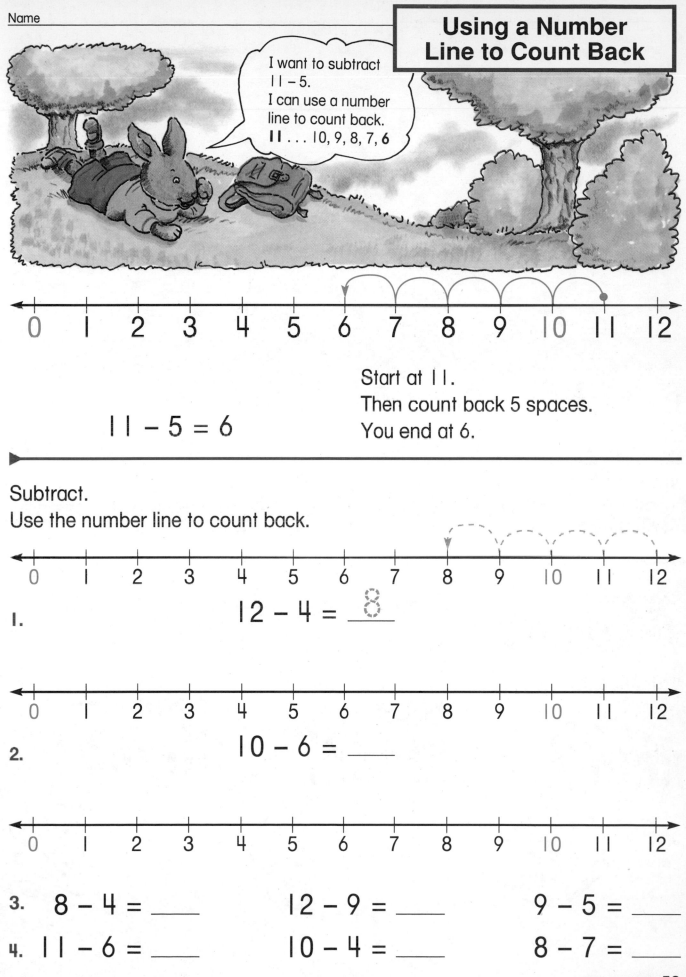

I want to subtract
11 − 5.
I can use a number
line to count back.
11 . . . 10, 9, 8, 7, **6**

0 1 2 3 4 5 6 7 8 9 10 11 12

11 − 5 = 6

Start at 11.
Then count back 5 spaces.
You end at 6.

Subtract.
Use the number line to count back.

0 1 2 3 4 5 6 7 8 9 10 11 12

1. 12 − 4 = _8_

0 1 2 3 4 5 6 7 8 9 10 11 12

2. 10 − 6 = ___

0 1 2 3 4 5 6 7 8 9 10 11 12

3. 8 − 4 = ___   12 − 9 = ___   9 − 5 = ___

4. 11 − 6 = ___   10 − 4 = ___   8 − 7 = ___

```
← 0   1   2   3   4   5   6   7   8   9   10   11   12 →
```

Subtract.

1.   10   9   7   12   6   9
     − 2   −2   −1   − 2   −3   −1

2.   8   8   11   11   9   9
      −2   −3   − 3   − 4   −3   −4

Problem Solving   Write a number sentence for each story.

3. The park has 12 swings. Rabbits
   are sitting on 5 of the swings.
   How many swings have no rabbits
   on them?

   _____

4. Jody sees 6 blue kites and 2 pink
   kites up in the sky. She also sees
   3 birds. How many kites does
   Jody see?

   _____

Maintain • **Number Sense**

Write how many.

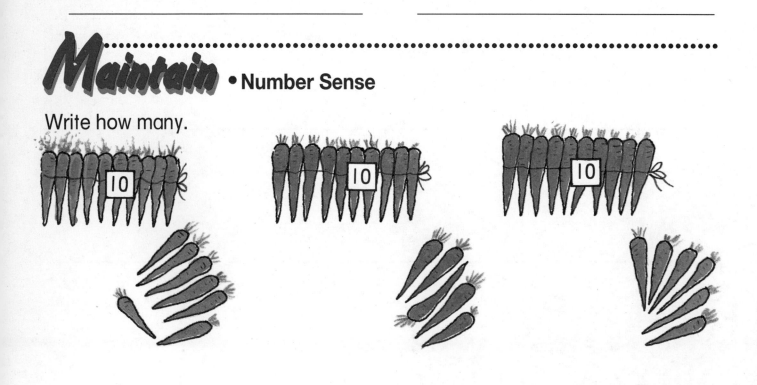

___   ___   ___

You need crayons. ▬▬▷   ▭▷
Add or subtract.

8 +4 **12**	9 −5	11 − 2	12 − 2	9 −8	11 − 5
11 − 10	4 +4	5 +5	9 −9	10 − 2	6 +4
3 +2	4 +7	11 − 9	7 +0	6 +6	2 +2

1. Use green to color boxes with answers greater than 9.

2. Use yellow to color boxes with answers less than 5.

Critical Thinking 💡 Talk with a friend.
Can you see a pattern?

3. Pick a fact from the top of the page.
Make up a story that uses the fact.

Problem Solving Work with a partner.

1. Jody and 2 friends get on the bus. They ride the bus for 8 blocks. Then Jody gets off the bus and walks 3 blocks. How many blocks

   did Jody travel? _____ blocks

2. It is 12 blocks from Karla's house to the school. She walks 3 blocks. Then she rides the rest of the way on a bus. How far does

   she ride the bus? _____ blocks

3. There are 5 rabbits on the bus. Then 2 more rabbits get on. At the next stop, 2 rabbits get off the bus. How many rabbits are on

   the bus now? _____ rabbits

4. Jake walks 2 blocks to the park. Then he walks 3 blocks to the bus stop. He rides the bus for 6 blocks. Does Jake walk more

   blocks than he rides? _____

5. Rob leaves the park and rides his bike for 3 blocks. His house is still 5 blocks away.

   How far is his house from the park? _____ blocks

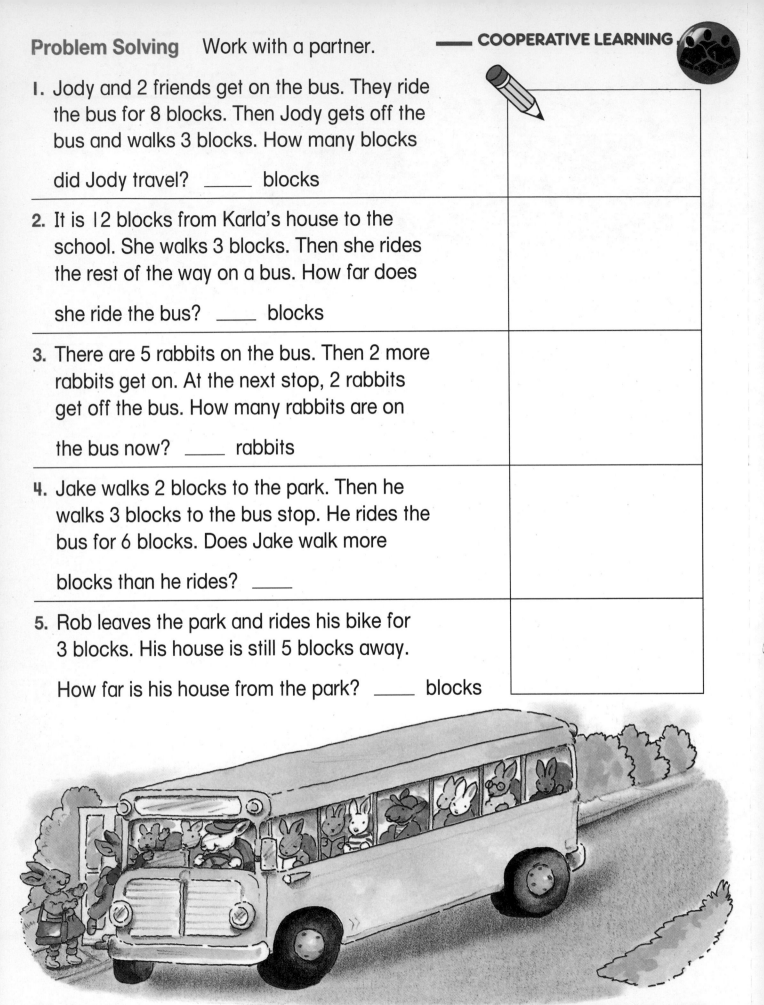

56 (fifty-six)

More Practice Set 2.15, page 393

Name _____

You need counters.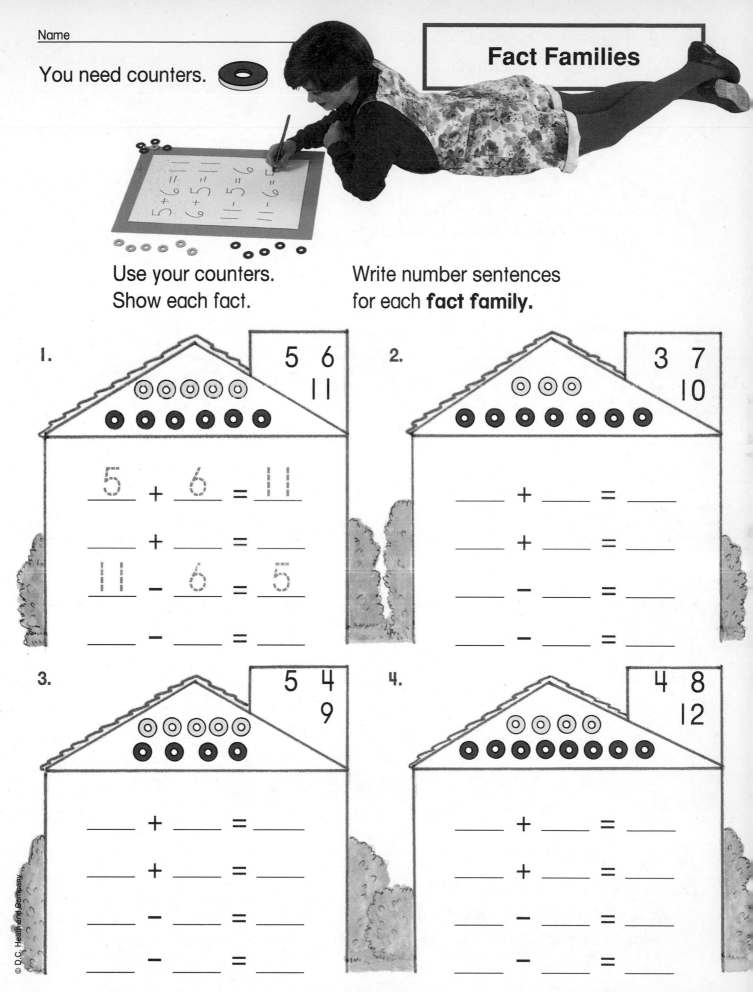

Fact Families

Use your counters.
Show each fact.

Write number sentences
for each **fact family.**

1.

| 5 | 6 |
| 11 | |

___5___ + ___6___ = ___11___

_____ + _____ = _____

__11__ – ___6___ = ___5___

_____ – _____ = _____

2.

| 3 | 7 |
| 10 | |

_____ + _____ = _____

_____ + _____ = _____

_____ – _____ = _____

_____ – _____ = _____

3.

| 5 | 4 |
| 9 | |

_____ + _____ = _____

_____ + _____ = _____

_____ – _____ = _____

_____ – _____ = _____

4.

| 4 | 8 |
| 12 | |

_____ + _____ = _____

_____ + _____ = _____

_____ – _____ = _____

_____ – _____ = _____

Use 12 or fewer counters to
show a fact. Write the number
sentences for the fact family.

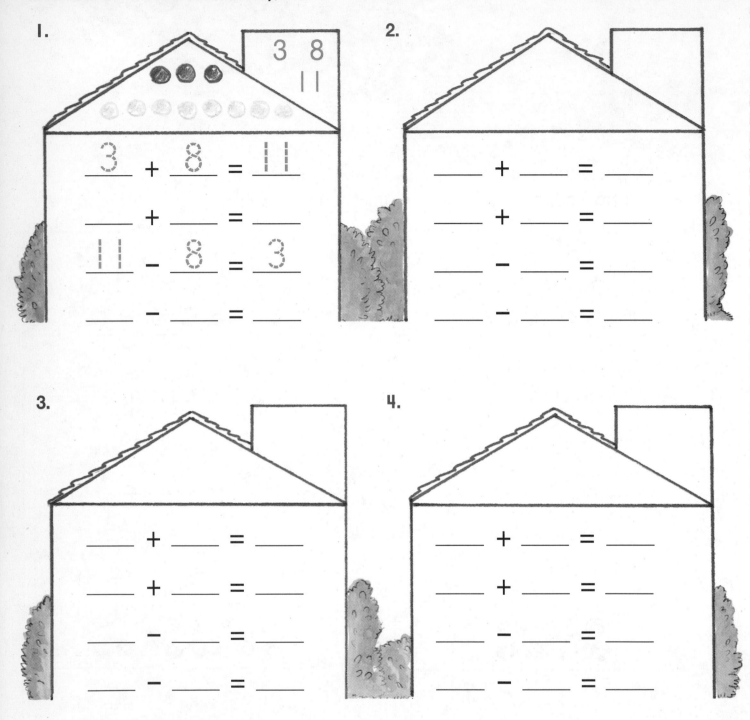

1.

3 8
11

__3__ + __8__ = __11__

____ + ____ = ____

__11__ − __8__ = 3

____ − ____ = ____

2.

____ + ____ = ____

____ + ____ = ____

____ − ____ = ____

____ − ____ = ____

3.

____ + ____ = ____

____ + ____ = ____

____ − ____ = ____

____ − ____ = ____

4.

____ + ____ = ____

____ + ____ = ____

____ − ____ = ____

____ − ____ = ____

MATH LOG
Show 6 red counters and 6 yellow
counters. Find the fact family.
How many facts did you find? Why?

Work with a partner.
Solve each problem.

1. Jody is 7 years old today. When will she be

   10 years old? in _____ years

2. Rob brings 10 cookies to the party. Jake eats
   some. Now there are 4 cookies. How many

   cookies did Jake eat? _____ cookies

3. Rob has 7 grapes and Jody has 3. Rob wants
   to give some of his grapes to Jody. He
   wants them both to have the same number of
   grapes. How many grapes should Rob give to Jody?

   _____ grapes

4. Jake wins 9 stickers in a balloon toss. He
   gives 3 of them to Jody. Jody gives
   1 sticker to Rob. How many stickers does Jake

   have now? _____ stickers

5. There are 12 hats. Four of them are red. The rest
   are blue. Are there more red hats or blue hats?

   _____ hats

Work with a partner.
Solve each problem.

1. There are 8 muffins on a plate. Three of them are banana muffins. How many muffins are not banana muffins? _____ muffins

2. Jody has 2 toy bears. The small bear is 3 inches tall. The big bear is 6 inches tall. How much taller is the big bear?

_____ inches taller

3. There are 3 plates of apples on the table. One plate has 3 red apples. The other plates have 4 green apples each. How many apples are on the table?

_____ apples

4. Rob brings 9 records to the party. He gives 3 of them to Karla. Karla gives 2 of her records to Rob. How many records does Rob have now? _____ records

5. There are 6 gifts. Each gift has 2 bows. Are there more gifts or more bows? _____

CHAPTER TEST

Write the sum or difference.

1. $6 + 2 =$ _____

2. $9 - 5 =$ _____

3. $12 - 7 =$ _____

4. $3 + 5 =$ _____

5. $7 - 4 =$ _____

6. $10 - 0 =$ _____

7. $\begin{array}{r} 8 \\ -4 \\ \hline \end{array}$

8. $\begin{array}{r} 10 \\ -1 \\ \hline \end{array}$

9. $\begin{array}{r} 5 \\ -3 \\ \hline \end{array}$

10. $\begin{array}{r} 5 \\ 1 \\ +6 \\ \hline \end{array}$

11. $\begin{array}{r} 3 \\ 3 \\ +4 \\ \hline \end{array}$

12. $\begin{array}{r} 2 \\ 5 \\ +4 \\ \hline \end{array}$

Complete the number sentence.

13. $7 +$ ____ $= 9$

14. $8 =$ ____ $+ 3$

15. ____ $+ 6 = 12$

16. $8 +$ ____ $= 11$

17. $10 = 0 +$ ____

18. ____ $+ 2 = 11$

Write a number sentence for the fact family.

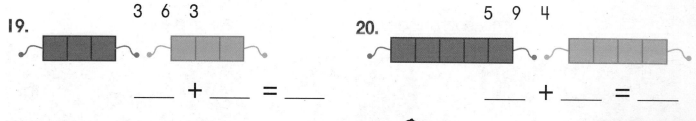

19. 3 6 3

____ $+$ ____ $=$ ____

20. 5 9 4

____ $+$ ____ $=$ ____

Write the number sentences for the fact family.

3   9

12

21. ____ $+$ ____ $=$ ____

22. ____ $+$ ____ $=$ ____

23. ____ $-$ ____ $=$ ____

24. ____ $-$ ____ $=$ ____

Fruit in a Box

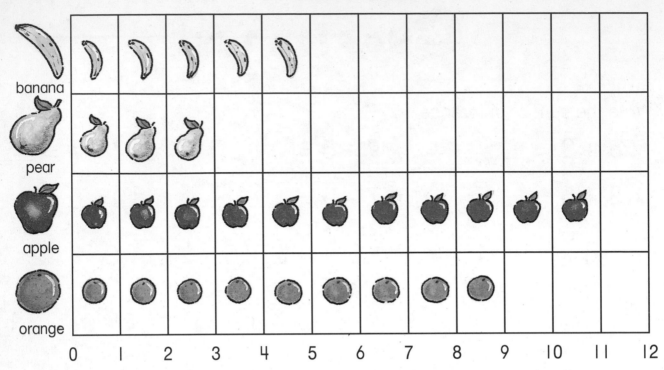

Use the graph.
Write a number sentence.

25. How many more oranges than bananas are there?

_____

_____ more oranges

26. How many fewer pears than apples are there?

_____

_____ fewer pears

Chapter Test

EXCURSION
CULTURAL DIVERSITY

You need a calculator.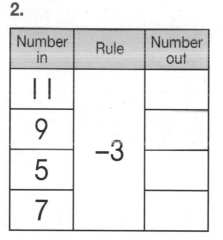

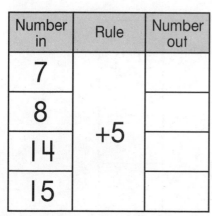

I used my calculator to fill in the table this way.

I used my calculator this way.

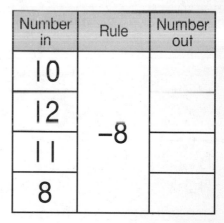

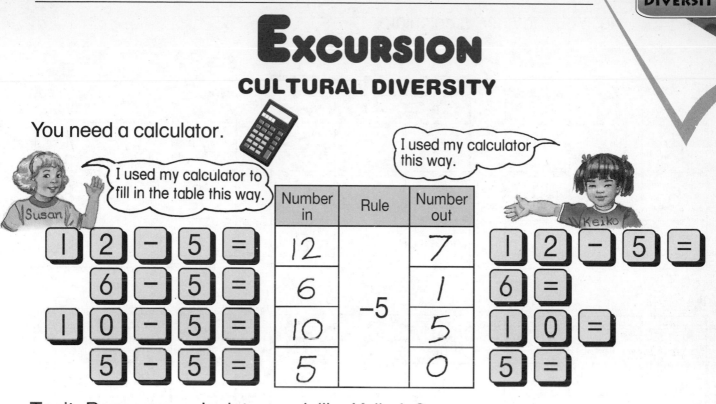

Number in	Rule	Number out
12		7
6	−5	1
10		5
5		0

Try it. Does your calculator work like Keiko's? _____

Use a calculator to fill in each table.

1.

Number in	Rule	Number out
7		11
2	+4	
8		
4		

2.

Number in	Rule	Number out
11		
9	−3	
5		
7		

3.

Number in	Rule	Number out
10		
12	−8	
11		
8		

4.

Number in	Rule	Number out
7		
8	+5	
14		
15		

5.

Number in	Rule	Number out
12		
36	−6	
40		
29		

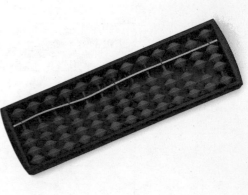

Work in pairs.
Find the rule. You may use a calculator.

1.

Number in	Rule	Number out
11		10
5	– 1	4
7		6

2.

Number in	Rule	Number out
4		9
6		11
3		8

3.

Number in	Rule	Number out
7		3
12		8
4		0

4.

Number in	Rule	Number out
11		8
3		0
7		4

5.

Number in	Rule	Number out
9		1
12		4
8		0

6.

Number in	Rule	Number out
		9
	+6	12
		10

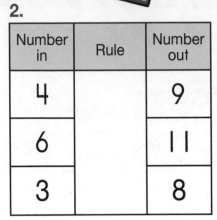
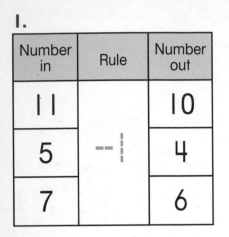

Take turns.
Think of a rule. Fill in a table.
Let your partner find the rule.

7.

Number in	Rule	Number out

Number in	Rule	Number out

Note to the Family

Your child has been learning addition and subtraction facts through 12. This activity sheet gives your child an opportunity to share new skills with you.

PICTURE-STORY CARDS

You will need construction paper and crayons.

1. Help your child make up addition and subtraction stories for facts through 12. Encourage your child to create both take-away (There are 8 bunnies. Then 3 bunnies hop away. How many bunnies are left?) and comparative (There are 10 bunnies. There are 7 carrots. How many more bunnies than carrots?) subtraction stories.

2. Use these stories to create picture-story cards. Help your child record a picture story on the front of a piece of construction paper, using words and drawings or pictures cut out from magazines. Write the addition or subtraction fact for the picture story on the back of the card.

3. As your child works on his or her story cards, you can make some of your own. When a sufficient number of cards has been finished, exchange cards and take turns solving each other's examples.

4. As a variation, identify the operation needed to solve each example (addition or subtraction) before giving the answer.

3 red
8 blue
How many in all?

(front)

3 + 8 = 11

(back)

5. You may wish to keep these picture stories for future practice of addition and subtraction facts through 12.

Note to the Family

In the next few weeks, your child will be learning about place value through 100. Among the topics taught will be tens and ones (for example, 4 tens 9 ones = 49), comparing and ordering numbers through 100, estimating 20, counting by 2's, 5's, and 10's, and ordinal numbers (first through thirty-first).

It is important for your child to see place-value concepts used outside of school. You can help your child at home by encouraging him or her to notice 2-digit numbers we use everyday; for example, the page numbers in a book or newspaper, days in a calendar, lunch money, and so on.

Thank you for helping us teach your child about place value through 100.

It might be fun to do the following activity with your child.

STRAW MODELS

You will need 20 index cards or small pieces of paper, markers or crayons, plastic straws, scissors, and rubber bands.

1. Help your child make 9 bundles of 10 straws each (you may wish to cut the straws in half to make them a more manageable size). Use rubber bands to hold the bundles together. Leave 9 loose straws.

2. Help your child make number cards. Write a different 2-digit number on each of 15 index cards. Leave 5 other cards blank, or write the words *wild card* on each of these cards.

3. Shuffle the cards, and put them face down in a pile on the table.

4. One player picks a card and uses the straws to model the number on the card chosen. If the card chosen is a wild card, the player can model any number she or he wants. The other player then identifies the number modeled.

5. Take turns picking cards and modeling numbers.

PLACE VALUE THROUGH 100

Listen to the story.

Free Rides on Bomba!

Loop sets of 10.

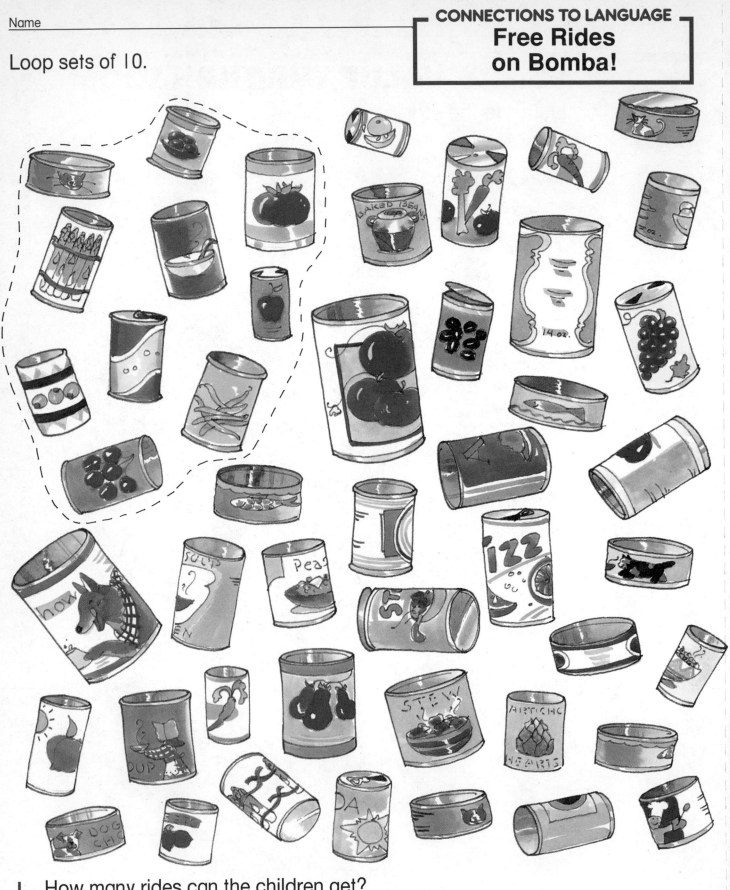

1. How many rides can the children get? _____
2. How many more cans do they need to get

   5 rides? _____

Tens

_1_ ten = _10_
ten

_5_ tens = _50_
fifty

Write how many tens.
Write the number.

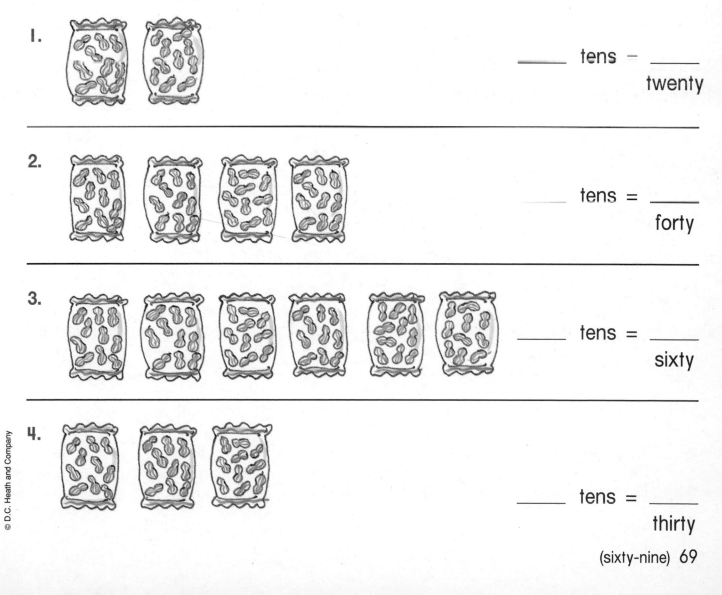

1. _____ tens – _____
twenty

2. _____ tens = _____
forty

3. _____ tens = _____
sixty

4. _____ tens = _____
thirty

Write how many tens.
Write the number.

1.

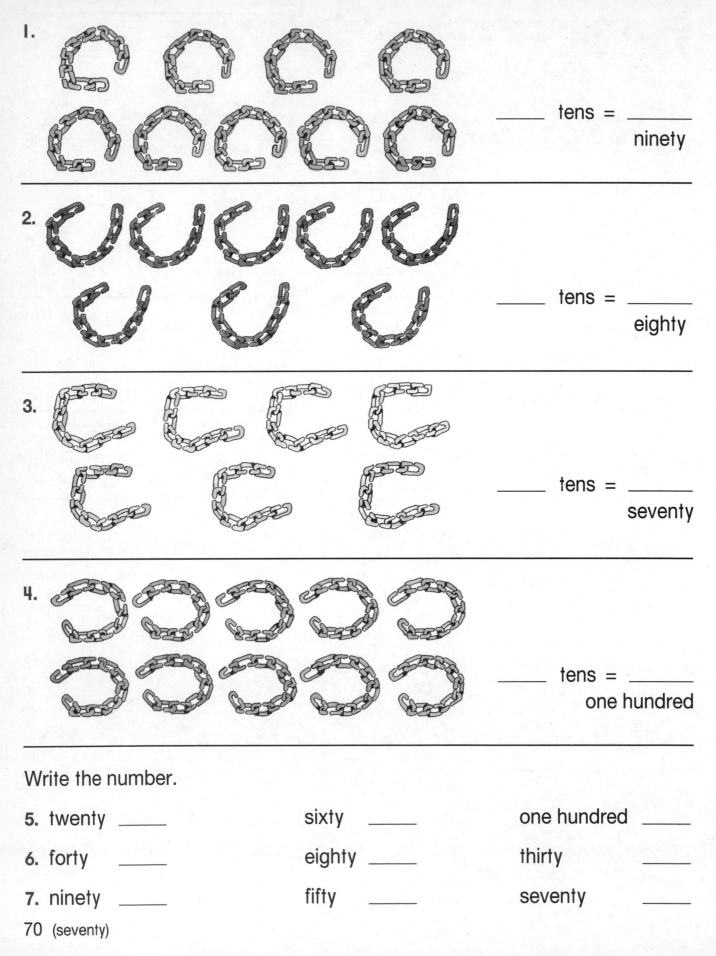

_____ tens = _____
ninety

2.

_____ tens = _____
eighty

3.

_____ tens = _____
seventy

4.

_____ tens = _____
one hundred

Write the number.

5. twenty _____   sixty _____   one hundred _____

6. forty _____   eighty _____   thirty _____

7. ninety _____   fifty _____   seventy _____

70 (seventy)

Tens and Ones

There are 4 tens and 5 ones.
That is 45 in all.

Write how many tens and ones.
Write the number.

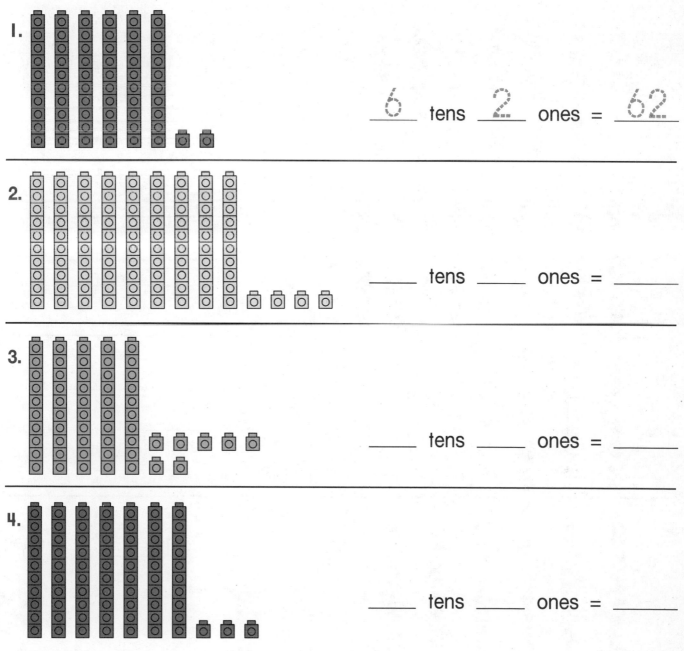

1. _6_ tens _2_ ones = _62_

2. ____ tens ____ ones = ____

3. ____ tens ____ ones = ____

4. ____ tens ____ ones = ____

4 tens 2 ones
40 + 2
42

Write the number in 3 different ways.

1.

_____ tens _____ ones

_____ + _____

_____

2.

_____ tens _____ ones

_____ + _____

_____

3.

_____ tens _____ ones

_____ + _____

_____

4.

_____ tens _____ ones

_____ + _____

_____

More Practice Set 3.2, page 394

You may use blocks.
Look at each pair of numbers.

| Compare the tens. | The tens are the same. Compare the ones. | The tens and the ones are the same. |

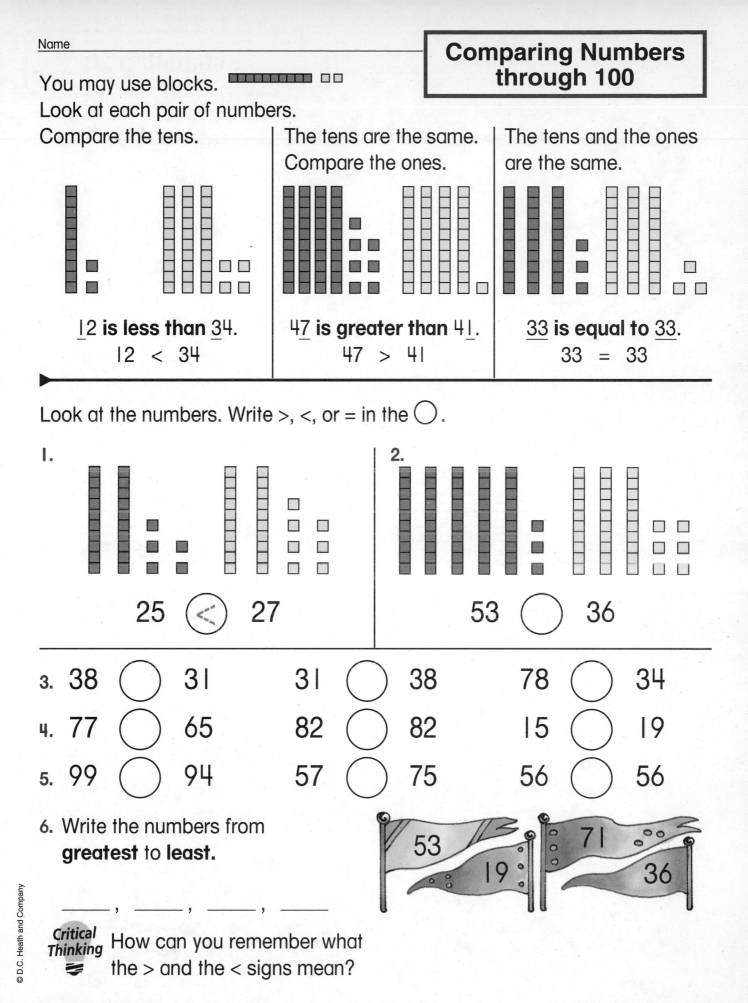

12 **is less than** 34.
12 < 34

47 **is greater than** 41.
47 > 41

33 **is equal to** 33.
33 = 33

Look at the numbers. Write >, <, or = in the ◯.

1.

25 ◯< 27

2.

53 ◯ 36

3. 38 ◯ 31   31 ◯ 38   78 ◯ 34

4. 77 ◯ 65   82 ◯ 82   15 ◯ 19

5. 99 ◯ 94   57 ◯ 75   56 ◯ 56

6. Write the numbers from **greatest** to **least**.

53   19   71   36

_____ , _____ , _____ , _____

Critical Thinking How can you remember what the > and the < signs mean?

More Practice Sets 3.3, page 394

This poster has 20 stars.

You can be a star!

Recycle

Estimate. Put a check next to each set that you think shows about 20 stars.

1. ☐

2. ☐

3. ☐

4. ☐

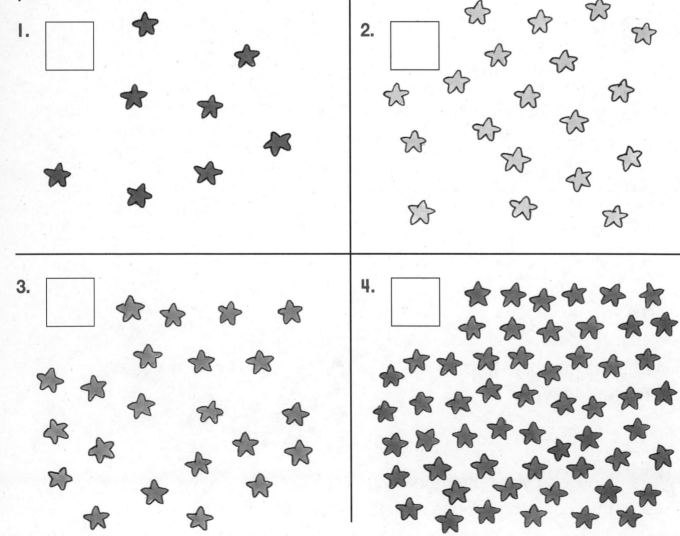

74 (seventy-four)

Name _____

1. Write the missing numbers.

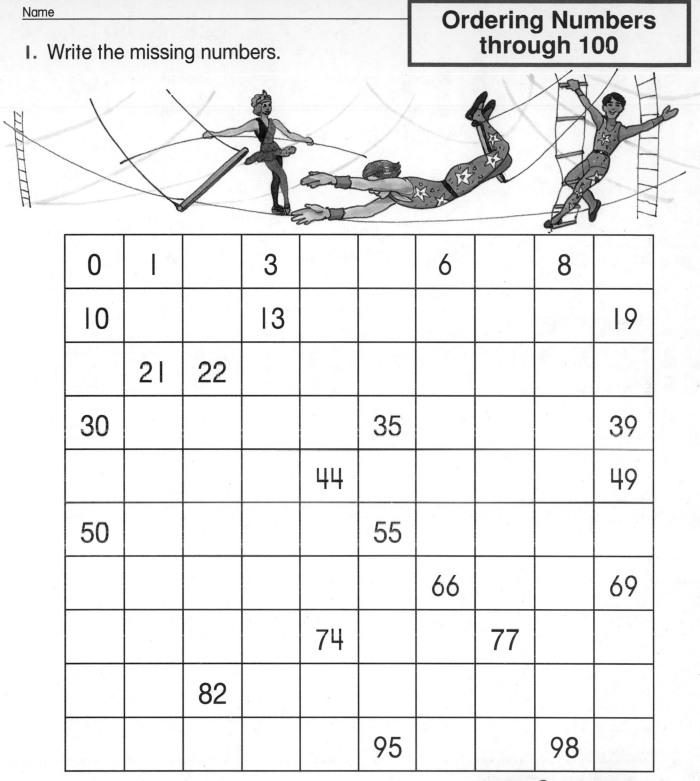

0	1		3			6		8	
10			13						19
	21	22							
30					35				39
				44					49
50					55				
						66			69
				74			77		
	82								
					95			98	

2. Which number is 1 more than 99? _____

3. Which number is 10 more than 46? _____

4. Which number is 1 less than 83? _____

5. Which number is 10 less than 83? _____

You may use blocks.

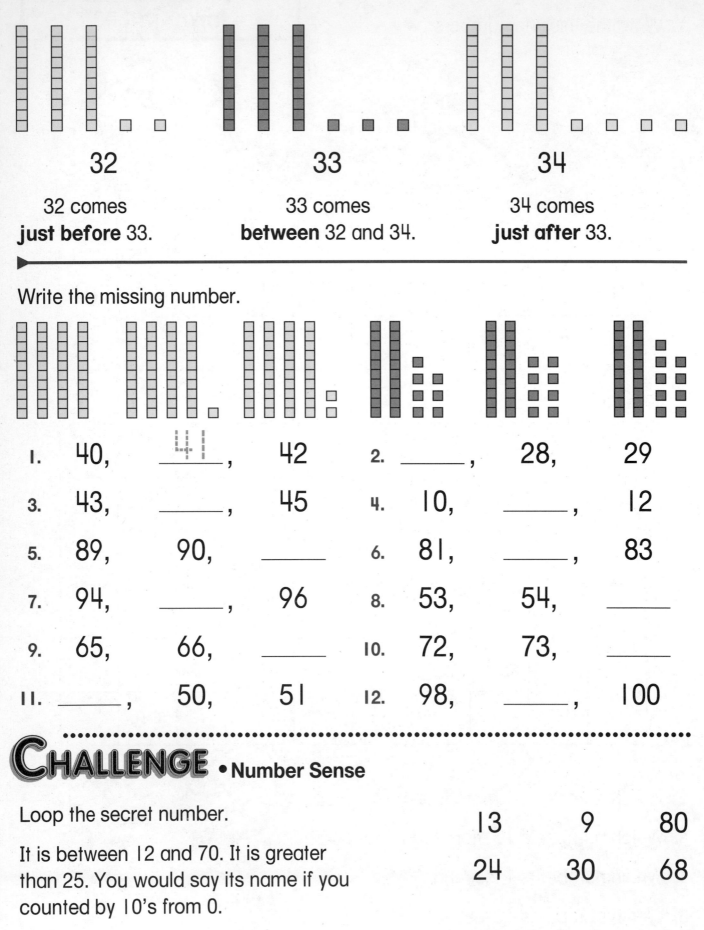

32

33

34

32 comes
just before 33.

33 comes
between 32 and 34.

34 comes
just after 33.

Write the missing number.

1. 40, __41__, 42   2. ____, 28, 29

3. 43, ____, 45   4. 10, ____, 12

5. 89, 90, ____   6. 81, ____, 83

7. 94, ____, 96   8. 53, 54, ____

9. 65, 66, ____   10. 72, 73, ____

11. ____, 50, 51   12. 98, ____, 100

CHALLENGE • Number Sense

Loop the secret number.

It is between 12 and 70. It is greater than 25. You would say its name if you counted by 10's from 0.

13   9   80

24   30   68

More Practice Set 3.5, page 395

You need a crayon.
Color to continue the pattern.

Odd   Even

1.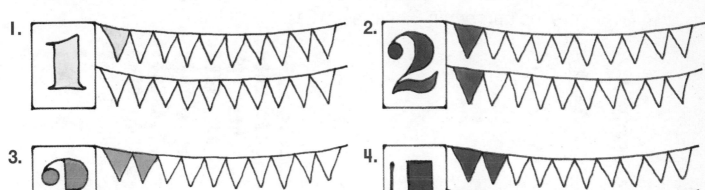

2.

3.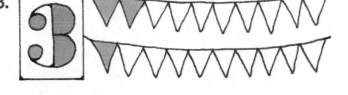

4.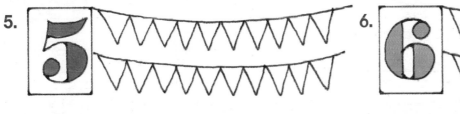

5.

6.

7.

8.

9.

10.

Now try these numbers.

11. Is 17 odd or even?

_____

12. Is 28 odd or even?

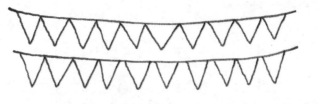
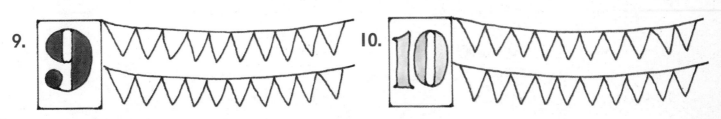
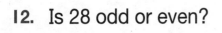
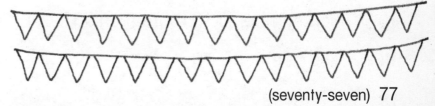

_____

MID-CHAPTER REVIEW

for pages 69–76

Write the number in 3 different ways.

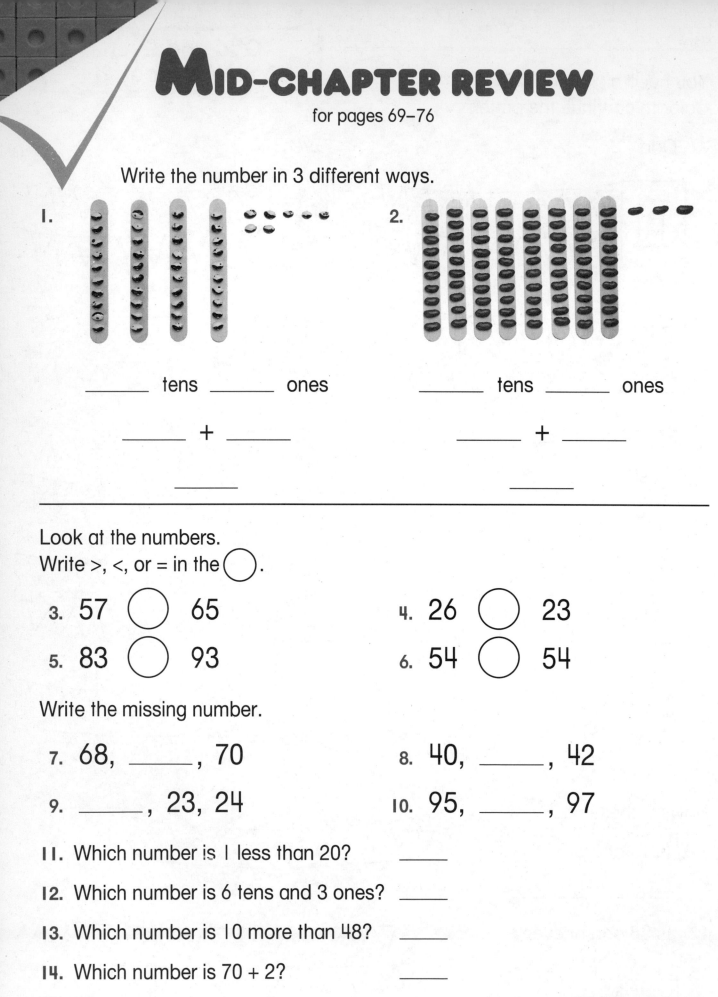

1. _____ tens _____ ones

_____ + _____

_____

2. _____ tens _____ ones

_____ + _____

_____

Look at the numbers.
Write >, <, or = in the ◯.

3. 57 ◯ 65

4. 26 ◯ 23

5. 83 ◯ 93

6. 54 ◯ 54

Write the missing number.

7. 68, _____, 70

8. 40, _____, 42

9. _____, 23, 24

10. 95, _____, 97

11. Which number is 1 less than 20? _____

12. Which number is 6 tens and 3 ones? _____

13. Which number is 10 more than 48? _____

14. Which number is 70 + 2? _____

Work with a partner.
Match each person with the things she needs.

1.

I make children laugh.

I am afraid of lions.

I work with an animal.

Match each trainer with her animal.

2.

My animal is standing on a ball.

My animal is gray.

My animal has small ears.

Work with a partner.
Match each person to his animal.

1.

2.

MATH LOG

Make up your own puzzle.
Give it to a friend to solve.

You need crayons.

Ordinal Numbers

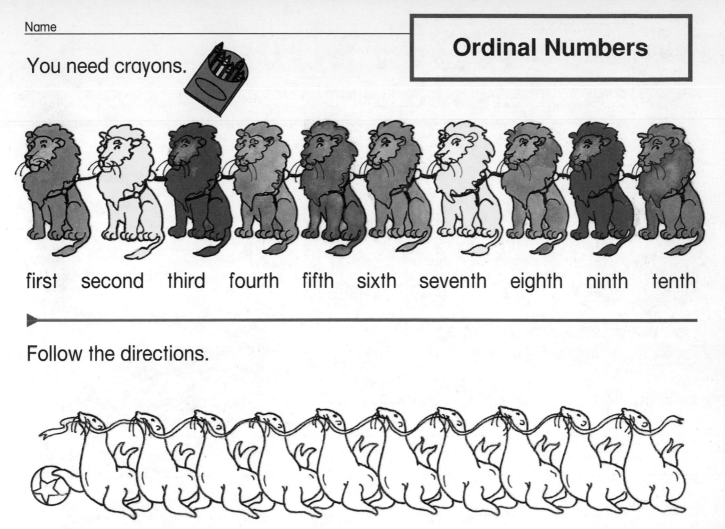

first   second   third   fourth   fifth   sixth   seventh   eighth   ninth   tenth

Follow the directions.

first

1. Color the second seal blue.

2. Color the ninth seal red.

3. Color the fifth seal orange.

4. Color the eighth seal green.

first

5. Color the fourth elephant green.

6. Color the seventh elephant yellow.

7. Color the tenth elephant orange.

8. Color the third elephant blue.

NOVEMBER

SUNDAY	MONDAY	TUESDAY	WEDNESDAY	THURSDAY	FRIDAY	SATURDAY
		1	2	3	4	5
6	7	8	9	10	11	12
13	14	15	16	17	18	19
20	21	22	23	24	25	26
27	28	29	30			

Use the calendar to answer each question.
Loop the answer.

1. What is the date of Emily's birthday?

   second   fifth   ninth

2. What day of the week is the sixteenth?

   Monday   Wednesday   Sunday

3. Ben wants to go to the circus again on the twenty-first. What day is that?

   Thursday   Monday   Saturday

4. Emily has a soccer game on the last Tuesday of November. What is the date?

   twenty-ninth   fourteenth   first

 • **Mixed Practice**

Complete the number sentence.

1. $4 + \underline{\hspace{1cm}} = 12$ 2. $8 + \underline{\hspace{1cm}} = 12$ 3. $11 - 7 = \underline{\hspace{1cm}}$

4. $9 + 2 = \underline{\hspace{1cm}}$ 5. $9 - 9 = \underline{\hspace{1cm}}$ 6. $9 - 2 = \underline{\hspace{1cm}}$

More Practice Set 3.8, page 395

You need crayons. ▭▷ ▭▷

Skip-Counting

0	1	2	3	4	5	6	7	8	9
10	11	12	13	14	15	16	17	18	19
20	21	22	23	24	25	26	27	28	29
30	31	32	33	34	35	36	37	38	39
40	41	42	43	44	45	46	47	48	49
50	51	52	53	54	55	56	57	58	59
60	61	62	63	64	65	66	67	68	69
70	71	72	73	74	75	76	77	78	79
80	81	82	83	84	85	86	87	88	89
90	91	92	93	94	95	96	97	98	99

1. Start at 0. Count by 2's. Color those boxes yellow.

2. Then count by 5's. Color those boxes blue.

Critical Thinking Talk with a friend.

Do you see any patterns?

What else do you see?

You need a calculator.

You can use a calculator to count by 3's.

6	9	12	15	18
[6]	[+][3][=]	[=]	[=]	[=]

Use a calculator to count.

1. Count by 4's.

12	16			
[1][2]	[+][4][=]	[=]	[=]	[=]

2. Count back by 3's.

47, _____, _____, _____, _____

[4][7] [−][3][=] [=] [=] [=]

3. Count by 10's. Write the numbers.

26, _____, _____, _____, _____, _____

4. Count back by 10's. Write the numbers.

63, _____, _____, _____, _____, _____

●●

CHALLENGE • Number Sense

Guess my rule. Continue the pattern.

23,   27,   31, _____, _____, _____, _____

More Practice Set 3.9, page 396

Counting Money

You may use coins.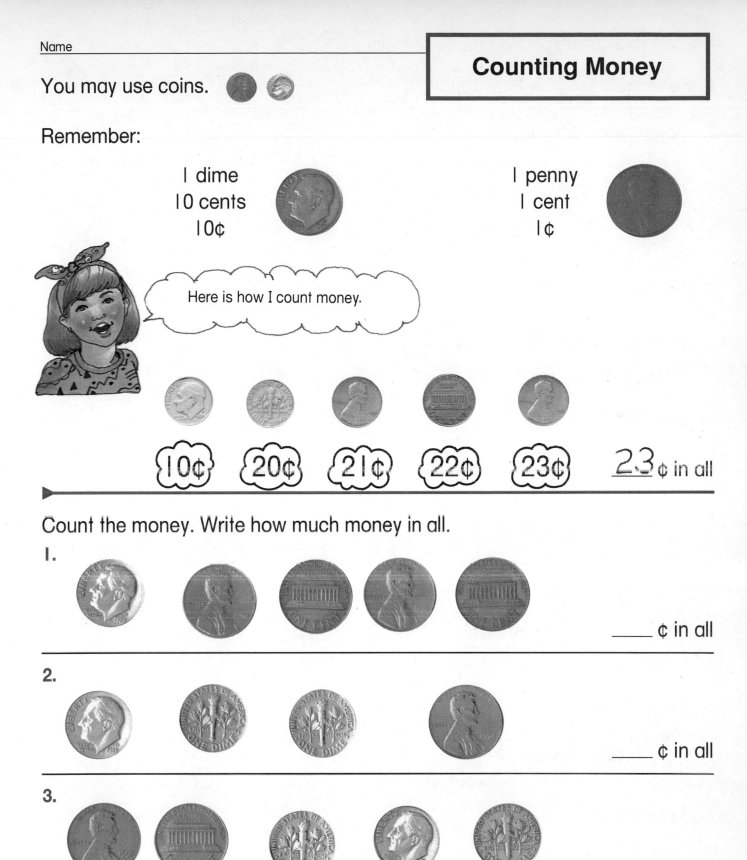

Remember:

I dime
10 cents
10¢

I penny
I cent
I¢

Here is how I count money.

(10¢) (20¢) (21¢) (22¢) (23¢) __23__ ¢ in all

Count the money. Write how much money in all.

1.

_____ ¢ in all

2.

_____ ¢ in all

3.

_____ ¢ in all

4.

_____ ¢ in all

Problem Solving You may use coins.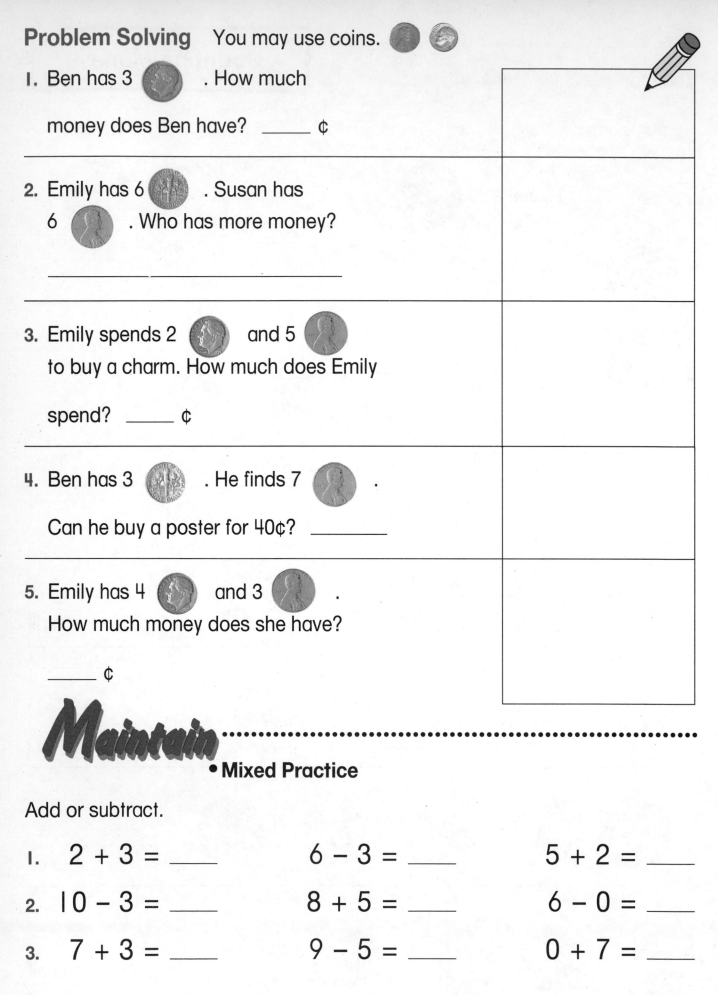

1. Ben has 3 ![dime] . How much

money does Ben have? _____ ¢

2. Emily has 6 ![dime] . Susan has

6 ![penny] . Who has more money?

_____

3. Emily spends 2 ![dime] and 5 ![penny]

to buy a charm. How much does Emily

spend? _____ ¢

4. Ben has 3 ![dime] . He finds 7 ![penny] .

Can he buy a poster for 40¢? _____

5. Emily has 4 ![dime] and 3 ![penny] .

How much money does she have?

_____ ¢

Maintain

• **Mixed Practice**

Add or subtract.

1. 2 + 3 = ___   6 − 3 = ___   5 + 2 = ___

2. 10 − 3 = ___   8 + 5 = ___   6 − 0 = ___

3. 7 + 3 = ___   9 − 5 = ___   0 + 7 = ___

You need 10 cans for 1 ticket.
You need 20 cans for 2 tickets.
How many cans do you need for 4 tickets?

You can make a table to help you to solve this problem.

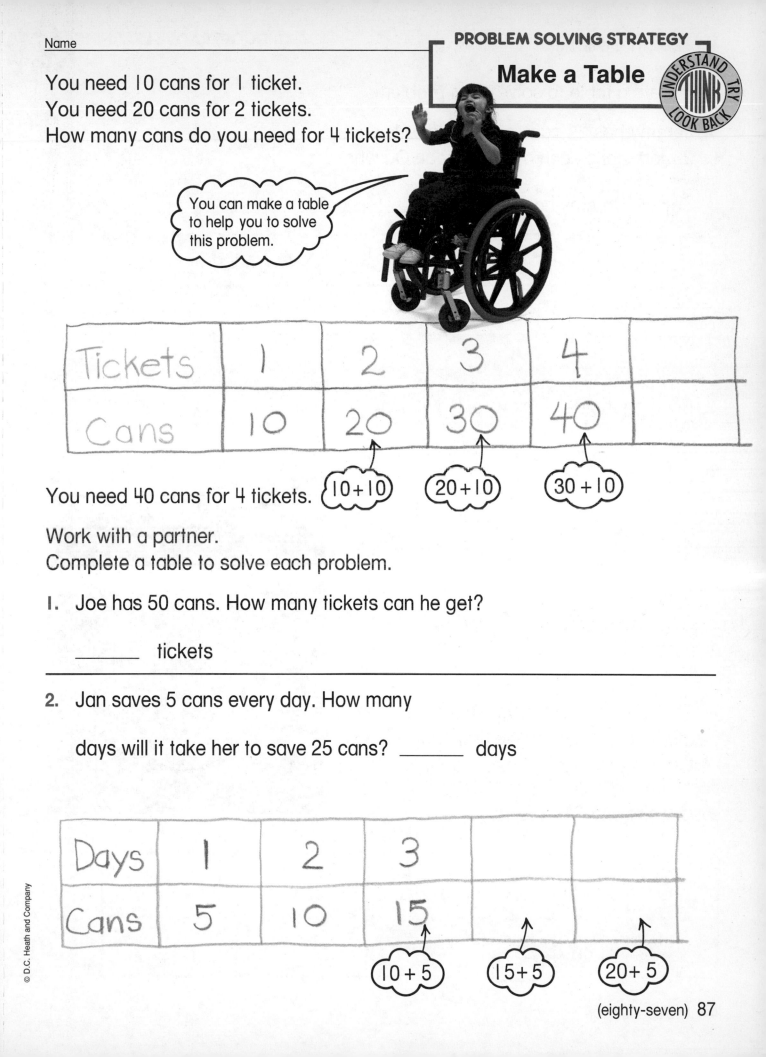

Tickets	1	2	3	4	
Cans	10	20	30	40	

10+10 20+10 30+10

You need 40 cans for 4 tickets.

Work with a partner.
Complete a table to solve each problem.

1. Joe has 50 cans. How many tickets can he get?

   _____ tickets

2. Jan saves 5 cans every day. How many

   days will it take her to save 25 cans? _____ days

Days	1	2	3		
Cans	5	10	15		

10+5 15+5 20+5

Work with a partner.

Complete a table to solve each problem.

1. Jeremy has 24 cans on Monday. He saves
   2 more cans each day after that. On what

   day will Jeremy have 30 cans? _____

Days	Monday	Tuesday	Wednesday	
Cans	24	26		

2. Each car holds 10 clowns. How many

   cars are needed to hold 40 clowns? _____ cars

Cars				
Clowns				

3. How many cars are needed to

   hold 37 clowns? _____ cars

4. There will be 10 shows. There are
   2 shows each day. The first show
   is on Wednesday. When will the

   last show be? _____

Day	Wednesday	Thursday	Friday		
Shows	1 and 2	3 and 4			

CHAPTER TEST

Write how many tens and ones.

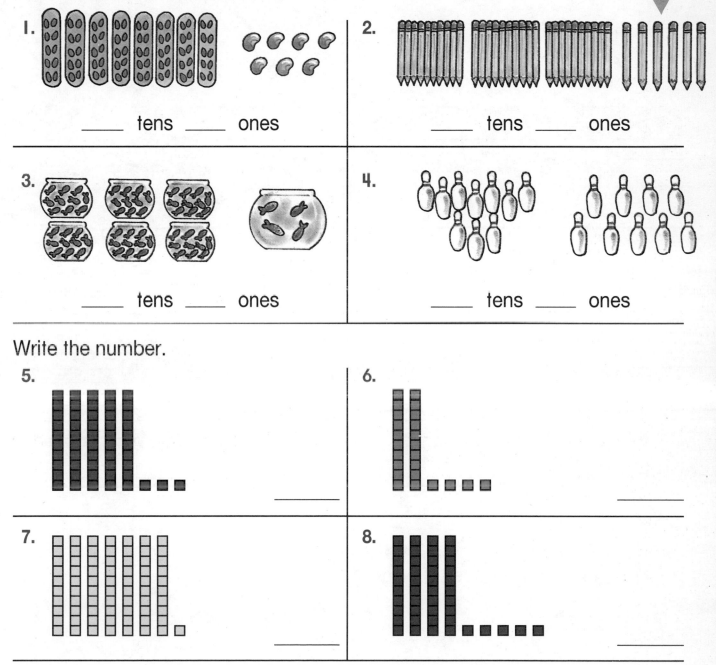

1. _____ tens _____ ones

2. _____ tens _____ ones

3. _____ tens _____ ones

4. _____ tens _____ ones

Write the number.

5. _____

6. _____

7. _____

8. _____

Write the missing number.

9. 56, _____, 58

10. 91, 92, _____

11. _____, 14, 15

12. 64, _____, 66

Write >, <, or =.

13. 74◯72   14. 31◯33   15. 18◯18   16. 43◯47

Loop the odd number.

17. 1, 2, 4   18. 2, 5, 6

Loop the even number.

19. 17, 16, 13   20. 16, 17, 19

MAY						
SUNDAY	MONDAY	TUESDAY	WEDNESDAY	THURSDAY	FRIDAY	SATURDAY
		1	2	3	4	5
6	7	8	9	10	11	12
13	14	15	16	17	18	19

Use the calendar to answer each question.

21. Karen wants to go sailing on the thirteenth. What day is that?

Saturday   Sunday

22. Pedro's birthday is the first Thursday in May. What is the date?

May first   May third

Solve each problem.

23. Pat has 4 dimes and 3 pennies. How much money does she have?

_____ ¢

24. You need 10¢ to buy 1 pencil. You need 20¢ to buy 2 pencils. Finish the table to find out how many pencils Pat can buy.

_____ pencils

pencils	1	2		
cents (¢)	10	20		

CUMULATIVE TEST

Count each object. Write how many.

1.
_____ frogs

2.
_____ birds

3.
_____ flowers

4.
_____ squirrels

Write the sum.

5. 9
   +2

6. 4
    3
   +2

7. 4
   +8

8. 7
    2
   +3

9. 5
   +3

10. $2 + 6 + 2 =$ _____   11. $4 + 6 + 1 =$ _____   12. $7 + 2 + 3 =$ _____

Write the missing number.

13. 96, _____, 98

14. 52, 53, _____

15. _____, 61, 62

(ninety-one) 91

Write number sentences
for the fact family.

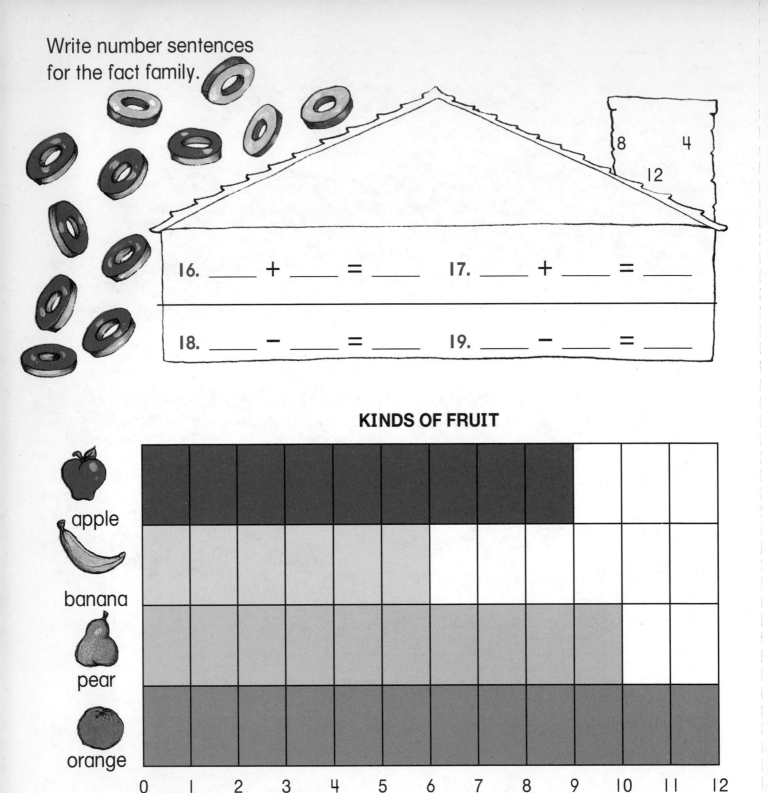

8   4
12

16. ____ + ____ = ____   17. ____ + ____ = ____

18. ____ – ____ = ____   19. ____ – ____ = ____

KINDS OF FRUIT

apple

banana

pear

orange

0 1 2 3 4 5 6 7 8 9 10 11 12

Look at the graph.
Write a number sentence.

20. How many more pears are
    there than bananas?

21. How many fewer apples are
    there than oranges?

_____   _____

Note to the Family

Your child has been learning about place value through 100. This activity sheet gives your child an opportunity to share new skills with you.

CIRCUS PICTURE

You will need crayons. Complete this picture with your child.

1. Color all numbers 0–33 red.

2. Color all numbers 34–66 blue.

3. Color all numbers 67–99 brown.

4. Think of a name for the picture.

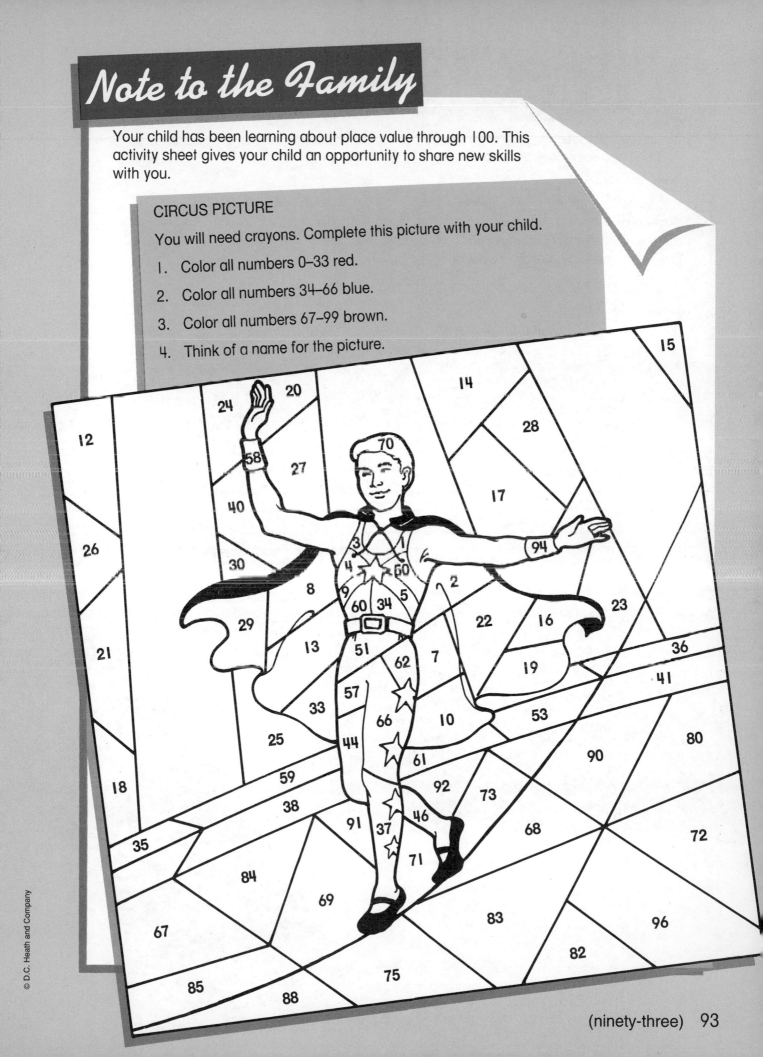

Note to the Family

In the next few weeks, your child will be continuing to learn about addition and subtraction by computing with addition and subtraction facts through 20.

It is important for your child to see addition and subtraction used outside of school. Your child can practice these skills by participating in daily activities, such as putting away the dishes and playing games using ordinary household items.

Thank you for helping us teach your child about addition and subtraction through 20!

It might be fun to do this activity with your child.

MORE EGG FACTS

You will need two empty egg cartons, scissors, and assorted buttons or other small objects.

1. Help your child cut two sections off each egg carton to make two cartons with ten sections each.

2. Put a button in each of the ten compartments of one carton.

3. Ask your child to put from one to ten buttons in the second carton, and tell you how many are in the two cartons. Repeat many times, always starting with ten in the first carton and adding from one to ten buttons to the second carton.

4. Then start with from eleven to twenty buttons altogether in the two cartons, take away buttons, and let your child tell you how many are left.

CHAPTER 4

ADDITION AND SUBTRACTION FACTS THROUGH 20

Listen to the story.

The Sand Castle Contest

Name

You need a crayon.

Draw a circle around a dot
for each shell.

Jimmy

Tasha

Carl

Donna

96 (ninety-six)

Make dots to show the second addend.
Write the sum.

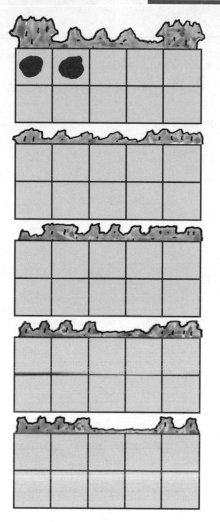

$10 + 2 =$ __12__

$10 + 7 =$ _____

$10 + 10 =$ _____

$10 + 6 =$ _____

$10 + 4 =$ _____

Write the sum.

6.
$$\begin{array}{r} 10 \\ + 8 \\ \hline \end{array} \qquad \begin{array}{r} 6 \\ +10 \\ \hline \end{array} \qquad \begin{array}{r} 10 \\ + 5 \\ \hline \end{array} \qquad \begin{array}{r} 4 \\ +10 \\ \hline \end{array} \qquad \begin{array}{r} 9 \\ +10 \\ \hline \end{array} \qquad \begin{array}{r} 3 \\ +10 \\ \hline \end{array}$$

7.
$$\begin{array}{r} 7 \\ +10 \\ \hline \end{array} \qquad \begin{array}{r} 10 \\ + 9 \\ \hline \end{array} \qquad \begin{array}{r} 2 \\ +10 \\ \hline \end{array} \qquad \begin{array}{r} 8 \\ +10 \\ \hline \end{array} \qquad \begin{array}{r} 10 \\ + 3 \\ \hline \end{array} \qquad \begin{array}{r} 5 \\ +10 \\ \hline \end{array}$$

Problem Solving   Write a number sentence for each story.

1. There are 5 green sailboats and 7 blue sailboats in the water. How many sailboats are in the water altogether?

_____

2. Jimmy and Tasha find 10 little pebbles and 7 bigger pebbles. Two of the pebbles are blue. How many pebbles do they find?

_____

3. In 1 hour, Carl takes 8 pictures of his castle and 4 pictures of the ocean. How many pictures does he take?

_____

4. Tasha finds some shells. She gives 5 of them away to Jimmy. She has 7 left. How many shells did Tasha find?

_____

Maintain • Number Sense

Write the number.

_____   _____   _____

1. Which number is less than 50? _____

2. Which number has 7 ones? _____

3. Which number has 7 tens? _____

98 (ninety-eight)

Use your counters
and a workmat.

**Making Tens
for Addition**

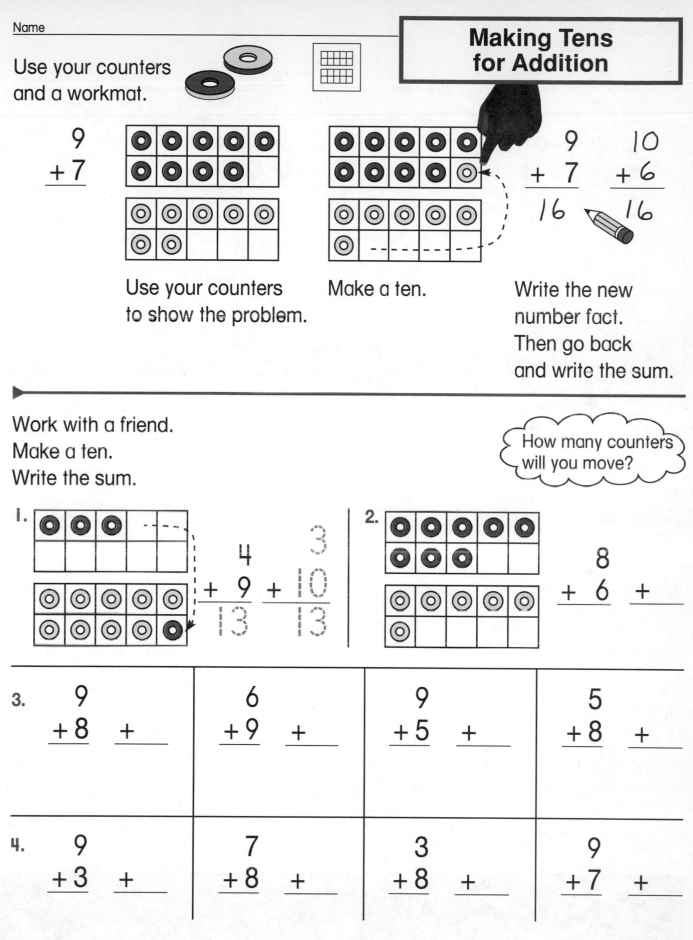

9
+ 7

Use your counters
to show the problem.

Make a ten.

9   10
+ 7   + 6
16   16

Write the new
number fact.
Then go back
and write the sum.

Work with a friend.
Make a ten.
Write the sum.

How many counters
will you move?

1.

4   3
+ 9   + 10
13   13

2.

8
+ 6 + ___

3.   9
+ 8 + ___

6
+ 9 + ___

9
+ 5 + ___

5
+ 8 + ___

4.   9
+ 3 + ___

7
+ 8 + ___

3
+ 8 + ___

9
+ 7 + ___

Make a 10. Add.

1.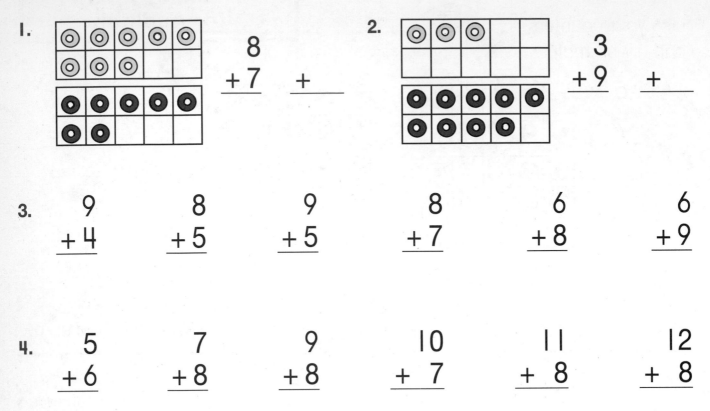
$$8 + 7 \quad +$$

2.
$$3 + 9 \quad +$$

3.
$$9 + 4 \qquad 8 + 5 \qquad 9 + 5 \qquad 8 + 7 \qquad 6 + 8 \qquad 6 + 9$$

4.
$$5 + 6 \qquad 7 + 8 \qquad 9 + 8 \qquad 10 + 7 \qquad 11 + 8 \qquad 12 + 8$$

Remember you can add numbers in any order.
Add. Loop the 10's.

5.

$$\begin{array}{c} (2) \\ 3 \\ +8 \\ \hline 13 \end{array} \qquad \begin{array}{c} 5 \\ 5 \\ +5 \\ \hline \end{array} \qquad \begin{array}{c} 9 \\ 3 \\ +7 \\ \hline \end{array} \qquad \begin{array}{c} 1 \\ 8 \\ +7 \\ \hline \end{array} \qquad \begin{array}{c} 2 \\ 6 \\ +8 \\ \hline \end{array} \qquad \begin{array}{c} 10 \\ 4 \\ +5 \\ \hline \end{array}$$

6.

$$\begin{array}{c} 9 \\ 4 \\ +6 \\ \hline \end{array} \qquad \begin{array}{c} 8 \\ 2 \\ +8 \\ \hline \end{array} \qquad \begin{array}{c} 1 \\ 9 \\ +8 \\ \hline \end{array} \qquad \begin{array}{c} 8 \\ 0 \\ +7 \\ \hline \end{array} \qquad \begin{array}{c} 6 \\ 1 \\ +8 \\ \hline \end{array} \qquad \begin{array}{c} 2 \\ 8 \\ +8 \\ \hline \end{array}$$

More Practice Set 4.2, page 396

You can draw a picture to help you solve a problem.

Work with a partner.
Finish the picture to solve each problem.

1. Jimmy and Tasha make another castle. It is shaped like a triangle. They want 6 shells along each side. How many shells do they

   need? _____ shells

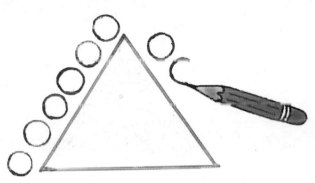

2. Carl makes a row of shells. The third shell is black. The ninth shell is blue. How many shells are between the black shell and the

   blue shell? _____ shells

3. Donna made a square cake out of sand. She made 2 cuts in the cake. How many pieces are

   there? _____

Work with a partner.
Finish the picture to solve each problem.

1. Donna finds 10 shells. There are
    5 brown shells and 2 pink shells.
    The rest are white. How many
    white shells does Donna find?

    _____ white shells

2. Jimmy is making shapes using
    shells. His triangle will have
    3 shells on each side. His square
    will have 2 shells on each side.
    How many shells will Jimmy need

    in all? _____ shells

3. The children make a pattern with
    shells. There are 5 rows with
    5 shells in each row. They put
    1 brown shell in each corner and
    1 in the middle. The rest of the
    shells are white. How many white

    shells are there? _____ white shells

4. Tasha puts 5 green shells in a
    row. Between each 2 green shells
    she puts a blue shell. How many

    shells does she use? _____ shells

Using Doubles for Addition Facts through 20

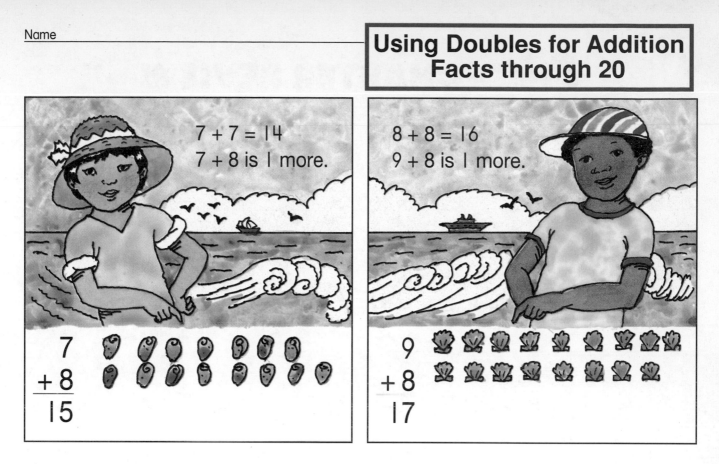

$7 + 7 = 14$
$7 + 8$ is 1 more.

$8 + 8 = 16$
$9 + 8$ is 1 more.

$$\begin{array}{r} 7 \\ +\,8 \\ \hline 15 \end{array}$$

$$\begin{array}{r} 9 \\ +\,8 \\ \hline 17 \end{array}$$

Write the sum. You may write a double to help you.

1.
$$\begin{array}{r} 8 \\ +\,9 \\ \hline 17 \end{array} \qquad \begin{array}{r} 8 \\ +\,8 \\ \hline 16 \end{array}$$

2.
$$\begin{array}{r} 5 \\ +\,6 \\ \hline \end{array}$$

3.
$$\begin{array}{r} 6 \\ +\,7 \\ \hline \end{array}$$

4.
$$\begin{array}{r} 4 \\ +\,5 \\ \hline \end{array}$$

5.
$$\begin{array}{r} 7 \\ +\,6 \\ \hline \end{array}$$

6.
$$\begin{array}{r} 7 \\ +\,8 \\ \hline \end{array}$$

7.
$$\begin{array}{r} 6 \\ +\,5 \\ \hline \end{array}$$

8.
$$\begin{array}{r} 8 \\ +\,7 \\ \hline \end{array}$$

9.
$$\begin{array}{r} 8 \\ +\,6 \\ \hline \end{array}$$

Critical Thinking Do you like to use a double to add? Why?

More Practice Set 4.4, page 397

MID-CHAPTER REVIEW

for pages 97–102

Write the sum.

1. 8 + 11 = ___   5 + 9 = ___   7 + 7 = ___

2. 6 + 5 = ___   7 + 4 = ___   6 + 4 = ___

3.
$$\begin{array}{r} 8 \\ +5 \\ \hline \end{array}\qquad \begin{array}{r} 7 \\ +8 \\ \hline \end{array}\qquad \begin{array}{r} 6 \\ +7 \\ \hline \end{array}\qquad \begin{array}{r} 7 \\ +6 \\ \hline \end{array}\qquad \begin{array}{r} 10 \\ +10 \\ \hline \end{array}\qquad \begin{array}{r} 7 \\ +3 \\ \hline \end{array}$$

4.
$$\begin{array}{r} 5 \\ +8 \\ \hline \end{array}\qquad \begin{array}{r} 9 \\ +5 \\ \hline \end{array}\qquad \begin{array}{r} 7 \\ +2 \\ \hline \end{array}\qquad \begin{array}{r} 7 \\ +9 \\ \hline \end{array}\qquad \begin{array}{r} 10 \\ +8 \\ \hline \end{array}\qquad \begin{array}{r} 8 \\ +6 \\ \hline \end{array}$$

5.
$$\begin{array}{r} 5 \\ 3 \\ +7 \\ \hline \end{array}\qquad \begin{array}{r} 10 \\ 1 \\ +8 \\ \hline \end{array}\qquad \begin{array}{r} 5 \\ 3 \\ +9 \\ \hline \end{array}\qquad \begin{array}{r} 8 \\ 2 \\ +7 \\ \hline \end{array}\qquad \begin{array}{r} 4 \\ 4 \\ +4 \\ \hline \end{array}\qquad \begin{array}{r} 6 \\ 1 \\ +9 \\ \hline \end{array}$$

Write a number sentence for the story.

6. Jimmy finds 6 starfish. Tasha finds 1 more than Jimmy. How many starfish do Tasha and Jimmy find?

7. Donna finds 8 yellow shells. So does Carl. How many shells do the children find?

_____   _____

Cross out to subtract.

Write the difference.

1.

$18 - 8 = \underline{10}$

2.

$15 - 5 = \underline{}$

3.

$12 - 2 = \underline{}$

4.

$16 - 6 = \underline{}$

5. $13 - 3 = \underline{}$ $17 - 7 = \underline{}$ $20 - 10 = \underline{}$

6. $19 - 9 = \underline{}$ $14 - 4 = \underline{}$ $11 - 1 = \underline{}$

Critical Thinking   What pattern do you see?

Problem Solving

1. Carl finds 8 white shells, 3 pebbles, and 6 black shells. How many shells does Carl find?

   _____ shells

2. A beach store had 17 pails. Some were sold. Now the store has 7 pails left. How many pails did the store sell? _____ pails

3. The children have 12 oranges. They eat 4 and give away 6. How many oranges do they have left?

   _____ oranges

4. Jimmy had more shells than Tasha. Jimmy finds 2 shells. So does Tasha. Who has more shells?

   _____

5. There are 6 children swimming in the ocean. One of them goes to play in the sand. Now there are 5 children playing in the sand. How many children are there in all? _____

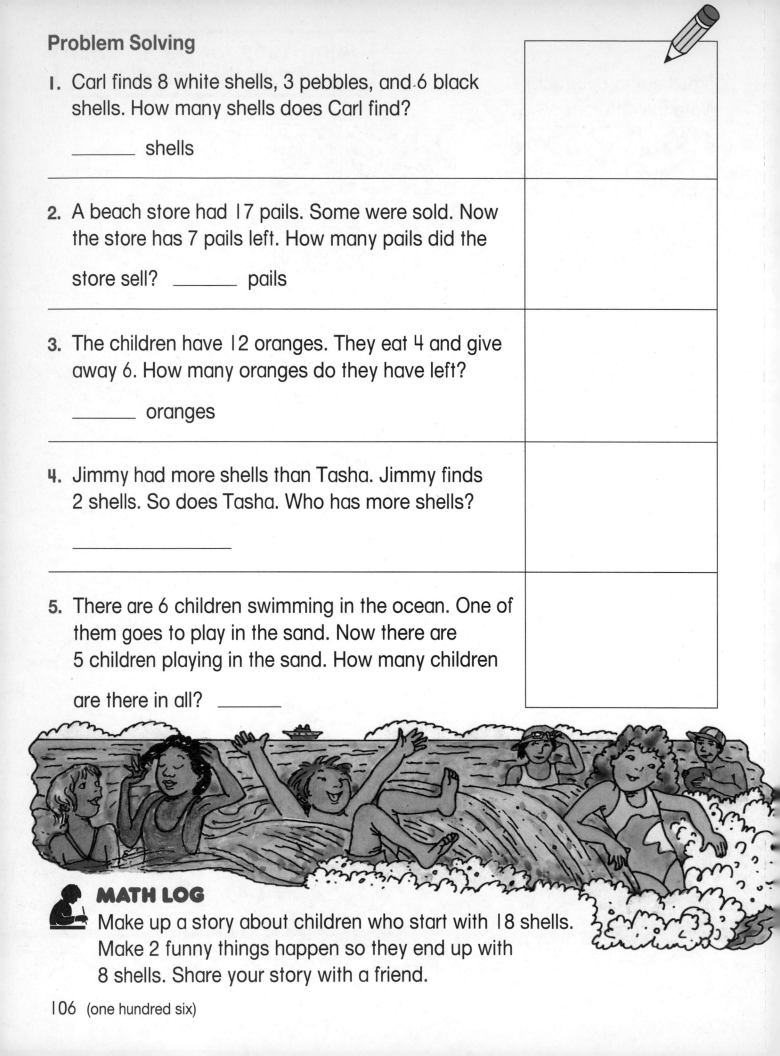

MATH LOG

Make up a story about children who start with 18 shells. Make 2 funny things happen so they end up with 8 shells. Share your story with a friend.

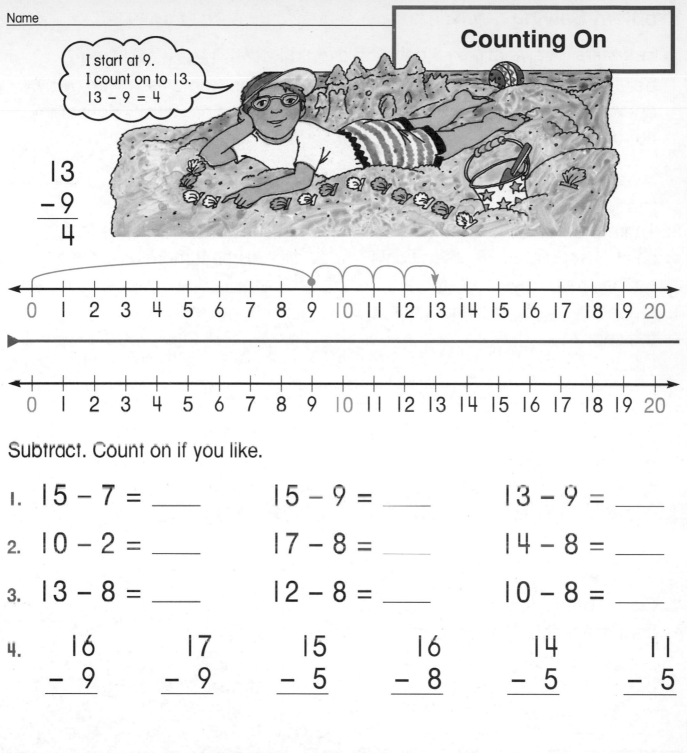

Counting On

I start at 9.
I count on to 13.
13 – 9 = 4

$$\begin{array}{r} 13 \\ -9 \\ \hline 4 \end{array}$$

Subtract. Count on if you like.

1. 15 – 7 = ____   15 – 9 = ____   13 – 9 = ____

2. 10 – 2 = ____   17 – 8 = ____   14 – 8 = ____

3. 13 – 8 = ____   12 – 8 = ____   10 – 8 = ____

4.
$$\begin{array}{r} 16 \\ -9 \\ \hline \end{array}$$
$$\begin{array}{r} 17 \\ -9 \\ \hline \end{array}$$
$$\begin{array}{r} 15 \\ -5 \\ \hline \end{array}$$
$$\begin{array}{r} 16 \\ -8 \\ \hline \end{array}$$
$$\begin{array}{r} 14 \\ -5 \\ \hline \end{array}$$
$$\begin{array}{r} 11 \\ -5 \\ \hline \end{array}$$

Now try these. You may use the number line.

5. 16 – 11 = ____   19 – 12 = ____   18 – 14 = ____

6.
$$\begin{array}{r} 18 \\ -12 \\ \hline \end{array}$$
$$\begin{array}{r} 17 \\ -11 \\ \hline \end{array}$$
$$\begin{array}{r} 19 \\ -11 \\ \hline \end{array}$$
$$\begin{array}{r} 16 \\ -10 \\ \hline \end{array}$$
$$\begin{array}{r} 20 \\ -9 \\ \hline \end{array}$$
$$\begin{array}{r} 18 \\ -8 \\ \hline \end{array}$$

Problem Solving   Write a number sentence for each story.

1. There are 15 umbrellas on the beach. There are 8 umbrellas open. How many umbrellas are not open?

_____

2. There are 16 fish swimming together. Some fish swim away. Now there are 9 fish. How many fish swam away?

_____

3. There are 9 red floats on the store shelf. Keisha puts 15 green floats on the shelf. How many more green floats than red floats are on the shelf?

_____

4. Eight children are in line to buy juice. Then 9 more children get in the line. How many children are in line altogether?

_____

5. There are 13 towels on the sand. A big wave gets 3 towels wet. How many towels stay dry?

_____

6. Jimmy needs 20 shells to make a road to his castle. He has 15 shells. How many more shells does he need?

_____

7. Donna brings 4 apples to the beach. So does Jimmy. Carl brings 4 pears. How many pieces of fruit do the children bring?

_____

More Practice Set 4.6, page 397

Name _____

Use counters and ten frames.

14 − 6	14 − 6	14 − 6 = 8

Put 14 counters in the ten frames.

Take away 6.

Count and write the difference.

Write the difference.

1.

13	14	17	15	11	17
− 7	− 6	− 9	− 9	− 9	− 8
6					

2.

14	16	12	18	16	13
− 8	− 7	− 3	− 9	− 9	− 8

Try these.

3.

19	18	15	20	19	18
− 9	− 5	− 10	− 11	− 10	− 7

Problem Solving

1. There are 14 seagulls on the sand. Four of them fly away. Later 2 more fly away. How many seagulls are on the sand now? _____ seagulls

2. Carl makes 7 sand pies. Then he makes 5 more. Donna makes 9 sand pies. Who makes more sand pies? _____

3. Donna puts ten flags on the castle. Then she puts on 3 shells and 2 pebbles. How many flags are on the castle? _____ flags

4. Jimmy sees 18 swimmers. Three of them get out of the water. Then 2 of them go back in. How many swimmers are in the water now? _____ swimmers

Maintain • Mixed Practice

Add or subtract.

1. $6 + 5 =$ ___ $12 - 5 =$ ___ $7 + 5 =$ ___

2. $12 - 7 =$ ___ $4 + 7 =$ ___ $11 - 4 =$ ___

More Practice Set 4.7, page 398

Name _____

You need two-sided counters.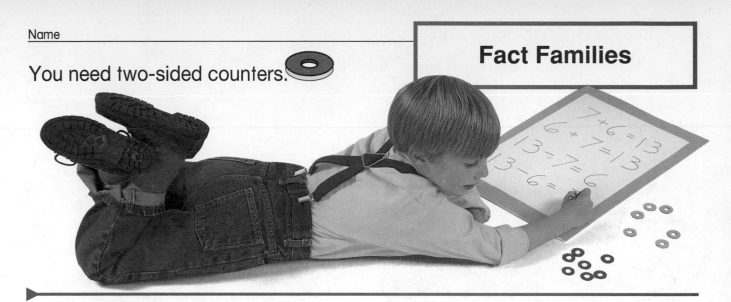

Use your counters to show each fact.

Write number sentences for each fact family.

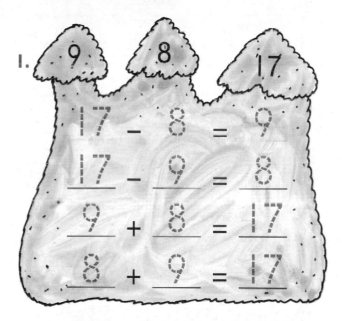

1. 9   8   17

$17 - 8 = 9$

$17 - 9 = 8$

$9 + 8 = 17$

$8 + 9 = 17$

2. 8   6   14

___ + ___ = ___

___ + ___ = ___

___ − ___ = ___

___ − ___ = ___

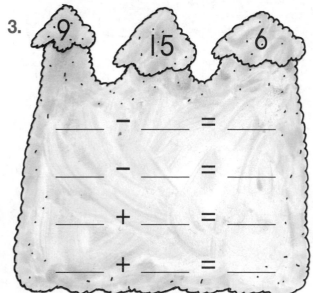

3. 9   15   6

___ − ___ = ___

___ − ___ = ___

___ + ___ = ___

___ + ___ = ___

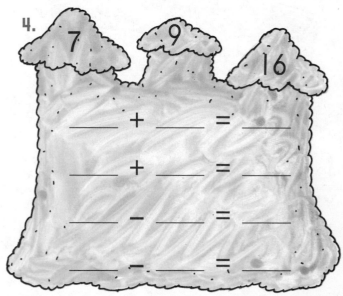

4. 7   9   16

___ + ___ = ___

___ + ___ = ___

___ − ___ = ___

___ − ___ = ___

Use your counters to show each fact.
Write number sentences for each fact family.

1.
3   12   9

____ + ____ = ____
____ + ____ = ____
____ − ____ = ____
____ − ____ = ____

2.
9   4   13

____ − ____ = ____
____ − ____ = ____
____ + ____ = ____
____ + ____ = ____

3.
13   5   8

____ − ____ = ____
____ − ____ = ____
____ + ____ = ____
____ + ____ = ____

4.
8   14   6

____ + ____ = ____
____ + ____ = ____
____ − ____ = ____
____ − ____ = ____

More Practice Set 4.8, page 398

You need counters.

8 plus 6 is __?__

Write a number from
3 to 20 in each square.

Listen to your teacher.
Find the sum or the
difference. Put a counter
on that number.

Get 4 counters in a line
and you win!

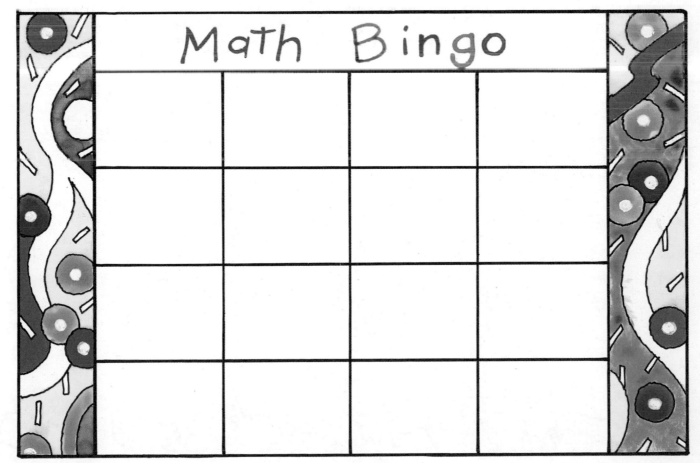

Math Bingo

Add or subtract.

1.
$$9 + 5$$
$$18 - 9$$
$$13 - 7$$
$$4 + 9$$
$$17 - 9$$
$$19 - 7$$

2.
$$7 + 9$$
$$13 - 6$$
$$8 + 7$$
$$15 - 9$$
$$6 + 8$$
$$11 + 9$$

3.
$$8 \; 2 + 5$$
$$7 \; 7 + 2$$
$$6 \; 5 + 9$$
$$5 \; 4 + 8$$
$$3 \; 8 + 7$$
$$7 \; 8 + 4$$

....

CHALLENGE • Operation Sense

Write the missing number.

4.
$$10 + \underline{} = 18$$
$$\underline{} + 5 = 14$$
$$8 + \underline{} = 20$$
$$\underline{} + 8 = 13$$
$$8 + \underline{} = 17$$
$$10 + \underline{} = 16$$

5.
$$13 - \underline{} = 9$$
$$\underline{} - 4 = 5$$
$$\underline{} - 10 = 10$$
$$17 - \underline{} = 10$$
$$19 - \underline{} = 8$$
$$14 - \underline{} = 7$$

We can write many number sentences for a number.

Write addition and subtraction sentences for each number.

| 13 |

1. _____

_____

_____

| 15 |

2. _____

_____

_____

| 16 |

3. _____

_____

_____

| 9 |

4. _____

_____

_____

Critical Thinking Share your number sentences with a friend. Talk about the different number sentences for each number.

Problem Solving

1. Donna had 10 beach toys. She gave some to Jimmy and some to Carl. Then she had 3 toys left. How many beach toys did she give away altogether?

   _____ beach toys

2. Jimmy's castle has 15 flags. Tasha's castle has 6 flags. Then Tasha puts on 7 more flags. Whose castle has more flags?

   _____ castle

3. Carl has 6 shells. Donna has 3 more shells than Carl. How many shells do they have altogether?

   _____ shells

CHALLENGE • Operation Sense

Is it addition or subtraction?
Write the sign in the circle.

1. $18 \bigcirc 5 = 13$ $6 \bigcirc 5 = 11$ $4 \bigcirc 14 = 18$

2. $19 \bigcirc 7 = 12$ $8 \bigcirc 8 = 16$ $15 \bigcirc 5 = 10$

3. $9 \bigcirc 8 = 17$ $14 \bigcirc 7 = 7$ $3 \bigcirc 9 = 12$

4. $13 \bigcirc 6 = 7$ $11 \bigcirc 5 = 6$ $6 \bigcirc 7 = 13$

More Practice Set 4.10, page 399

Name _____

Work with a partner.
Solve each problem.

1. Carl caught a small fish in his pail. Donna caught
   5 fish in her pail, and Jimmy caught 9 fish in his.

   How many fish did they catch? _____ fish

2. Tasha wants to make 16 castles by the end of the
   day. She makes 9 in the morning. How many castles
   must she make in the afternoon?

   _____ castles

3. There were 14 castles on the beach. A wave took
   away 4 of them. A puppy stepped on 1. The children
   took apart 3. How many castles are left?

   _____ castles

4. The children find 16 blue shells and 12 red shells.
   They use 6 shells of each color to make a picture
   about their day at the beach. How many blue shells

   do they have left? _____ blue shells

5. Three of the children find pennies at the beach. Carl
   found more than Jimmy. Tasha found more than
   Carl. Who found the most pennies?

   _____

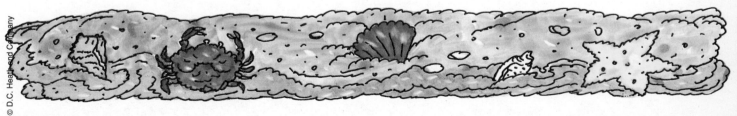

Work with a partner.
Solve each problem.

1. The store had 17 beach balls. Carl looked at 3 of them. Then he bought 1. How many beach balls are

    in the store now? _____ beach balls

2. The children find 18 pebbles. They put 10 in a pail. They leave 6 on the beach. They give away the rest. How many pebbles do they give away?

    _____ pebbles

3. At one o'clock, there were 9 children at the beach. At two o'clock, 7 more children came. At three o'clock, 2 children went home. How many children

    are still at the beach? _____ children

4. Tasha and Donna made a big castle. Nine of their friends helped. One friend had to leave early. How many children worked on the castle in all?

    _____ children

5. Jimmy has 1 more flag than Donna. If Jimmy gives 1 of his flags to Donna, who will have more flags?

    _____

CHAPTER TEST

Write the sum.

1. $\begin{array}{r} 9 \\ +9 \\ \hline \end{array}$
2. $\begin{array}{r} 5 \\ +9 \\ \hline \end{array}$
3. $\begin{array}{r} 12 \\ +\ 8 \\ \hline \end{array}$
4. $\begin{array}{r} 10 \\ +\ 3 \\ \hline \end{array}$

5. $\begin{array}{r} 5 \\ 5 \\ +5 \\ \hline \end{array}$
6. $\begin{array}{r} 9 \\ 2 \\ +8 \\ \hline \end{array}$
7. $\begin{array}{r} 10 \\ 6 \\ +\ 4 \\ \hline \end{array}$
8. $\begin{array}{r} 7 \\ 1 \\ +2 \\ \hline \end{array}$

9. $7 + 5 = \underline{\qquad}$

10. $4 + 11 = \underline{\qquad}$

11. $13 + 6 = \underline{\qquad}$

12. $14 + 3 = \underline{\qquad}$

Write the difference.

13. $\begin{array}{r} 12 \\ -\ 5 \\ \hline \end{array}$
14. $\begin{array}{r} 16 \\ -11 \\ \hline \end{array}$
15. $\begin{array}{r} 20 \\ -17 \\ \hline \end{array}$
16. $\begin{array}{r} 15 \\ -\ 7 \\ \hline \end{array}$

17. $17 - 8 = \underline{\qquad}$

18. $13 - 8 = \underline{\qquad}$

19. $20 - 2 = \underline{\qquad}$

20. $16 - 5 = \underline{\qquad}$

Write a number sentence for each fact family.

21.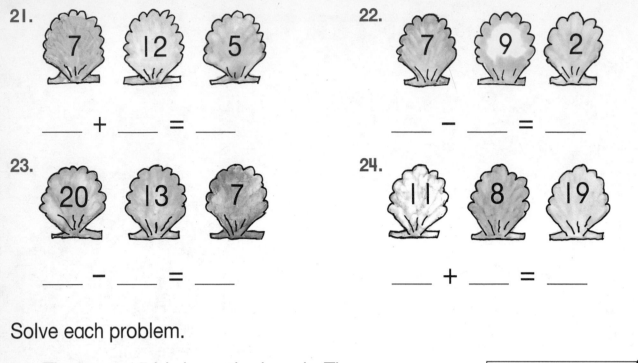

7   12   5

___ + ___ = ___

22.

7   9   2

___ − ___ = ___

23.

20   13   7

___ − ___ = ___

24.

11   8   19

___ + ___ = ___

Solve each problem.

25. There are 15 birds on the beach. Then 4 birds fly away. Soon, 3 more birds land. How many birds are on the beach?

_____ birds

26. While on the beach, Rhea finds 7 shells and Carlos finds 5 shells. Donna finds some too. The children count 20 shells in all. How many shells did Donna find?

_____ shells

Chapter Test

EXCURSION
CULTURAL DIVERSITY

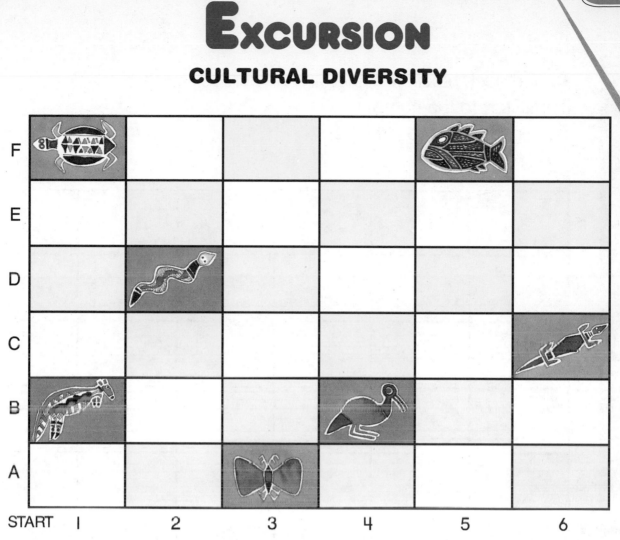

START   1   2   3   4   5   6

Find the fish.

From Start, go across (——►) to 5. Then go
up (⬆) 6 spaces to F. The fish is in box 5,F.

Write the answer. Remember: Always begin at Start.

1. Find the snake.
   From Start, go across to _____ .

   Then go up to _____ .

   The snake is in box _____ .

2. Find the bird.
   From Start, go across to _____ .

   Then go up to _____ .

   The bird is in box _____ .

3. Find the lizard.
   The lizard is in box _____ .

4. Find the tortoise.
   The tortoise is in box _____ .

5. Find the butterfly.
   The butterfly is in box _____ .

6. Find the kangaroo.
   The kangaroo is in box _____ .

Graphing

You need scissors and glue or tape.

To find each box in the grid, first go across (—▶)
from Start to the number.
Then go up (↑) to the letter.

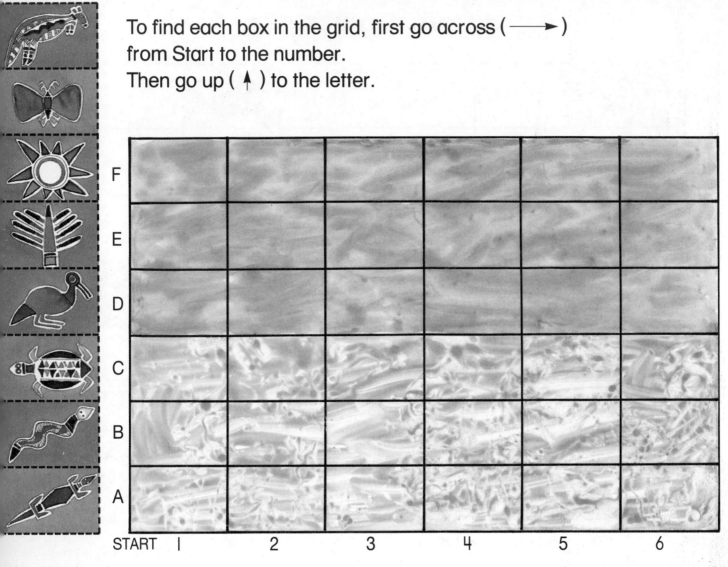

F
E
D
C
B
A

START   1   2   3   4   5   6

Cut out the pictures. Put them in the grid.

1. Put the bird in box 3,C.

2. Put the lizard in box 1,B.

3. Put the snake in box 6,A.

4. Put the sun in box 2,F.

5. Put the tortoise in box 5,C.

6. Put the butterfly in box 4,E.

7. Put the kangaroo in box 4,B.

8. Put the tree in box 2,D.

Your child has been learning about addition and subtraction through 20. This activity sheet gives your child an opportunity to share new skills with you.

FACTS RACE

You need 2 markers to move along the game board (for example: 2 different, small buttons) and 1 coin.

1. Toss the coin to determine how many spaces to move along the game board. If the coin lands heads up, move 1 space. If it lands tails up, move 2 spaces.

2. Take turns tossing the coin, moving the markers along the game board, and solving the addition or subtraction problem in the space where the marker lands. If a player solves a problem incorrectly, he or she must remain on that space for another turn to try and solve the problem again.

3. Players can use a paper and pencil, or beans or other small objects to help solve the problems.

4. If a marker lands on a happy face, the player slides the marker across the game board to the space indicated. If a marker lands on a sad face, the player must slide the marker across the game board to the space indicated.

5. The first player to reach the end wins.

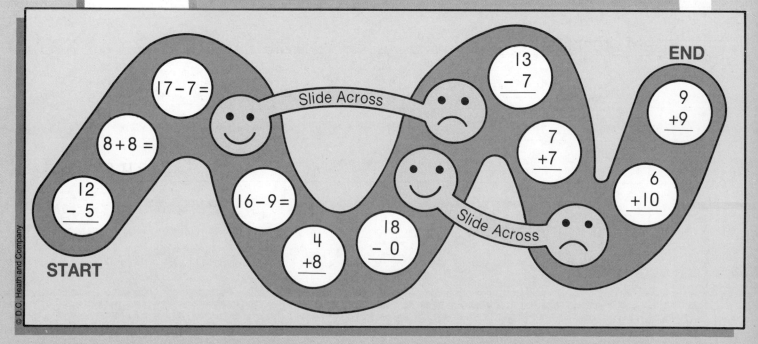

Note to the Family

In the next few weeks your child will be learning about time and money. Among the topics taught will be telling time, elapsed time, the value of money, with amounts to $1.00.

It is important for children to see time and money used outside of school. Your child can practice related skills by participating in daily household activities, such as helping to time something cooking for dinner, setting timers on a microwave oven or VCR, and helping you shop for groceries.

You may enjoy doing the following activity with your child.

HOW LONG DOES IT TAKE?

You will need a pencil and a clock or a watch.

Help your child complete this chart. Ask your child about other activities and add them to the chart.

Activity	Start Time	End Time	How long did it take?
brush teeth	:	:	:
make a bed	:	:	:
set a table	:	:	:
eat breakfast	:	:	:
do homework	:	:	:
	:	:	:
	:	:	:

CHAPTER 5

TIME AND MONEY

Listen to the story.

Time Will Tell

Plan a day at the museum.

Choose the things you would like to do.

Fill in the schedule.

10:00 – 11:00	Time Will Tell exhibit
11:00 – 12:00	
12:00 – 1:00	
1:00 – 2:00	
2:00 – 3:00	
3:00 – 4:00	Ride home.

Name _____

minute
hand

hour
hand

7:00
7 o'clock

Write the time 2 ways.

1. $4 : 00$

____4____ o'clock

2. ___ : ___

_____ o'clock

3. ___ : ___

_____ o'clock

4. ___ : ___

_____ o'clock

5. ___ : ___

_____ o'clock

6. ___ : ___

_____ o'clock

Draw the hands on the clock to show the time.

7. 11 o'clock

8. 5 : 00

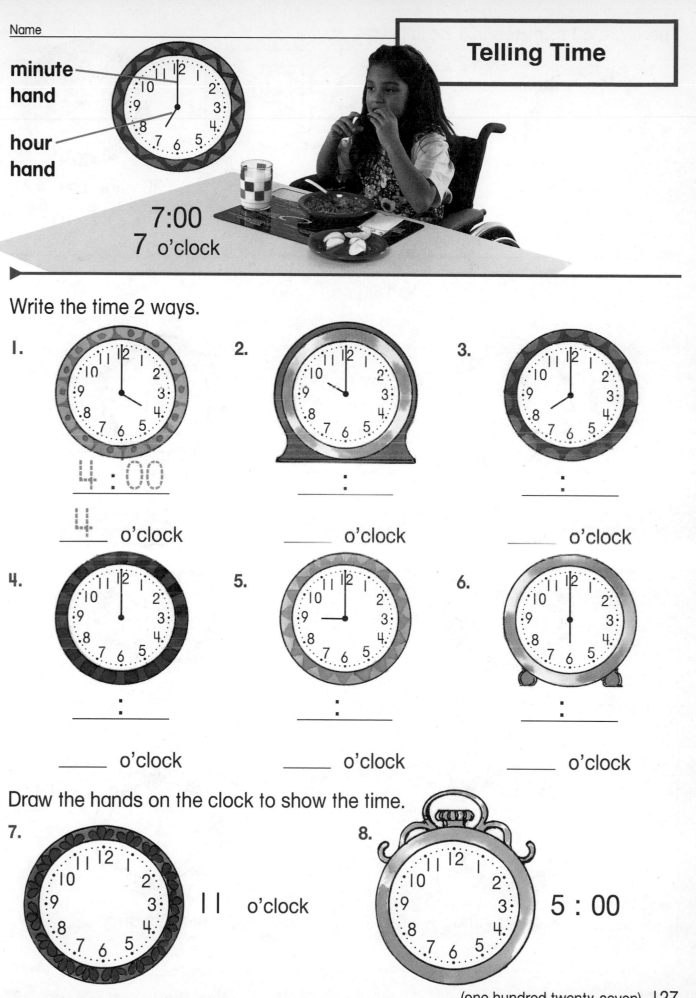

There are **60 minutes** in **1 hour.**

9 : 00

I can count by 5's to tell time.

20 minutes after 9

9 : 20

Count by 5's. Write the time 2 ways.

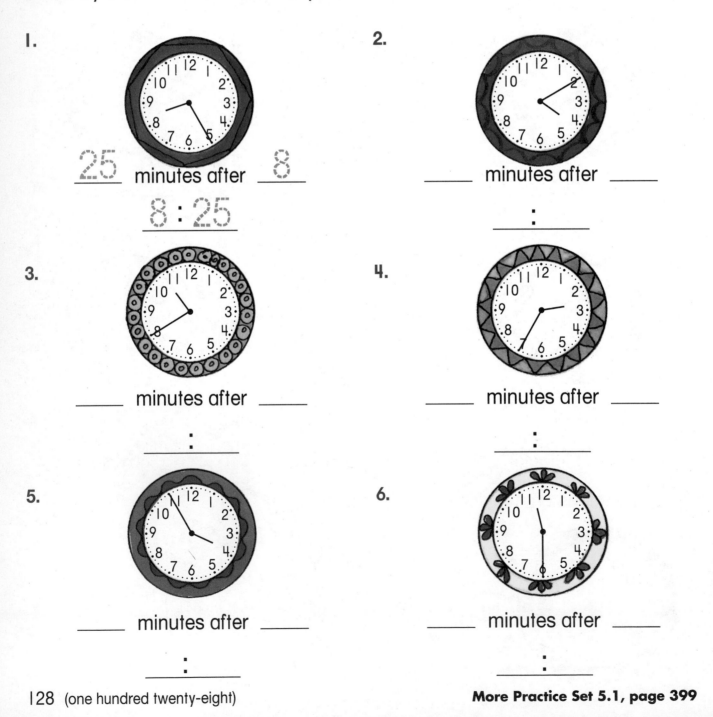

1.

_25_ minutes after _8_

_8_ : _25_

2.

_____ minutes after _____

_____ : _____

3.

_____ minutes after _____

_____ : _____

4.

_____ minutes after _____

_____ : _____

5.

_____ minutes after _____

_____ : _____

6.

_____ minutes after _____

_____ : _____

More Practice Set 5.1, page 399

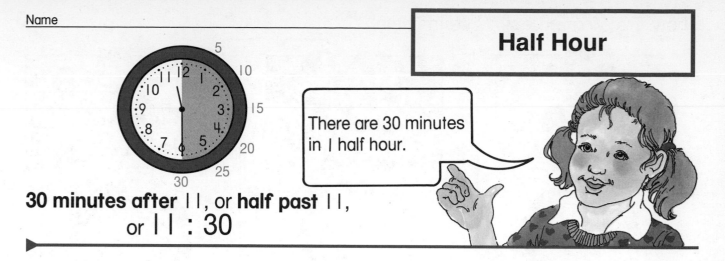

Half Hour

There are 30 minutes in 1 half hour.

30 minutes after 11, or **half past** 11,
or 11 : 30

Write the time 2 ways.

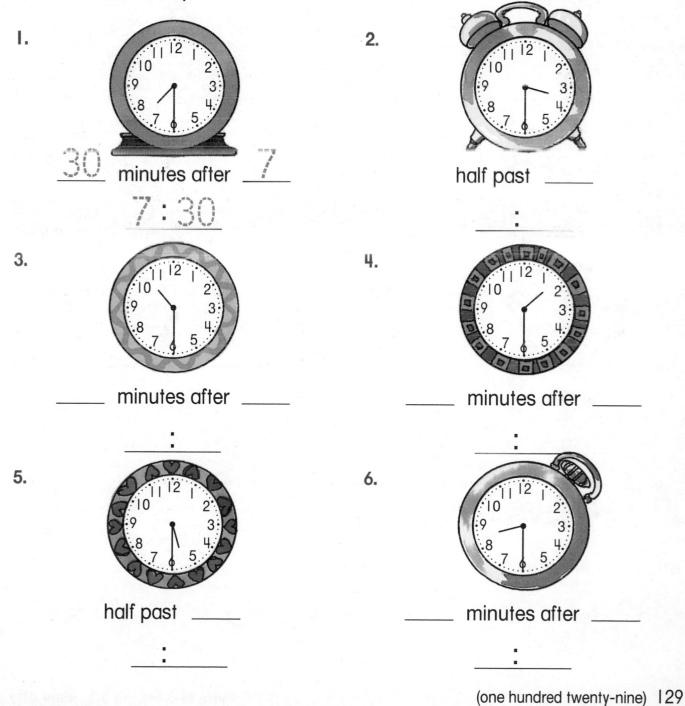

1.

___30___ minutes after ___7___

___7 : 30___

2.

half past _____

_____ : _____

3.

_____ minutes after _____

_____ : _____

4.

_____ minutes after _____

_____ : _____

5.

half past _____

_____ : _____

6.

_____ minutes after _____

_____ : _____

Draw the minute hand. Write the time.

1. 25 minutes after 11

$11:25$

2. 50 minutes after 2

___ : ___

3. 55 minutes after 12

___ : ___

4. half past 4

___ : ___

5. 30 minutes after 6

___ : ___

6. 35 minutes after 8

___ : ___

Maintain • Mixed Practice

Add or subtract.

1. $8 + 6 =$ _____ $12 - 6 =$ _____ $8 + 10 =$ _____

2. $15 - 8 =$ _____ $16 - 7 =$ _____ $9 + 8 =$ _____

More Practice Set 5.2, page 400

Telling Time to Fifteen Minutes

Count by 5's to tell the time.

45 minutes after 1

1 : 45

Write the time 2 ways.

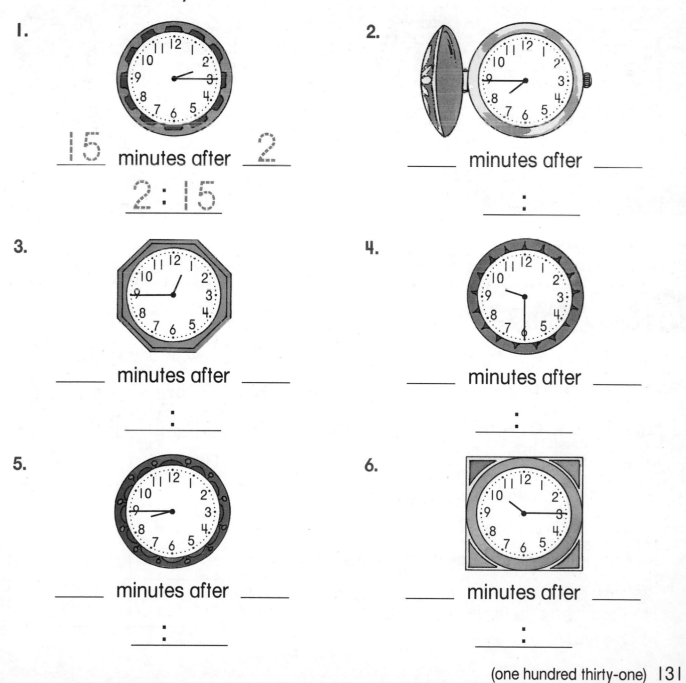

1.

_15_ minutes after _2_

_2 : 15_

2.

____ minutes after ____

____ : ____

3.

____ minutes after ____

____ : ____

4.

____ minutes after ____

____ : ____

5.

____ minutes after ____

____ : ____

6.

____ minutes after ____

____ : ____

The 2 watches tell the same time. The time is 4:45.

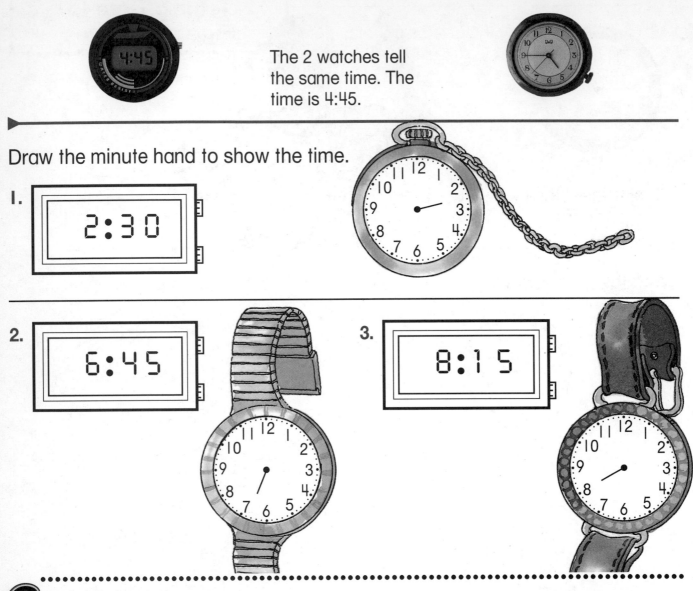

▶ Draw the minute hand to show the time.

1.

2:30

2.

6:45

3.

8:15

CHALLENGE • Time

Work with a partner. You need a digital watch. How long is a minute?

Li says that she can count to 100 in a minute. Do you think you can? Try it.

Guess and check with a watch. In 1 minute:

How many numbers can you write?
How many times could you clap your hands?
How many times could you clap your hands and touch your nose?

Guess	Real

Sequencing Events

Look at the pictures of Nora's day.
Write the numbers 1 through 6 to
put the pictures in order.

Think about your day.
Write the time you do each activity.
Write the numbers 1 through 6
to put the pictures in order.

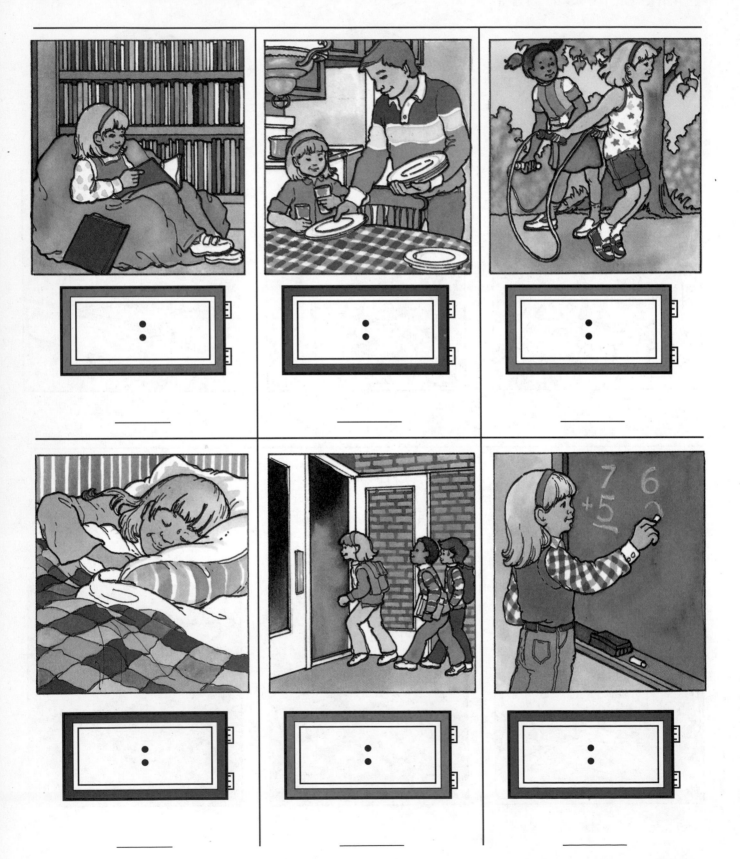

More Practice Set 5.4, page 400

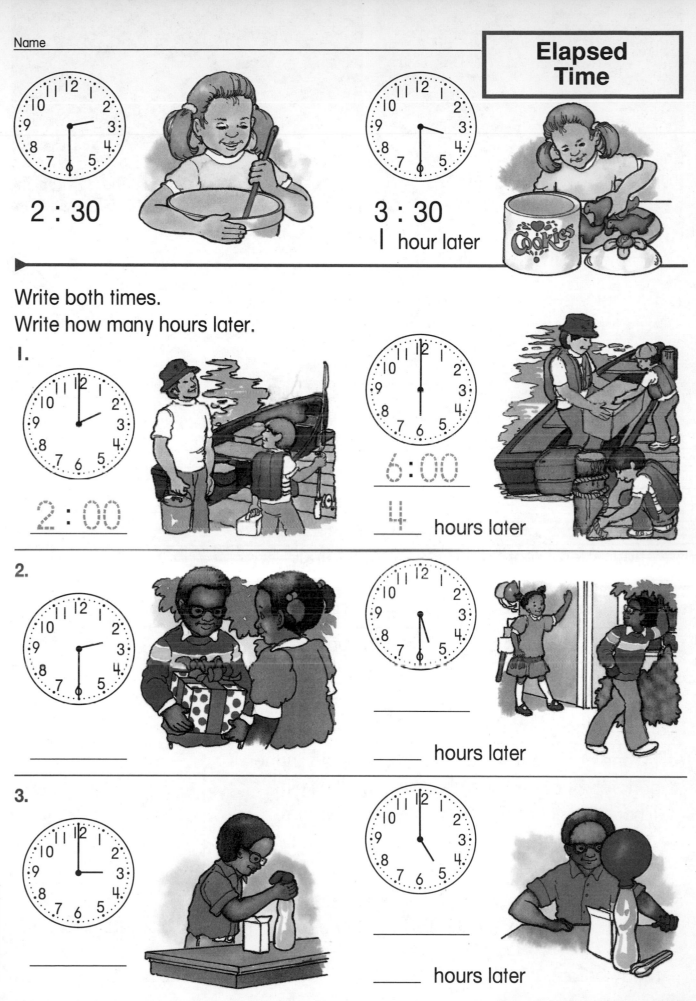

2 : 30

3 : 30
1 hour later

Write both times.
Write how many hours later.

1.

2 : 00

6:00

4 hours later

2.

_____

_____ hours later

3.

_____

_____

_____ hours later

Problem Solving   You may use a
clock to solve these problems.

1. Tyrone gets to school at 8:30 in the morning. He
   eats lunch 4 hours later. What time does Tyrone

   eat lunch? _____

2. Jack gets to Nora's house at 1:00. After 4 hours
   Jack leaves. What time does Jack leave Nora's

   house? _____

3. Nora goes to swim class at 3:30. The class ends
   1 hour later. What time does the class end?

   _____

4. Jack and his mom start to clean the garage at
   10:30. They finish cleaning 3 hours later. What

   time do Jack and his mom finish? _____

5. Tyrone goes to the park at 3:00. He plays in the
   park for 2 hours. Then he leaves. It takes him
   1 hour to get home. What time does Tyrone

   get home? _____

6. Nora's mother begins to fix dinner at 4:00. It will
   take 2 hours to fix dinner. Will dinner be

   ready before 6:30? _____

136 (one hundred thirty-six)

More Practice Set 5.5, page 401

Using a Calendar

Use the calendar to answer each question.

1. What month comes just after March? __April__

2. What month and day is Thanksgiving?

_____ , _____

3. What is the fifth month of the year? _____

4. Name a month that is in the winter.

_____

5. Circle your birthday. Write the month and the date.

_____ , _____

Sunday	Monday	Tuesday	Wednesday	Thursday	Friday	Saturday

Complete the calendar for this month.
Answer each question.

1. How many days are in this month? _____

2. What day will it be tomorrow? _____

3. How many days are in a week? _____

4. What is the first day of next month? _____

5. How many Tuesdays are in this month? _____

6. What day was it yesterday? _____

7. What is the date of the first Tuesday? _____

8. How many Saturdays are in this month? _____

More Practice Set 5.6, page 401

Nora visited the museum. The clocks show a time that Nora was in each room. Write each time. Draw a line to show the path Nora took.

Start

11:00

_____

_____

_____

_____

_____

MID-CHAPTER REVIEW

Write the time 2 ways.

1.

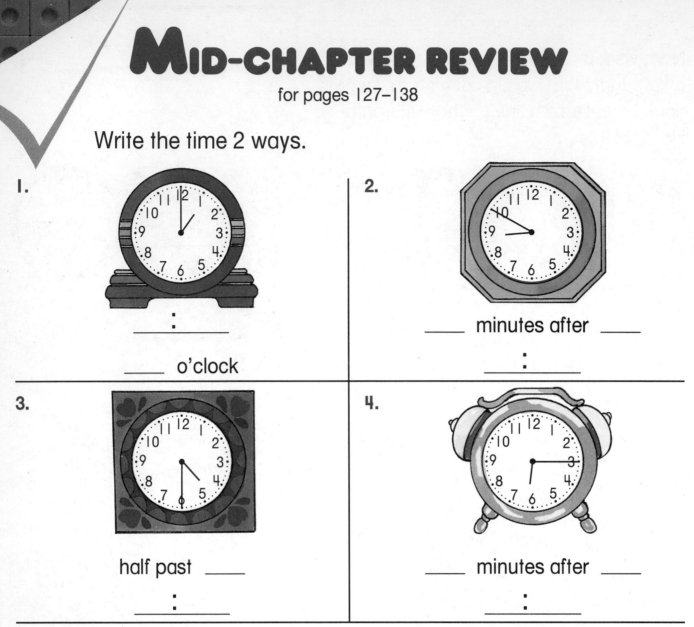

_____ : _____

_____ o'clock

2.

_____ minutes after _____

_____ : _____

3.

half past _____

_____ : _____

4.

_____ minutes after _____

_____ : _____

Write the time. Write how many hours later.

5.

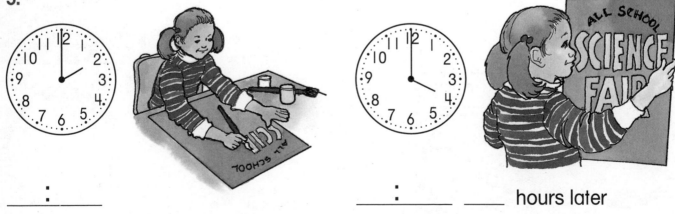

_____ : _____   _____ : _____ _____ hours later

6. Write today's date with the month, day, and year.

_____

Work with a partner.

1. In how many different ways can Jack,
   Tyrone, and Nora sit for their picture?
   Here are 2 ways.

You can **make a list** to help you solve some problems.

Jack	Tyrone	Nora
Jack	Nora	Tyrone

List the other ways.

_____ _____ _____

_____ _____ _____

_____ _____ _____

_____ _____ _____

How many different ways are there? _____

2. In how many ways can Jack see the 3 shows? _____
   Finish the list to answer the question.

First Show	Second Show	Third Show
Light	Space	Robot

SPACE SHOW

Robot SHOW

LIGHT SHOW

Work with a partner.
Finish the list to solve each problem.

1. The Dino-Maker kit from the gift shop lets you make different models. How many models can you make?

_____ models

Head	Body
red	blue

2. How many different paths can you take from the Main Hall to the Robot Show?

_____ paths

First Path	Second Path
red	green

You need coins.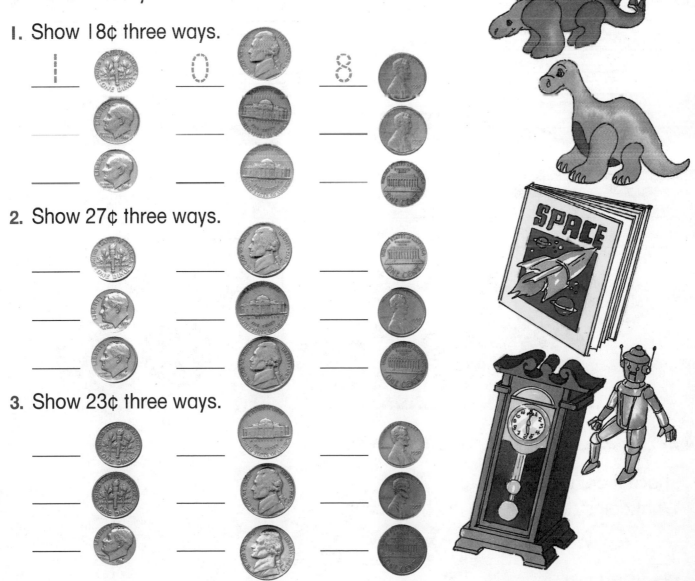

Penny, Nickel, and Dime

dime	**nickel**	**penny**
10 cents	5 cents	1 cent
10¢	5¢	1¢

Use coins to show each amount.
Write how many.

1. Show 18¢ three ways.

____ 1   ____ 0   ____ 8

____   ____   ____

____   ____   ____

2. Show 27¢ three ways.

____   ____   ____

____   ____   ____

____   ____   ____

3. Show 23¢ three ways.

____   ____   ____

____   ____   ____

____   ____   ____

(one hundred forty-three) 143

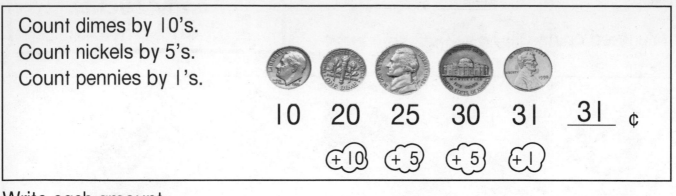

Count dimes by 10's.
Count nickels by 5's.
Count pennies by 1's.

10   20   25   30   31   _31_ ¢

(+10) (+5) (+5) (+1)

Write each amount.

1.

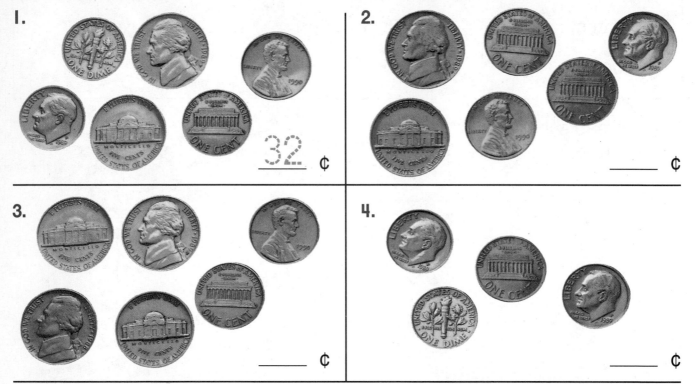

_32_ ¢

2.

_____ ¢

3.

_____ ¢

4.

_____ ¢

Loop the set with more money.

5.

I have 4 coins. I have 25¢ in all.
What coins do I have? Write how many.

 _____   _____   _____

You need coins.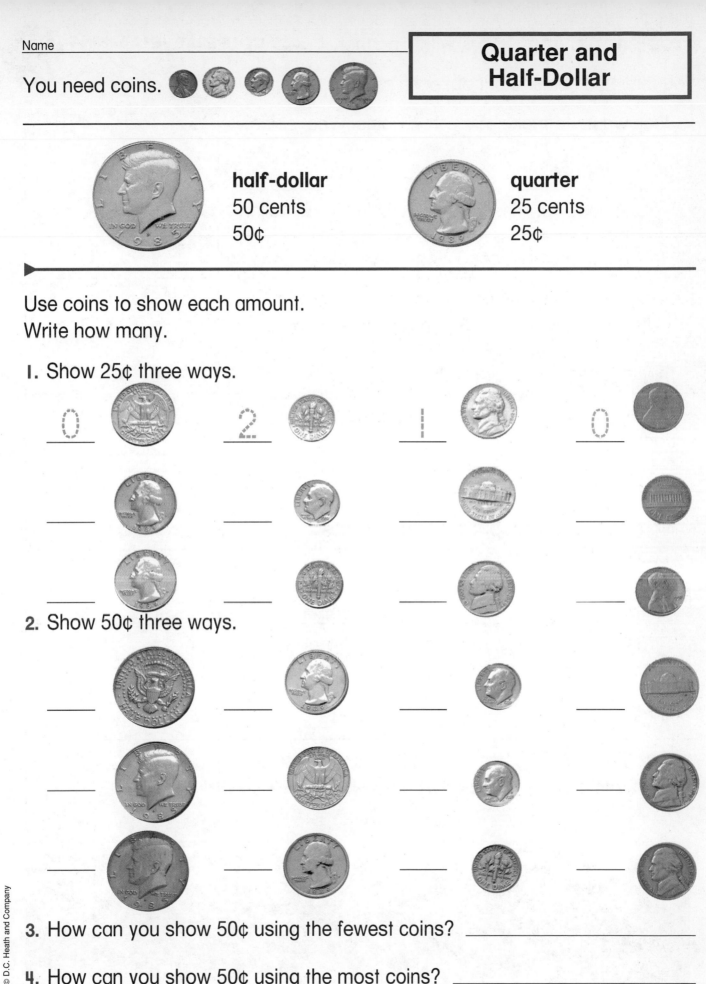

Quarter and Half-Dollar

half-dollar
50 cents
50¢

quarter
25 cents
25¢

Use coins to show each amount.
Write how many.

1. Show 25¢ three ways.

| 0 | (quarter) | 2 | (dime) | 1 | (nickel) | 0 | (penny) |

| ___ | (quarter) | ___ | (dime) | ___ | (nickel) | ___ | (penny) |

| ___ | (quarter) | ___ | (dime) | ___ | (nickel) | ___ | (penny) |

2. Show 50¢ three ways.

| ___ | (half-dollar) | ___ | (quarter) | ___ | (dime) | ___ | (nickel) |

| ___ | (half-dollar) | ___ | (quarter) | ___ | (dime) | ___ | (nickel) |

| ___ | (half-dollar) | ___ | (quarter) | ___ | (dime) | ___ | (nickel) |

3. How can you show 50¢ using the fewest coins? _____

4. How can you show 50¢ using the most coins? _____

Problem Solving Work with a partner. ── COOPERATIVE LEARNING

You may use coins to act out each problem.

1. Jack wants to make 15¢ with 3 coins. What coins does Jack use? _____	
2. Tyrone has 25¢. His mother gives him 1 half-dollar. How much money does Tyrone have now? _____ ¢	
3. Jack is saving money to buy a book. He saves 1 dime, 2 quarters, and 3 pennies. How much money does Jack have so far? _____ ¢	
4. Nora and Jack have the same number of coins. Jack has quarters. Nora has dimes. Who has more money? _____	
5. Nora has 70¢ in her pocket. She only has 3 coins. What coins does Nora have? _____	
6. Tyrone has 80¢ to spend. He has 1 half-dollar. He has 2 other coins. What other coins does Tyrone have? _____	
7. Nora has 70¢. She has 6 coins that are the same and 2 more coins. What coins does Nora have?	

Estimating Costs

Can I buy the book?
I do not need to count.
I can estimate. I have
a quarter. I know I
have enough money.

Can you buy the item? Estimate.
Check *yes* or *no*.

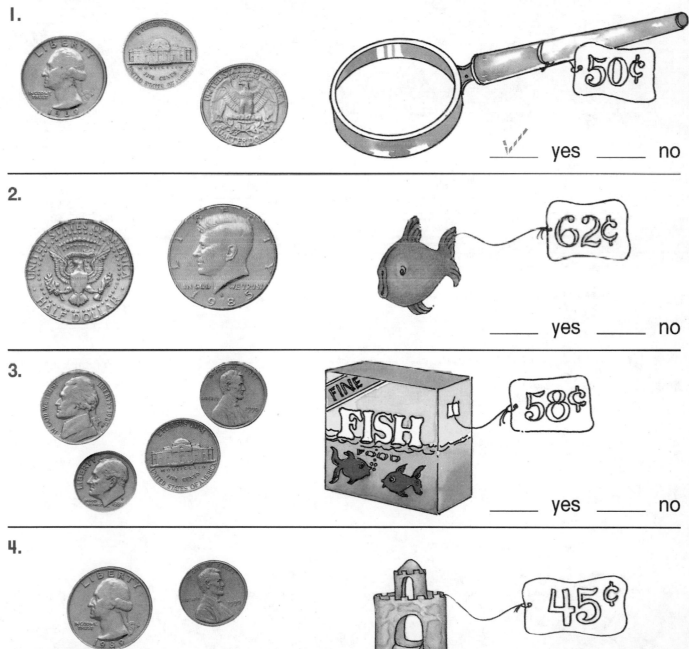

1. 50¢

_____ yes _____ no

2. 62¢

_____ yes _____ no

3. 58¢

_____ yes _____ no

4. 45¢

_____ yes _____ no

Can you buy both items? Estimate.
Check *yes* or *no*.

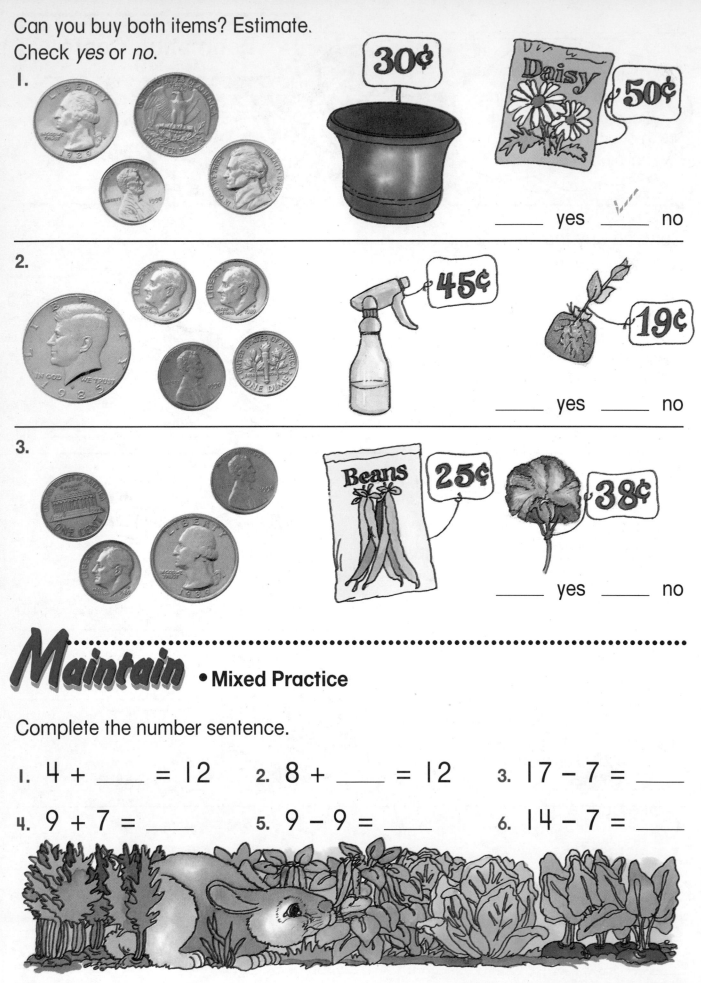

1. 30¢ Daisy 50¢

_____ yes __✓__ no

2. 45¢ 19¢

_____ yes _____ no

3. Beans 25¢ 38¢

_____ yes _____ no

Maintain •Mixed Practice

Complete the number sentence.

1. $4 + \underline{\quad} = 12$ 2. $8 + \underline{\quad} = 12$ 3. $17 - 7 = \underline{\quad}$

4. $9 + 7 = \underline{\quad}$ 5. $9 - 9 = \underline{\quad}$ 6. $14 - 7 = \underline{\quad}$

Name _____

You need coins.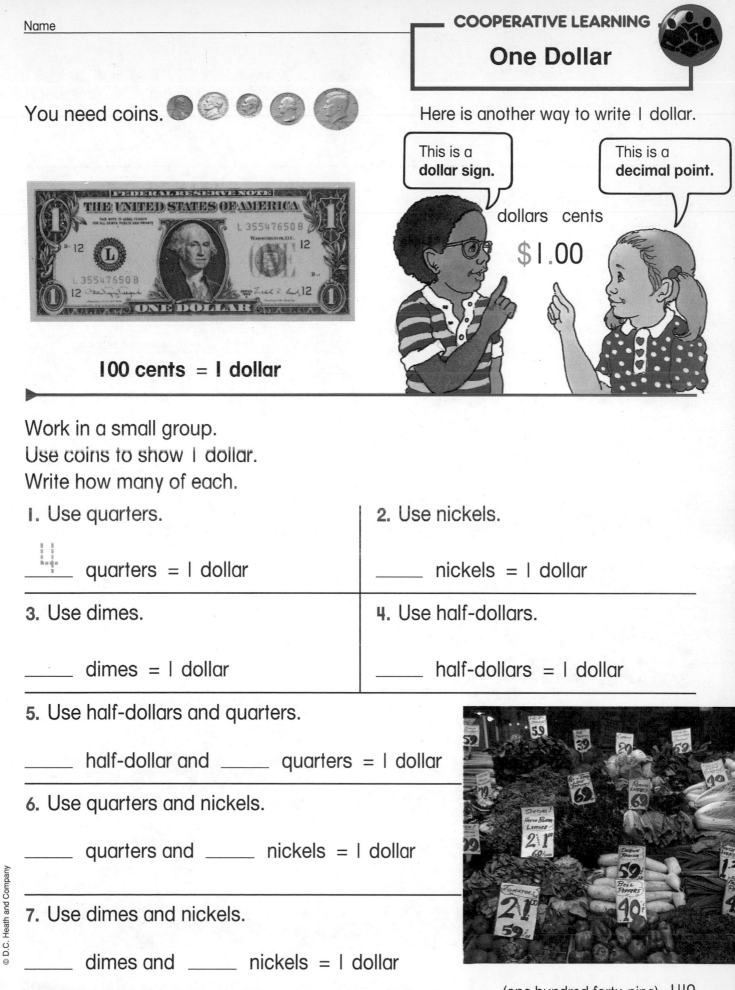

Here is another way to write 1 dollar.

This is a **dollar sign.**

This is a **decimal point.**

dollars   cents

$1.00

100 cents = 1 dollar

Work in a small group.
Use coins to show 1 dollar.
Write how many of each.

1. Use quarters.

_____ quarters = 1 dollar

2. Use nickels.

_____ nickels = 1 dollar

3. Use dimes.

_____ dimes = 1 dollar

4. Use half-dollars.

_____ half-dollars = 1 dollar

5. Use half-dollars and quarters.

_____ half-dollar and _____ quarters = 1 dollar

6. Use quarters and nickels.

_____ quarters and _____ nickels = 1 dollar

7. Use dimes and nickels.

_____ dimes and _____ nickels = 1 dollar

23¢
You can use the dollar sign and decimal point to write the amount.

$0.23

Write the amount. Use the dollar sign and decimal point.

1.  $ 0.32

2. $.

3. $.

· ·

CHALLENGE • Math Sense

Use all the coins to buy only 2 items.
Loop the items you buy.

$0.15

$0.75

$0.45

150 (one hundred fifty)

More Practice Set 5.12, page 403

Work with a partner.
You may use coins or a clock to solve each problem.

1. At the gift shop, Ella wants to buy a sticker for 25¢ and a pin for 65¢. She has 2 quarters and 5 dimes.

   Does she have enough money? _____

2. Tyrone goes to the gift shop at 2 o'clock. His father is coming to pick him up in 1 hour. At what time will his father arrive at the museum?

   _____

3. Nora leaves home for the museum at 8:00. Her mother says to be home in 5 hours. By what time should Nora be home? _____

4. Jack waits in the lunch line for 10 minutes. He spends $2.00 for lunch. It takes him 30 minutes to eat lunch and clean his space. How long is Jack in the lunchroom? _____ minutes

5. Nora buys a magnet. She gives the clerk a one-dollar bill. She gets 2 quarters in change. How much does the magnet cost? _____

6. A dinosaur kit costs $5.00. Tyrone has 4 one-dollar bills and 1 half-dollar. How much more money does Tyrone need to buy the kit? _____

Work with a partner.

You may use coins or a clock to solve each problem.

1. The film about the planet Mars is 45 minutes long. Nora must leave for home in half an hour. Does she

   have enough time to watch the film? _____

2. Jack has 2 one-dollar bills to spend at the gift shop. He wants to buy a set of stickers for $0.95 and a note card for $0.85. Does Jack have

   enough money to buy both? _____

3. Jon arrives at the museum at 9:00. He leaves the museum at 1:00. How many hours does Jon

   spend at the museum? _____ hours

4. Nora has 4 quarters. Sam has 8 dimes. Who has

   more money? _____

5. Tyrone wants to buy 6 postcards that are 10¢ each. He has only 1 quarter and 1 nickel. How

   many postcards can he really buy? ___ postcards

6. Jack begins a project for his mother at 11:30. He cuts out paper shapes until 12:30. Then he glues them down until 1:00. Does Jack spend more time

   cutting or gluing? _____

CHAPTER TEST

Look at the pictures.
Write the time.

1.   2.

3.   4.

Look at the pictures in problems 1–4.
Write the numbers 1 through 4 to put the
pictures in order.

5. Picture 1   6. Picture 2   7. Picture 3   8. Picture 4

_____   _____   _____   _____

Draw hands on the clock to show the time.

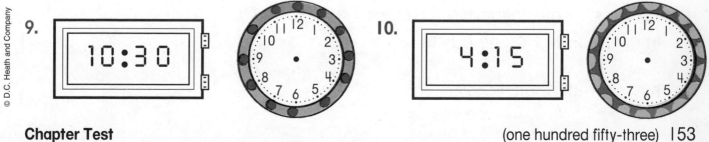

9. `10:30`   10. `4:15`

Think about a calendar. Loop the correct answer.

11. What month comes between August and October?

September   November

12. What is the fifth month of the year?

April   May

Write the amount. Use a dollar sign and decimal point.

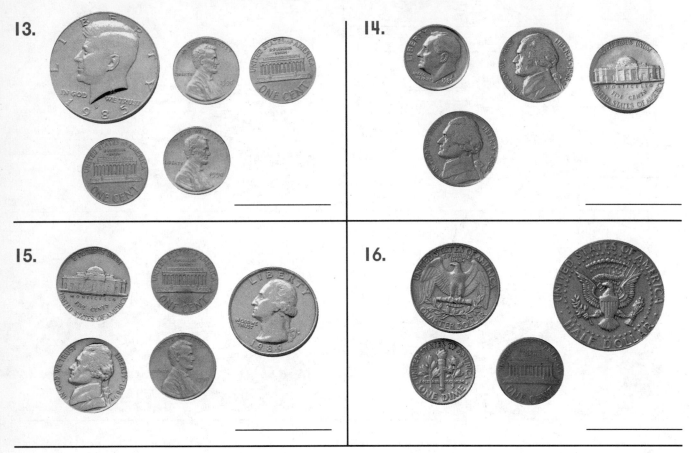

13. _____

14. _____

15. _____

16. _____

Solve each problem.

17. The swimming pool opens at 12:00. It stays open for 4 hours. At what time does the pool close?

_____

18. Lee has 1 half-dollar and 4 nickels in his pocket. Can he buy a

marker that costs $0.89? _____

EXCURSION
CULTURAL DIVERSITY

You need a paper clip, a pencil, and crayons.

Hold the paper clip on the dot with the pencil to make a spinner.

1. Spin the paper clip 20 times. Color a box red or blue to show each spin.

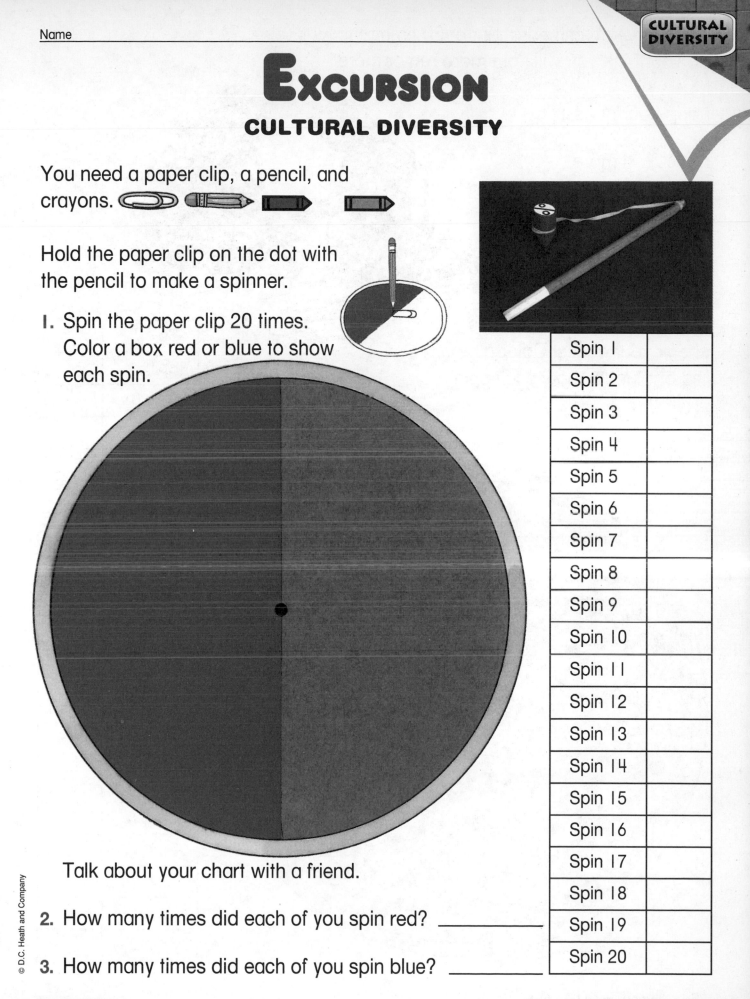

Talk about your chart with a friend.

2. How many times did each of you spin red? _____

3. How many times did each of you spin blue? _____

Spin 1	
Spin 2	
Spin 3	
Spin 4	
Spin 5	
Spin 6	
Spin 7	
Spin 8	
Spin 9	
Spin 10	
Spin 11	
Spin 12	
Spin 13	
Spin 14	
Spin 15	
Spin 16	
Spin 17	
Spin 18	
Spin 19	
Spin 20	

Guess. If you spin this spinner 20 times,
do you think you will spin more red or more
blue?
Loop your guess.

| more | more |
| red | blue |

Spin the paper clip 20 times to
check your guess. Color a box
red or blue to show each spin.

Spin 1	
Spin 2	
Spin 3	
Spin 4	
Spin 5	
Spin 6	
Spin 7	
Spin 8	
Spin 9	
Spin 10	
Spin 11	
Spin 12	
Spin 13	
Spin 14	
Spin 15	
Spin 16	
Spin 17	
Spin 18	
Spin 19	
Spin 20	

Your child has been learning about time and money. This activity sheet gives your child an opportunity to share new skills with you.

COIN COUNT

You need a minimum of 9 pennies, 5 nickels, 5 dimes, 5 quarters, and 1 half-dollar. Also, you need some household objects with prices up to $1.00, a pad of paper, and a pencil or pen.

1. Put the household items on a table or counter. These can be items with real price tags or items you tag yourself. You might want to use food items so that your child can "order" dinner or an afternoon snack. Be sure the price of each item is less than a dollar.

2. Let your child pick out the items. Have your child pay for each item using the exact amount of coins.

3. You can vary the activity by picking the items and then paying your child.

25¢

MILK 40¢

CALENDAR TIME

You and your child can use a calendar to plan next month's activities. Your child can write in family and friend's birthdays, holidays, appointments, trips, sporting events, or other activities. Your child can use crayons or cut out pictures to decorate the calendar.

November

Sunday	Monday	Tuesday	Wednesday	Thursday	Friday	Saturday
1	2 Jack's party	3	4 Lauren's game 3:00	5	6	7 Grandpa for Dinner 7:30
8 Circus Day	9 No school	10 Doctor's 4:00	11	12	13	14 Cub Scout Can Day

Note to the Family

In the next few weeks, your child will be learning about addition of 2-digit numbers.

It is important for children to see addition used outside of school. Your child can practice the addition skills by participating in daily household activities such as adding prices of items in the kitchen cabinet, and adding money that is spent daily on lunch, milk, and the newspaper.

It might be fun to play this game with your child.

ADDITION SPIN

You will need the two number wheels at the bottom of this page, two pencils, and two small paper clips.

1. Use the number wheels as spinners. Place a paper clip on the center of each wheel. Place a pencil through the clip on top of the dot in the center of each wheel. Spin one paper clip and write the number on a piece of lined paper.

2. Repeat with the second wheel. Write the number indicated by the paper clip.

3. Add the numbers. Let your child tell you the steps he or she took while adding.

4. To make the game more competitive, you and your child spin, record, and add the two numbers in each turn. The player with the higher sum at the end of a turn scores a point. If a player adds incorrectly, she or he forfeits that turn, and the other player automatically scores a point for that turn. The player with the most points at the end of a specified number of turns wins.

CHAPTER 6

ADDITION OF 2-DIGIT NUMBERS

Listen to the story.

The Princess Wants a Puppy

(one hundred fifty-nine) 159

Add or take away from each gift.
Make gifts that can be counted
into sets of 10. Write how many.

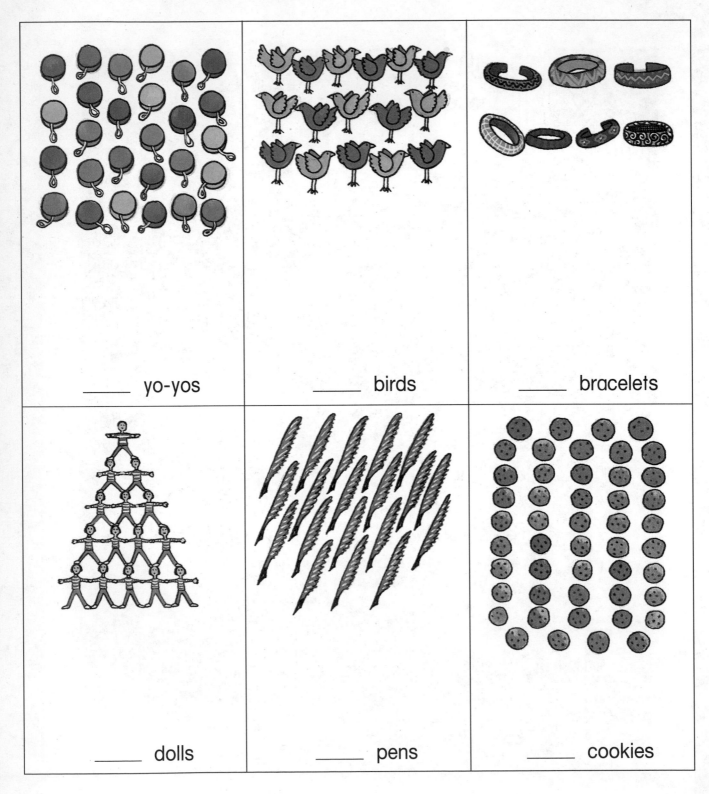

_____ yo-yos

_____ birds

_____ bracelets

_____ dolls

_____ pens

_____ cookies

Which gift did you change the least? _____

Add.

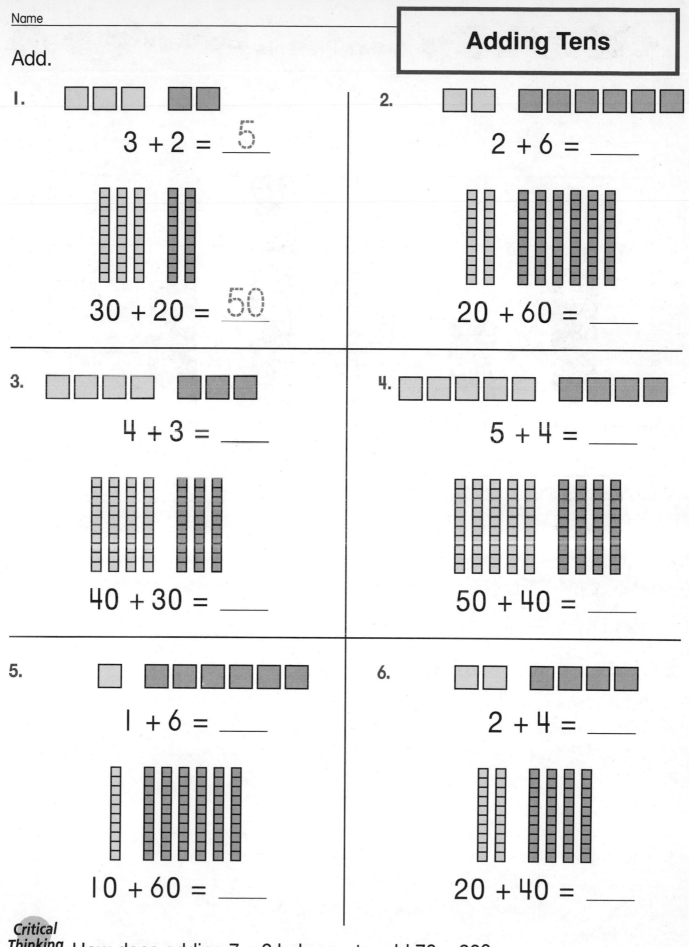

1. $3 + 2 = \underline{5}$

$30 + 20 = \underline{50}$

2. $2 + 6 = \underline{}$

$20 + 60 = \underline{}$

3. $4 + 3 = \underline{}$

$40 + 30 = \underline{}$

4. $5 + 4 = \underline{}$

$50 + 40 = \underline{}$

5. $1 + 6 = \underline{}$

$10 + 60 = \underline{}$

6. $2 + 4 = \underline{}$

$20 + 40 = \underline{}$

Critical Thinking How does adding $7 + 2$ help you to add $70 + 20$?

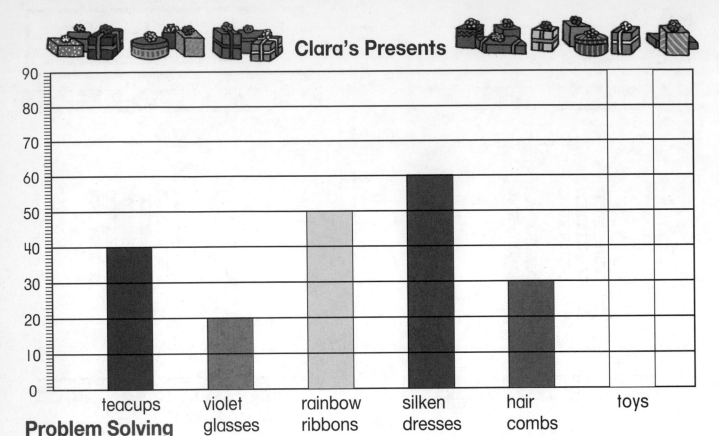

Clara's Presents

Problem Solving

The Royal Counters made a graph of the
gifts Princess Clara received. Use the
graph to solve each problem.

1. Clara can put hair combs and ribbons in her hair.
How many things did Clara get that she

can use in her hair? _____

2. Clara can also put the ribbons on the dresses she
got. Can Clara put 1 ribbon on every dress?

_____

3. How many more teacups than glasses did Clara

get? _____

4. The children of the kingdom gave Clara toys. One
group gave her 50 balls. Another group gave her 40
jacks. Fill in the graph to show how many toys the
children gave Clara.

More Practice Set 6.1, page 403

Write a number sentence for the coins.

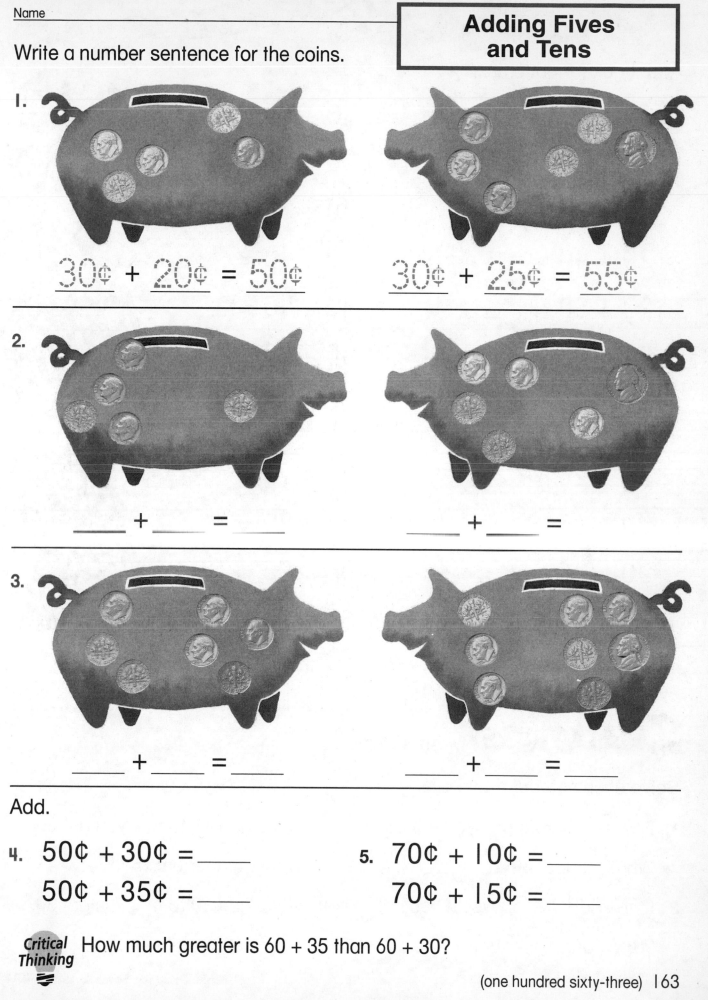

1. 30¢ + 20¢ = 50¢   30¢ + 25¢ = 55¢

2. ___ + ___ = ___   ___ + ___ = ___

3. ___ + ___ = ___   ___ + ___ = ___

Add.

4. 50¢ + 30¢ = ____

    50¢ + 35¢ = ____

5. 70¢ + 10¢ = ____

    70¢ + 15¢ = ____

Critical Thinking How much greater is 60 + 35 than 60 + 30?

Add. Look for patterns.

1. 20 + 10 = _30_

   20 + 20 = _40_

   20 + 30 = ___

   20 + 40 = ___

   20 + 50 = ___

   20 + 60 = ___

2. 40 + 25 = ___

   40 + 30 = ___

   40 + 35 = ___

   40 + 40 = ___

   40 + 45 = ___

   40 + 50 = ___

3. 20 + 15 = ___

   20 + 25 = ___

   20 + 35 = ___

   20 + 45 = ___

   20 + 55 = ___

   20 + 65 = ___

4. 35 + 10 = ___

   35 + 15 = ___

   35 + 20 = ___

   35 + 25 = ___

   35 + 30 = ___

   35 + 35 = ___

CHALLENGE • Mental Math

Solve each number riddle.

1. If you add 10 to me, you get 35.

   What number am I? _____

2. If you add 10 to me, you get 50.

   What number am I? _____

3. If you add me to myself, you get

   20. What number am I? _____

4. If you add 30 to me, you get 30.

   What number am I? _____

More Practice Set 6.2, page 404

Work with a partner.
Make cards to help you guess.

The palace helpers need to put
3 stacks of plates at each end of
the party table. Each end of the
table should get the same
number of plates. Which stacks
should go at each end of the
table?

Try this guess:

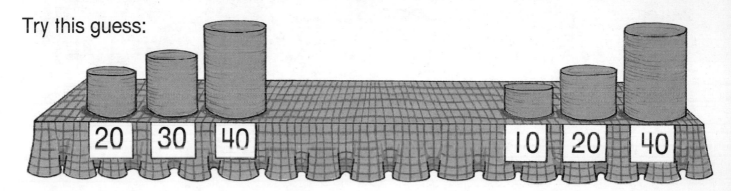

Check the guess.

$$
\begin{array}{r} 20 \\ 30 \\ +\,40 \\ \hline 90 \end{array}
\qquad
\begin{array}{r} 10 \\ 20 \\ +\,40 \\ \hline 70 \end{array}
$$

Is the guess right? _____

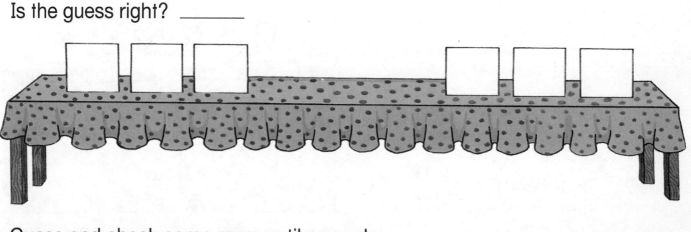

Guess and check some more until you solve
the problem. Write the answers in the boxes.

Work with a partner.
Solve each problem.
You may guess and check.
You may use number cards.

1. It will cost 80¢ for Clara's Aunt Marta to mail her a present. Aunt Marta has these stamps. Loop the stamps Aunt Marta should use.

2. Tomás played bag toss at Clara's party. He made 2 tosses and scored a total of 50 points. His second toss was 30 points higher than his first toss. What did he score on each toss?

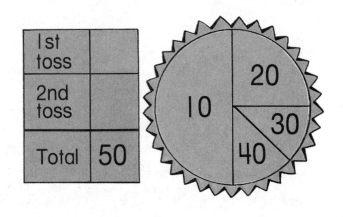

1st toss	
2nd toss	
Total	50

3. Clara got bags of marbles. She wants to share them with Tomás so they both have the same number of marbles. Which bags should each one get?

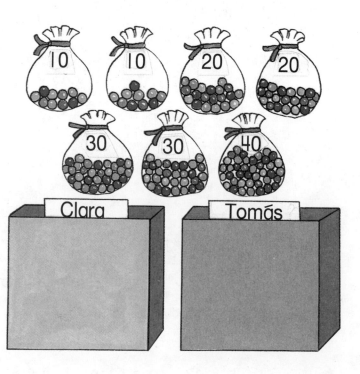

Clara wanted to share her marbles with 3 friends. Then all four friends would have the same number of marbles. How many would each child get?

_____ marbles

Use blocks
and a workmat.

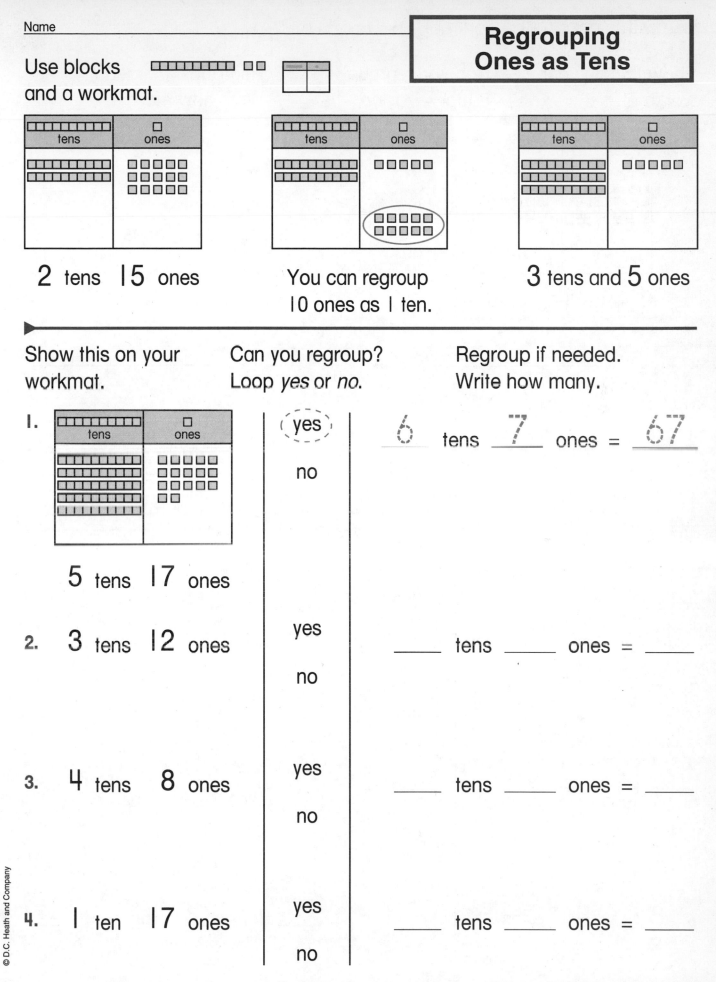

2 tens 15 ones

You can regroup
10 ones as 1 ten.

3 tens and 5 ones

Show this on your
workmat.

Can you regroup?
Loop *yes* or *no*.

Regroup if needed.
Write how many.

1.
5 tens 17 ones

(yes)

no

6 tens __7__ ones = __67__

2. 3 tens 12 ones

yes

no

____ tens ____ ones = ____

3. 4 tens 8 ones

yes

no

____ tens ____ ones = ____

4. 1 ten 17 ones

yes

no

____ tens ____ ones = ____

Use with blocks and a workmat.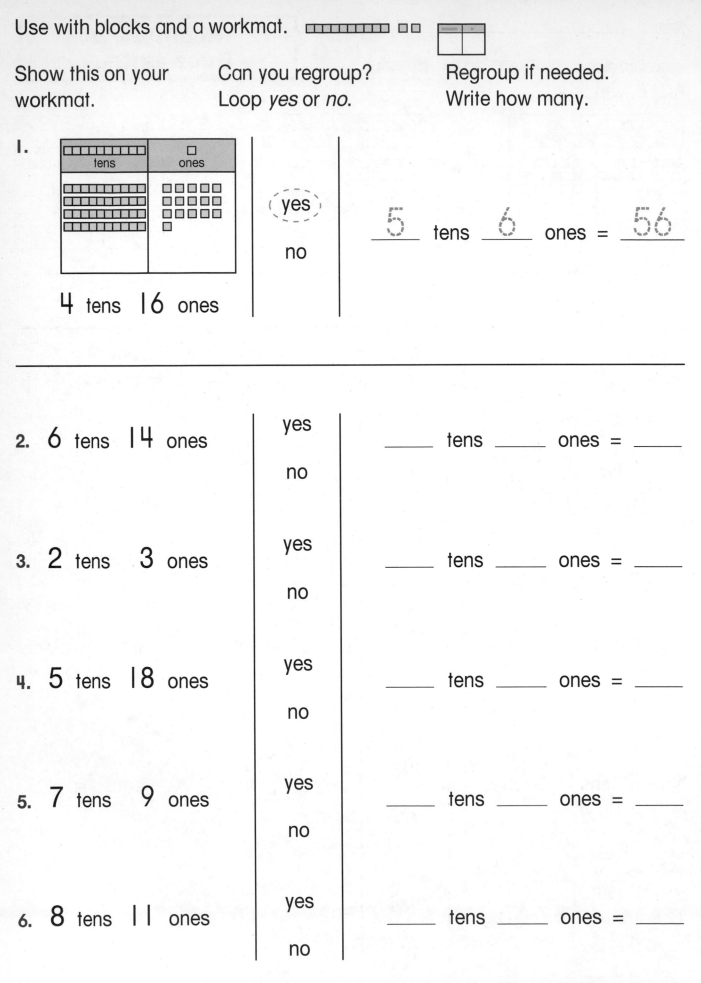

Show this on your workmat.   Can you regroup? Loop *yes* or *no*.   Regroup if needed. Write how many.

1.

tens	ones

4 tens 16 ones

(yes)

no

___5___ tens ___6___ ones = ___56___

---

2. 6 tens 14 ones

yes

no

_____ tens _____ ones = _____

3. 2 tens 3 ones

yes

no

_____ tens _____ ones = _____

4. 5 tens 18 ones

yes

no

_____ tens _____ ones = _____

5. 7 tens 9 ones

yes

no

_____ tens _____ ones = _____

6. 8 tens 11 ones

yes

no

_____ tens _____ ones = _____

168 (one hundred sixty-eight)

More Practice Set 6.4, page 404

Adding Tens and Ones

You may use blocks ▭▭▭▭▭ ▭▭ and a workmat.

47 + 25	47 + 25	47 + 25
tens / ones	tens / ones	tens / ones

The sum is 72.

| Show the addends with blocks on your workmat. | Look at the ones. Regroup 10 ones as 1 ten if you can. | Regroup if needed. Write the sum. |

Show the addends with blocks on your workmat.

| | Can you regroup? Loop *yes* or *no*. | Regroup if needed. Write the sum. |

32 + 16

1. tens / ones

                       yes   (no)   The sum is _48_ .

2.   44 + 19   yes   no   The sum is ____ .

3.   49 + 5   yes   no   The sum is ____ .

4.   36 + 23   yes   no   The sum is ____ .

5.   28 + 13   yes   no   The sum is ____ .

Show the addends with blocks on your workmat.	Can you regroup? Loop *yes* or *no*.	Regroup if needed. Write the sum.

19 + 33

1.

| tens | ones ☐ |

                      yes   no   19 + 33 = ____

2.   15 + 16   yes   no   15 + 16 = ____

3.   38 + 27   yes   no   38 + 27 = ____

4.   42 + 6   yes   no   42 + 6 = ____

5.   27 + 45   yes   no   27 + 45 = ____

Maintain • Money Sense

Write each amount. Loop the set with more money.

____ ¢ | ____ ¢

More Practice Set 6.5, page 405

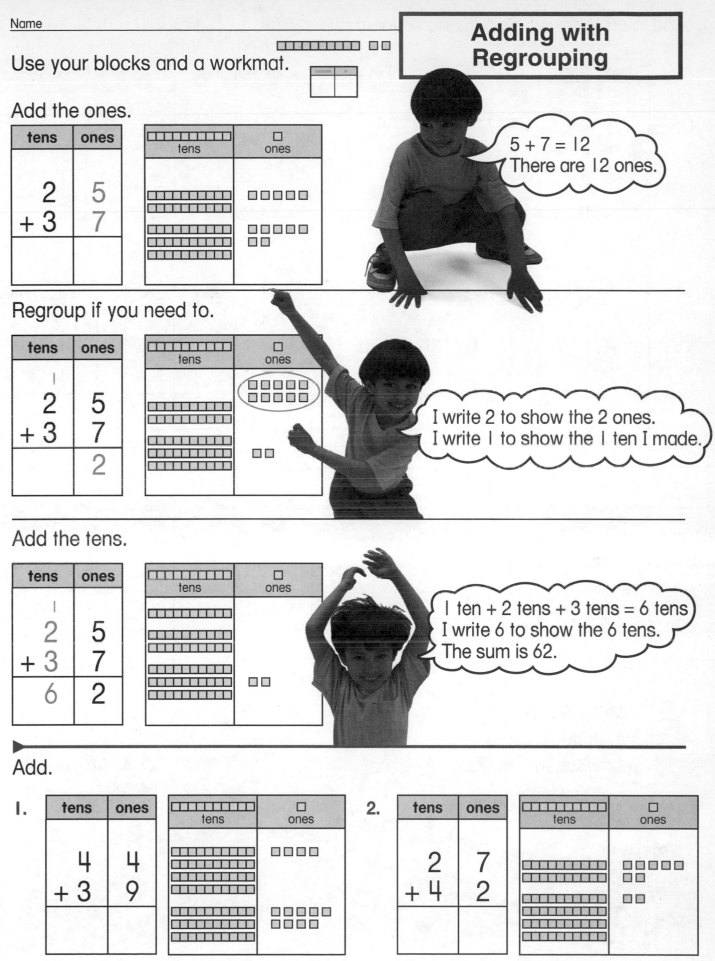

Adding with Regrouping

Use your blocks and a workmat.

Add the ones.

tens	ones
2	5
+ 3	7

5 + 7 = 12
There are 12 ones.

Regroup if you need to.

tens	ones
¹	
2	5
+ 3	7
	2

I write 2 to show the 2 ones.
I write 1 to show the 1 ten I made.

Add the tens.

tens	ones
¹	
2	5
+ 3	7
6	2

1 ten + 2 tens + 3 tens = 6 tens
I write 6 to show the 6 tens.
The sum is 62.

Add.

1.

tens	ones
4	4
+ 3	9

2.

tens	ones
2	7
+ 4	2

Add. You may use blocks and a workmat.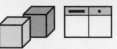

1.

tens	ones
1	6
+ 1	3

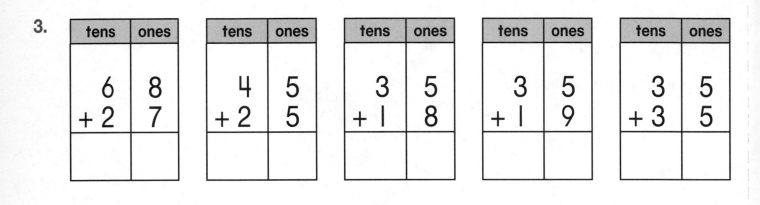

2.

tens	ones
3	4
+	6

3.

tens	ones
6	8
+ 2	7

tens	ones
4	5
+ 2	5

tens	ones
3	5
+ 1	8

tens	ones
3	5
+ 1	9

tens	ones
3	5
+ 3	5

4.

tens	ones
1	8
+ 2	3

tens	ones
5	6
+ 3	4

tens	ones
3	6
+ 3	6

tens	ones
4	1
+	8

tens	ones
2	9
+ 5	7

MATH LOG

What steps do you
follow when you add?

More Practice Set 6.6, page 405

Adding 2-Digit Numbers

$\begin{array}{r} 56 \\ +38 \\ \hline \end{array}$ $6 + 8 = 14$	$\overset{1}{\begin{array}{r} 56 \\ +38 \\ \hline 4 \end{array}}$ $14 = 1 \text{ ten } 4 \text{ ones}$	$\overset{1}{\begin{array}{r} 56 \\ +38 \\ \hline 94 \end{array}}$
Add the ones.	Regroup if you need to.	Add the tens.

▶

Write the sum.

1.
$\begin{array}{r} 32 \\ +55 \\ \hline \end{array}$
$\begin{array}{r} 17 \\ +29 \\ \hline \end{array}$
$\begin{array}{r} 46 \\ + 8 \\ \hline \end{array}$
$\begin{array}{r} 60 \\ +38 \\ \hline \end{array}$

2.
$\begin{array}{r} 26 \\ +37 \\ \hline \end{array}$
$\begin{array}{r} 59 \\ +15 \\ \hline \end{array}$
$\begin{array}{r} 44 \\ +23 \\ \hline \end{array}$
$\begin{array}{r} 68 \\ + 7 \\ \hline \end{array}$
$\begin{array}{r} 28 \\ +28 \\ \hline \end{array}$
$\begin{array}{r} 39 \\ +11 \\ \hline \end{array}$

3.
$\begin{array}{r} 71 \\ +18 \\ \hline \end{array}$
$\begin{array}{r} 27 \\ + 5 \\ \hline \end{array}$
$\begin{array}{r} 36 \\ +49 \\ \hline \end{array}$
$\begin{array}{r} 51 \\ +20 \\ \hline \end{array}$
$\begin{array}{r} 63 \\ + 8 \\ \hline \end{array}$
$\begin{array}{r} 16 \\ +15 \\ \hline \end{array}$

4.
$\begin{array}{r} 47 \\ +43 \\ \hline \end{array}$
$\begin{array}{r} 34 \\ +18 \\ \hline \end{array}$
$\begin{array}{r} 62 \\ +24 \\ \hline \end{array}$
$\begin{array}{r} 56 \\ + 7 \\ \hline \end{array}$
$\begin{array}{r} 22 \\ +19 \\ \hline \end{array}$
$\begin{array}{r} 85 \\ + 6 \\ \hline \end{array}$

Problem Solving

1. Aunt Elena was the only one at the party who ate peanuts. She ate 10 peanuts. There are 35 peanuts left in the bowl. How many peanuts were in the bowl before Aunt Elena ate some? _____ peanuts

2. There are 16 people waiting in a line for food at the party. There are 29 people already sitting down. When all of the people are sitting down, will each table have exactly 10 people? _____

3. There are 45 chairs on the castle lawn. Only 2 chairs are empty. How many people are sitting on chairs?

   _____ people

4. Clara gives a pen and a pencil to each child at the party. She gives out 40 pens and 40 pencils. Besides Clara, how many children are at the party?

   _____ children

5. There are 50 streamers at the party. Twenty of them are red. The rest are blue. Are there more red streamers or blue streamers? _____ streamers

More Practice Set 6.7, page 406

You need a paper clip and a pencil to use on the spinner.
You may use a calculator.

**Play Spin 50.
The player who
comes closer to
50 wins!**

11	13
9	15
18	Sorry! 0
10	16

Work in pairs.
Take turns. Spin the spinner.
Write the numbers in the table.

Add the numbers.

Continue spinning and adding.
Stop when you think you
are close enough to 50.

Players		
Spin 1		
Spin 2	+	+
Sum		
Spin 3	+	+
Sum		
Spin 4	+	+
Sum		
Spin 5	+	+
Sum		

MID-CHAPTER REVIEW

for pages 161–174

Write the sum.

1.

tens	ones
3	7
+ 2	5

☐☐☐☐☐☐☐☐☐☐ tens	☐ ones

2.

tens	ones
1	6
+ 2	7

☐☐☐☐☐☐☐☐☐☐ tens	☐ ones

3.

56	74	45	33	34	17
+38	+ 9	+24	+ 7	+43	+38

4.

52	32	47	35	73	29
+26	+39	+ 6	+25	+22	+29

Problem Solving

5. Each yo-yo costs 35 cents. How much do 2 yo-yos

cost? _____ cents

6. There are 25 cats, 15 dogs, and 35 trees in the
yard. How many animals are in the yard?

_____ animals

Mid-Chapter Review

Addition with Money

You may use coins.

15¢ +59¢	1 15¢ +59¢ 4	1 15¢ +59¢ 74¢
Show the problem with coins. Add the pennies.	Regroup pennies for dimes if you need to.	Add the dimes.

Remember to write the cents sign!

Add.

1. 46¢   67¢   34¢   25¢
   +14¢   + 5¢   +59¢   +14¢
    60¢

2. 38¢   73¢   23¢   28¢   23¢   37¢
   +36¢   +16¢   + 9¢   +52¢   +17¢   +35¢

3. 55¢   42¢   38¢   22¢   15¢   72¢
   +27¢   + 5¢   +27¢   +63¢   +39¢   +26¢

Loop the addends that make 10¢. Add.

4.   6¢   8¢   2¢
     1¢   9¢   1¢   8¢   6¢
     7¢   3¢   1¢   5¢   2¢
   + 3¢   + 7¢   + 6¢   + 5¢   + 4¢

It is easier to add tens and ones when I write them this way!

34¢

34¢ + 22¢ =
    34¢
  +22¢
    56¢

castle

27¢

train

12¢
puppet

55¢
flowers

Write how much each item costs.
Find the total cost.

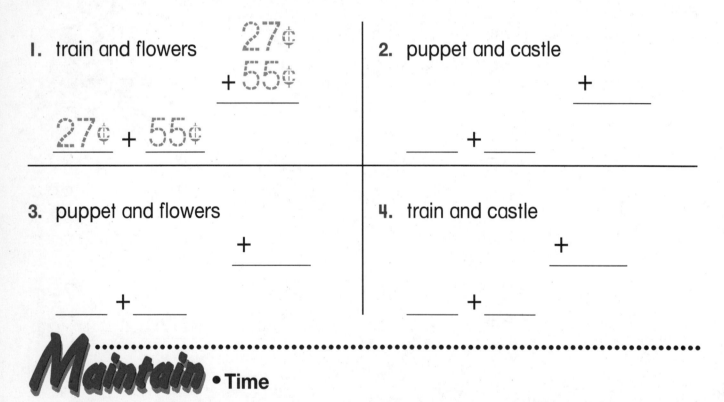

1. train and flowers

27¢
+ 55¢
_____

27¢ + 55¢

2. puppet and castle

_____ + _____

_____ + _____

3. puppet and flowers

_____ + _____

_____ + _____

4. train and castle

_____ + _____

_____ + _____

Maintain • Time

Write the time. Write how many hours later.

____ : ____

____ : ____

____ hours later

More Practice Set 6.9, page 406

tens	ones
1	
3	6
2	9
+ 1	3
7	8

Adding 3 numbers is like adding 2 numbers. First add the ones. Regroup if you need to. Then add the tens.

Three Addends

Write the sum.

1.
```
  40      12      24      45      14      52
  34      63       3      15      27      12
+ 15    +  7    + 37    + 15    + 32    + 19
  89
```

2.
```
  42      24      23      16      33      19
  16      24      15      18      22      43
+ 25    + 24    +  8    + 20    + 44    + 17
```

3. 16 + 53 + 7 = ___

4. 25 + 12 + 19 = ___

5. 42 + 29 + 11 = ___

3.	4.	5.

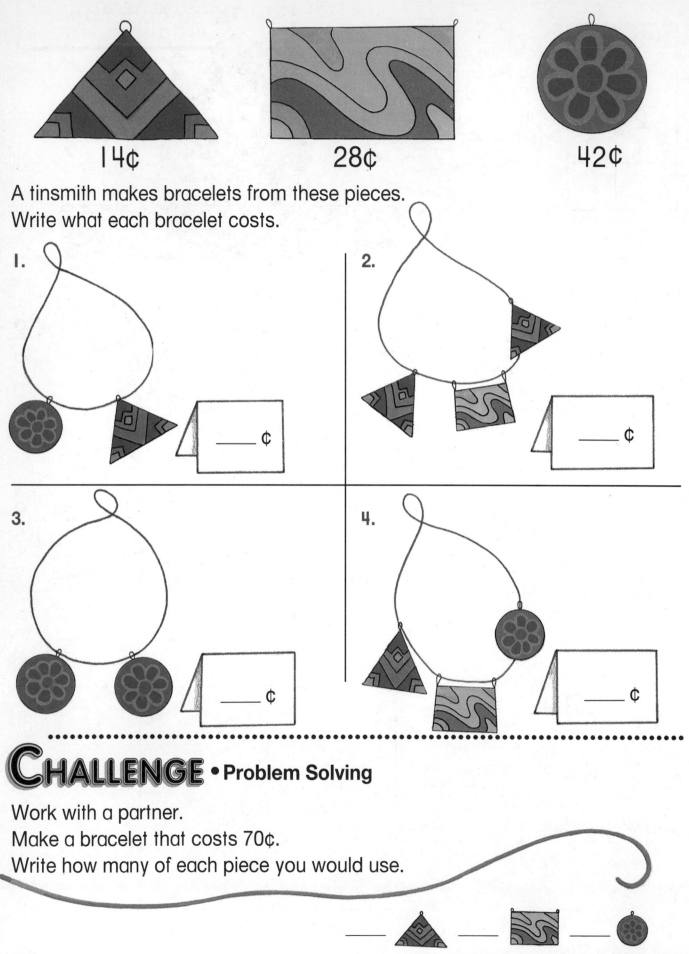

14¢ 28¢ 42¢

A tinsmith makes bracelets from these pieces.
Write what each bracelet costs.

1. _____ ¢

2. _____ ¢

3. _____ ¢

4. _____ ¢

CHALLENGE • Problem Solving

Work with a partner.
Make a bracelet that costs 70¢.
Write how many of each piece you would use.

_____ △ _____ ▭ _____ ◉

More Practice Set 6.10, page 407

I did not have to add.
I found a pattern. So
I can just write the sums.

30	+1	31	+1	32	+1	33	+1	34
+39		+39		+39		+39		+39
69	+1	70	+1	71	+1	72	+1	73

Look for a pattern.
Use the pattern to find the sums.

1.

40	41	42	43	44
+40	+39	+38	+37	+36
80				

2.

18	18	18	18	18
+ 7	+17	+27	+37	+47
25				

3.

9	19	29	39	49
+ 5	+15	+25	+35	+45
14				

Critical Thinking Talk with a friend.
Explain how you did these without adding.

4. Make up a pattern. Share it with a friend.

30	+ ___	+ ___	+ ___	+ ___
+30				
60				

	Team 1	
	Clara	Anne
Egg Toss	24	46
Bull's-Eye	32	18

	Team 2	
	Isabel	Tomás
Egg Toss	41	17
Bull's-Eye	43	37

Problem Solving   Use the tables to solve each problem.

1. How many points did Team 1 score in the Egg

   Toss? _____ points

2. Which team won the Egg Toss? _____

3. How many points did Tomás score altogether?

   _____ points

4. Which player scored the most points altogether?

   _____

5. Which player scored the fewest points altogether?

   _____

6. Which player scored 20 points higher in the
   Bull's-Eye than in the Egg Toss?

   _____

MATH LOG

How can you tell which team won the
Bull's-Eye without adding?

PROBLEM SOLVING
Too Much Information

UNDERSTAND
TRY
THINK
LOOK BACK

Name _____

Work with a partner.
Solve each problem.
Do you need all the information?
Loop what you do not need.

1. Tomás wants to buy 3 whistles. Each whistle has 7 holes. Each whistle costs 20¢. How much will he pay? _____ cents

2. Clara and Tomás bring toys out to the lawn. Tomás brings 14 yo-yos. So does Clara. Each yo-yo has 4 stripes. How many yo-yos can Clara and Tomás give out? _____ yo-yos

3. The castle library has 30 books. Ten of the books are about dogs. The library would like to have 70 books in all. Kristin brings 5 books. How many more books are needed? _____ more books

4. The tallest person at the party is 65 inches tall. Juan is 45 inches tall. Gretta is 5 inches taller than Juan. Is Gretta the tallest person at the party? _____

5. Clara has 60 minutes before bedtime. She wants to play with her puppy for 30 minutes and read for 20 minutes. Does she have enough time? _____

Work with a partner.
Solve each problem.
Do you need all the information?
Loop what you do not need.

1. Anne buys streamers for 20¢. She buys 4 balloons, too. They cost 10¢ each. Two of the balloons are gold. How much does Anne spend? _____ ¢

2. There are 40 children at the party. Kristin brings 18 flowers for them. Jeanne brings 12 flowers. How many more flowers are needed so each child will have a flower? _____ flowers

3. Maria walks 10 miles to the party. She stays 5 hours. Then she walks back. How far does she walk altogether? _____ miles

4. There are 18 children watching a puppet show in the Grand Room. The Grand Room has 60 seats. There are 20 puppets in the show. How many more people could be seated in the Grand Room?

   _____ people

5. Tomás fills 3 boxes with balls. One box has 10 balls. The other 2 boxes have 20 balls in each.

   How many balls are in the boxes? _____ balls

CHAPTER TEST

Write the sum.

1. 40
   +15

2. 60
   +20

3. 30
   +45

4. 34
   + 8

5. 46
   +13

6. 58
   +22

7. 15¢
   +30¢

8. 69¢
   +27¢

9. 41¢
   +29¢

10. 70¢
   + 6¢

11. 25
   +45

12. 11¢
   +88¢

13. 41¢
   +34¢

14. 39¢
   +27¢

15. 79¢
   +11¢

16. 10
    74
   +11

17. 40
    51
   + 3

18. 53
    16
   +24

19. 32
    12
   +14

20. 27
    23
   +38

Chapter Test

Write each sum.

21. $80 + 10 =$ _____

22. $45 + 30 =$ _____

23. $58¢ + 24¢ =$ _____

24. $16¢ + 34¢ =$ _____

Solve each problem.

25. David found 23 seashells yesterday. Today he found 10 more than yesterday. How many seashells has David found in the two days?

_____ seashells

26. A yo-yo costs 45¢. Kia buys one yo-yo for herself and one for her brother. How much money does Kia spend on yo-yos? _____

27. Mari bought a shovel for 29¢, a pail for 49¢, and a hat for 21¢. Did she spend more than one dollar?

_____

Chapter Test

CUMULATIVE TEST

Write the sum.

1. $\begin{array}{r} 8 \\ +6 \\ \hline \end{array}$
2. $\begin{array}{r} 11 \\ +\ 9 \\ \hline \end{array}$
3. $\begin{array}{r} 43 \\ +\ 8 \\ \hline \end{array}$
4. $\begin{array}{r} 15 \\ +\ 4 \\ \hline \end{array}$
5. $\begin{array}{r} 36 \\ +37 \\ \hline \end{array}$
6. $\begin{array}{r} 13 \\ +\ 8 \\ \hline \end{array}$

7. $4 + 16 =$ _____

8. $14 + 3 =$ _____

9. $52 + 47 =$ _____

10. $36 + 7 =$ _____

Write the difference.

11. $\begin{array}{r} 18 \\ -11 \\ \hline \end{array}$
12. $\begin{array}{r} 19 \\ -\ 7 \\ \hline \end{array}$
13. $\begin{array}{r} 16 \\ -\ 6 \\ \hline \end{array}$
14. $\begin{array}{r} 13 \\ -\ 8 \\ \hline \end{array}$
15. $\begin{array}{r} 11 \\ -\ 4 \\ \hline \end{array}$
16. $\begin{array}{r} 20 \\ -\ 8 \\ \hline \end{array}$

17. $20 - 9 =$ _____

18. $19 - 10 =$ _____

19. $14 - 2 =$ _____

20. $15 - 11 =$ _____

Write the time.

21.

_____ : _____

22.

_____ : _____

Write the time.

23.

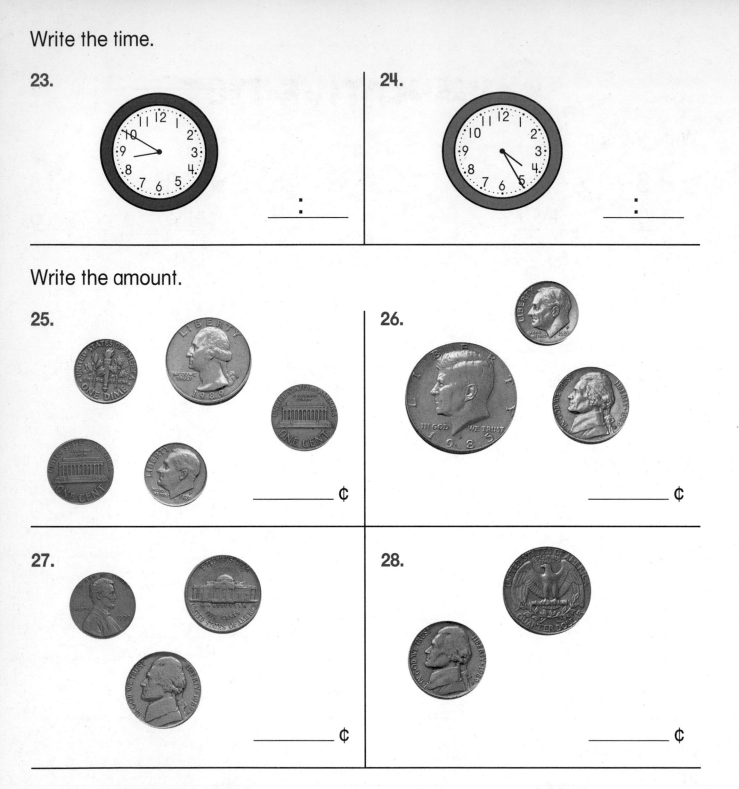

_____ : _____

24.

_____ : _____

Write the amount.

25.

_____ ¢

26.

_____ ¢

27.

_____ ¢

28.

_____ ¢

Solve each problem.

29. Ima's art class starts at 9:45. It lasts for 2 hours. At what time is the class over?

_____ : _____

30. Jacy buys an orange for $0.30 and a plum for $0.45. How much money does Jacy spend in all?

_____

Note to the Family

Your child has been learning about addition of 2-digit numbers. This activity sheet gives your child an opportunity to share new skills with you.

SHOPPING SPREE

You need a variety of small household items (items that are in reality priced under $1); price tags; a minimum of 5 pennies, 5 nickels, 5 dimes, 5 quarters, 1 half-dollar; 1 paper bag; paper, and a pencil.

1. Set up a "store" with various common household items for sale, each of which has a price tag. (Use the original price tag from the store, if possible. If you make the price tags, make each price realistic.)

2. Put all the coins into the paper bag.

3. The first player closes his or her eyes and takes a handful of money from the bag. This player then counts the total amount of money picked.

4. The first player tries to "buy" as many items with the money as possible. Record the items bought and the amount spent on a piece of paper.

5. Return the money to the bag and the items to the store before the next player has a turn, to give everyone an equal chance to purchase items.

6. After everyone has had a turn, the player who was able to buy the most items wins. (The winner is not necessarily determined by who picked the largest amount of money from the bag.)

Note to the Family

In the next few weeks, your child will be learning about geometry and fractions. It is important for children to see geometry and fractions used outside of school. You and your child can talk about geometry and fractions while participating in daily household activities such as folding napkins for the dinner table to make triangles or cutting a pie into 8 equal parts and telling how much of the pie is eaten at dinner (for example, six eighths).

It might be fun to do this activity with your child.

GEOMETRY SORT

You will need common household objects and scissors.

1. Gather some household objects.

2. Cut out the labels below and set them up on a table.

3. Have your child sort the objects and place them behind the labels. (Note: Some objects may go in 2 places—the end of a crayon is like a cylinder, while the point is like a cone.)

Things That Are Round		Things That Have Corners		
Cylinder	Sphere	Rectangular Prism	Cube	Pyramid
Circle	Cone	Triangle	Square	Rectangle

CHAPTER 7

GEOMETRY AND FRACTIONS

Listen to the story.

Fair Is Fair

Loop how Peter and Paul should share.
If they cut, draw a line to show it.

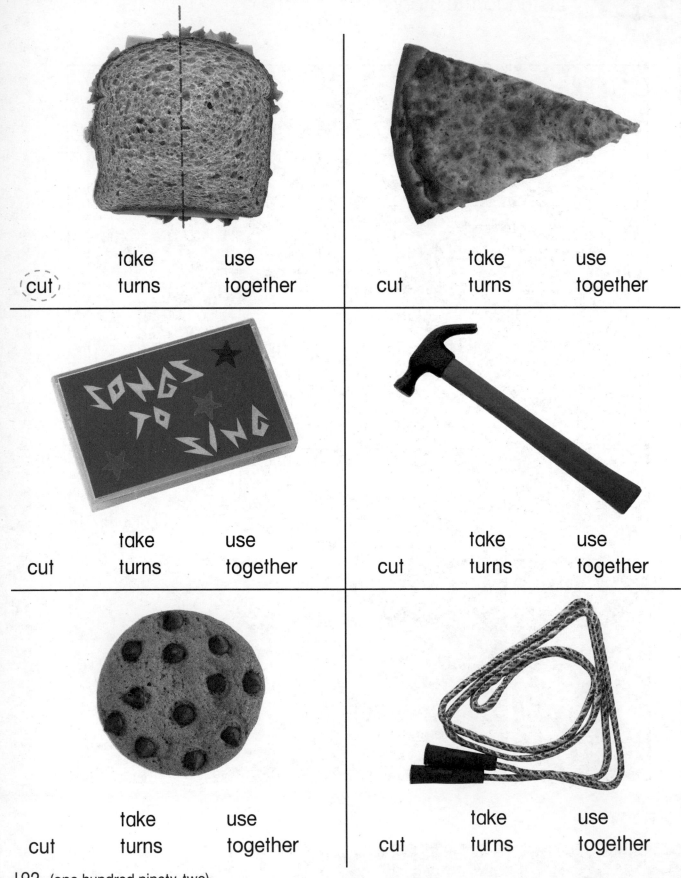

(cut)   take   use
       turns   together

cut   take   use
       turns   together

cut   take   use
       turns   together

cut   take   use
       turns   together

cut   take   use
       turns   together

cut   take   use
       turns   together

Solids

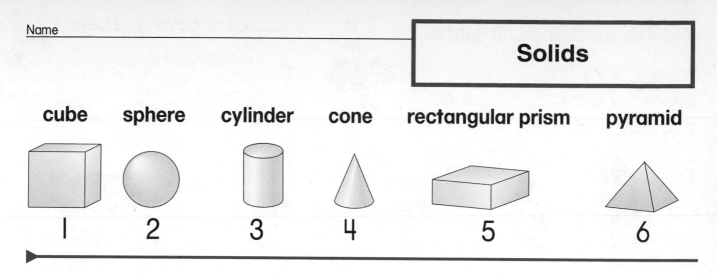

cube   sphere   cylinder   cone   rectangular prism   pyramid

1   2   3   4   5   6

Write the number of the solid
to match the object.

You may use solids and cubes.

Work in pairs.
Loop the solid that is missing.
You may make these with solids first.

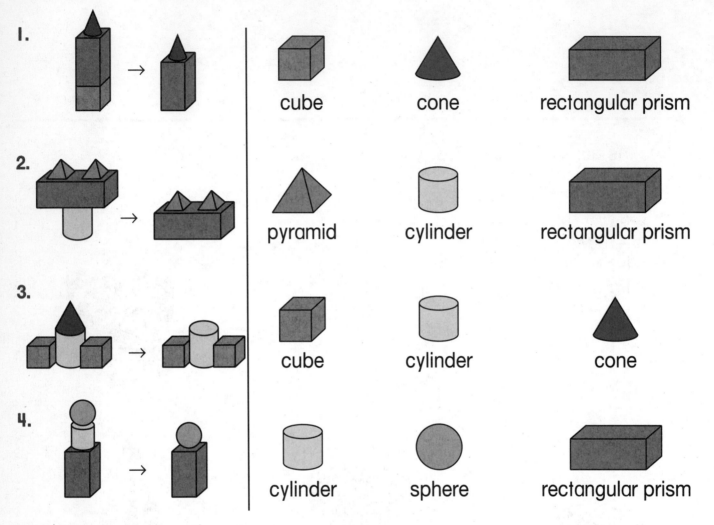

1. cube   cone   rectangular prism

2. pyramid   cylinder   rectangular prism

3. cube   cylinder   cone

4. cylinder   sphere   rectangular prism

Try to make these with cubes.
Write how many cubes you use.

5.

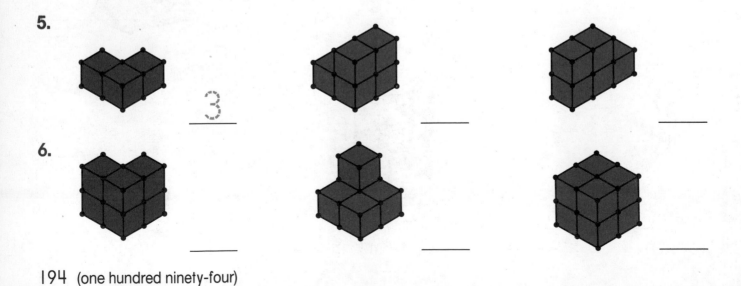

3

6.

194 (one hundred ninety-four)

You may use a geoboard and dot paper.

Plane Figures

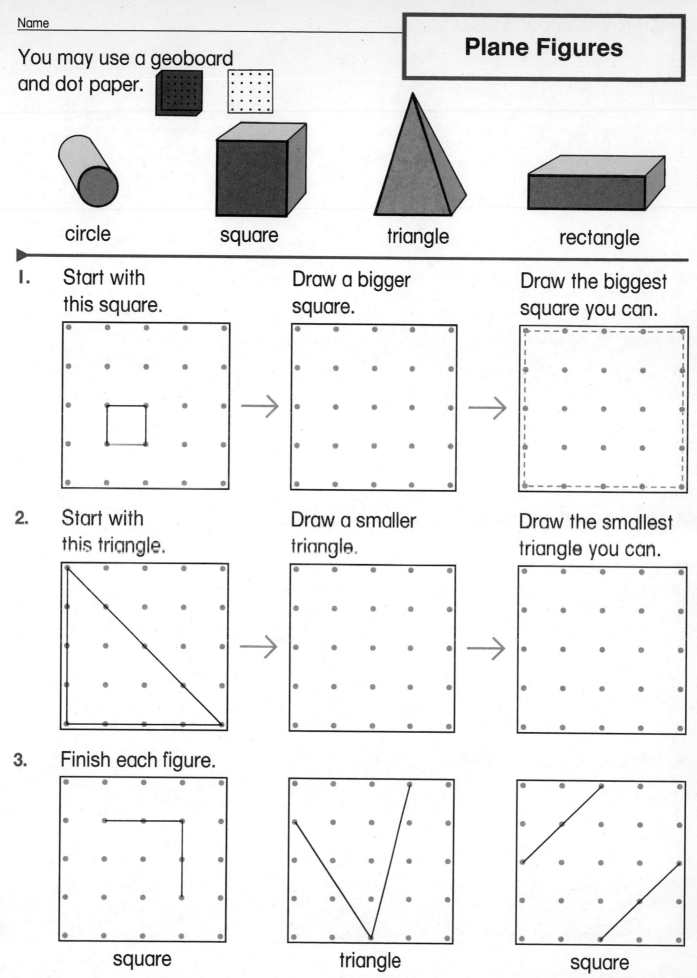

circle   square   triangle   rectangle

1. Start with this square.

Draw a bigger square.

Draw the biggest square you can.

2. Start with this triangle.

Draw a smaller triangle.

Draw the smallest triangle you can.

3. Finish each figure.

square   triangle   square

(one hundred ninety-five) 195

1. Write how many squares ☐ .

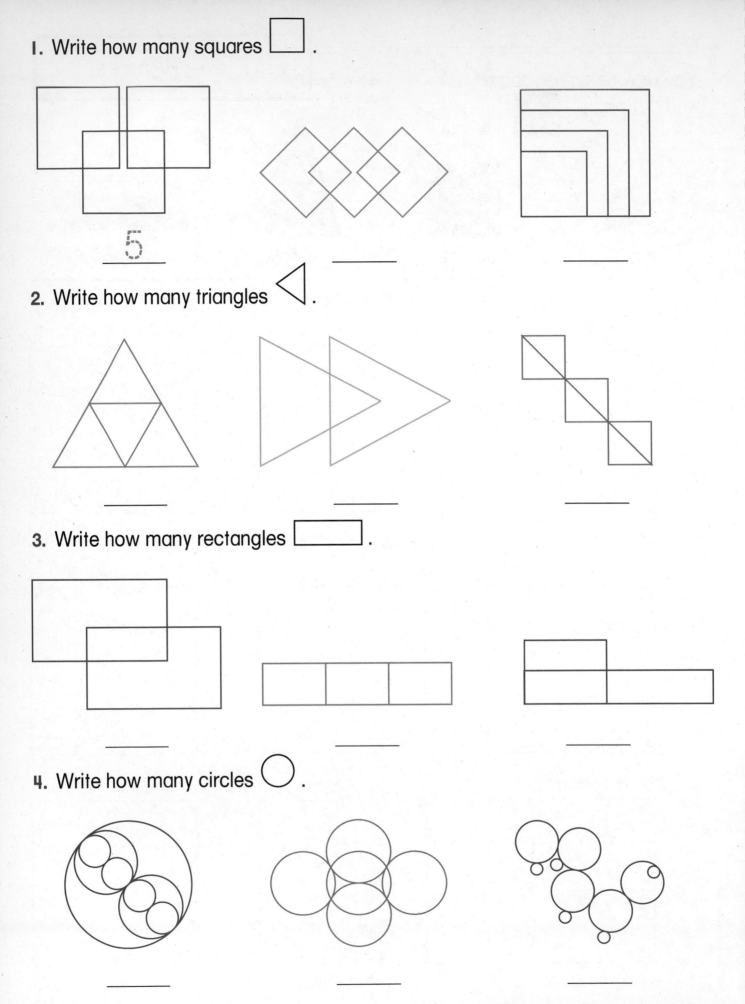

5 ____   ____   ____

2. Write how many triangles ◁ .

____   ____   ____

3. Write how many rectangles ▭ .

____   ____   ____

4. Write how many circles ◯ .

____   ____   ____

More Practice Set 7.2, page 407

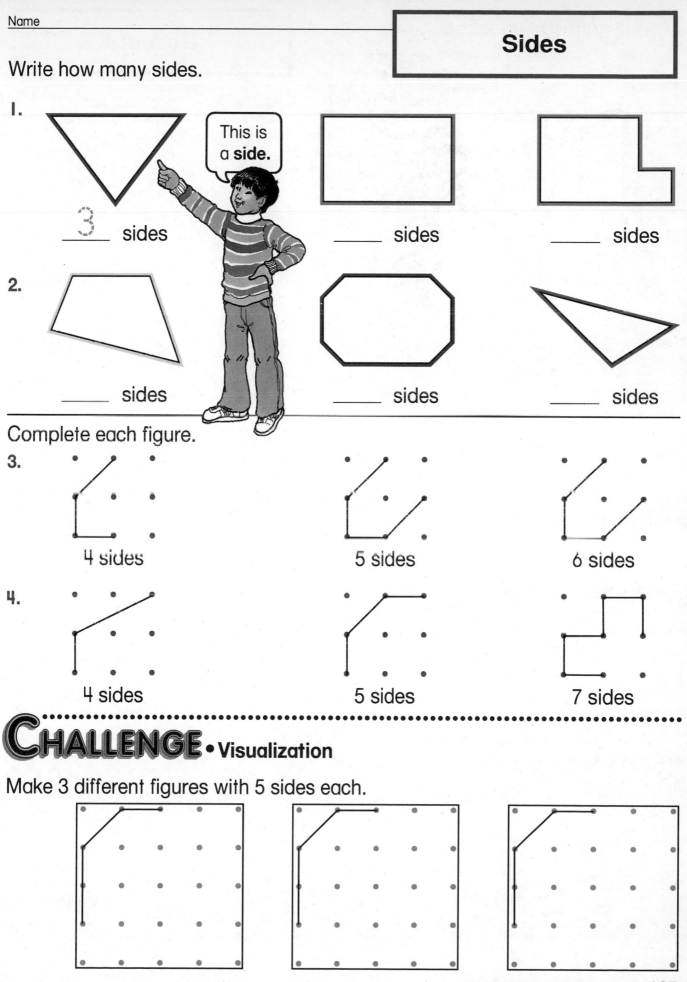

Sides

Write how many sides.

1.

3 _____ sides

_____ sides

_____ sides

2.

_____ sides

_____ sides

_____ sides

This is a **side.**

Complete each figure.

3.

4 sides

5 sides

6 sides

4.

4 sides

5 sides

7 sides

CHALLENGE • Visualization

Make 3 different figures with 5 sides each.

Write how many corners.

Corners

1.

This is a **corner.**

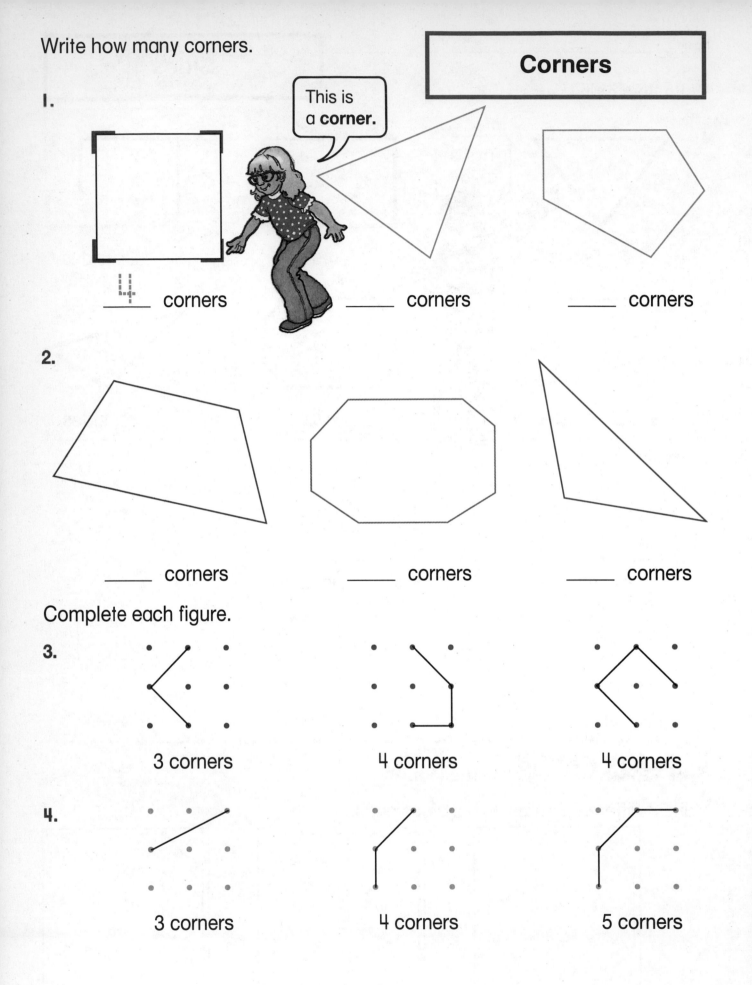

___4___ corners   _____ corners   _____ corners

2.

_____ corners   _____ corners   _____ corners

Complete each figure.

3.

3 corners   4 corners   4 corners

4.

3 corners   4 corners   5 corners

More Practice Set 7.4, page 408

You need crayons.

**Same Shape
and Same Size**

I traced the circles that are
the same size and same
shape as this one!

1. Trace this rectangle.

Make a ✓ on all the rectangles that are the same
as your tracing.

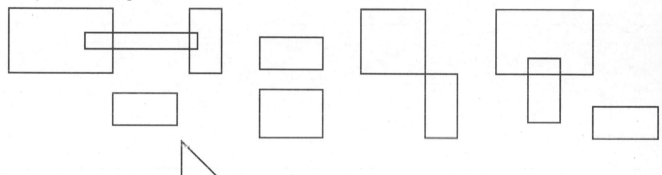

2. Trace this triangle.

Make a ✓ on all the triangles that are the same
as your tracing.

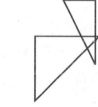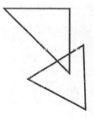

3. Trace this square.

Make a ✓ on all the squares that are the
same as your tracing.

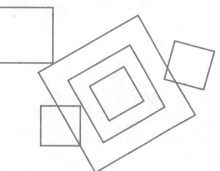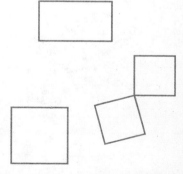

Loop the one that is different.

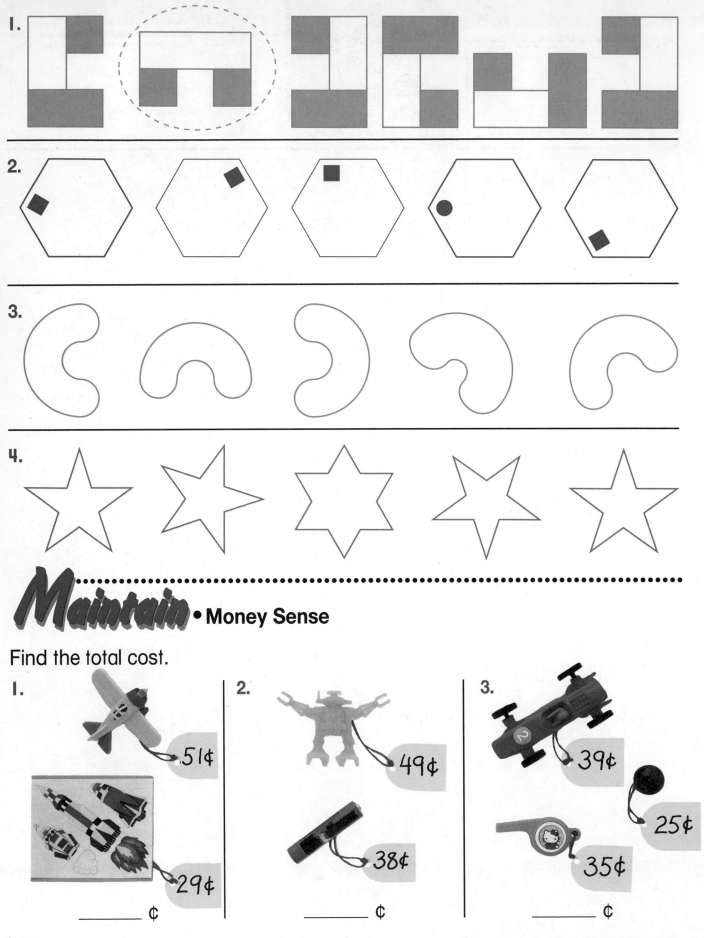

1.

2.

3.

4.

Maintain • Money Sense

Find the total cost.

1. 51¢ 29¢ _____ ¢

2. 49¢ 38¢ _____ ¢

3. 39¢ 25¢ 35¢ _____ ¢

More Practice Set 7.5, page 408

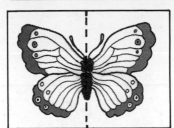

Symmetry

The two parts match
when folded on the line.
This is a **line of symmetry.**

The two parts
do not match
when folded on the line.

Loop the pictures that show a line of symmetry.

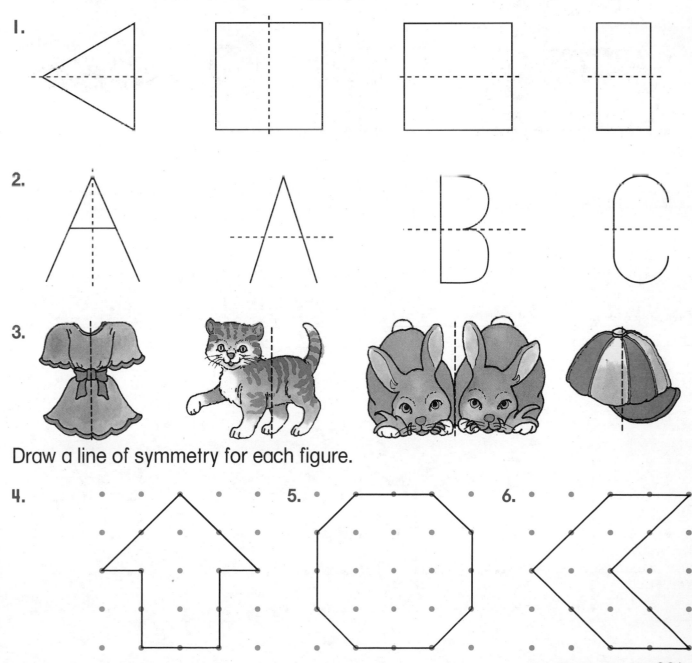

1.

2.

3.

Draw a line of symmetry for each figure.

4.

5.

6.

The fold line is a line of symmetry.
Loop the correct figure.

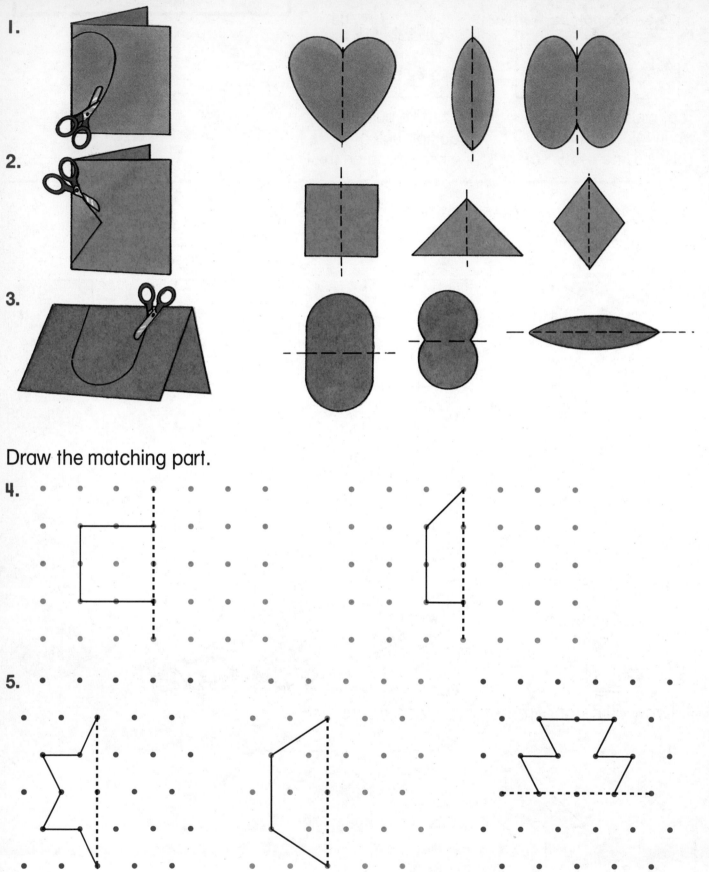

1.

2.

3.

Draw the matching part.

4.

5.

More Practice Set 7.6, page 409

Slides, Flips, and Turns

Here are some patterns I made with this figure.

Draw more figures to continue the pattern.

1.

2.

3.

4.

5.

Critical Thinking Can you think of some words that tell how Paul made each pattern?

MID-CHAPTER REVIEW

for pages 193–202

Write how many of each figure.

1. _____

_____

_____

2. _____

_____

_____

3.

_____ circles

_____ triangles

_____ squares

_____ rectangles

---

4. Draw a figure with 5 sides.

5. Draw a figure with 4 corners.

---

6. Loop each figure that shows a line of symmetry.

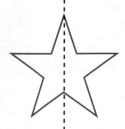

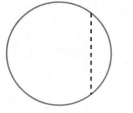

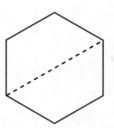

Mid-Chapter Review

Work with a partner.
Find the pattern.
Finish the picture.

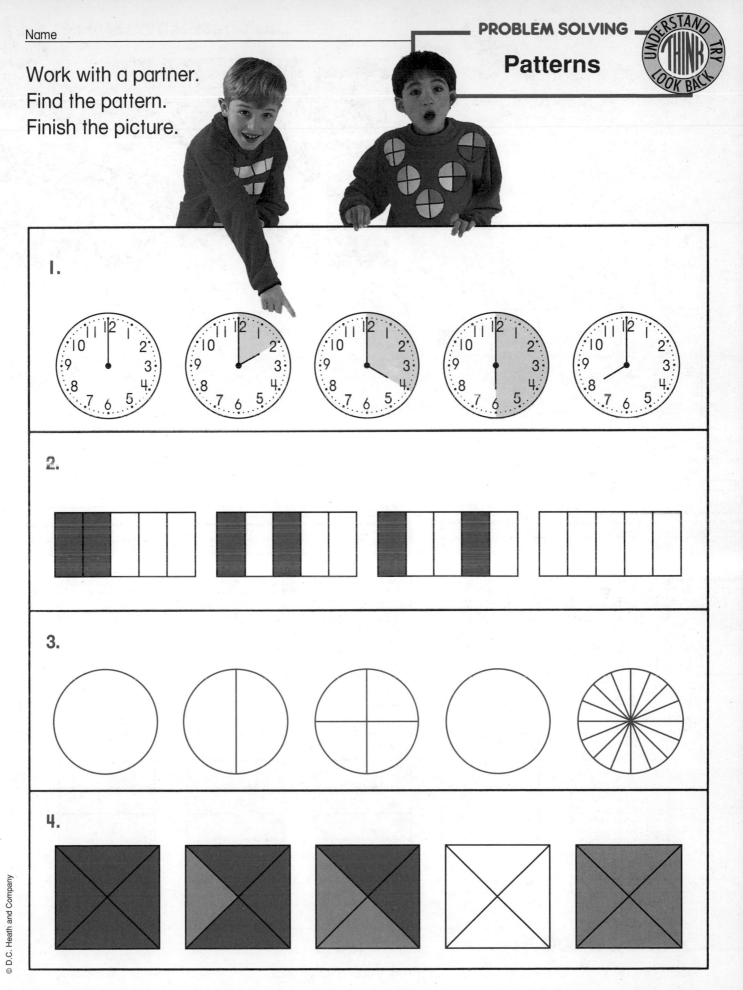

1.

2.

3.

4.

You need crayons.

Work with a partner.

Color the figures to make a pattern.

1.

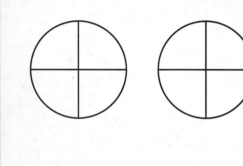

2.

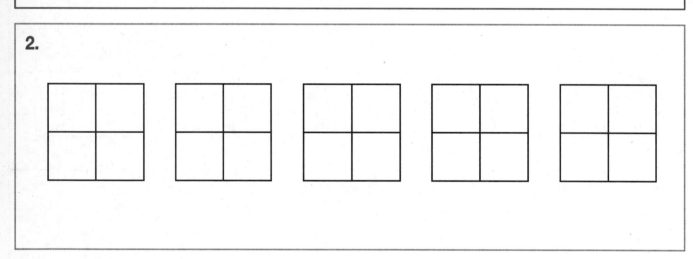

3.

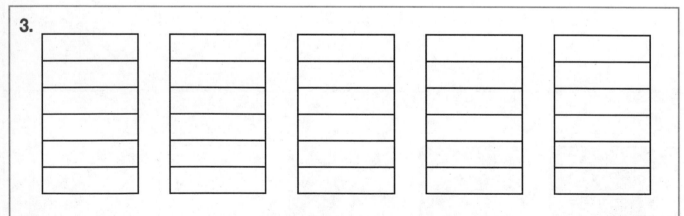

 MATH LOG

Talk with a friend about one of your patterns.

Name _____

You need pattern blocks.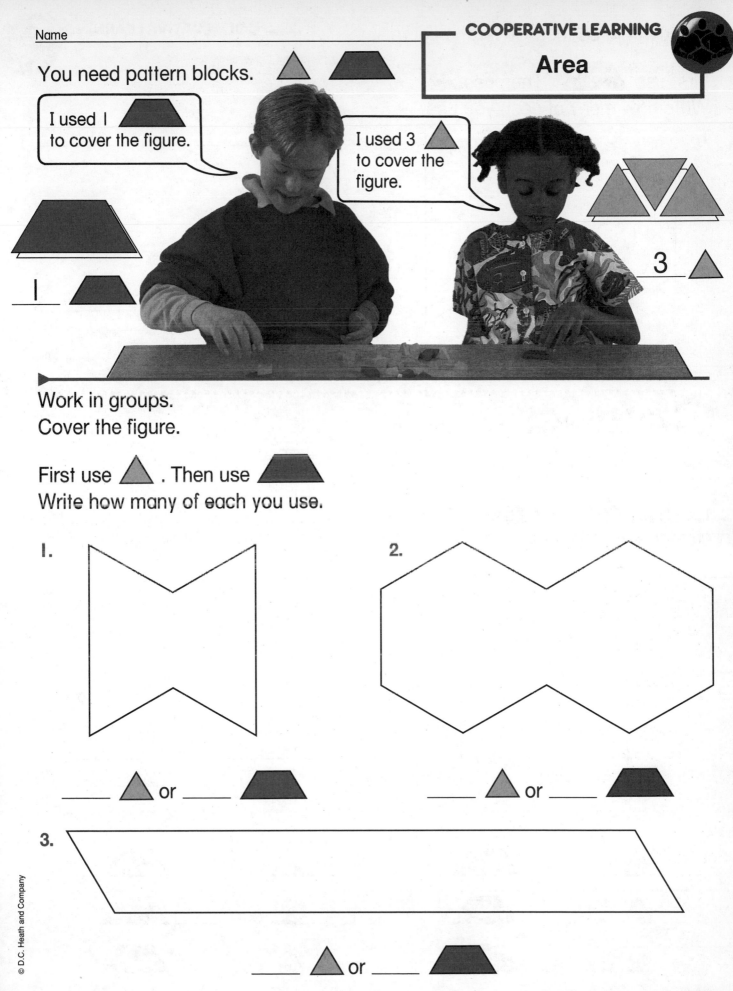

I used 1 to cover the figure.

I used 3 to cover the figure.

1

3

Work in groups.
Cover the figure.

First use △ . Then use ⬢
Write how many of each you use.

1.

_____ △ or _____ ⬢

2.

_____ △ or _____ ⬢

3.

_____ △ or _____ ⬢

Work with a partner. Cover the figure.

First use 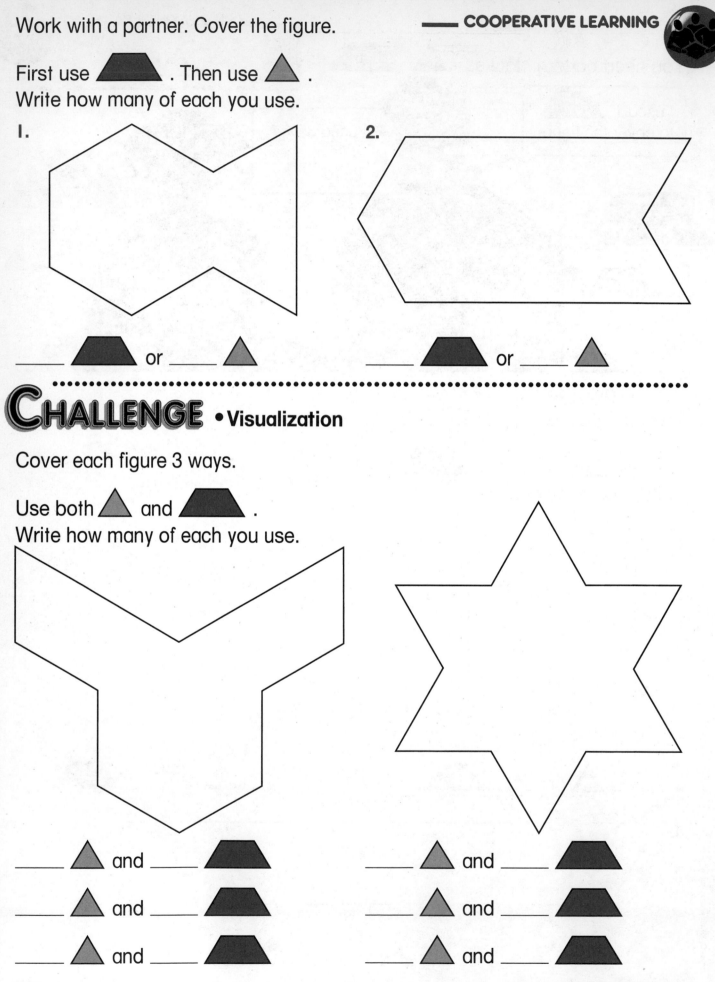. Then use ▲.
Write how many of each you use.

1.

_____ 🔷 or _____ ▲

2.

_____ 🔷 or _____ ▲

• •

CHALLENGE • Visualization

Cover each figure 3 ways.

Use both ▲ and 🔷.
Write how many of each you use.

_____ ▲ and _____ 🔷

_____ ▲ and _____ 🔷

_____ ▲ and _____ 🔷

_____ ▲ and _____ 🔷

_____ ▲ and _____ 🔷

_____ ▲ and _____ 🔷

More Practice Set 7.9, page 409

Equal Parts

If you use 4 squares to cover this rectangle

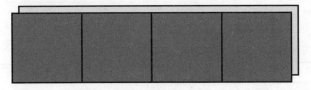

the 4 parts match. They are all the same size.
They are **equal parts.**

If you use 1 square and 2 triangles to cover this figure

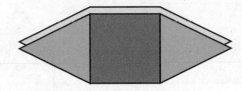

the 3 parts do not match. They are not the same size.
They are not equal parts.

▶ Loop each figure that shows equal parts.
Write how many equal parts.

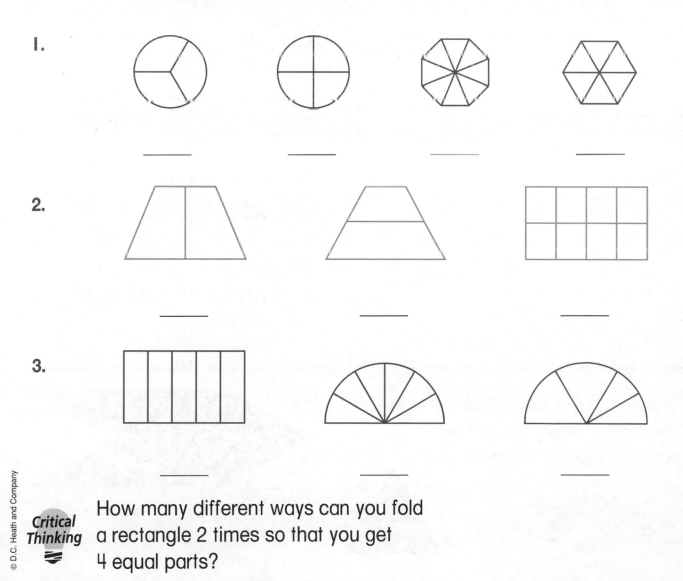

1.

_____ _____ _____ _____

2.

_____ _____ _____

3.

_____ _____ _____

Critical Thinking How many different ways can you fold a rectangle 2 times so that you get 4 equal parts?

More Practice Set 7.10, page 410

You need pattern block punchouts.

2 equal parts are called **halves.**

One half of the figure is covered.

3 equal parts are called **thirds.**

One third of the figure is covered.

4 equal parts are called **fourths.**

One fourth of the figure is covered.

Put one block on the figure.
How much of the figure does it cover?
Loop the answer.

1.

Use △ .
one half
one third
one fourth

Use ◆ .
one half
one third
one fourth

2.

Use ▰ .
one half
one third
one fourth

Use ◆ .
one half
one third
one fourth

3. Which one of these pattern blocks separates this figure into equal parts? Loop the answer.

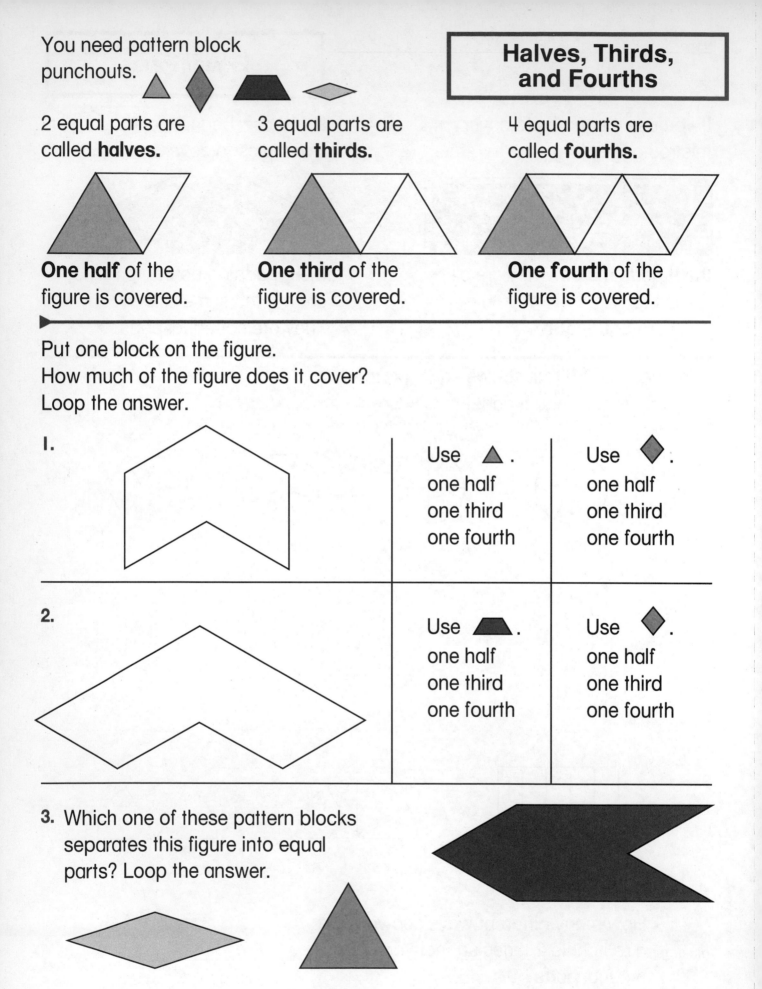

You need crayons.

One half, one third, and one fourth are called **fractions.**
You can write the fractions another way.

One half of the
rectangle is red.

One third of the
circle is green.

One fourth of the
square is blue.

$\frac{1 \text{ red part}}{2 \text{ equal parts}}$

$\frac{1 \text{ green part}}{3 \text{ equal parts}}$

$\frac{1 \text{ blue part}}{4 \text{ equal parts}}$

$\frac{1}{2}$ of the rectangle
is red.

$\frac{1}{3}$ of the circle
is green.

$\frac{1}{4}$ of the square
is blue.

What fraction of the figure is red?
Loop the answer.

1.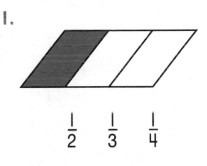

$\frac{1}{2}$ $\frac{1}{3}$ $\frac{1}{4}$

2.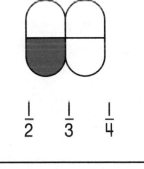

$\frac{1}{2}$ $\frac{1}{3}$ $\frac{1}{4}$

3.

$\frac{1}{2}$ $\frac{1}{3}$ $\frac{1}{4}$

Draw to make equal parts. Color the figure to match the fraction.

4.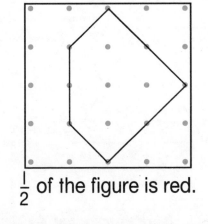

$\frac{1}{2}$ of the figure is red.

5.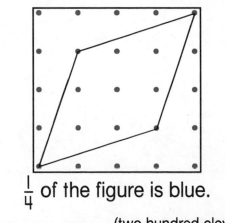

$\frac{1}{4}$ of the figure is blue.

You need crayons.

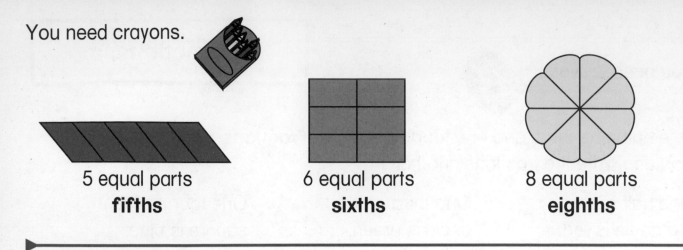

5 equal parts
fifths

6 equal parts
sixths

8 equal parts
eighths

Color the figure to show the fraction.
Write the fraction for the shaded part.

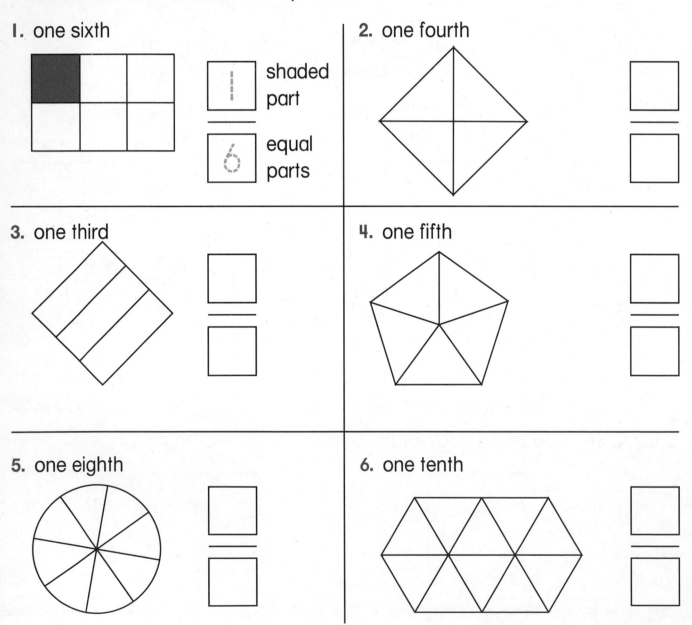

1. one sixth

shaded
part

equal
parts

2. one fourth

3. one third

4. one fifth

5. one eighth

6. one tenth

212 (two hundred twelve)

More Practice Set 7.12, page 410

You need crayons.

three sixths

$\dfrac{3}{6}$ $\dfrac{\text{shaded parts}}{\text{equal parts}}$

$\dfrac{3}{6}$ of the figure is shaded.

Color the figure to show the fraction.
Write the fraction for the shaded part.

1. three eighths

$\dfrac{3}{8}$ $\dfrac{\text{shaded parts}}{\text{equal parts}}$

2. two fourths

$\dfrac{}{}$ $\dfrac{\text{shaded parts}}{\text{equal parts}}$

3. seven tenths

4. five sixths

5. three fifths

6. two thirds

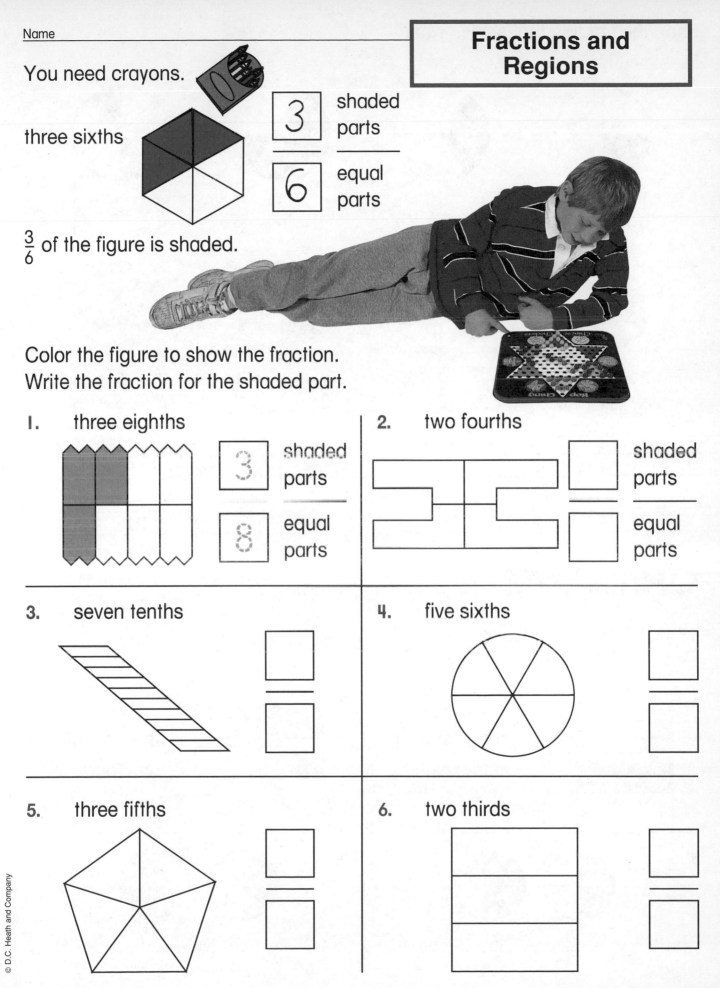

Loop the fraction that shows what part is shaded.

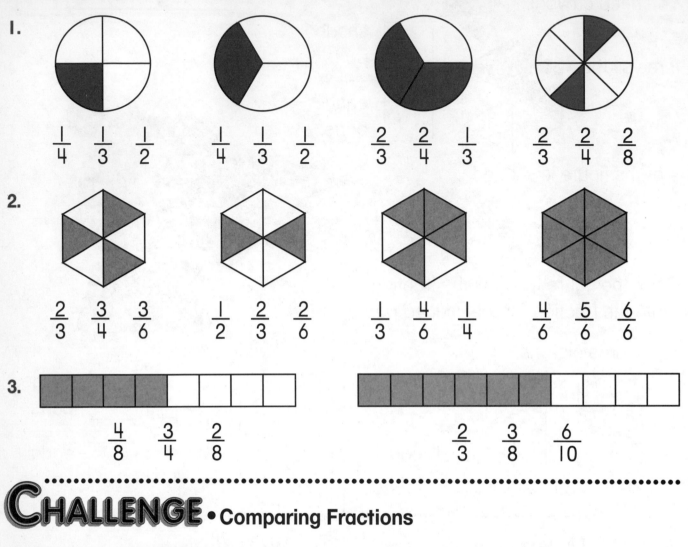

1.

$\dfrac{1}{4}$ $\dfrac{1}{3}$ $\dfrac{1}{2}$

$\dfrac{1}{4}$ $\dfrac{1}{3}$ $\dfrac{1}{2}$

$\dfrac{2}{3}$ $\dfrac{2}{4}$ $\dfrac{1}{3}$

$\dfrac{2}{3}$ $\dfrac{2}{4}$ $\dfrac{2}{8}$

2.

$\dfrac{2}{3}$ $\dfrac{3}{4}$ $\dfrac{3}{6}$

$\dfrac{1}{2}$ $\dfrac{2}{3}$ $\dfrac{2}{6}$

$\dfrac{1}{3}$ $\dfrac{4}{6}$ $\dfrac{1}{4}$

$\dfrac{4}{6}$ $\dfrac{5}{6}$ $\dfrac{6}{6}$

3.

$\dfrac{4}{8}$ $\dfrac{3}{4}$ $\dfrac{2}{8}$

$\dfrac{2}{3}$ $\dfrac{3}{8}$ $\dfrac{6}{10}$

CHALLENGE • Comparing Fractions

Look at the shaded parts.
Loop the greater fraction.

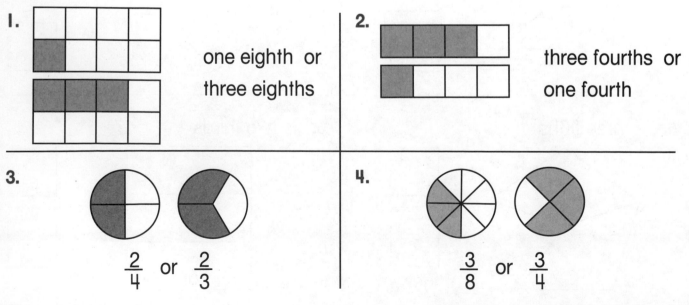

1.

one eighth or
three eighths

2.

three fourths or
one fourth

3.

$\dfrac{2}{4}$ or $\dfrac{2}{3}$

4.

$\dfrac{3}{8}$ or $\dfrac{3}{4}$

More Practice Set 7.13, page 411

Using Fractions

There are eight children in the playground.
Two of them are wearing glasses.
Two eighths of the children are wearing glasses.

Look at the picture. Loop the correct fraction.

1. What fraction of the children are girls?   five eighths   or
                                                 three eighths

2. What fraction of the children are boys?   five eighths   or
                                               three eighths

3. What fraction of the boys are wearing jackets?   one third   or
                                                      two thirds

4. What fraction of the girls are on the swings?   one fifth   or
                                                     two fifths

5. Paul is about _____ of the way up the steps. $\frac{2}{3}$ or $\frac{2}{6}$

6. Molly is about _____ of the way up the steps. $\frac{4}{6}$ or $\frac{1}{3}$

Problem Solving Peter, Paul, and Molly have a race.
Use the picture to answer each question.

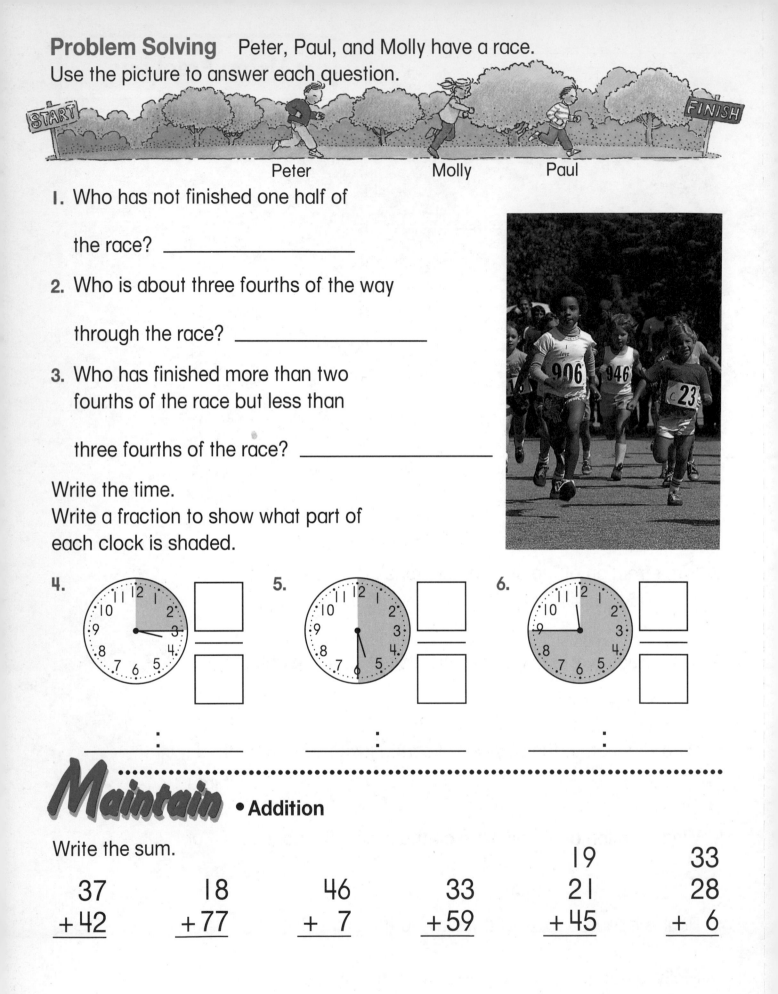

START   FINISH

Peter   Molly   Paul

1. Who has not finished one half of

   the race? _____

2. Who is about three fourths of the way

   through the race? _____

3. Who has finished more than two
   fourths of the race but less than

   three fourths of the race? _____

Write the time.
Write a fraction to show what part of
each clock is shaded.

4.   5.   6.

   [clock] [ ]   [clock] [ ]   [clock] [ ]
          [ ]   [ ]   [ ]

   ___:___   ___:___   ___:___

Maintain • Addition

Write the sum.

				19	33
37	18	46	33	21	28
+42	+77	+ 7	+59	+45	+ 6

Name _____

You may use cubes.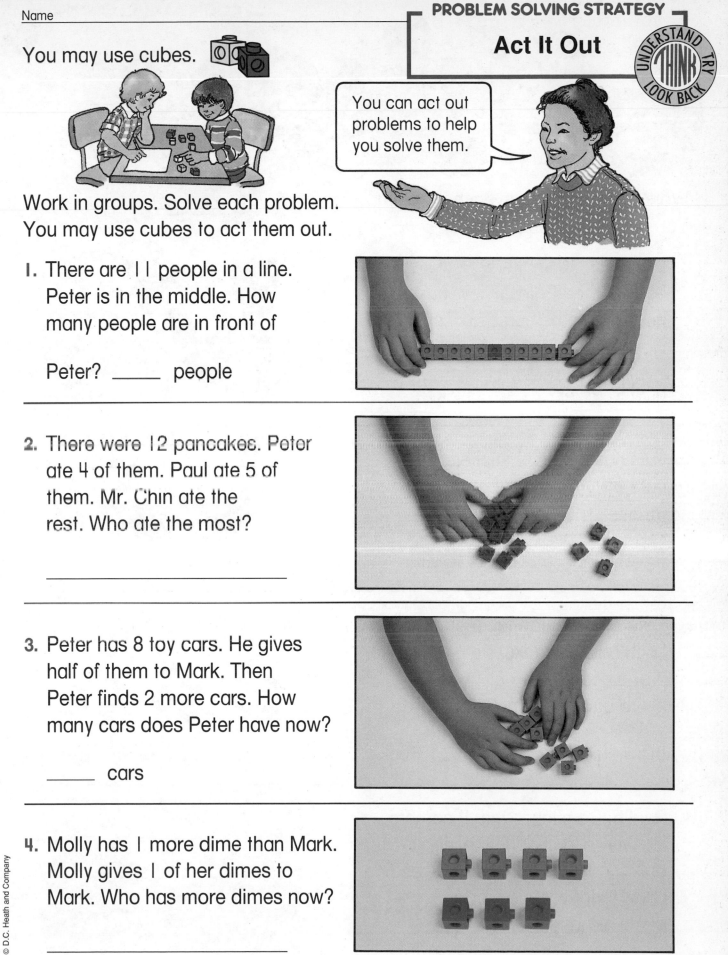

You can act out problems to help you solve them.

Work in groups. Solve each problem. You may use cubes to act them out.

1. There are 11 people in a line. Peter is in the middle. How many people are in front of

   Peter? _____ people

2. There were 12 pancakes. Peter ate 4 of them. Paul ate 5 of them. Mr. Chin ate the rest. Who ate the most?

   _____

3. Peter has 8 toy cars. He gives half of them to Mark. Then Peter finds 2 more cars. How many cars does Peter have now?

   _____ cars

4. Molly has 1 more dime than Mark. Molly gives 1 of her dimes to Mark. Who has more dimes now?

   _____

Work in groups. Solve each problem. You may use cubes or paper.

1. Peter has 10 stickers. Paul has 4 more than Peter. They want to have the same number of stickers. How many stickers should Paul give to Peter? _____ stickers

2. Luis has a square sticker. If he cuts off 1 of the corners, how many corners will there be on the sticker? _____ corners

3. Peter, Paul, and their friend Luis each have 4 trucks. Peter gives 2 of his to Paul. Paul gives 2 of his to Luis. How many trucks do the 3 children have? _____ trucks

4. Paul has a sticker with 4 corners. He wants to change it so it has only 3 corners. What can he do? Draw what you would do on the piece of paper.

CHAPTER TEST

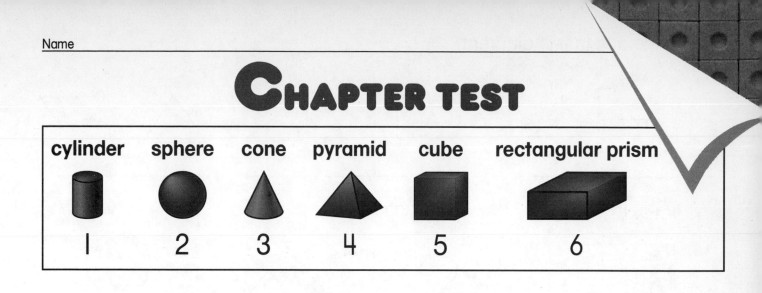

cylinder	sphere	cone	pyramid	cube	rectangular prism
1	2	3	4	5	6

Write the number to match each object.

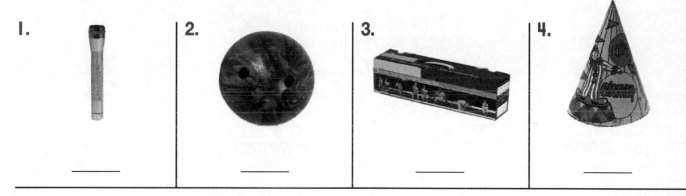

1. _____

2. _____

3. _____

4. _____

Write how many sides.

5. _____ sides

6. _____ sides

Write how many corners.

7. _____ corners

8. _____ corners

Loop the one that is the same as the red figure.

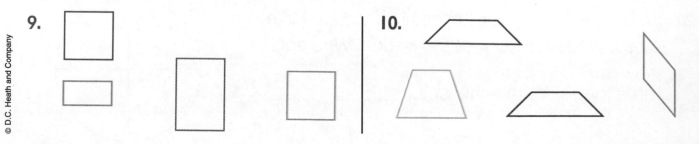

9.

10.

Loop the one that is different.

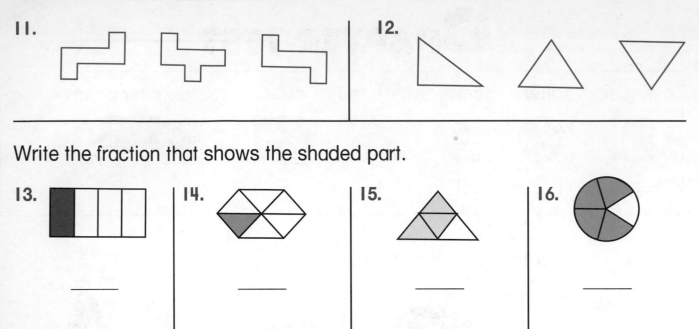

11.

12.

Write the fraction that shows the shaded part.

13.

14.

15.

16.

_____

_____

_____

_____

Color the figure to show the fraction.

17. two thirds

18. five eighths

Solve each problem.

19. There are three swings at the playground. One of
the swings is not being used. What fraction of the

swings are being used? _____

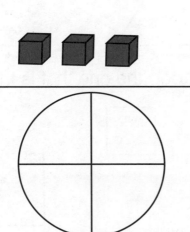

20. There are 4 wedges of cheese on a dish. Mike
eats 3 wedges. Mary eats 1 wedge. Who eats

three fourths of the cheese? _____

Chapter Test

EXCURSION
TECHNOLOGY

Work with a partner to
teach the turtle how to draw.
Type these steps.
Fill in the missing steps.

Forward	F D	Back	B K
Right	R T	Left	L T

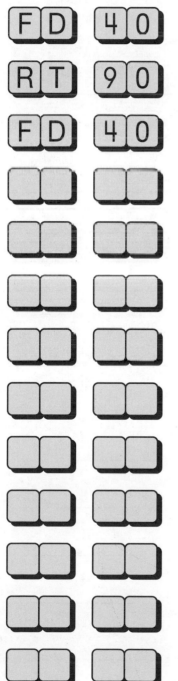

F D 40
R T 90
F D 40

Computer

1. Read the steps. What do you think the turtle will draw? Draw a picture. Then type in each step to check your picture.

LT 90

FD 40

LT 90

FD 40

LT 90

FD 40

2. These steps tell the turtle to draw a square. Change the steps so that the turtle will draw a larger square. Write each step you typed.

LT 90

FD 15

RT 90

FD 15

RT 90

FD 15

RT 90

FD 15

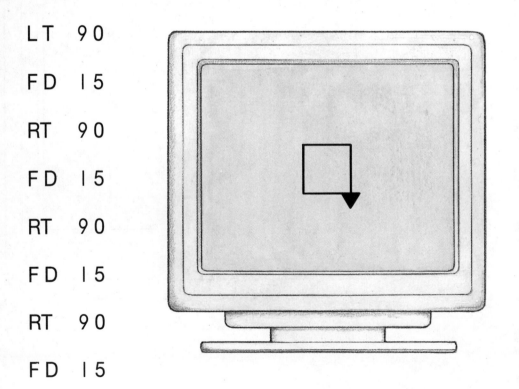

_____

_____

_____

_____

_____

_____

_____

_____

Note to the Family

Your child has been learning about geometry and fractions. This activity sheet gives your child an opportunity to share new skills with you.

PIZZA BAKE

You will need a large paper plate, a small paper plate (or you could substitute two different-sized sheets of paper), and crayons.

1. Have your child use red and yellow crayons to decorate each paper plate to look like a cheese pizza. Fold the large paper plate into 8 equal parts. Fold the small paper plate into 6 equal parts. (This could be a whole family project with each person making individual pizzas.)

2. Tell your child to put toppings on the pizzas. Your child can use crayons to color the toppings. (Or your child could cut the toppings out of construction paper and tape them on.)

Some possible toppings:

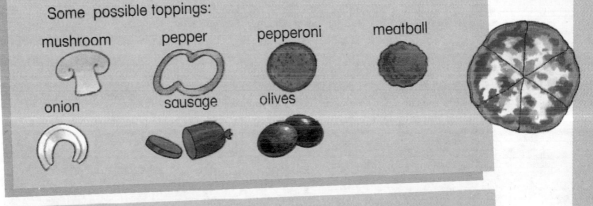

mushroom   pepper   pepperoni   meatball

onion   sausage   olives

3. Use sentences such as "I like mushrooms on my pizza. Put some mushrooms on three slices of the large pizza. How much of the pizza has mushrooms?" (three eighths); or "Your sister likes meatballs and peppers on her pizza. Put some meatballs and peppers on three sixths of the small pizza. Does more than half of the pizza have meatballs and peppers?" (no) Check to see that your child places the toppings correctly.

4. Then, have your child choose toppings to put on the pizzas and describe what he or she has done. For example: "I like pepperoni, so I put pepperoni on 3 pieces of the large pizza. So, three eighths of the large pizza has pepperoni."

Note to the Family

In the next few weeks, your child will be learning about subtraction of 2-digit numbers. It is important for children to see subtraction used outside of school. Your child can practice subtraction skills by participating in daily household activities such as playing games, making change for purchases, stating how much taller or shorter family members are, or stating how many are left in packages of paper plates or sandwich bags after using a certain amount.

It might be fun to play this game with your child.

TIC-TAC-TOE

You will need at least 21 small pieces of paper, a large sheet of paper, a pencil, different small markers for each player (such as different colored buttons, macaroni, beans), and a paper bag.

1. Help your child write the numbers 0–20 on the paper.

2. Draw a tic-tac-toe game board on a sheet of paper. Write any number from 5–25 in one of the 9 spaces on the board. Then let your child fill in a number. Take turns. Keep writing numbers until the board is filled in. Use each number only once. A sample game board is shown.

25	6	15
20	22	11
5	12	10

3. Put all the paper numbers in a bag. Players take turns reaching in and picking two pieces of paper. After adding or subtracting the numbers picked, players see if the sum or difference matches a number on the game board. (It may not always be possible to place a marker in each turn.) For example, if 13 and 8 were the numbers picked, then a marker could be put only on the numbers 5 (13 − 8) or 21 (13 + 8). Return the numbers to the bag after each turn.

4. Continue picking 2 numbers and placing markers. The first player to get 3 markers in a row wins.

5. Remove the markers and play the game again. Let the winner decide whether to use the same game board or to make another. The player who wins two out of three games can be named the grand winner.

SUBTRACTION OF 2-DIGIT NUMBERS

Listen to the story.

Eucalyptus Stew

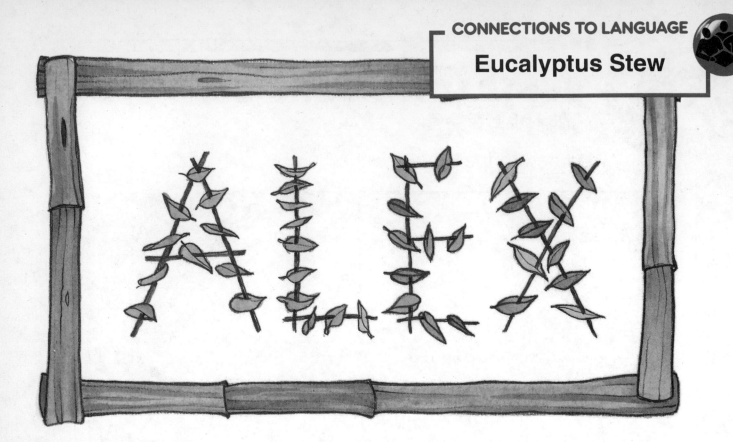

How many leaves are on the sign? _____ leaves

Work with a friend.
Each of you should write your name here
and on a sheet of paper.
On the paper, draw 10 leaves on each letter of your name.

My Name _____

My Friend's Name _____

1. How many leaves are on your name? _____ leaves

2. How many are on your friend's name? _____ leaves

3. Who has more leaves? _____

4. How many more? _____ more

Subtract. Cross out to show it.

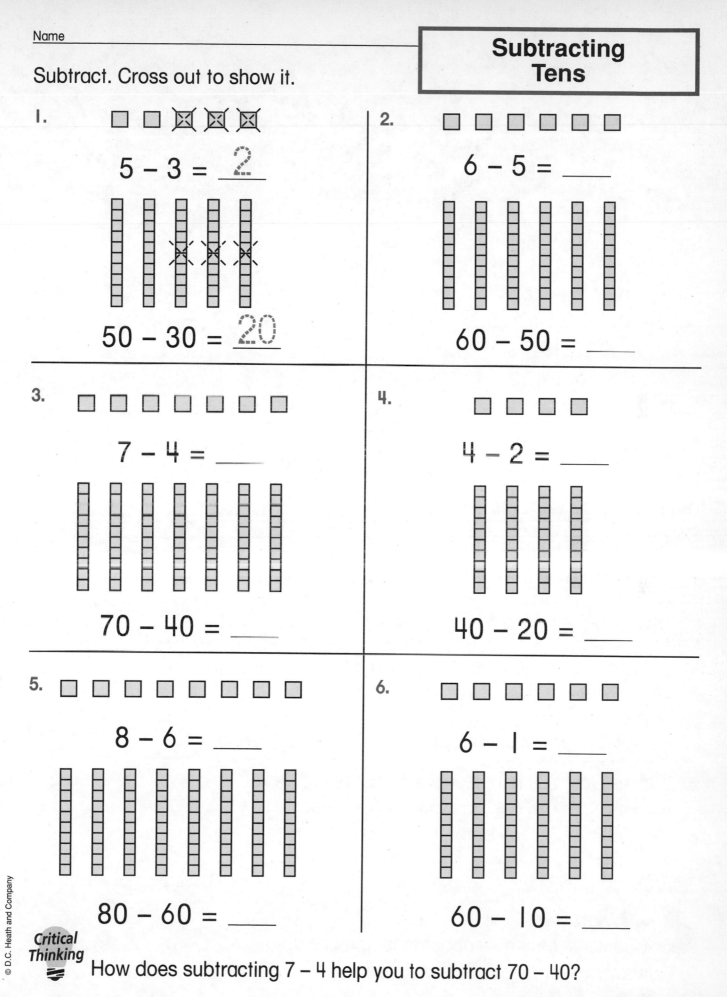

1. □ □ ⊠ ⊠ ⊠

$5 - 3 =$ _2_

$50 - 30 =$ _20_

2. □ □ □ □ □ □

$6 - 5 =$ ___

$60 - 50 =$ ___

3. □ □ □ □ □ □ □

$7 - 4 =$ ___

$70 - 40 =$ ___

4. □ □ □ □

$4 - 2 =$ ___

$40 - 20 =$ ___

5. □ □ □ □ □ □ □ □

$8 - 6 =$ ___

$80 - 60 =$ ___

6. □ □ □ □ □ □

$6 - 1 =$ ___

$60 - 10 =$ ___

Critical Thinking

How does subtracting $7 - 4$ help you to subtract $70 - 40$?

Subtract. You may use place-value blocks.

1.

40	90	70	80	30	60
− 30	− 50	− 20	− 40	− 10	− 30

Problem Solving

2. Alex counts 80 leaves on a tree. The wind blows some away. There are 20 leaves left on the tree.

   How many leaves blew away? _____ leaves

3. There are 50 koalas in Koala Corner. One week 30 koalas come to visit them. How many koalas are

   now in Koala Corner? _____ koalas

4. Cathy has some leaves for a snack. She shares 10 of them with Alex. Now she has 20 leaves left.

   How many leaves did she start with? _____ leaves

5. It takes Dawn 20 minutes to walk to the big rock. It takes Cathy 20 minutes to walk there, too. How long will it take both of them to walk to the

   rock together? _____ minutes

 MATH LOG
Use what you know about tens to make up a number story. Ask a friend to solve it.

You need dimes and nickels.

Use your coins.
Subtract. Cross out to show it.

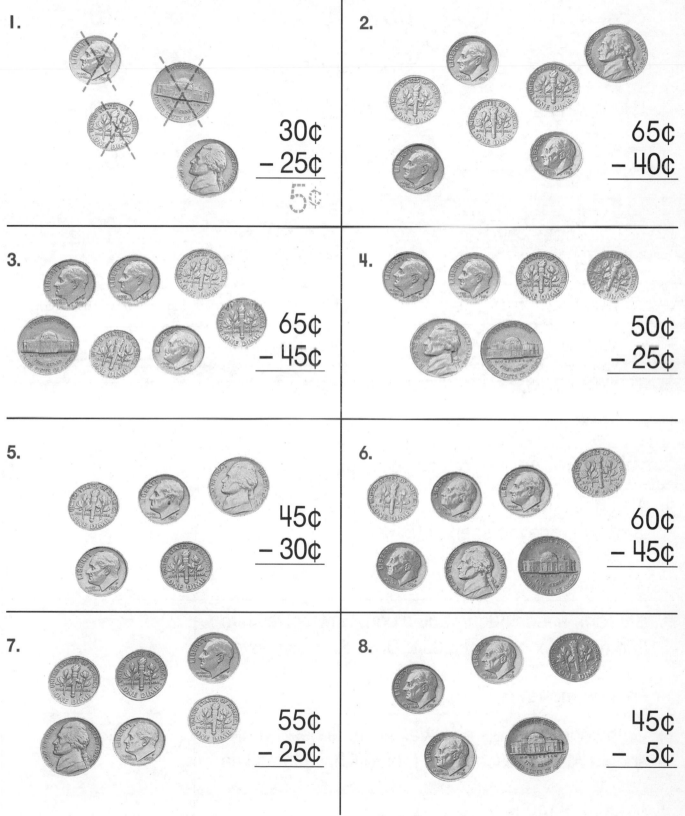

1.

$$\begin{array}{r} 30¢ \\ -\ 25¢ \\ \hline 5¢ \end{array}$$

2.

$$\begin{array}{r} 65¢ \\ -\ 40¢ \\ \hline \end{array}$$

3.

$$\begin{array}{r} 65¢ \\ -\ 45¢ \\ \hline \end{array}$$

4.

$$\begin{array}{r} 50¢ \\ -\ 25¢ \\ \hline \end{array}$$

5.

$$\begin{array}{r} 45¢ \\ -\ 30¢ \\ \hline \end{array}$$

6.

$$\begin{array}{r} 60¢ \\ -\ 45¢ \\ \hline \end{array}$$

7.

$$\begin{array}{r} 55¢ \\ -\ 25¢ \\ \hline \end{array}$$

8.

$$\begin{array}{r} 45¢ \\ -\ 5¢ \\ \hline \end{array}$$

Subtract. Look for a pattern.

1. 85 – 30 = _55_   2. 85 – 35 = ___   3. 60 – 30 = ___

   75 – 30 = _45_   85 – 40 = ___   60 – 35 = ___

   65 – 30 = ___   85 – 45 = ___   60 – 40 = ___

   55 – 30 = ___   85 – 50 = ___   60 – 45 = ___

   45 – 30 = ___   85 – 55 = ___   60 – 50 = ___

   35 – 30 = ___   85 – 60 = ___   60 – 55 = ___

Problem Solving   You may use coins.

4. Alex has 3 dimes and 5 nickels. Does Alex have enough money to spend 60¢ on a plate?

   _____

5. Brandon needs 50¢ to buy a pan. Dawn gives him 25¢ and Alex gives him 35¢. Does Brandon have

   enough money? _____

6. Cathy has 4 nickels and Alex has 4 dimes. What should Alex give Cathy so they will have the same

   amount of money? _____

Name _____

Use blocks and a workmat.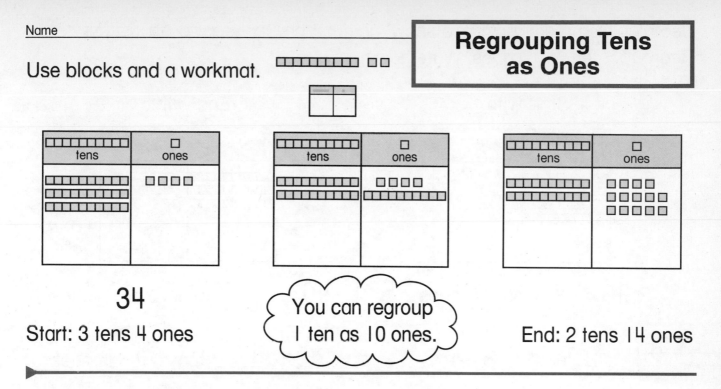

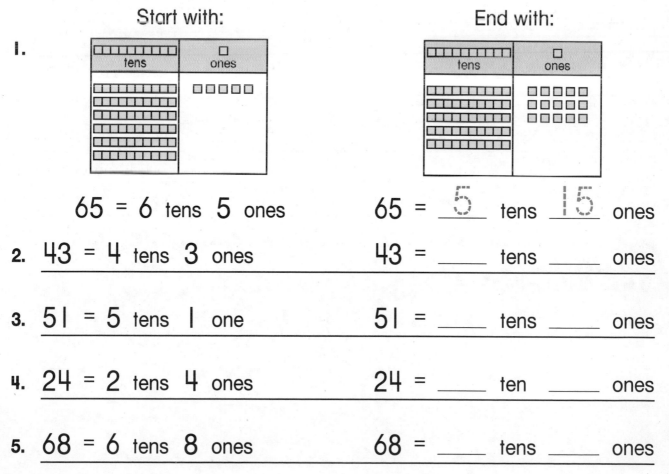

34

Start: 3 tens 4 ones

You can regroup 1 ten as 10 ones.

End: 2 tens 14 ones

Use your blocks and workmat to show the numbers.
Regroup 1 ten as 10 ones.
Write how many.

Start with: End with:

1.

$65 = 6$ tens 5 ones $65 = \underline{5}$ tens $\underline{15}$ ones

2. $43 = 4$ tens 3 ones $43 = \underline{}$ tens $\underline{}$ ones

3. $51 = 5$ tens 1 one $51 = \underline{}$ tens $\underline{}$ ones

4. $24 = 2$ tens 4 ones $24 = \underline{}$ ten $\underline{}$ ones

5. $68 = 6$ tens 8 ones $68 = \underline{}$ tens $\underline{}$ ones

Use blocks and a workmat to show the numbers.
Regroup I ten as 10 ones. Write how many.

Start with: End with:

I.

40 = 4 tens 0 ones   40 = __3__ tens __10__ ones

2. 24 = 2 tens 4 ones   24 = _____ ten _____ ones

3. 62 = 6 tens 2 ones   62 = _____ tens _____ ones

4. 20 = 2 tens 0 ones   20 = _____ ten _____ ones

5. 35 = 3 tens 5 ones   35 = _____ tens _____ ones

6. 77 = 7 tens 7 ones   77 = _____ tens _____ ones

7. 59 = 5 tens 9 ones   59 = _____ tens _____ ones

Maintain • Geometry

Complete the figure.

I.   2.   3.   4.

4 corners   3 corners   6 sides   5 sides

More Practice Set 8.3, page 411

Use blocks and a workmat.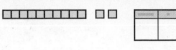

31 – 17

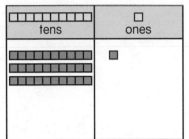

Show 31.
Look at the ones.
Are there enough to
subtract 7 ones?

31 – 17

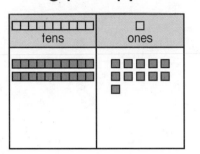

Regroup 1 ten as
10 ones.

31 – 17

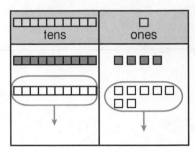

Subtract 7 ones.
Subtract 1 ten.
14 are left.

Show the larger
number. Look at
the ones.

Do you need to
regroup? Loop
yes or *no*.

Subtract the ones.
Subtract the tens.
Write how many are left.

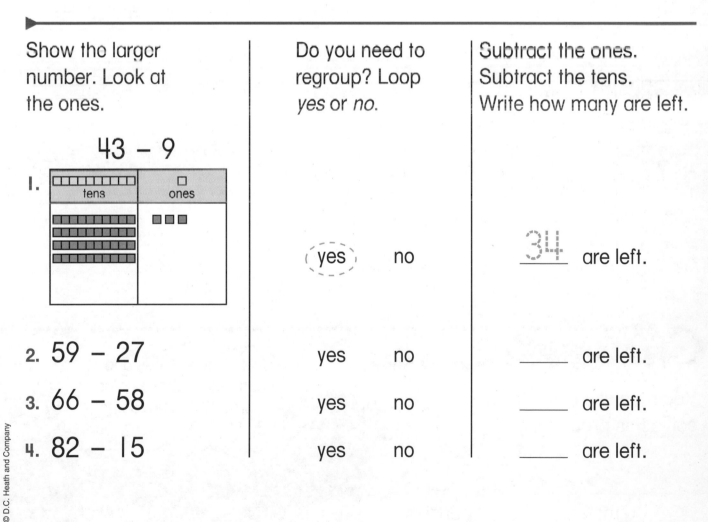

43 – 9

1.

(yes)   no   34 ___ are left.

2. **59 – 27**   yes   no   ___ are left.

3. **66 – 58**   yes   no   ___ are left.

4. **82 – 15**   yes   no   ___ are left.

Use blocks and a workmat. ▭▭▭▭▭▭▭ ▭▭ ▭▭▭

Show the larger number. Look at the ones.	Do you need to regroup? Loop *yes* or *no*.	Subtract the ones. Subtract the tens. Write how many are left.
1. 48 – 5	yes (no)	__43__ are left.
2. 85 – 38	yes no	_____ are left.
3. 25 – 17	yes no	_____ are left.
4. 69 – 8	yes no	_____ are left.
5. 32 – 17	yes no	_____ are left.
6. 77 – 9	yes no	_____ are left.
7. 29 – 7	yes no	_____ are left.

CHALLENGE •Money Sense

You may use coins to solve this problem.

I have only dimes and pennies. I have 8 coins worth 35¢. What coins do I have?

_____ dimes and _____ pennies

234 (two hundred thirty-four)

More Practice Set 8.4, page 412

Subtracting with Regrouping

Do you have enough ones to subtract?

tens	ones
4	2
− 2	7

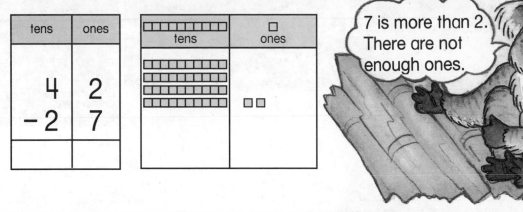

7 is more than 2. There are not enough ones.

Regroup if you need to.

tens	ones
3	12
4̶	2̶
− 2	7

Write a 3 and a 12 to show 3 tens and 12 ones.

Subtract the ones.

tens	ones
3	12
4̶	2̶
− 2	7
	5

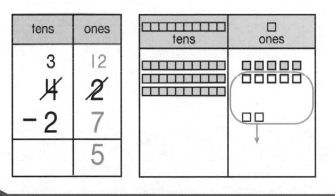

Subtract the tens.

tens	ones
3	12
4̶	2̶
− 2	7
1	5

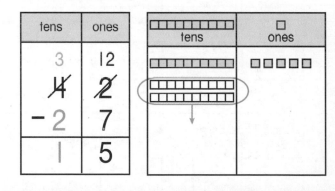

Subtract. Use blocks and a workmat if you like.

1.

tens	ones
5	14
6̶	4̶
− 1	9
4	5

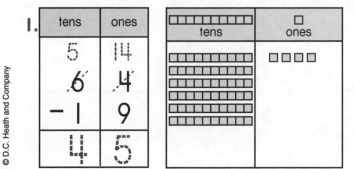

2.

tens	ones
3	3
−	7

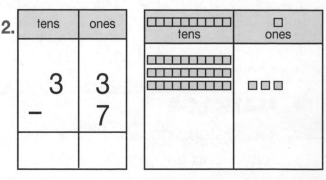

Subtract. You may use blocks.

1.

tens	ones
8	9
−5	6
3	*3*

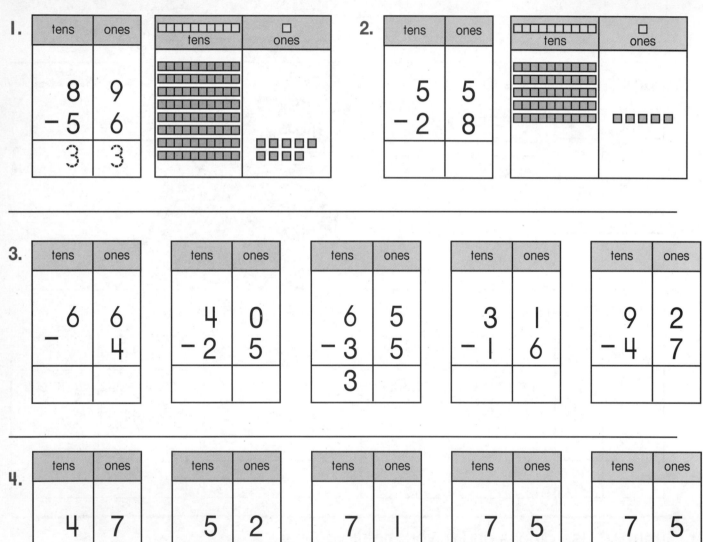

2.

tens	ones
5	5
−2	8

3.

tens	ones
− 6	6
	4

tens	ones
4	0
−2	5

tens	ones
6	5
−3	5
	3

tens	ones
3	1
−1	6

tens	ones
9	2
−4	7

4.

tens	ones
4	7
−3	8

tens	ones
5	2
−3	8

tens	ones
7	1
−6	8

tens	ones
7	5
−	9

tens	ones
7	5
−2	9

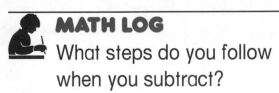

MATH LOG

What steps do you follow
when you subtract?

More Practice Set 8.5, page 412

Subtracting 2-Digit Numbers

$\overset{4}{\cancel{5}}\overset{10}{\cancel{0}}$	$\overset{4}{\cancel{5}}\overset{10}{\cancel{0}}$	$\overset{4}{\cancel{5}}\overset{10}{\cancel{0}}$
$-\ 1\ 8$	$-\ 1\ 8$	$-\ 1\ 8$
	2	$3\ 2$
Enough ones? Regroup if you need to.	Subtract the ones.	Subtract the tens.

Subtract.

1.

$$\begin{array}{r} \overset{7}{\cancel{8}}\overset{11}{\cancel{1}} \\ -\ 1\ 7 \\ \hline 6\ 4 \end{array} \qquad \begin{array}{r} 70 \\ -\ 25 \\ \hline \end{array} \qquad \begin{array}{r} 33 \\ -\ 12 \\ \hline \end{array} \qquad \begin{array}{r} 62 \\ -\ 7 \\ \hline \end{array} \qquad \begin{array}{r} 28 \\ -\ 18 \\ \hline \end{array} \qquad \begin{array}{r} 41 \\ -\ 9 \\ \hline \end{array}$$

2.

$$\begin{array}{r} 99 \\ -\ 5 \\ \hline \end{array} \qquad \begin{array}{r} 66 \\ -\ 48 \\ \hline \end{array} \qquad \begin{array}{r} 47 \\ -\ 39 \\ \hline \end{array} \qquad \begin{array}{r} 30 \\ -\ 14 \\ \hline \end{array} \qquad \begin{array}{r} 42 \\ -\ 18 \\ \hline \end{array} \qquad \begin{array}{r} 25 \\ -\ 4 \\ \hline \end{array}$$

3.

$$\begin{array}{r} 80 \\ -\ 56 \\ \hline \end{array} \qquad \begin{array}{r} 75 \\ -\ 27 \\ \hline \end{array} \qquad \begin{array}{r} 58 \\ -\ 34 \\ \hline \end{array} \qquad \begin{array}{r} 58 \\ -\ 6 \\ \hline \end{array} \qquad \begin{array}{r} 63 \\ -\ 59 \\ \hline \end{array} \qquad \begin{array}{r} 32 \\ -\ 6 \\ \hline \end{array}$$

4. $36 - 27 = $ ___

$$\begin{array}{r} 36 \\ -27 \\ \hline \end{array}$$

5. $55 - 8 = $ ___

6. $93 - 39 = $ ___

You need these pattern blocks.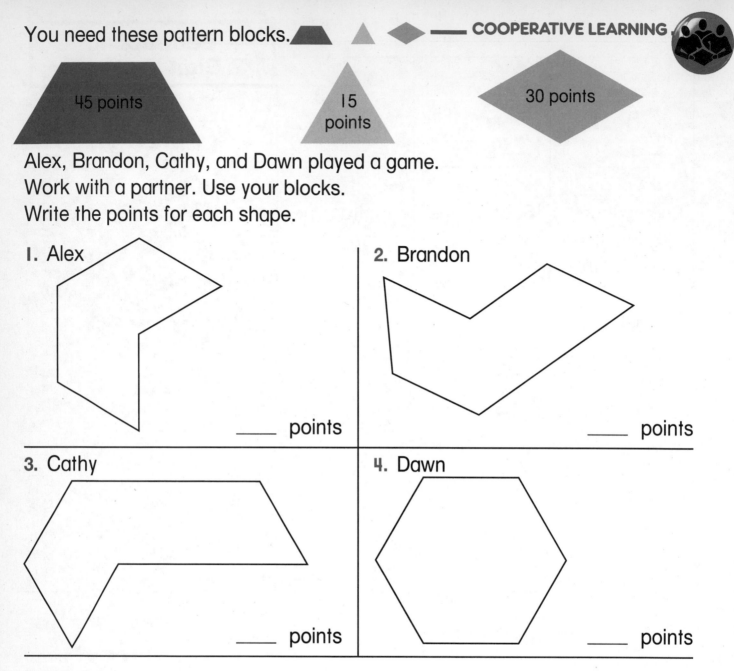

COOPERATIVE LEARNING

45 points

15 points

30 points

Alex, Brandon, Cathy, and Dawn played a game.
Work with a partner. Use your blocks.
Write the points for each shape.

1. Alex

_____ points

2. Brandon

_____ points

3. Cathy

_____ points

4. Dawn

_____ points

Write the answer.

5. Who got 15 more points than Alex? _____

6. Who got 30 fewer points than Dawn? _____

7. What block can Brandon add to make his shape have the same number of points as Cathy's? Loop the answer.

8. What block can Dawn take away to make her shape have 15 fewer points than Alex's? Loop the answer.

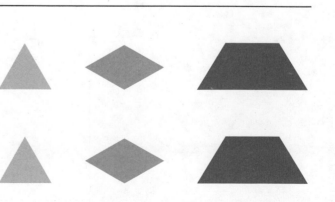

More Practice Set 8.6, page 413

You may use a calculator.

Look for a pattern. Write the differences.

1.
31	32	33	34	35	36
− 16	− 17	− 18	− 19	− 20	− 21
15					

2.
22	32	42	52	62	72
− 8	− 18	− 28	− 38	− 48	− 58
14					

3.
60	60	60	60	60	60
− 24	− 25	− 26	− 27	− 28	− 29
36					

4.
80	80	80	80	80	80
− 41	− 39	− 37	− 35	− 33	− 31
39					

5. Use a calculator to check row 4. Was your pattern right?

CHALLENGE • Number Patterns

You may use a calculator.
Look for a pattern. Write the missing number.

1.
| 95 | 80 | 64 | 47 | | 10 |

2.
| 6 | 15 | 26 | | 54 | 71 |

3.
| 94 | 85 | 73 | 58 | 40 | |

MID-CHAPTER REVIEW

for pages 227–238

Subtract.

1.

tens	ones
3	2
– 1	7

tens	□ ones

2.

tens	ones
5	8
– 2	9

tens	□ ones

3.

35	26	47	71	86	91
– 18	– 9	– 32	– 43	– 5	– 22

4.

40	32	55	95	76	63
– 13	– 6	– 11	– 47	– 4	– 35

Problem Solving

5. Alex needs 22 berries for his stew. He picks 8 berries. Then Dawn gives him 7 berries. How many more berries does Alex need?

_____ berries

6. There are 82 koalas at the feast. After eating, 44 of the koalas dance. How many of the koalas do not

dance? _____ koalas

Mid-Chapter Review

Work with a partner. Solve each problem.

1. There are 3 tables at the feast. The largest table has room for 20 koalas. Can 60 koalas sit at the

   3 tables? _____

2. Dawn needs 40 leaves. She has a branch with 18 leaves and a branch with 19 leaves. Does she

   have all the leaves she needs? _____

3. There are 2 teams for a race. Alex's team has 22 koalas. Brandon's team has 18. Alex and Brandon need the same number of koalas on each team. How many koalas should move from

   Alex's team to Brandon's? _____ koalas

4. Alex has only dimes and pennies. He has more dimes than pennies. He has 4 dimes. Can he

   buy a bowl that costs 45¢? _____

5. A big spoon costs 25¢, a big fork costs 21¢, and a cup costs 30¢. Cathy has 50¢ to spend. What 2 things can she buy?

   _____

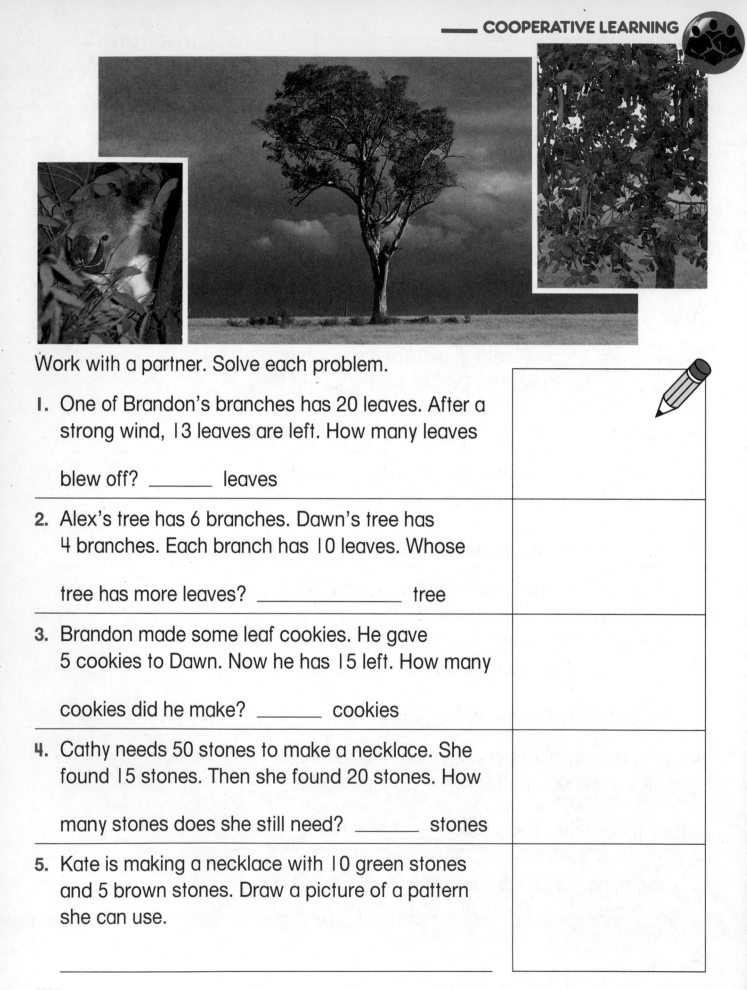

Work with a partner. Solve each problem.

1. One of Brandon's branches has 20 leaves. After a strong wind, 13 leaves are left. How many leaves

   blew off? _____ leaves

2. Alex's tree has 6 branches. Dawn's tree has 4 branches. Each branch has 10 leaves. Whose

   tree has more leaves? _____ tree

3. Brandon made some leaf cookies. He gave 5 cookies to Dawn. Now he has 15 left. How many

   cookies did he make? _____ cookies

4. Cathy needs 50 stones to make a necklace. She found 15 stones. Then she found 20 stones. How

   many stones does she still need? _____ stones

5. Kate is making a necklace with 10 green stones and 5 brown stones. Draw a picture of a pattern she can use.

You may use dimes and pennies.

Subtract. You may use coins.

1.
67¢	39¢	88¢	96¢	68¢	44¢
− 9¢	− 27¢	− 49¢	− 38¢	− 38¢	− 29¢
58¢					

2.
56¢	87¢	76¢	62¢	53¢	72¢
− 5¢	− 59¢	− 33¢	− 8¢	− 14¢	− 51¢

3.
85¢	95¢	36¢	75¢	43¢	85¢
− 17¢	− 38¢	− 25¢	− 4¢	− 38¢	− 25¢

Problem Solving

4. Alex has 50¢. He wants to buy 2 mugs that cost 35¢ each. How much more money does Alex need?

_____ ¢

Koala Corner Kitchen Store

CUP 10¢
Pan 86¢
basket 39¢
Spices 17¢
Bowl 82¢
FORK 59¢
Spoon 25¢

Problem Solving

1. Alex has 91¢. He buys a bowl. Will he have enough

money to buy spices also? _____

2. Brandon has 75¢. If he buys a fork and a cup,

how much money will he have left? _____

3. Cathy has 49¢. She buys a basket. Can she

also buy a cup? _____

4. Dawn has 64¢. She buys 2 things. Now she has no money. What did she buy?

_____

5. How much more does a pan cost than a fork and

a spoon? _____

6. If you had 56¢, what would you buy?

_____

More Practice Set 8.9, page 414

You need crayons.

Add or subtract. Find the addition and subtraction pairs.
Color the matching pairs the same color.

$$\begin{array}{r} 0 \\ +27 \\ \hline \end{array}$$

$$\begin{array}{r} 16 \\ +83 \\ \hline \end{array}$$

$$\begin{array}{r} 18 \\ -13 \\ \hline \end{array}$$

$$\begin{array}{r} 39 \\ +\ 1 \\ \hline \end{array}$$

$$\begin{array}{r} 60 \\ -35 \\ \hline 25 \end{array}$$

$$\begin{array}{r} 75 \\ -50 \\ \hline \end{array}$$

$$\begin{array}{r} 25 \\ +50 \\ \hline \end{array}$$

$$\begin{array}{r} 22 \\ +20 \\ \hline \end{array}$$

$$\begin{array}{r} 72 \\ -\ 9 \\ \hline \end{array}$$

$$\begin{array}{r} 25 \\ +35 \\ \hline 60 \end{array}$$

$$\begin{array}{r} 63 \\ +\ 9 \\ \hline \end{array}$$

$$\begin{array}{r} 99 \\ -83 \\ \hline \end{array}$$

$$\begin{array}{r} 27 \\ -27 \\ \hline \end{array}$$

$$\begin{array}{r} 40 \\ -\ 1 \\ \hline \end{array}$$

$$\begin{array}{r} 5 \\ +13 \\ \hline \end{array}$$

$$\begin{array}{r} 42 \\ -20 \\ \hline \end{array}$$

Critical Thinking Do you think that $72 - 6 = 66$? What addition sentence will help you to check your answer?

_____

Problem Solving   Write a number sentence for each story.

1. It took Brandon 25 minutes to get home. He ran for 6 minutes and walked the rest of the way. How long did he walk?

_____

2. Alex uses 36 leaves to make stew. Then he uses 25 leaves for a cake. How many leaves does Alex use in all?

_____

3. It takes Cathy 15 minutes to walk from her tree to the hill. It is 80 steps. How many minutes does it take Cathy to get to the hill and then back to her tree?

_____

4. Dawn sorts long tree branches from short ones. She has 85 branches to sort. She puts 40 branches in the long pile. How many branches are in the short pile?

_____

Maintain • Fractions

Loop the fraction for the shaded part.

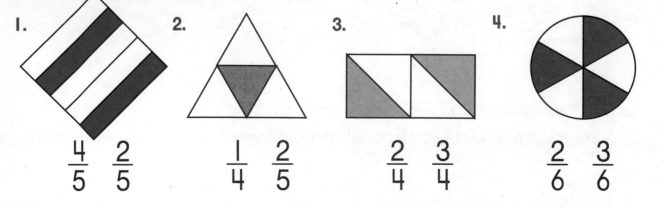

1. $\frac{4}{5}$ $\frac{2}{5}$

2. $\frac{1}{4}$ $\frac{2}{5}$

3. $\frac{2}{4}$ $\frac{3}{4}$

4. $\frac{2}{6}$ $\frac{3}{6}$

More Practice Set 8.10, page 414

Name _____

The koalas decided to count the leaves they had found each day for 5 days. Alex and Dawn made this table to show how many leaves they each found. Then Alex spilled juice on it.

Leaves Found

	Monday	Tuesday	Wednesday	Thursday	Friday	TOTAL
Alex	6	6		7	10	37
Dawn	6	10	9		8	43

Work with a partner. Find out what numbers the juice covers. Complete the table. Answer each question.

1. Who found more leaves on Tuesday, Dawn or

   Alex? _____

2. How many leaves were found on Wednesday?

   _____ leaves

3. On which day did Dawn find the fewest leaves?

   _____

4. On which day were more than 20 leaves found?

   _____

5. Were more than 70 leaves found in the 5 days?

   _____

6. On which day were the most leaves found?

   _____

The bar graph shows how many leaves each of the koalas had found by the end of Friday.

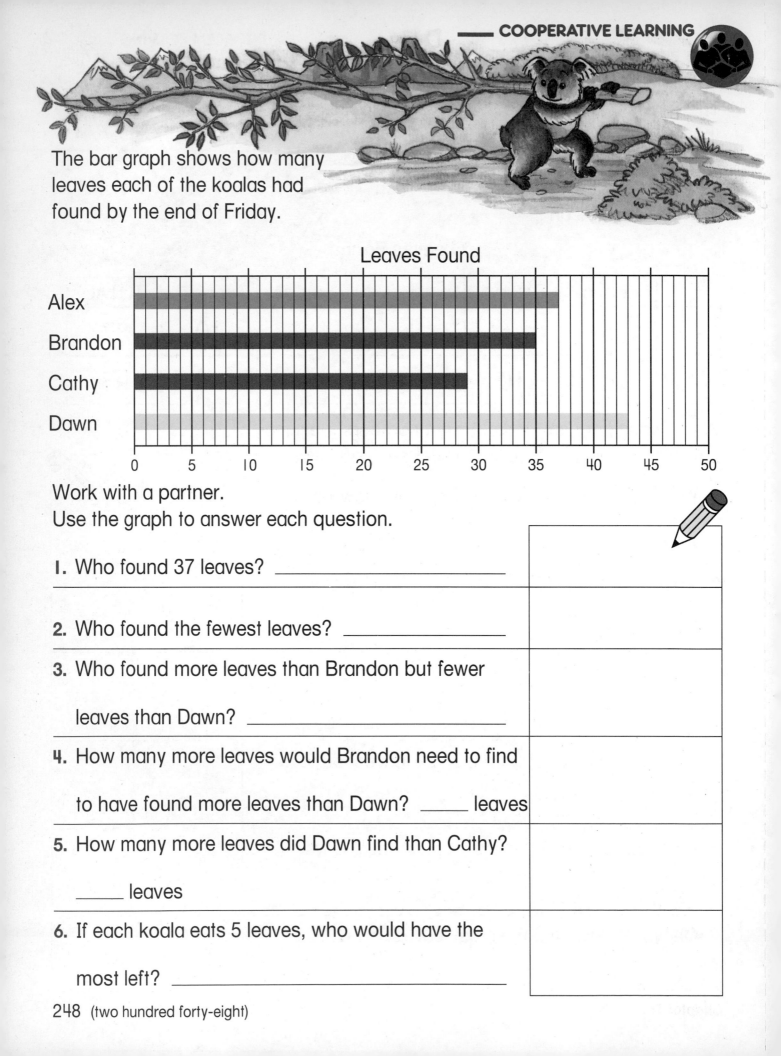

Leaves Found

Alex	
Brandon	
Cathy	
Dawn	

0   5   10   15   20   25   30   35   40   45   50

Work with a partner.
Use the graph to answer each question.

1. Who found 37 leaves? _____

2. Who found the fewest leaves? _____

3. Who found more leaves than Brandon but fewer

   leaves than Dawn? _____

4. How many more leaves would Brandon need to find

   to have found more leaves than Dawn? _____ leaves

5. How many more leaves did Dawn find than Cathy?

   _____ leaves

6. If each koala eats 5 leaves, who would have the

   most left? _____

CHAPTER TEST

Subtract.

1. $\begin{array}{r} 70 \\ -50 \\ \hline \end{array}$ 2. $\begin{array}{r} 85 \\ -25 \\ \hline \end{array}$ 3. $\begin{array}{r} 97 \\ -56 \\ \hline \end{array}$ 4. $\begin{array}{r} 78¢ \\ -39¢ \\ \hline \end{array}$

5. $\begin{array}{r} 60 \\ -30 \\ \hline \end{array}$ 6. $\begin{array}{r} 88 \\ -9 \\ \hline \end{array}$ 7. $\begin{array}{r} 90 \\ -80 \\ \hline \end{array}$ 8. $\begin{array}{r} 54¢ \\ -8¢ \\ \hline \end{array}$

9. $\begin{array}{r} 80¢ \\ -30¢ \\ \hline \end{array}$ 10. $\begin{array}{r} 72 \\ -47 \\ \hline \end{array}$ 11. $\begin{array}{r} 50 \\ -20 \\ \hline \end{array}$ 12. $\begin{array}{r} 95 \\ -20 \\ \hline \end{array}$

13. $\begin{array}{r} 45 \\ -5 \\ \hline \end{array}$ 14. $\begin{array}{r} 90 \\ -10 \\ \hline \end{array}$ 15. $\begin{array}{r} 63¢ \\ -19¢ \\ \hline \end{array}$ 16. $\begin{array}{r} 56¢ \\ -3¢ \\ \hline \end{array}$

17. $\begin{array}{r} 87 \\ -9 \\ \hline \end{array}$ 18. $\begin{array}{r} 50 \\ -40 \\ \hline \end{array}$

19. $\begin{array}{r} 75¢ \\ -15¢ \\ \hline \end{array}$ 20. $\begin{array}{r} 99¢ \\ -17¢ \\ \hline \end{array}$

Write each difference.

21. 60 – 40 = _____

22. 80¢ – 5¢ = _____

23. 98¢ – 77¢ = _____

24. 65 – 56 = _____

Solve each problem.

25. Ray has 65¢. He wants to buy 2 erasers that cost 35¢ each. How much more money does Ray

need? _____

26. Tanya had 80 short sticks to build a small house of sticks. She lost some. Now she has 67 sticks.

How many sticks is Tanya missing? _____ sticks

27. Marie needs 90¢ to buy a large cup of juice. Kim gives her 45¢, and Corey gives her 50¢. Does

Marie have enough money? _____

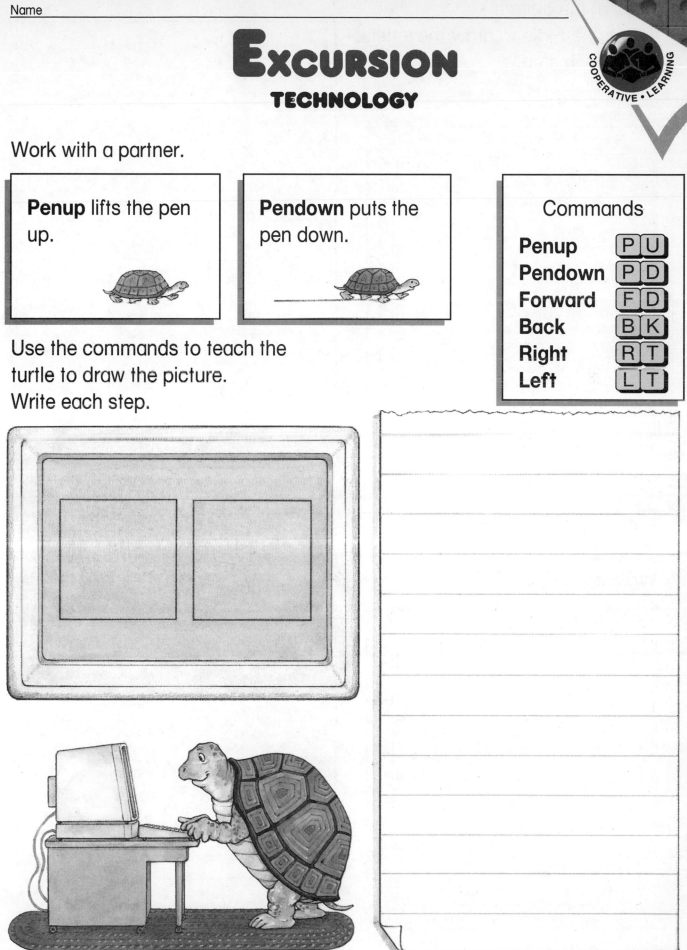

Work with a partner.

Penup lifts the pen up.

Pendown puts the pen down.

Commands

Penup	P U
Pendown	P D
Forward	F D
Back	B K
Right	R T
Left	L T

Use the commands to teach the turtle to draw the picture.
Write each step.

Computer

(two hundred fifty-one) 251

1. Look at the picture.
Teach the turtle to draw the letters.
Write each step.

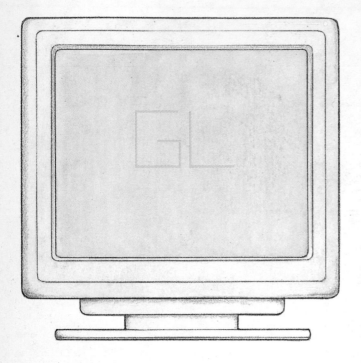

2. Write your initials on this screen.
Teach the turtle to draw your initials.
Write each step.

Note to the Family

Your child has been learning about subtraction of 2-digit numbers. This activity sheet gives your child an opportunity to share new skills with you.

COUPON MATH

You will need lined paper, food advertisement pages from newspapers or magazines, cents-off coupons, scissors, small pieces of paper, and pencils.

1. You need to make a shopping list for each player. (See below.) Use the food advertisement pages.

2. You and your child can look in the food advertisement pages for coupons that could be used to buy items on the list. Cut out as many coupons as you can find. You might want to include some of your own coupons. For example:

5¢ off for every "a" in the word	10¢ off anything that comes in a box	15¢ off when you buy at least 2	20¢ off anything you can eat

3. Place all the coupons face up between the players.

4. Players take turns choosing coupons and filling in each line of the chart by writing the value of the coupon under "How much saved?" (For example, you could write 15¢ for buying 2 cans of cat food, or you could write 10¢ because there are 2 *a*'s in "cans of cat food.") Then players complete the row by writing the new price.

5. Players can use only 1 coupon at a time. Each player keeps the used coupons. At the end of the game, each player adds up how much he or she saved. The player who saved the most wins.

Things I Need to Get	Price	How much saved?	New Price
box of macaroni	89¢		
bar of soap	54¢		
2 small bottles of juice	98¢		
a bag of apples	99¢		

Note to the Family

In the next few weeks, your child will be learning about measurement. Among the topics emphasized will be length and height, weight, and capacity.

It is important for children to see measurement used outside of school. Your child can practice measurement by watching or helping with cooking and repair projects and by measuring ordinary household items.

It might be fun to do this activity with your child.

ALL ABOUT ME

You will need a yardstick or measuring tape, a bathroom scale, and a measuring cup.

Help your child use the yardstick, scale, and cup to fill in the chart. You can ask for additional measurements such as heights of siblings and other family members, heights and weights of pets, lengths of rooms, amount of juice or milk used in a day, and so on.

All About Me

My name _____

1. I am about _____ inches tall.

2. I can stretch about _____ inches.

3. I weigh about _____ pounds.

4. I drink about _____ cups of milk a day.

5. My room is about _____ feet long.

MEASUREMENT

Listen to the story.

Hats Off

Name _____

You need string.

Can you match each color string with an animal's head?
Bear has the biggest head.
Mouse has the smallest head.
Use real string to help you.

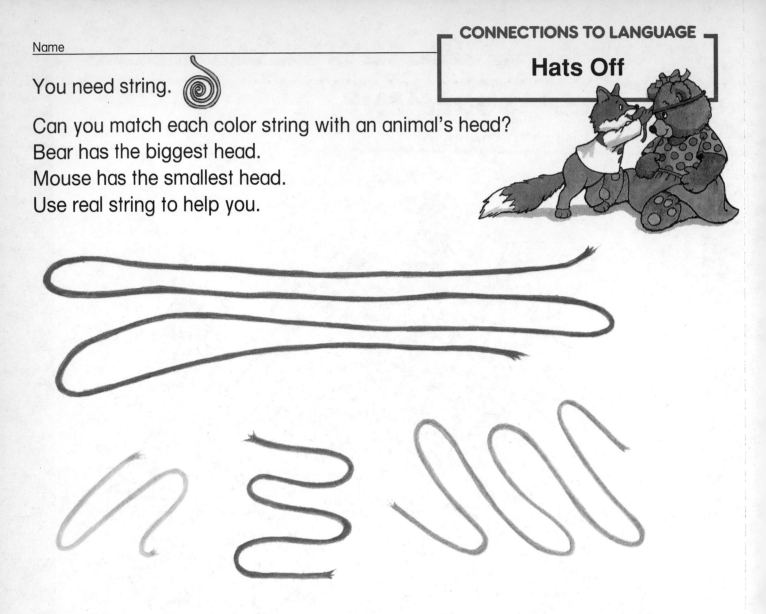

Write the colors.

1.	red _____ string	2.	_____ string
3.	_____ string	4.	_____ string

You need string, scissors, and inch units.

Frog wanted to know how many **inches** around his head was. He used inch units to measure.

My head is about 6 **inches** around.

Work with a partner to fill in the chart.
Use string to wrap around your head.
Then use inch units to measure the string.

How Big Around Is My Head?

_____ about ___ inches
Name

_____ about ___ inches
Name

1. Look at your chart. Who has the bigger head? _____

2. Which is longer? Loop your guess.

   around your head
   or
   from your wrist to your elbow

3. Measure from your wrist to your elbow in inches. about _____ inches

4. Was your guess right? _____

Use inch units to measure along each path.
Write about how many inches.

1.

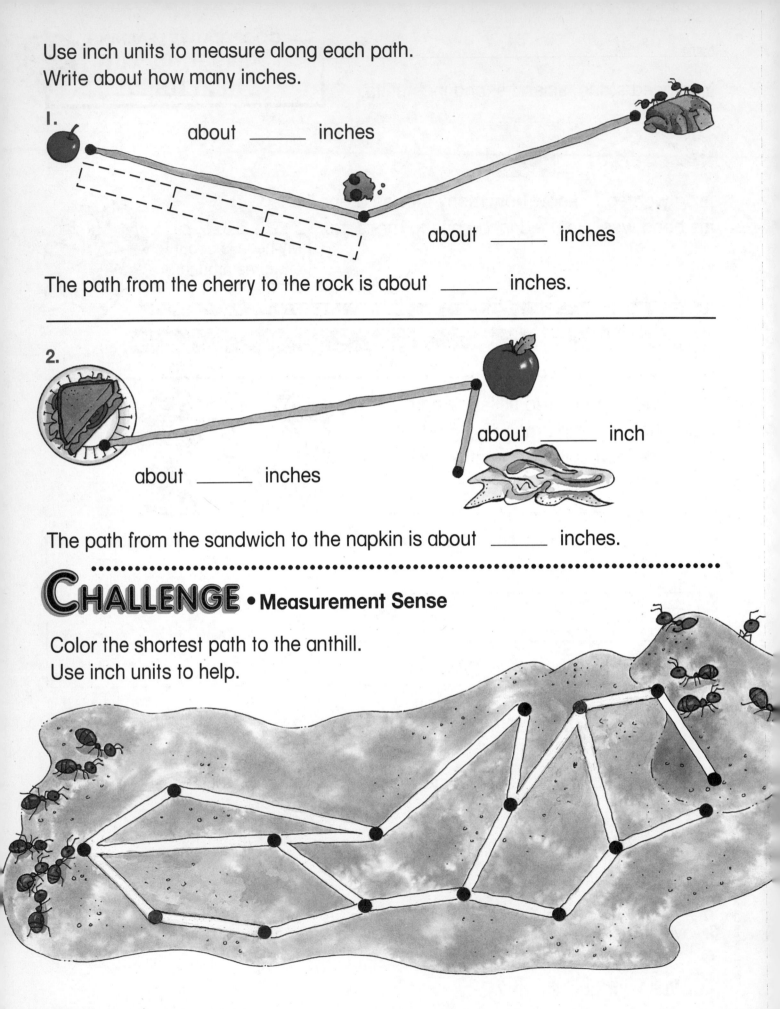

about _____ inches

about _____ inches

The path from the cherry to the rock is about _____ inches.

2.

about _____ inches

about _____ inch

The path from the sandwich to the napkin is about _____ inches.

CHALLENGE • Measurement Sense

Color the shortest path to the anthill.
Use inch units to help.

Name

You need crayons and an inch ruler.

inches

If you put the inch units together, you can make an **inch ruler.** The pencil is about 4 inches long.

Estimate. Color the things you think are shorter than 4 inches blue. Color the things you think are longer than 4 inches red.

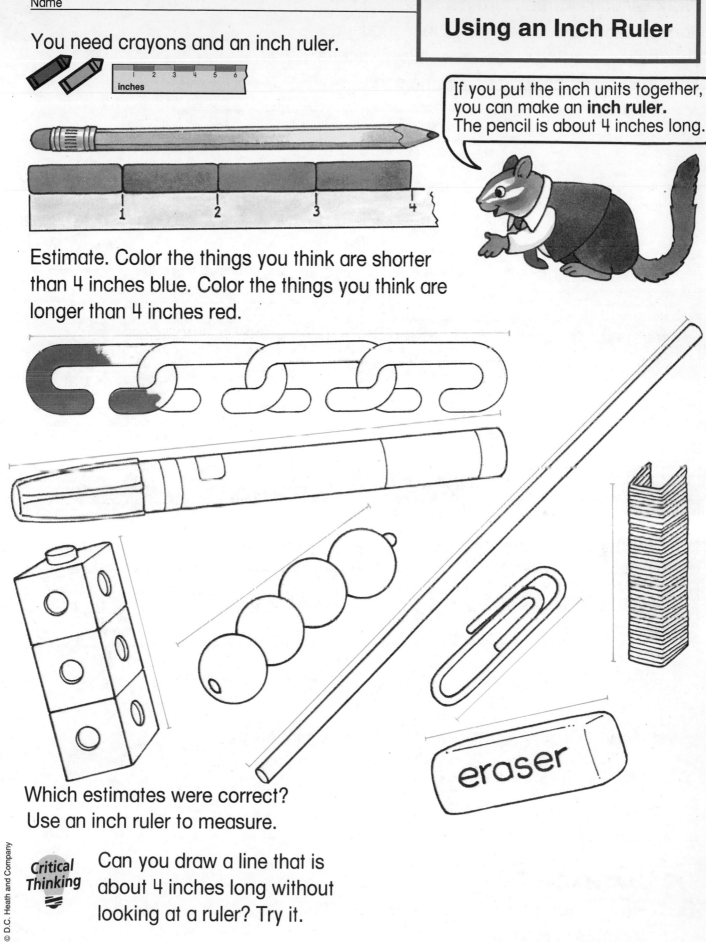

eraser

Which estimates were correct?
Use an inch ruler to measure.

Critical Thinking Can you draw a line that is about 4 inches long without looking at a ruler? Try it.

Work with a partner.
Look at the chart. Check (✓) those measures
you think are going to be more than 6 inches.
Then use an inch ruler to fill in the chart.

All About Me

from knee to heel about ____ inches	from heel to toe about ____ inches
from elbow to wrist about ____ inches	from elbow to shoulder about ____ inches
from forehead to chin about ____ inches	from wrist to top of little finger about ____ inches
length of little finger about ____ inches	hand spread about ____ inches
a step about ____ inches	a giant step about ____ inches

 MATH LOG

How is using an inch ruler easier
than using inch units?

Name _____

You need an inch ruler.

about 2 inches

about 1 inch

inches
1
2

I measured each side. Then I added. The shape is about 5 inches around.

about ___5___ inches around

Use a ruler to connect the dots.
Use an inch ruler to measure each side.
Write about how many inches around.

1.

about _____ inches

about _____ inch

about _____ inches

about _____ inches

about _____ inches around

2.

about _____ inches

about _____ inches

about _____ inches

about _____ inches around

1. Draw a square.
   Make each side 2 inches long.

   Estimate how many inches around.

   about _____ inches around
   Add to check your estimate.

   ____ + ____ + ____ + ____

   about _____ inches around

---

2. Draw a triangle.
   Make the bottom side 3 inches long.
   Make one side 4 inches long.
   Make the last side 5 inches long.

   Estimate how many inches around.

   about _____ inches around
   Add to check your estimate.

   ____ + ____ + ____

   about _____ inches around

Maintain • Subtraction

Subtract.

98	82	50	62	43	66
− 90	− 65	− 18	− 49	− 27	− 18

More Practice Set 9.3, page 415

You need crayons, an inch ruler, and a yardstick.

My paper is about I **yard** wide.

My folder is about I **foot** wide.

▶ Work in small groups.

Use an inch ruler to measure these things in your school.

Color the things longer than I foot green.

Color the things shorter than I foot yellow.

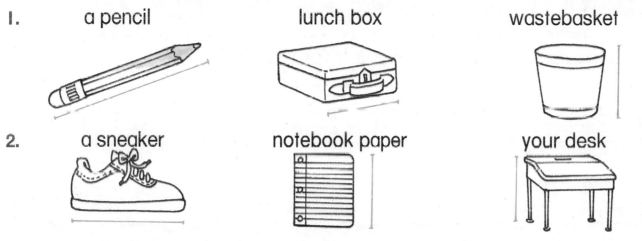

1.   a pencil   lunch box   wastebasket

2.   a sneaker   notebook paper   your desk

Use a **yardstick** to measure these things in your school.

Color the things longer than I yard red.

Color the things shorter than I yard blue.

3.   a bookcase   your desk   chalkboard

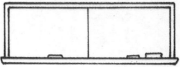

4.   a cabinet   a poster   wastebasket

Visit Maine

Work in small groups.
Look around your classroom.
List 3 things you think measure between 1 foot and 3 feet.
Use a ruler to check your answers.

Things Between 1 Foot and 3 Feet

1. _____

2. _____

3. _____

List 3 things that you think measure between 1 yard and 2 yards.
Use a yardstick to check your answer.

Things Between 1 Yard and 2 Yards

4. _____

5. _____

6. _____

Which would you use to measure these objects?
Loop your answer.

7.

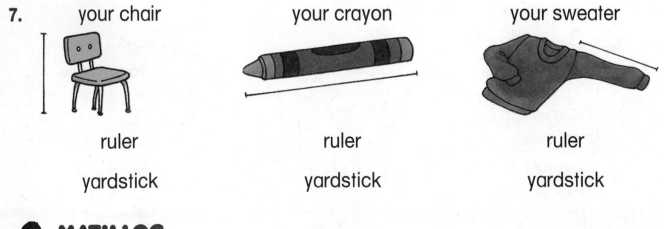

your chair	your crayon	your sweater
ruler	ruler	ruler
yardstick	yardstick	yardstick

MATH LOG
Tell why you picked the ruler or the yardstick to measure each object.

Pound

pound weight   bag of buns

light bulb   small plant   small dog

less than
I pound

about
I pound

more than
I pound

Loop the best estimate.

1. bicycle

less than
I pound

about
I pound

more than
I pound

2. sneakers

less than
I pound

about
I pound

more than
I pound

3. watch

less than
I pound

about
I pound

more than
I pound

4. bread

less than
I pound

about
I pound

more than
I pound

5. chair

less than
I pound

about
I pound

more than
I pound

6. 3 strawberries

less than
I pound

about
I pound

more than
I pound

You need a balance scale and pound weight.

Estimate whether each object is less than
1 pound, about 1 pound, or more than 1 pound.
Use a balance to compare.

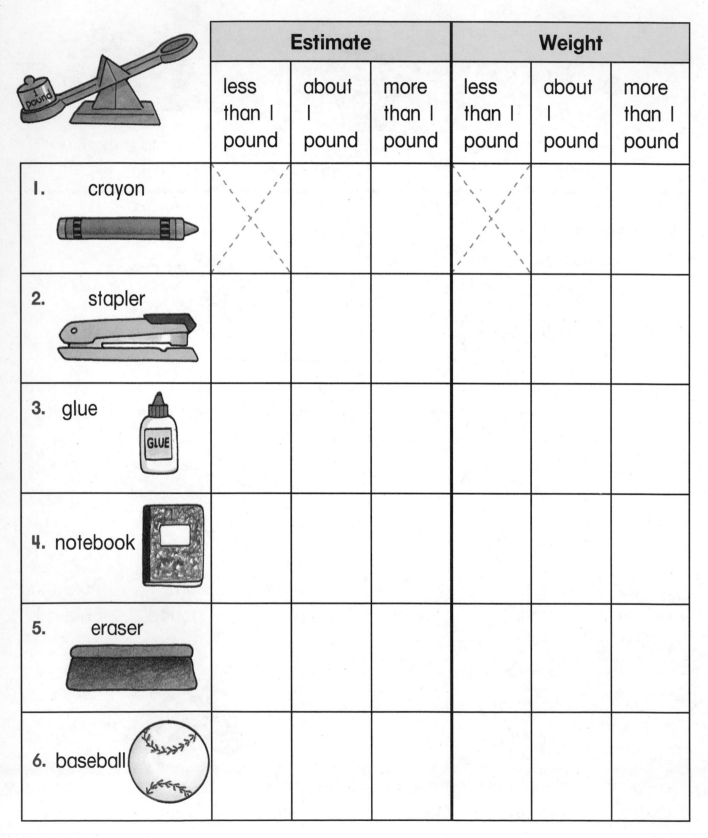

	Estimate			Weight		
	less than 1 pound	about 1 pound	more than 1 pound	less than 1 pound	about 1 pound	more than 1 pound
1. crayon	✕			✕		
2. stapler						
3. glue						
4. notebook						
5. eraser						
6. baseball						

Name _____

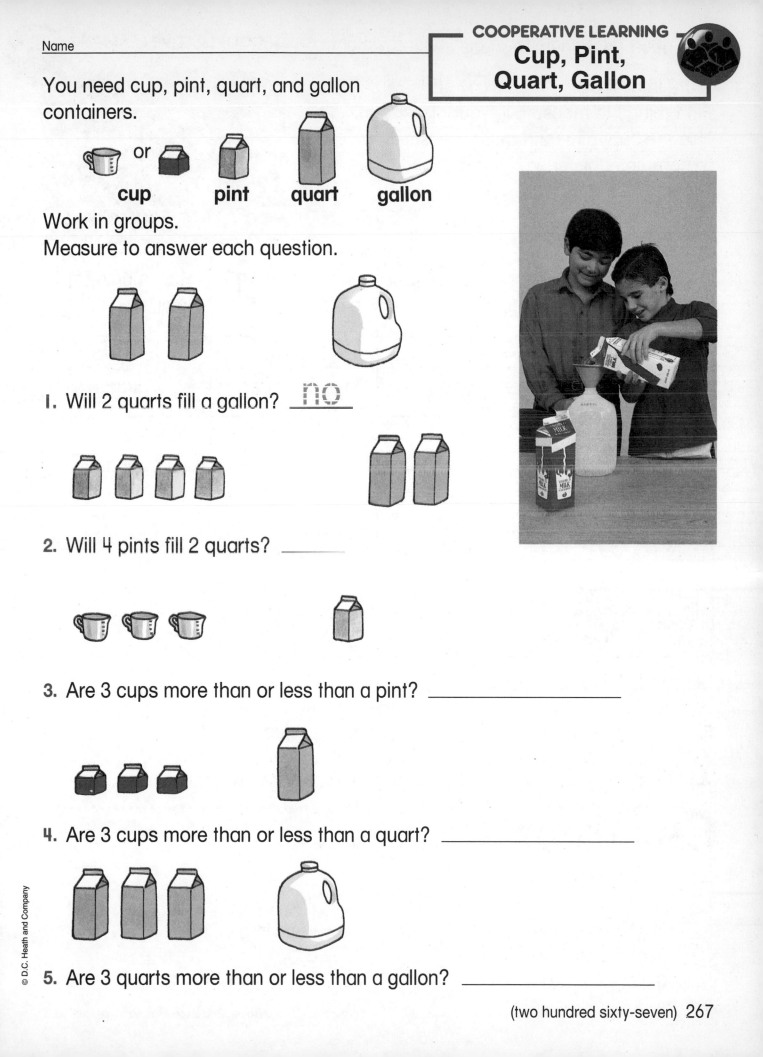

You need cup, pint, quart, and gallon containers.

cup **pint** **quart** **gallon**

Work in groups.
Measure to answer each question.

1. Will 2 quarts fill a gallon? __no__

2. Will 4 pints fill 2 quarts? _____

3. Are 3 cups more than or less than a pint? _____

4. Are 3 cups more than or less than a quart? _____

5. Are 3 quarts more than or less than a gallon? _____

© D.C. Heath and Company

You need containers to measure.

Work in groups.
Find things to measure in your classroom.
Use the cup, pint, and quart measures
to complete this chart.

Container	How many cups?	How many pints?	How many quarts?
1. pail	___ cups	___ pints	___ quarts
2. pan	___ cups	___ pints	___ quarts
3. bowl	___ cups	___ pints	___ quarts
4. pitcher	___ cups	___ pints	___ quarts

Measure. Write how many.

5. ___ cups in a pint

6. ___ cups in a quart

7. ___ pints in a quart

8. ___ pints in 2 quarts

CHALLENGE • Measurement Sense

Fill a gallon. Write how many.

___ cups in a gallon

___ pints in a gallon

___ quarts in a gallon

___ half gallons in a gallon

More Practice Set 9.6, page 415

Temperature

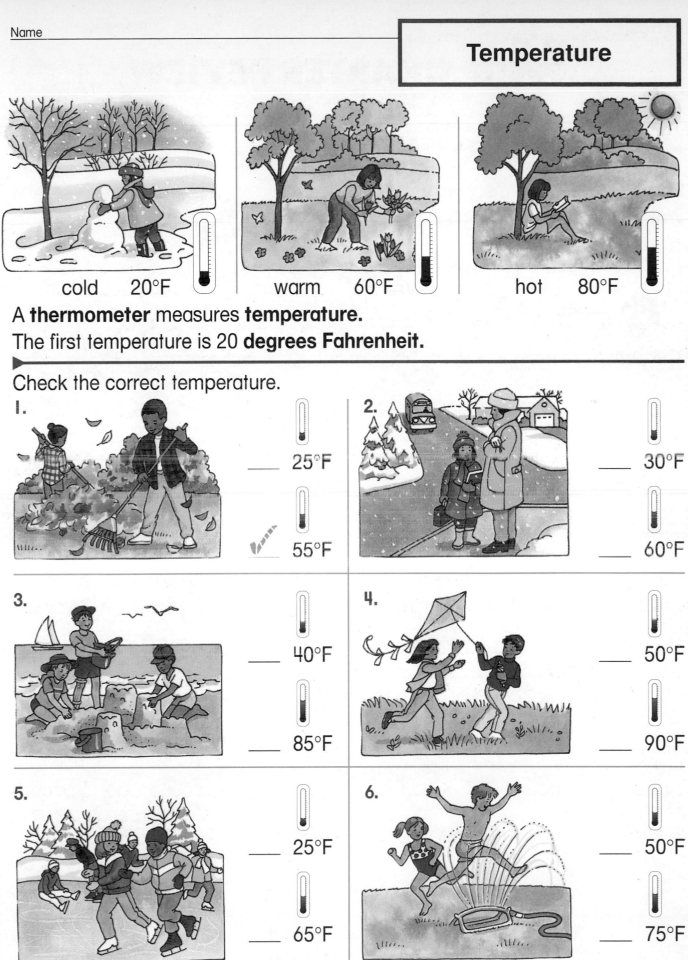

cold   20°F

warm   60°F

hot   80°F

A **thermometer** measures **temperature.**

The first temperature is 20 **degrees Fahrenheit.**

▶

Check the correct temperature.

1.
___ 25°F
___ 55°F

2.
___ 30°F
___ 60°F

3.
___ 40°F
___ 85°F

4.
___ 50°F
___ 90°F

5.
___ 25°F
___ 65°F

6.
___ 50°F
___ 75°F

MID-CHAPTER REVIEW

for pages 257–268

You need an inch ruler. [inches 1 2 3 4 5 6]

Use an inch ruler to measure each path.
Write about how many inches.

1.   about _____ inches

about _____ inch

The path from the apple to the fox is about _____ inches.

Loop the best estimate.

2. a phone book

about 1 inch	about 1 foot	about 1 yard

3. teacher's desk

about 1 yard	about 2 yards	about 3 yards

4. a cat

less than 1 pound	about 1 pound	more than 1 pound

5. a toy car

less than 1 pound	about 1 pound	more than 1 pound

6. a tall glass of milk

about 2 cups	about 2 pints	about 2 quarts

7. a small sink

about 2 pints	about 2 quarts	about 2 gallons

Mid-Chapter Review

Work with a partner. Loop the best answer.

Sometimes a problem does not have enough information for you to solve it.

1. Mouse started walking at 1 o'clock. Chipmunk started walking later. Both got to the pond at 3 o'clock. How long did Chipmunk walk?

2 hours   3 hours   not enough information

___

2. Bear had some nuts. She gave half of them to Mouse. She ate the rest. How many does she have left?

15 nuts   0 nuts   not enough information

___

3. Chipmunk went for a walk with 3 squirrels. Some skunks joined them. How many animals went for a walk?

5 animals   7 animals   not enough information

___

4. Fox planted this garden. It has the same number of flowers in each row. How many flowers are growing in the garden?

18 flowers   20 flowers   not enough information

___

5. Fox jumped higher than Mouse. Frog jumped higher than Fox. Which of the 3 animals jumped the highest?

Fox   Frog   not enough information

Work with a partner. Loop the best answer.

1. Mouse is at a mouse party. Seven mice at the party are black and white. The rest of the mice are brown. Are more than half of the mice brown?

   yes   no   not enough information

---

2. Chipmunk's new poster has 4 sides. How many corners does it have?

   4 corners   3 corners   not enough information

---

3. Fox went to visit his uncle. He started his trip on Monday morning. He got to his uncle's house on Friday night, that same week. How many days did it take Fox to get there?

   3 days   5 days   not enough information

---

4. Frog has a plant 7 inches tall. It has 20 leaves. Last week it had 12 leaves. How much taller has it grown since last week?

   8 inches   5 inches   not enough information

---

5. Bear has 1 more jar of honey than Fox. Bear gives Fox 1 of his jars. Who has more jars of honey now?

   Bear   Fox   not enough information

You need crayons 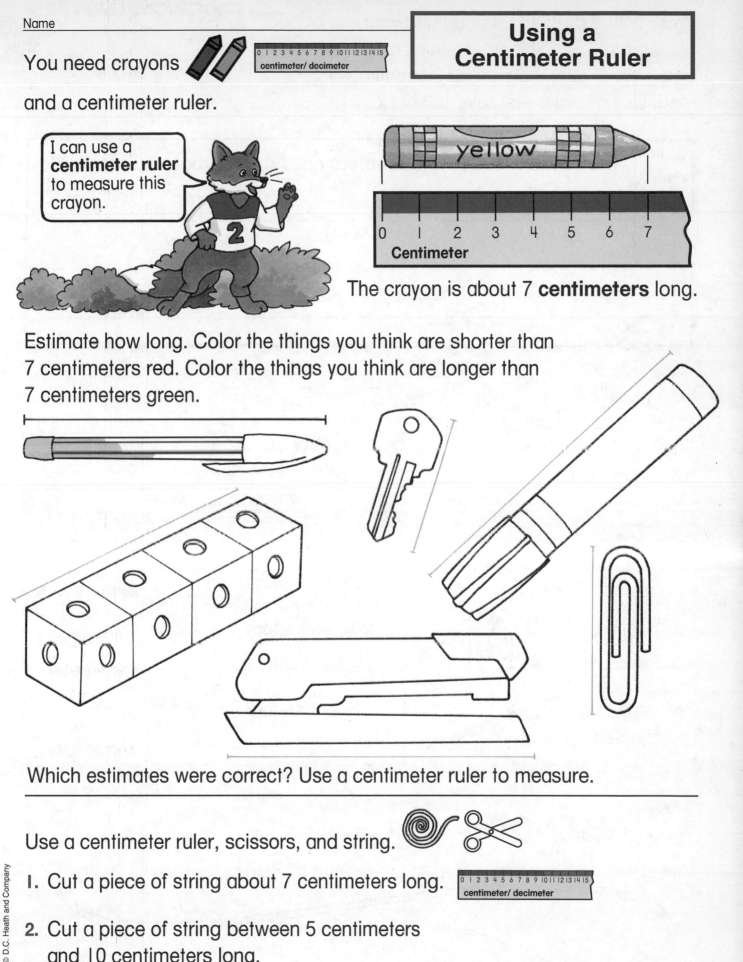 and a centimeter ruler.

I can use a **centimeter ruler** to measure this crayon.

yellow

Centimeter

The crayon is about 7 **centimeters** long.

Estimate how long. Color the things you think are shorter than 7 centimeters red. Color the things you think are longer than 7 centimeters green.

Which estimates were correct? Use a centimeter ruler to measure.

Use a centimeter ruler, scissors, and string.

1. Cut a piece of string about 7 centimeters long.

centimeter/ decimeter

2. Cut a piece of string between 5 centimeters and 10 centimeters long.

Work with a partner. Look around your classroom. List 3 things you think are between 15 centimeters and 30 centimeters long. Use a centimeter ruler to check.

Things Between 15 Centimeters and 30 Centimeters Long

1. _____

2. _____

3. _____

Find these classroom objects. Estimate how many centimeters. Then use a centimeter ruler to measure.

	Estimate Loop about how many centimeters.	Measure
4. length of a straw	20 centimeters 10 centimeters	about _____ centimeters
5. height of a glue jar	20 centimeters 10 centimeters	about _____ centimeters
6. length of a brush	20 centimeters 30 centimeters	about _____ centimeters

CHALLENGE • Measurement Sense

Use string and a centimeter ruler to measure this string.

about _____ centimeters

274 (two hundred seventy-four)

More Practice Set 9.9, page 416

You need crayons and a meterstick.

This side is about 1 **meter** long.

Meter

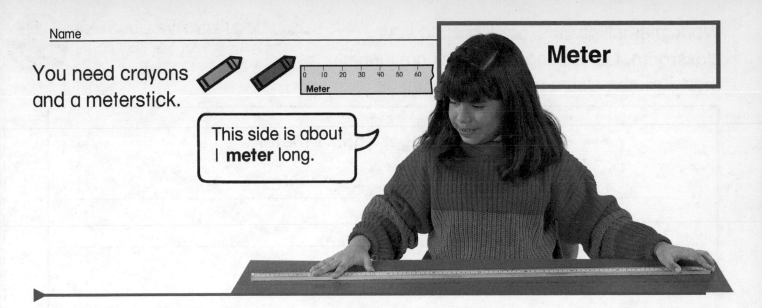

Use a meterstick to measure these things in your school.
Color the things longer than 1 meter green.
Color the things shorter than 1 meter purple.

1. your teacher's desk

large wall poster

box of crayons

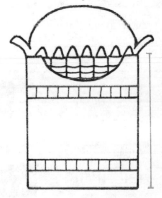

2.   a table

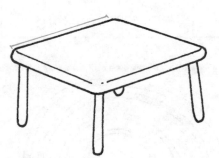

your desk

a knapsack

Critical Thinking What do you think you are closer to?
Loop your estimate. Then use a meterstick to measure.

1 meter tall
2 meters tall

Work in small groups. Look around your classroom. List 3 things you think are longer than I meter. Use a meterstick to check.

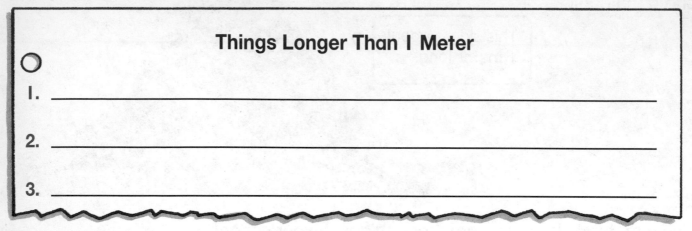

Things Longer Than I Meter

1. _____

2. _____

3. _____

Find these classroom objects. Estimate how many meters. Then use a meterstick to measure.

		Estimate Loop about how many meters.	**Measure**
4.	height of a door	I meter 2 meters	about _____ meters
5.	height of chalkboard	I meter 2 meters	about _____ meters
6.	length of classroom	I meter 3 meters	about _____ meters

● ●

CHALLENGE • Measurement Sense

How long is this string? Loop your guess. Use string and a meterstick to measure.

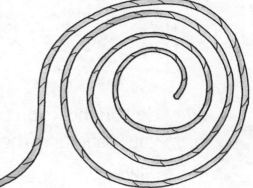

about I meter

about 60 centimeters

Name _____

Kilogram

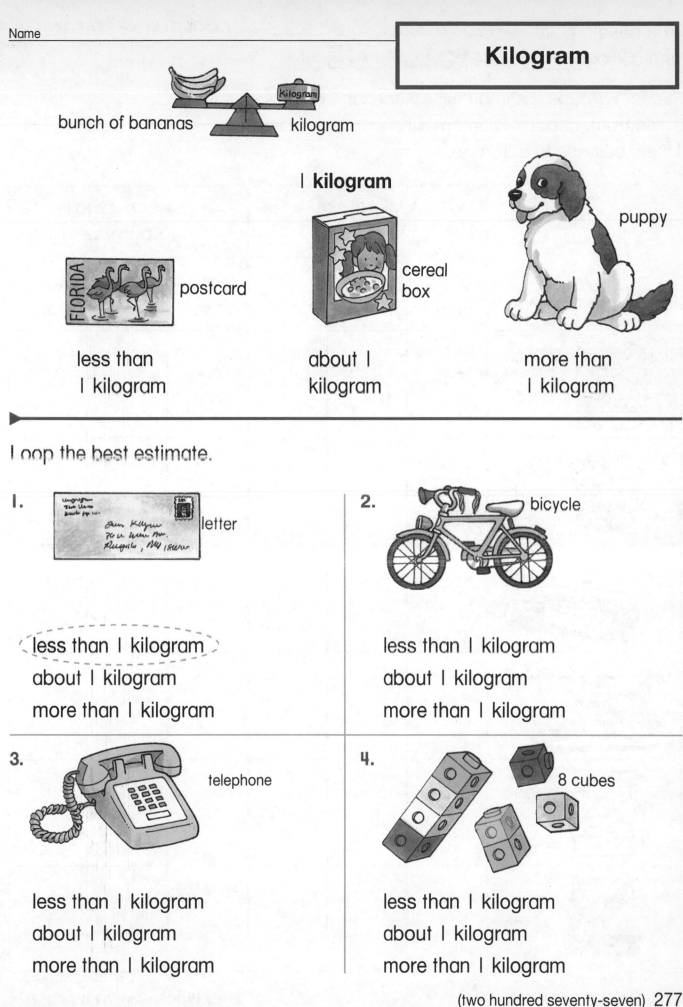

bunch of bananas   kilogram

I **kilogram**

postcard

cereal box

puppy

less than
I kilogram

about I
kilogram

more than
I kilogram

Loop the best estimate.

1. letter

(less than I kilogram)
about I kilogram
more than I kilogram

2. bicycle

less than I kilogram
about I kilogram
more than I kilogram

3. telephone

less than I kilogram
about I kilogram
more than I kilogram

4. 8 cubes

less than I kilogram
about I kilogram
more than I kilogram

You need a balance scale and a kilogram measure.

Work in groups. Estimate whether each object is less than 1 kilogram, about 1 kilogram, or more than 1 kilogram. Use a balance to compare.

		Estimate in Kilograms			Measure in Kilograms		
		less than 1	about 1	more than 1	less than 1	about 1	more than 1
1.	box of chalk	X			X		
2.	pail of sand						
3.	newspaper						
4.	sneaker						
5.	phone book						
6.	your lunch						

More Practice Set 9.11, page 416

Liter

Check the best estimate

container	less than 1 liter	about 1 liter	more than 1 liter

Loop the tool that best measures each thing.

1. How much milk is there?

meterstick   liter bottle   balance

2. How long is the baseball card?

meterstick   ruler   balance

3. How heavy are the apples?

meterstick   liter bottle   balance

4. How tall is your chair?

meterstick   ruler   balance

5. How much snow is there?

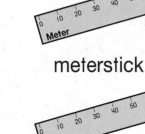

meterstick   ruler   balance

6. How much soda is there?

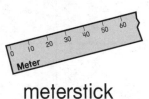

meterstick   liter bottle   balance

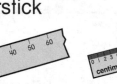

Maintain • Mixed Practice

Add or subtract.

$$
\begin{array}{cccccc}
53 & 45 & 60 & 72 & 66 & 38 \\
-27 & +15 & -18 & +9 & -59 & +29 \\
\end{array}
$$

Name _____

Work with a partner.
Read the problem.
Look at the pictures.
Finish one of the pictures
to solve the problem.

1. There are 5 rows in Fox's garden.
   There are 6 flowers in each row.

   How many flowers are there?   _____ flowers

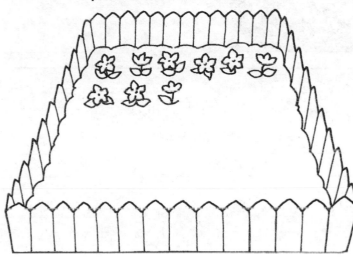

2. Bear has 3 dimes and 8 pennies. She wants to
   buy 3 apples. Each apple costs 12 cents. How

   much money will Bear have left?   _____ cents

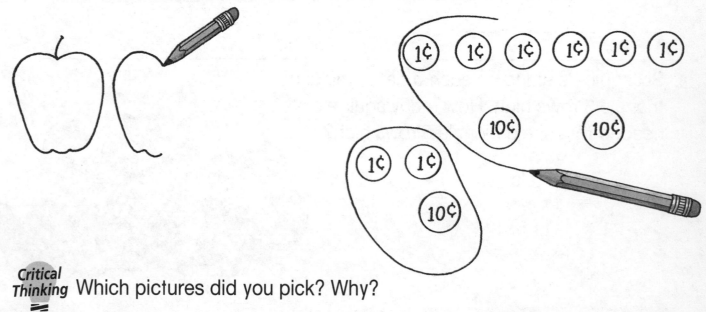

**Critical
Thinking** Which pictures did you pick? Why?

(two hundred eighty-one) 281

Work with a partner.
Solve each problem.
You can draw a picture to help you.

1. There are 3 mice. Each mouse ate 2 big nuts and 4 small nuts. How many nuts

   did they eat? _____ nuts

2. Frog lives 20 yards from a tall tree. Frog hops halfway there. Then he hops

   home. How far does he hop? _____ yards

3. Some squirrels build a square playground. They put up a fence to cut the playground in half. What shape is each half of the playground?

   _____

4. Six squirrels stand on each other to make a triangle 3 rows high. How many squirrels are needed to make a triangle 5 rows high?

   _____ squirrels

CHAPTER TEST

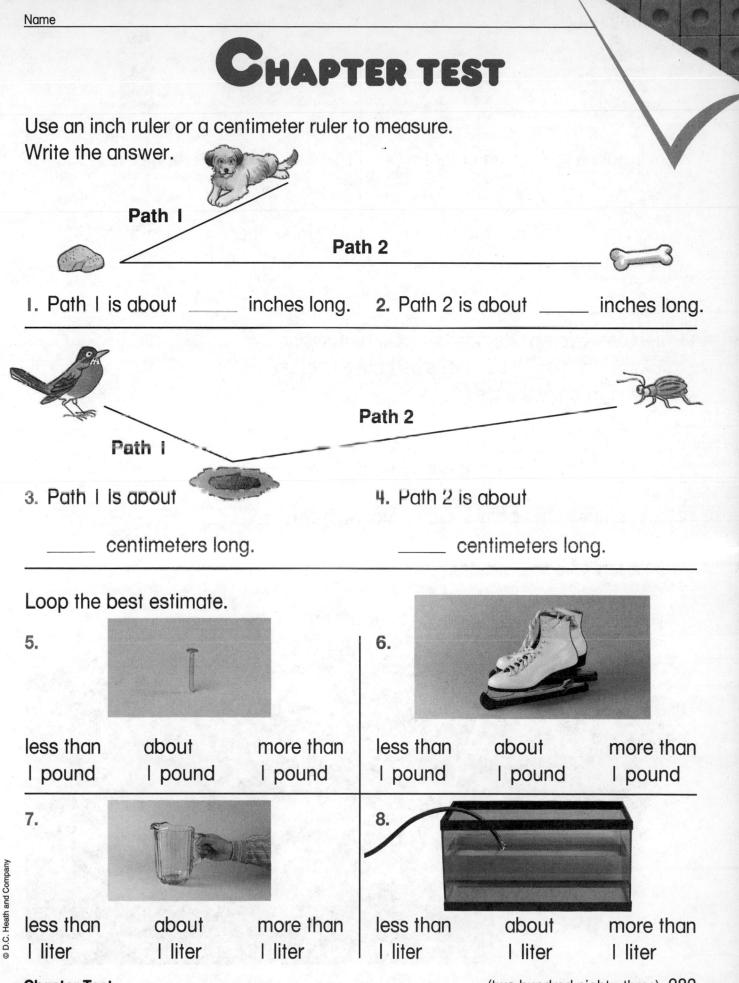

Use an inch ruler or a centimeter ruler to measure.
Write the answer.

Path 1

Path 2

1. Path 1 is about _____ inches long.   2. Path 2 is about _____ inches long.

Path 2

Path 1

3. Path 1 is about

_____ centimeters long.

4. Path 2 is about

_____ centimeters long.

Loop the best estimate.

5.

less than   about   more than
1 pound   1 pound   1 pound

6.

less than   about   more than
1 pound   1 pound   1 pound

7.

less than   about   more than
1 liter   1 liter   1 liter

8.

less than   about   more than
1 liter   1 liter   1 liter

Chapter Test

Loop the answer.

9.

Is 1 gallon more than or less than 1 cup?

more than   less than

10.

Is 1 pint more than or less than 1 quart?

more than   less than

Loop the answer.

11. Jeff has 1 raisin. He needs 1 pound of raisins in order to bake a pie. Does Jeff have enough raisins to bake the pie?

     yes   no   not enough information

12. Shara has 1 liter of milk. She needs to make 24 cookies for a party. Does Shara have enough milk to make the cookies?

     yes   no   not enough information

Chapter Test

CUMULATIVE TEST

Loop the one that is the same.

1.   2.

a   b   c   a   b   c

Loop the one that is different.

3.   4.

a   b   c   a   b   c

Loop the fraction that shows the shaded part.

5.   6.

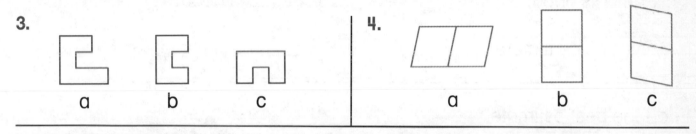

$\frac{1}{6}$ or $\frac{1}{8}$ $\frac{3}{6}$ or $\frac{3}{5}$

Subtract.

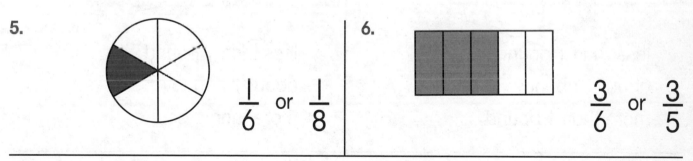

7.   75   8.   98¢   9.   43   10.   81¢   11.   98   12.   32¢
    – 5   – 6¢   – 39   – 8¢   – 9   – 8¢
  _____   _____   _____   _____   _____   _____

13. 54¢ – 3¢ = ____   14. 67 – 9 = ____

15. 25¢ – 6¢ = ____   16. 99 – 36 = ____

Use an inch ruler or a centimeter ruler.
Write the answer.

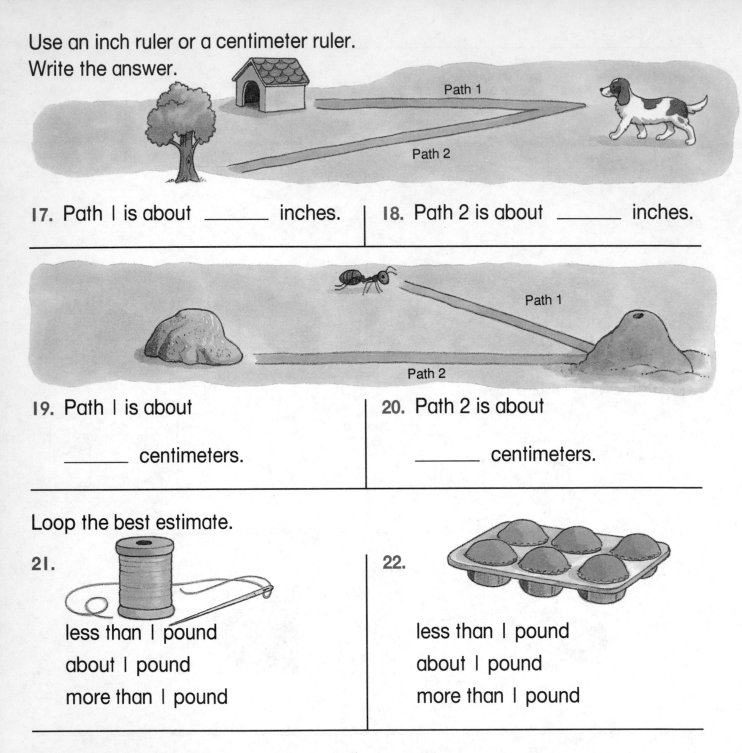

17. Path I is about _____ inches.

18. Path 2 is about _____ inches.

19. Path I is about

_____ centimeters.

20. Path 2 is about

_____ centimeters.

Loop the best estimate.

21.

less than I pound

about I pound

more than I pound

22.

less than I pound

about I pound

more than I pound

Solve each problem.

23. There are eight children in the yard. Five of them are playing catch. Loop the fraction that tells what part of the group is playing catch.

$\frac{2}{8}$ $\frac{3}{8}$ $\frac{5}{8}$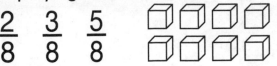

24. There are 3 slices of pie on a dish. Rachel takes I slice. Bert takes 2 slices. Who takes two thirds of the slices?

Rachel   Bert

Note to the Family

Your child has been learning about measurement. This activity sheet gives your child an opportunity to share new skills with you.

Help your child make one of the recipes below or use a favorite recipe of your own. Encourage your child to talk about the amount of each ingredient in each recipe. Talk about how and why you measure the amount of each ingredient.

FOOD FESTIVAL

YOGURT SQUARES

4 envelopes unflavored gelatin
2 cups apple yogurt
$\frac{1}{2}$ cup apple juice

1 cup boiling water
$1\frac{1}{4}$ cup honey
$\frac{1}{2}$ cup raisins or chopped walnuts

Using a large bowl, help your child sprinkle the gelatin into the apple juice. You add the boiling water and stir until gelatin is completely dissolved. Using a wire whisk or beater, blend in the apple yogurt and the honey. Pour into an 8-inch or 9-inch square pan. Sprinkle the top with raisins or chopped walnuts. Chill until firm. Cut into squares and serve. (As a variation, substitute pineapple-orange or orange yogurt and orange juice for apple yogurt and apple juice.)

EASY APPLESAUCE PIE

$\frac{1}{2}$ cup brown sugar
1 cup packaged pie crust mix
$\frac{1}{2}$ teaspoon cinnamon
$\frac{1}{2}$ teaspoon nutmeg

2 cups applesauce
1 tablespoon lemon juice
light cream or ice cream

Let your child do the measuring! You preheat the oven to 375°F. Then help your child grease an 8-inch pie plate. Combine the sugar, pie crust mix, cinnamon, and nutmeg in a bowl. Mix until crumbly. Pour the applesauce into the greased pie plate. Sprinkle with lemon juice, and spread the crumbly mixture over the top. Bake in oven for about 25 to 30 minutes. Serve warm, garnished with light cream or ice cream.

Note to the Family

In the next few weeks, your child will be learning about multiplication and division. Among the skills your child will be studying are making equal sets of objects; finding how many in all, given several equal sets; and separating a group of objects into equal sets, counting how many are in each set, and counting how many are left over.

Your child can be encouraged to notice that many everyday objects come in sets. For example, shoes, socks, pillow cases, and salt and pepper shakers come in sets of 2. Tennis balls often come in tubes of 3. Video cassette tapes are often sold in packages of 3 or 4. There are 4-packs of juice, 6-packs of soda or puddings, and 8-packs of crayons.

It might be fun to do the following activity with your child.

SETS OF THINGS

You will need common household objects and paper, pencils, and scissors.

1. Gather some household objects such as those listed above.

2. Cut out the labels below and set them up on a table.

3. Have your child sort the objects and place them behind the labels. If your child notices that furniture or lamps are in sets, he or she could write or draw the set on a piece of paper.

Sets of 2	Sets of 3	Sets of 4
Sets of 6	Sets of 8	

CHAPTER 10

MULTIPLICATION AND DIVISION READINESS

Listen to the story.

The Great Guppy Giveaway

(two hundred eighty-nine) 289

Name _____

You need 36 guppy punchouts and the story workmat.

1. How many guppies are there in all? _____

2. How many children will share the guppies? _____

3. Use your punchouts to make 5 equal sets.
   Draw a circle for each guppy.

4. How many guppies will each child get? _____

5. How many will be left over? _____

You need 25 links.

Make 4 sets of 2.
How many in all?

> I can count to find how many in all.

__2__, __4__, __6__, __8__ __8__ in all

Work with a partner.
Use links to make the sets.
Count. Write how many in all.

1. Make 4 sets of 3.

__3__, __6__, ____, ____

____ in all

2. Make 4 sets of 4.

____, ____, ____, ____

____ in all

3. Make 3 sets of 4.

____, ____, ____

____ in all

4. Make 3 sets of 5.

____, ____, ____

____ in all

5. Make 2 sets of 5.

____, ____

____ in all

6. Make 3 sets of 3.

____, ____, ____

____ in all

7. Make 4 sets of 5.

____, ____, ____, ____

____ in all

8. Make 4 sets of 6.

____, ____, ____, ____

____ in all

Work with a partner.
You may use counters and the story workmat.
Count. Write how many in all.

1. 4 sets of 5

_20_ in all

2. 5 sets of 4

_____ in all

3. 2 sets of 1

_____ in all

4. 1 set of 2

_____ in all

5. 2 sets of 9

_____ in all

6. 9 sets of 2

_____ in all

7. 4 sets of 0

_____ in all

8. 0 sets of 4

_____ in all

CHALLENGE • Number Sense

You will need squared paper and crayons.

Todd shaded 4 rows of 3 squares.
He shaded 12 squares in all.

Make other pictures that show 12 in all.
Color so that there are the same number
of squares in each row.

How many pictures did you make? _____

Name _____

How many are there?

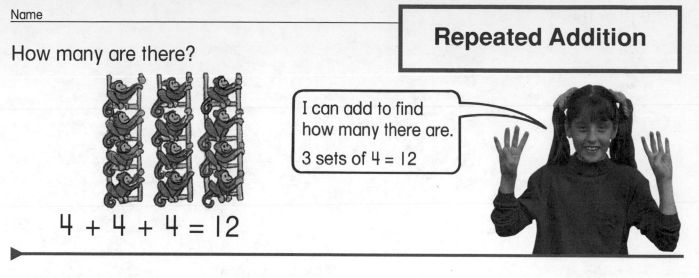

I can add to find how many there are.

3 sets of 4 = 12

4 + 4 + 4 = 12

Write how many.

1.
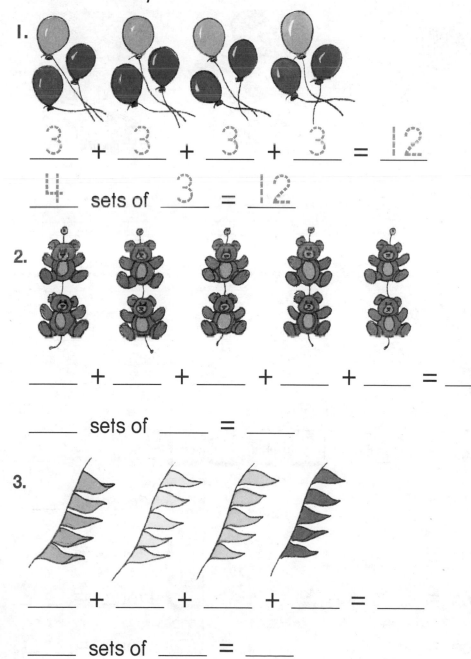

__3__ + __3__ + __3__ + __3__ = __12__

__4__ sets of __3__ = __12__

2.

___ + ___ + ___ + ___ + ___ = ___

___ sets of ___ = ___

3.

___ + ___ + ___ + ___ = ___

___ sets of ___ = ___

Write how many.

1.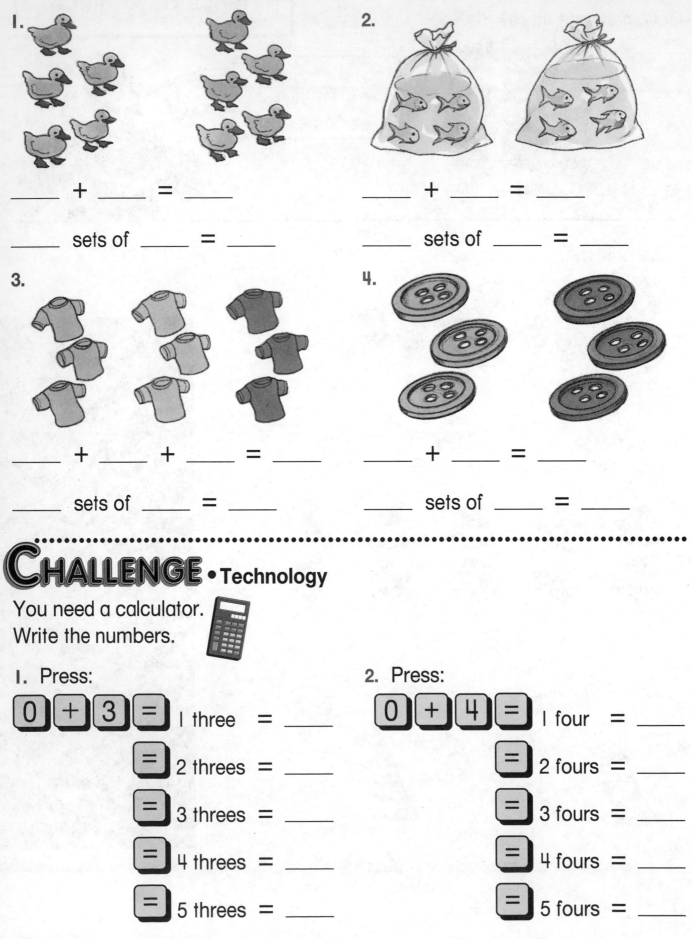

_____ + _____ = _____

_____ sets of _____ = _____

2.

_____ + _____ = _____

_____ sets of _____ = _____

3.

_____ + _____ + _____ = _____

_____ sets of _____ = _____

4.

_____ + _____ = _____

_____ sets of _____ = _____

··

CHALLENGE • Technology

You need a calculator.
Write the numbers.

1. Press:

| 0 | + | 3 | = | 1 three = _____

| = | 2 threes = _____

| = | 3 threes = _____

| = | 4 threes = _____

| = | 5 threes = _____

2. Press:

| 0 | + | 4 | = | 1 four = _____

| = | 2 fours = _____

| = | 3 fours = _____

| = | 4 fours = _____

| = | 5 fours = _____

Multiplication Sentences

Carla can multiply to find how many wheels.

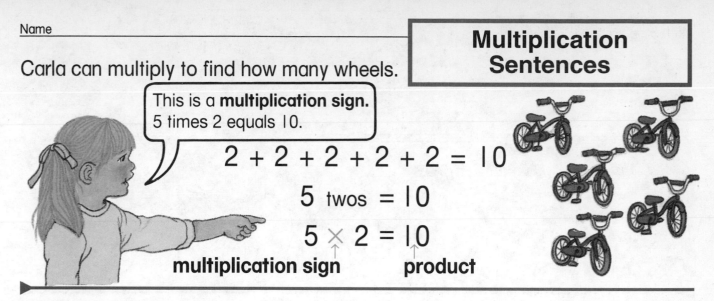

This is a **multiplication sign.**
5 times 2 equals 10.

2 + 2 + 2 + 2 + 2 = 10

5 twos = 10

5 × 2 = 10

multiplication sign   **product**

Write how many wheels.
Write the product.

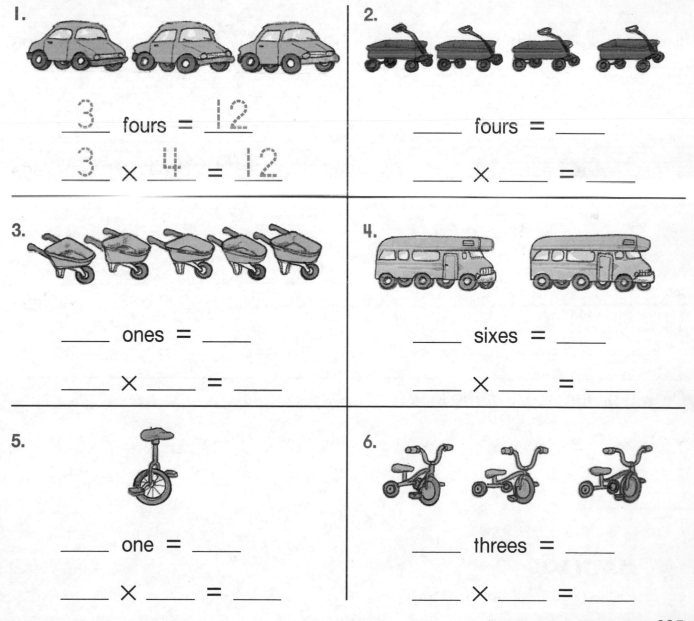

1.

___3___ fours = ___12___

___3___ × ___4___ = ___12___

2.

___ fours = ___

___ × ___ = ___

3.

___ ones = ___

___ × ___ = ___

4.

___ sixes = ___

___ × ___ = ___

5.

___ one = ___

___ × ___ = ___

6.

___ threes = ___

___ × ___ = ___

Write how many legs.
Write the multiplication sentence.

1. __3__ 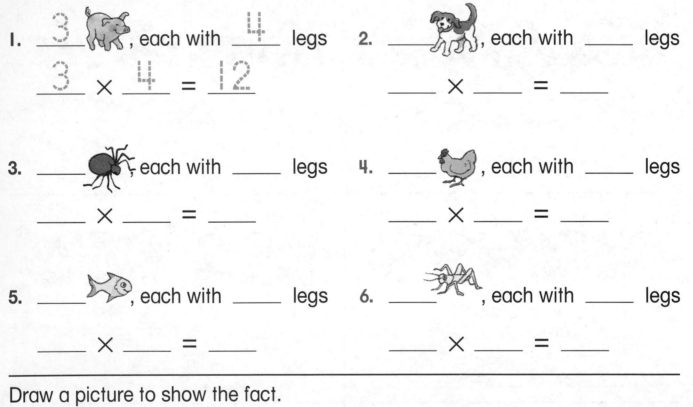, each with __4__ legs
   __3__ × __4__ = __12__

2. _____, each with _____ legs
   ____ × ____ = ____

3. _____, each with _____ legs
   ____ × ____ = ____

4. _____, each with _____ legs
   ____ × ____ = ____

5. _____, each with _____ legs
   ____ × ____ = ____

6. _____, each with _____ legs
   ____ × ____ = ____

Draw a picture to show the fact.

7. $4 \times 2 =$ ____

8. $2 \times 4 =$ ____

MATH LOG

Pick a fact. Make up a story.

More Practice Set 10.3, page 417

Name _____

Multiply. You may use counters.

1.

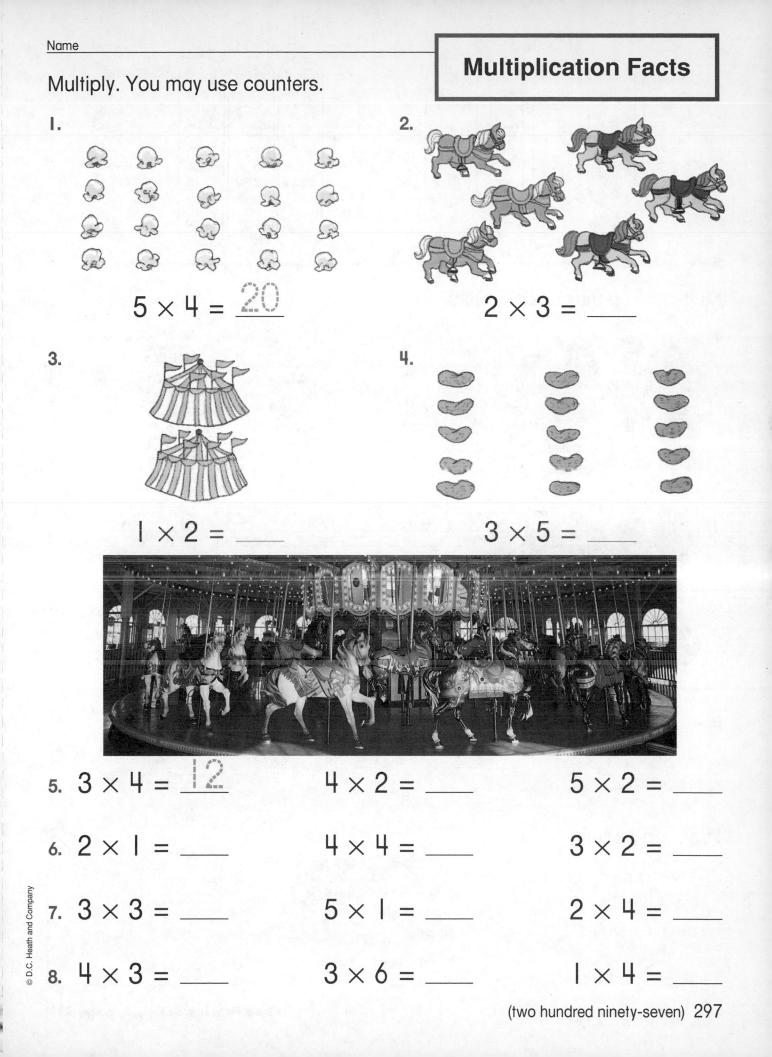

$5 \times 4 = \underline{20}$

2.

$2 \times 3 = \underline{}$

3.

$1 \times 2 = \underline{}$

4.

$3 \times 5 = \underline{}$

5. $3 \times 4 = \underline{12}$ $4 \times 2 = \underline{}$ $5 \times 2 = \underline{}$

6. $2 \times 1 = \underline{}$ $4 \times 4 = \underline{}$ $3 \times 2 = \underline{}$

7. $3 \times 3 = \underline{}$ $5 \times 1 = \underline{}$ $2 \times 4 = \underline{}$

8. $4 \times 3 = \underline{}$ $3 \times 6 = \underline{}$ $1 \times 4 = \underline{}$

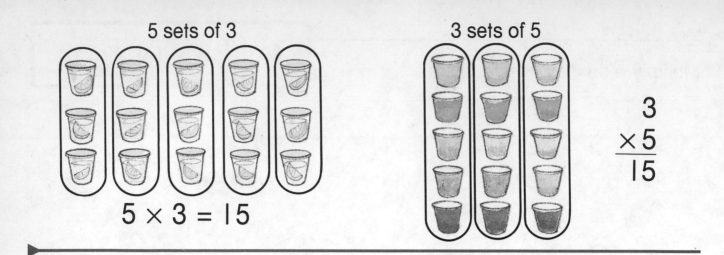

5 sets of 3

3 sets of 5

5 × 3 = 15

$$\begin{array}{r} 3 \\ \times 5 \\ \hline 15 \end{array}$$

Multiply. You may use counters.

1.
$$\begin{array}{r} 5 \\ \times 1 \\ \hline 5 \end{array}$$

2.
$$\begin{array}{r} 3 \\ \times 2 \\ \hline \end{array}$$

3.
$$\begin{array}{r} 5 \\ \times 2 \\ \hline \end{array}$$

4.
$$\begin{array}{r} 4 \\ \times 3 \\ \hline \end{array}$$

5.
$$\begin{array}{r} 5 \\ \times 5 \\ \hline \end{array}$$
$$\begin{array}{r} 1 \\ \times 3 \\ \hline \end{array}$$
$$\begin{array}{r} 2 \\ \times 4 \\ \hline \end{array}$$
$$\begin{array}{r} 6 \\ \times 2 \\ \hline \end{array}$$
$$\begin{array}{r} 5 \\ \times 3 \\ \hline \end{array}$$
$$\begin{array}{r} 2 \\ \times 2 \\ \hline \end{array}$$
$$\begin{array}{r} 4 \\ \times 5 \\ \hline \end{array}$$

Problem Solving

6. The carnival stays in town for 3 weeks. How many days does it stay?

_____ days

298 (two hundred ninety-eight)

More Practice Set 10.4, page 417

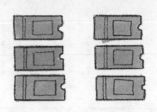
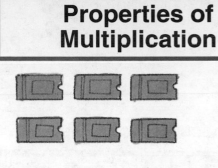

$2 \times 3 =$ __6__ $3 \times 2 =$ __6__

Multiply. You may use counters.

1.
$2 \times 4 =$ __8__ $3 \times 1 =$ ___ $2 \times 5 =$ ___

$4 \times 2 =$ __8__ $1 \times 3 =$ ___ $5 \times 2 =$ ___

2.
$3 \times 5 =$ ___ $3 \times 6 =$ ___ $1 \times 5 =$ ___

$5 \times 3 =$ ___ $6 \times 3 =$ ___ $5 \times 1 =$ ___

3.
$\begin{array}{r} 2 \\ \times 4 \\ \hline \end{array}$ $\begin{array}{r} 4 \\ \times 2 \\ \hline \end{array}$ $\begin{array}{r} 3 \\ \times 4 \\ \hline \end{array}$ $\begin{array}{r} 4 \\ \times 3 \\ \hline \end{array}$ $\begin{array}{r} 2 \\ \times 9 \\ \hline \end{array}$ $\begin{array}{r} 9 \\ \times 2 \\ \hline \end{array}$

4.
$\begin{array}{r} 1 \\ \times 3 \\ \hline \end{array}$ $\begin{array}{r} 3 \\ \times 1 \\ \hline \end{array}$ $\begin{array}{r} 5 \\ \times 2 \\ \hline \end{array}$ $\begin{array}{r} 2 \\ \times 5 \\ \hline \end{array}$ $\begin{array}{r} 2 \\ \times 6 \\ \hline \end{array}$ $\begin{array}{r} 6 \\ \times 2 \\ \hline \end{array}$

Critical Thinking Look at each pair of multiplication facts.
What do you notice?

You need a calculator.

To multiply:

Press these keys.

$2 \times 1 =$ ____

`2` `×` `1` `=`

```
2
```

Use a calculator to multiply.

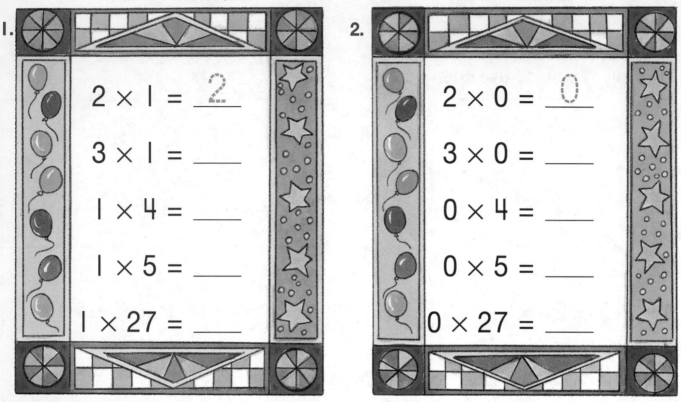

1.

$2 \times 1 =$ _2_

$3 \times 1 =$ ____

$1 \times 4 =$ ____

$1 \times 5 =$ ____

$1 \times 27 =$ ____

2.

$2 \times 0 =$ _0_

$3 \times 0 =$ ____

$0 \times 4 =$ ____

$0 \times 5 =$ ____

$0 \times 27 =$ ____

Critical Thinking Look at chart 1.
Look at chart 2. What do you notice?

Maintain • Measurement

What would you use to measure? Match.

1. How heavy is an orange?

2. How long is a fence?

3. How much juice is there?

Name _____

$$\begin{array}{r} 2 \\ \times 3 \\ \hline 6 \end{array}$$

$$\begin{array}{r} 5 \\ \times 2 \\ \hline 10 \end{array}$$

Write the product.

1.
$$\begin{array}{r} 4 \\ \times 3 \end{array}$$
$$\begin{array}{r} 2 \\ \times 5 \end{array}$$
$$\begin{array}{r} 4 \\ \times 2 \end{array}$$
$$\begin{array}{r} 2 \\ \times 9 \end{array}$$
$$\begin{array}{r} 0 \\ \times 2 \end{array}$$
$$\begin{array}{r} 2 \\ \times 8 \end{array}$$

2.
$$\begin{array}{r} 0 \\ \times 3 \end{array}$$
$$\begin{array}{r} 3 \\ \times 2 \end{array}$$
$$\begin{array}{r} 3 \\ \times 4 \end{array}$$
$$\begin{array}{r} 5 \\ \times 3 \end{array}$$
$$\begin{array}{r} 3 \\ \times 6 \end{array}$$
$$\begin{array}{r} 2 \\ \times 3 \end{array}$$

3.
$$\begin{array}{r} 3 \\ \times 5 \end{array}$$
$$\begin{array}{r} 1 \\ \times 3 \end{array}$$
$$\begin{array}{r} 2 \\ \times 1 \end{array}$$
$$\begin{array}{r} 2 \\ \times 4 \end{array}$$
$$\begin{array}{r} 5 \\ \times 4 \end{array}$$
$$\begin{array}{r} 9 \\ \times 2 \end{array}$$

4.
$$\begin{array}{r} 1 \\ \times 2 \end{array}$$
$$\begin{array}{r} 8 \\ \times 2 \end{array}$$
$$\begin{array}{r} 2 \\ \times 2 \end{array}$$
$$\begin{array}{r} 7 \\ \times 2 \end{array}$$
$$\begin{array}{r} 3 \\ \times 3 \end{array}$$
$$\begin{array}{r} 1 \\ \times 3 \end{array}$$

Problem Solving

1. There are 7 bumper cars. Each has 2 red lights. How many red lights are there?

   _____ red lights

2. There are 9 booths at the carnival. There are 3 people working in each booth. How many

   people are working in the booths? _____ people

3. It costs 4 tickets to ride the Ferris wheel. Henry has 18 tickets left. Can he go on the Ferris wheel

   8 times? _____

4. Two children can fit in each car on the Octopus ride. Seven of the cars are full. One car has only 1 child. How many children are on the ride?

   _____ children

....

CHALLENGE • Multiplication

Write the missing numbers.

$$
\begin{array}{r} 6 \\ \times \\ \hline 12 \end{array}
\qquad
\begin{array}{r} 3 \\ \times \\ \hline 12 \end{array}
\qquad
\begin{array}{r} \\ \times 7 \\ \hline 14 \end{array}
\qquad
\begin{array}{r} \\ \times 5 \\ \hline 15 \end{array}
\qquad
\begin{array}{r} 3 \\ \times \\ \hline 6 \end{array}
\qquad
\begin{array}{r} \\ \times 2 \\ \hline 8 \end{array}
$$

More Practice Set 10.6, page 418

Name _____

This graph shows how many buttons were won at different booths. One button stands for every 5 buttons that were won.

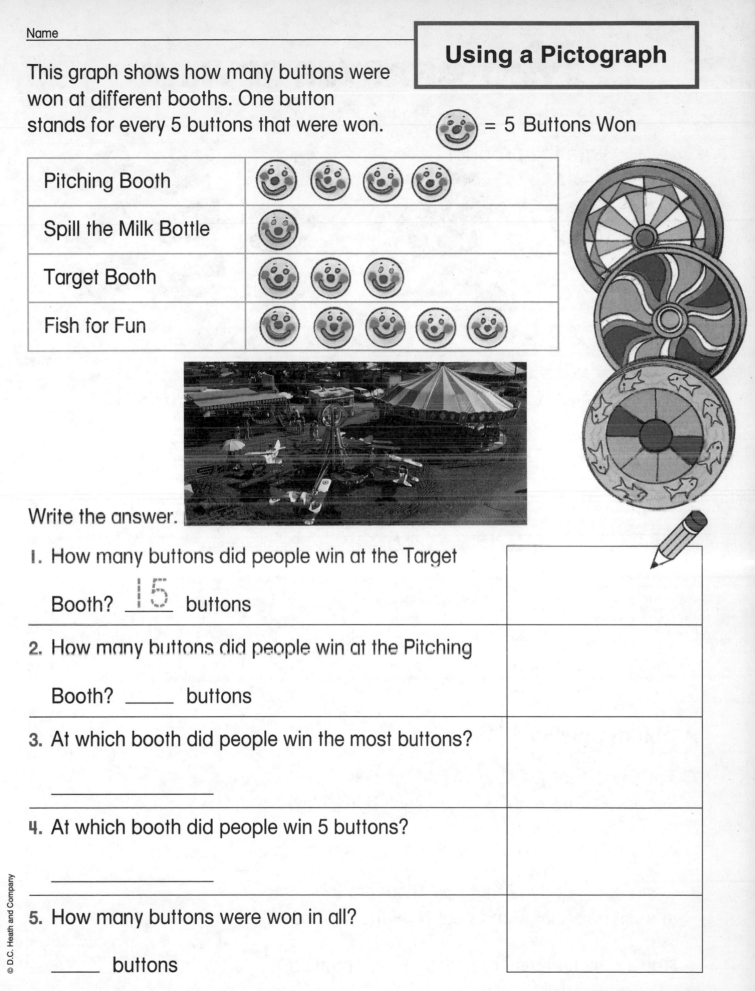

= 5 Buttons Won

Pitching Booth	😊 😊 😊 😊
Spill the Milk Bottle	😊
Target Booth	😊 😊 😊
Fish for Fun	😊 😊 😊 😊 😊

Write the answer.

1. How many buttons did people win at the Target

   Booth? _15_ buttons

2. How many buttons did people win at the Pitching

   Booth? _____ buttons

3. At which booth did people win the most buttons?

   _____

4. At which booth did people win 5 buttons?

   _____

5. How many buttons were won in all?

   _____ buttons

MID-CHAPTER REVIEW

Write the product.

1. $2 \times 3 =$ _____

2. $3 \times 3 =$ _____

3. $4 \times 4 =$ _____ $1 \times 2 =$ _____ $0 \times 1 =$ _____

4. $5 \times 2 =$ _____ $5 \times 5 =$ _____ $2 \times 6 =$ _____

5.
$$
\begin{array}{cccccc}
2 & 1 & 3 & 4 & 2 & 6 \\
\times 4 & \times 2 & \times 5 & \times 3 & \times 9 & \times 1 \\
\end{array}
$$

6.
$$
\begin{array}{cccccc}
4 & 3 & 5 & 2 & 0 & 4 \\
\times 0 & \times 1 & \times 4 & \times 2 & \times 6 & \times 4 \\
\end{array}
$$

Problem Solving

7. Todd has 1 large fishbowl and 2 small fishbowls. There are 3 fish in each bowl. How many fish does Todd have? _____ fish

8. Carla has 4 bags of muffins. There are 3 muffins in each bag. Her friends eat all of the muffins.

How many muffins are left? _____ muffins

Name _____

SCORE 2 POINTS GET A TICKET

Points	2	4	6	8	10
Tickets	1	2	3		

Work with a partner. Fill in the table.
Use it to solve each problem.

1. Amanda scores 10 points. How many tickets will

   she win? _____ tickets

2. Carla wins 3 tickets. How many points did she

   score? _____ points

3. Todd needs 5 tickets to get a toy truck. He scores

   8 points. Can he get the truck? _____

4. Rosita has 12 points. How many tickets will

   she win? _____ tickets

5. Henry scores 4 points in his first game. He scores
   6 points in his second game. How many tickets

   does he win? _____ tickets

6. Henry's mother plays 2 games. She wins 8 tickets.
   Show what her scores could have been.

   Game 1: _____ points   Game 2: _____ points

6 shots in a game
Win tickets for prizes with
every basket made

Baskets Made	1	2	3	4	5	6
Tickets Won	1	2	4	8	16	32

Work with a partner.
Use the table to solve each problem.

1. Amanda plays 1 game. She makes 2 baskets and misses 4 shots. How many tickets does she win?

   _____ tickets

2. Carla plays 1 game. She makes a basket every other time she shoots. How many tickets does

   she win? _____ tickets

3. Henry plays 1 game. He misses only 1 shot.

   How many tickets does he win? _____ tickets

4. Todd plays 2 games. In the first game, he makes 2 baskets. In the second game, he makes 3 baskets.

   How many tickets does he win? _____ tickets

5. Rosita plays 2 games. She wins 12 tickets. How many baskets did she make altogether?

   _____ baskets

MATH LOG
Make up a problem about this game.

Write how many.

1. How many balls? __12__
   Loop sets of 3.

   How many sets? __4__

   __4__ sets of __3__ in __12__

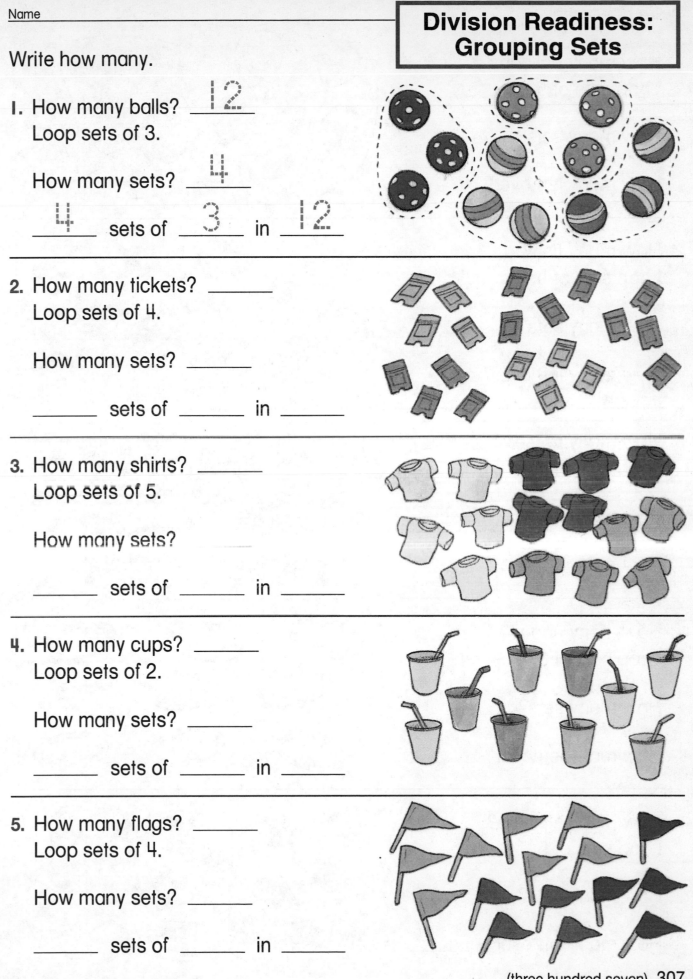

2. How many tickets? _____
   Loop sets of 4.

   How many sets? _____

   _____ sets of _____ in _____

3. How many shirts? _____
   Loop sets of 5.

   How many sets? _____

   _____ sets of _____ in _____

4. How many cups? _____
   Loop sets of 2.

   How many sets? _____

   _____ sets of _____ in _____

5. How many flags? _____
   Loop sets of 4.

   How many sets? _____

   _____ sets of _____ in _____

Write how many.

1. How many balloons? __11__
   Loop sets of 5.

   How many sets? __2__

   How many left over? __1__

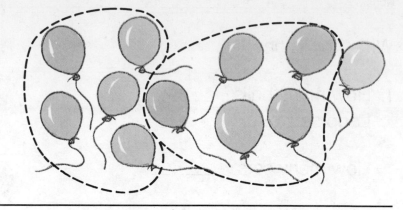

2. How many fish? _____
   Loop sets of 4.

   How many sets? _____

   How many left over? _____

3. How many horses? _____
   Loop sets of 2.

   How many sets? _____

   How many left over? _____

4. How many hoops? _____
   Loop sets of 3.

   How many sets? _____

   How many left over? _____

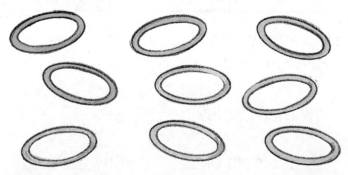

5. How many stickers? _____
   Loop sets of 5.

   How many sets? _____

   How many left over? _____

308 (three hundred eight)

More Practice Set 10.9, page 418

Name _____

You need punchout counters and the story workmat.

Work in groups. Write how many.

1. Use 13 counters.
Make 3 equal sets.

How many in each set? __4__

How many left over? __1__

2. Use 20 counters.
Make 4 equal sets.

How many in each set? _____

How many left over? _____

3. Use 11 counters.
Make 5 equal sets.

How many in each set? _____

How many left over? _____

4. Use 21 counters.
Make 3 equal sets.

How many in each set? _____

How many left over? _____

5. Use 8 counters.
Make 2 equal sets.

How many in each set? _____

How many left over? _____

6. Use 17 counters.
Make 5 equal sets.

How many in each set? _____

How many left over? _____

7. Use 14 counters.
Make 3 equal sets.

How many in each set? _____

How many left over? _____

8. Use 9 counters.
Make 3 equal sets.

How many in each set? _____

How many left over? _____

(three hundred nine) 309

Work in groups.

Use counters to complete each table.

1.

Number of Counters	20	20	20	20	20
Number of Equal Sets	6	5	4	3	2
Number in Each Set	3				
Number Left Over	2				

2.

Number of Counters	18	18	18	18	18
Number of Equal Sets	6	5	4	3	2
Number in Each Set					
Number Left Over					

Maintain • Mixed Practice

Add or subtract. Look for patterns.

1.

$$
\begin{array}{cccccc}
15 & 81 & 81 & 77 & 77 & 76 \\
+66 & -11 & -12 & +15 & +16 & +16 \\
\end{array}
$$

2.

$$
\begin{array}{cccccc}
15 & 30 & 94 & 94 & 58 & 57 \\
+30 & +15 & -50 & -49 & -28 & -28 \\
\end{array}
$$

More Practice Set 10.10, page 419

Name _____

Carla has 8 hats. She gives one half of her hats to Henry. How many hats does Henry get?

To find one half, I make 2 equal sets. Henry gets 4 hats.

$\frac{1}{2}$ of 8 = __4__

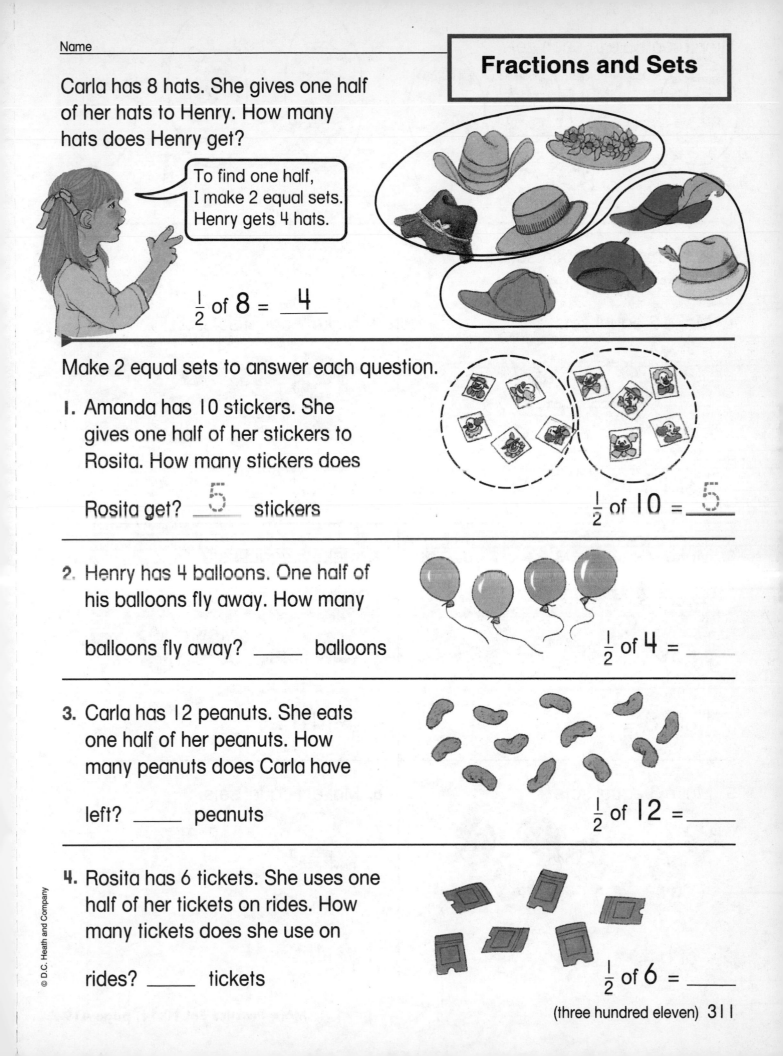

Make 2 equal sets to answer each question.

1. Amanda has 10 stickers. She gives one half of her stickers to Rosita. How many stickers does

   Rosita get? __5__ stickers

   $\frac{1}{2}$ of 10 = __5__

2. Henry has 4 balloons. One half of his balloons fly away. How many

   balloons fly away? _____ balloons

   $\frac{1}{2}$ of 4 = _____

3. Carla has 12 peanuts. She eats one half of her peanuts. How many peanuts does Carla have

   left? _____ peanuts

   $\frac{1}{2}$ of 12 = _____

4. Rosita has 6 tickets. She uses one half of her tickets on rides. How many tickets does she use on

   rides? _____ tickets

   $\frac{1}{2}$ of 6 = _____

How many are in each set?

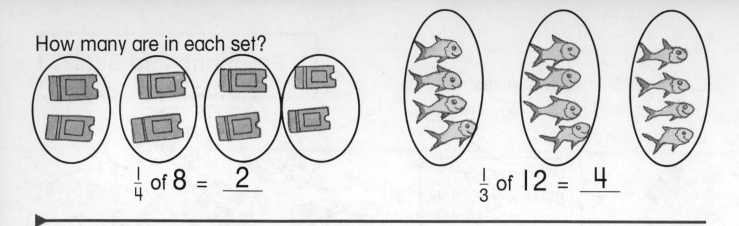

$\frac{1}{4}$ of 8 = __2__

$\frac{1}{3}$ of 12 = __4__

How many are in each set?
Write the missing number.

1. Make 2 equal sets.

$\frac{1}{2}$ of 10 = ____

2. Make 4 equal sets.

$\frac{1}{4}$ of 12 = ____

3. Make 6 equal sets.

$\frac{1}{6}$ of 18 = ____

4. Make 5 equal sets.

$\frac{1}{5}$ of 10 = ____

5. Make 3 equal sets.

$\frac{1}{3}$ of 6 = ____

6. Make 4 equal sets.

$\frac{1}{4}$ of 4 = ____

More Practice Set 10.11, page 419

You need coins. 🪙 🪙 🪙 🪙 🪙

Using Money

Problem Solving   Use coins to solve each problem.

1. A ticket for the merry-go-round costs 5¢. Todd

   has 2 dimes. Can he buy 3 tickets? _____

2. A ride on the Ferris wheel costs 10¢. Amanda has
   3 nickels. Can she go on the Ferris wheel twice?

   _____

3. Rosita has 5 nickels. She can only use dimes to
   play a game. How many dimes can Rosita get?

   _____ dimes

4. Henry has 4 nickels. Todd has half as much
   money. How much money do they have in all?

   _____ ¢

5. Amanda has 2 dimes and 4 pennies. She gives
   half of her money to her brother. What coins do
   they each have now?

   _____ dime _____ pennies

How many dimes can you get for these nickels?

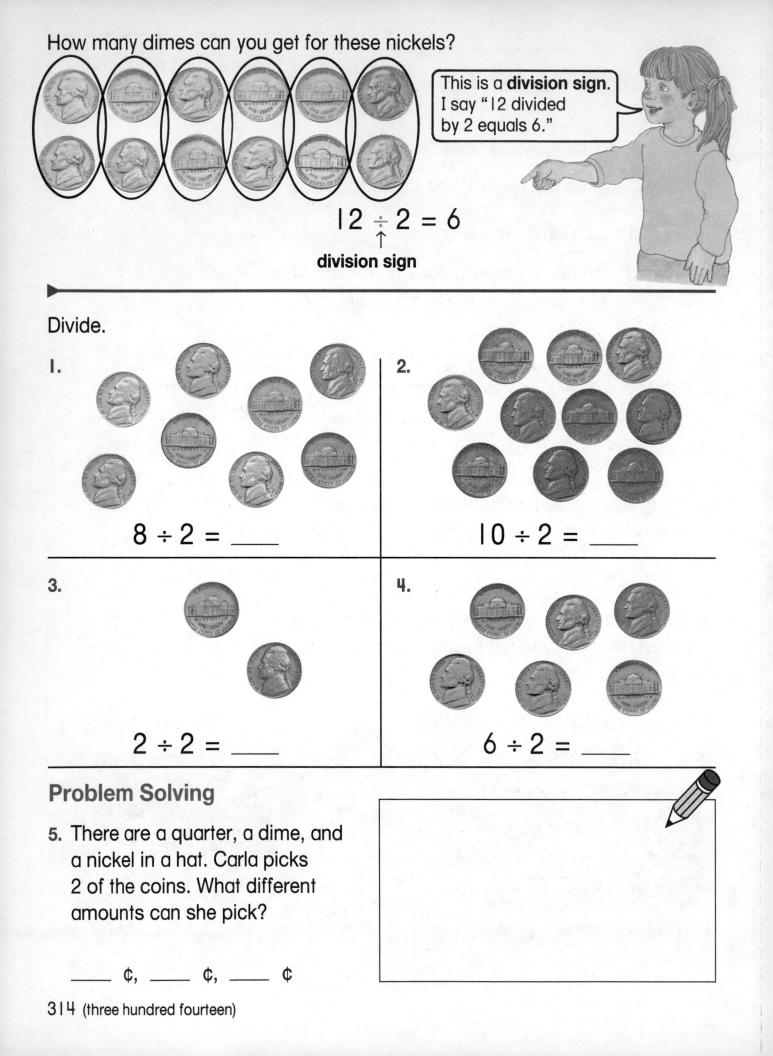

This is a **division sign**. I say "12 divided by 2 equals 6."

$$12 \div 2 = 6$$

↑
division sign

Divide.

1.

$8 \div 2 = \underline{}$

2.

$10 \div 2 = \underline{}$

3.

$2 \div 2 = \underline{}$

4.

$6 \div 2 = \underline{}$

Problem Solving

5. There are a quarter, a dime, and a nickel in a hat. Carla picks 2 of the coins. What different amounts can she pick?

____ ¢, ____ ¢, ____ ¢

Name

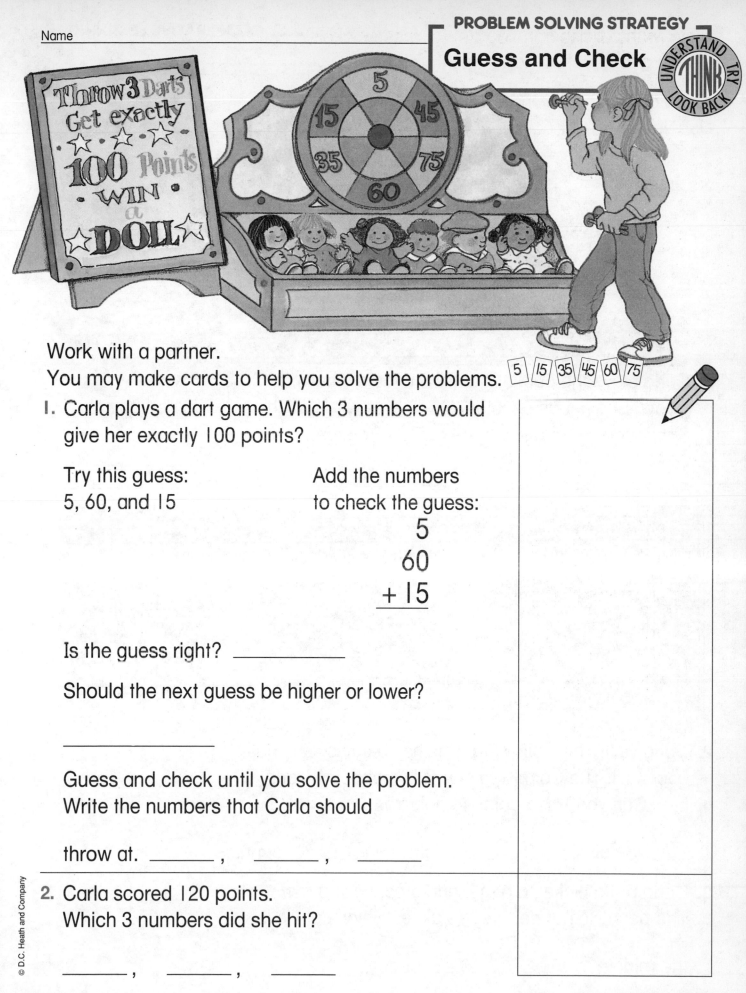

Throw 3 Darts
Get exactly
★ ★ ★
100 Points
· WIN ·
a
☆ DOLL ☆

Work with a partner.
You may make cards to help you solve the problems. 5 15 35 45 60 75

1. Carla plays a dart game. Which 3 numbers would give her exactly 100 points?

   Try this guess: Add the numbers
   5, 60, and 15   to check the guess:

$$
\begin{array}{r}
5 \\
60 \\
+\ 15 \\
\hline
\end{array}
$$

   Is the guess right? _____

   Should the next guess be higher or lower?

   _____

   Guess and check until you solve the problem.
   Write the numbers that Carla should

   throw at. _____ , _____ , _____

2. Carla scored 120 points.
   Which 3 numbers did she hit?

   _____ , _____ , _____

Work with a partner.

Guess and check to solve each problem.

Make cards. 5 10 25 35

Use your cards or coins.

1. Carla plays the bucket game. She gets 3 balls to throw. She needs exactly 75 points to win. Which 3 numbers would give her exactly 75 points?

_____ , _____ , _____

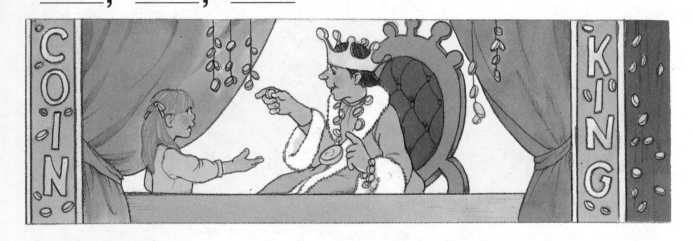

2. Carla visits the Coin King. She has 5 coins. She has 26¢ in all. The Coin King can tell what coins Carla has. Can you? Use coins to help you.

_____ dimes _____ nickels _____ pennies

3. Carla put a nickel, a dime, and a penny in a row. The penny is not next to the dime. Which coin is in

the middle? _____

316 (three hundred sixteen)

CHAPTER TEST

Write how many.

1.

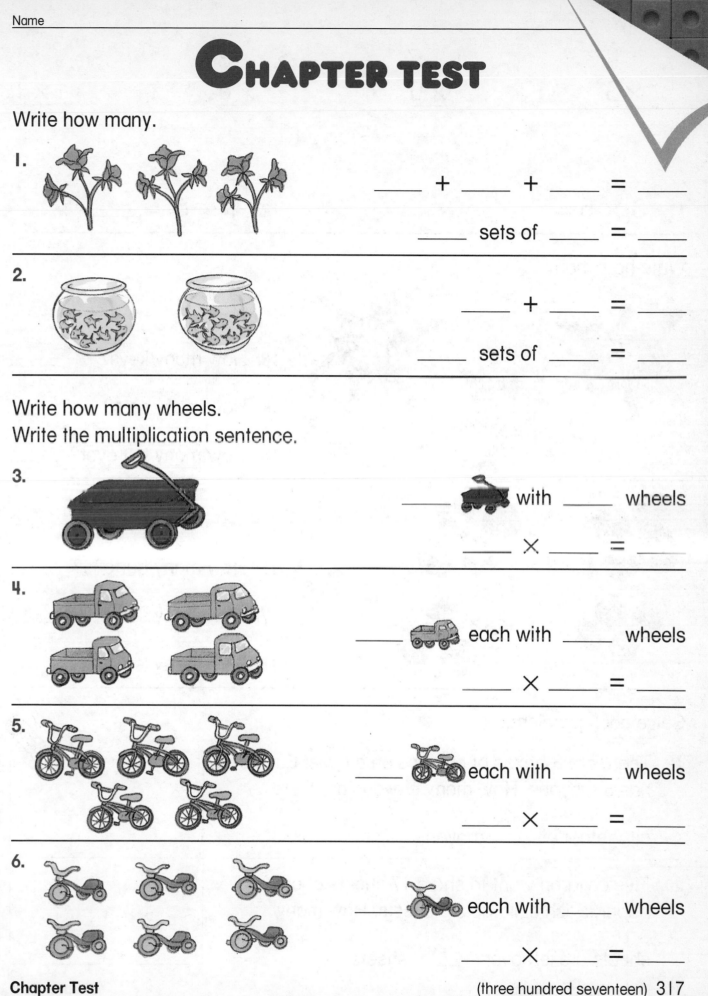

___ + ___ + ___ = ___

___ sets of ___ = ___

2.

___ + ___ = ___

___ sets of ___ = ___

Write how many wheels.
Write the multiplication sentence.

3.

___ with ___ wheels

___ × ___ = ___

4.

___ each with ___ wheels

___ × ___ = ___

5.

___ each with ___ wheels

___ × ___ = ___

6.

___ each with ___ wheels

___ × ___ = ___

Multiply.

7. $\begin{array}{r} 4 \\ \times 3 \\ \hline \end{array}$ 8. $\begin{array}{r} 5 \\ \times 0 \\ \hline \end{array}$ 9. $\begin{array}{r} 3 \\ \times 6 \\ \hline \end{array}$ 10. $\begin{array}{r} 1 \\ \times 1 \\ \hline \end{array}$

11. $3 \times 5 = \underline{}$ 12. $1 \times 6 = \underline{}$

Write how many.

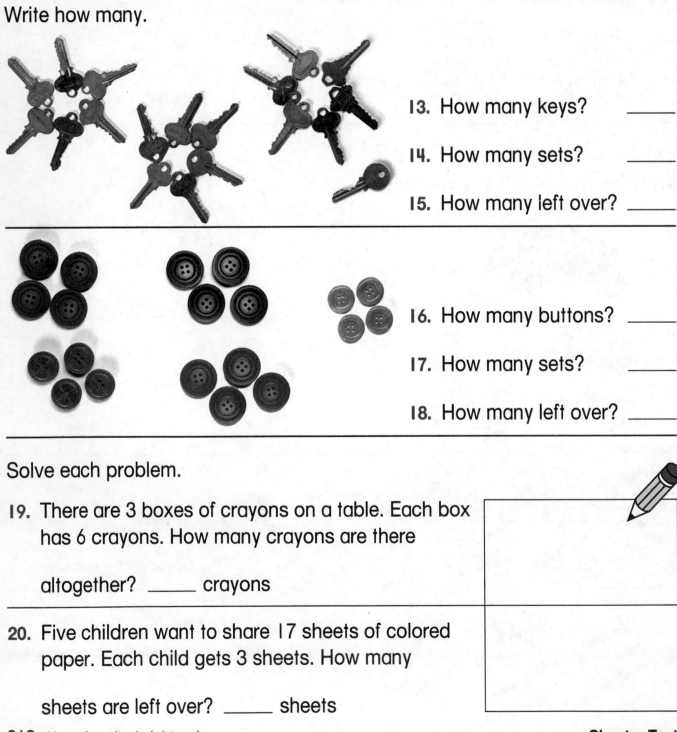

13. How many keys? _____

14. How many sets? _____

15. How many left over? _____

16. How many buttons? _____

17. How many sets? _____

18. How many left over? _____

Solve each problem.

19. There are 3 boxes of crayons on a table. Each box has 6 crayons. How many crayons are there altogether? _____ crayons

20. Five children want to share 17 sheets of colored paper. Each child gets 3 sheets. How many sheets are left over? _____ sheets

Chapter Test

EXCURSION
CULTURAL DIVERSITY

You need a centimeter ruler and crayons.

The tens block is about 10 centimeters long.
It is about 1 **decimeter** long.

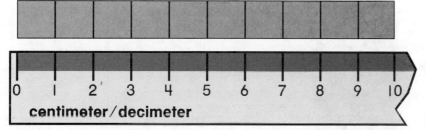

Use a centimeter ruler to measure each comb.
Loop the combs longer than 1 decimeter with red.
Loop the combs shorter than 1 decimeter with blue.

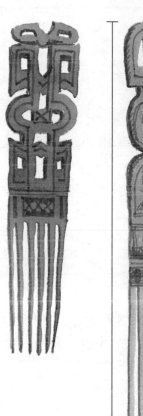

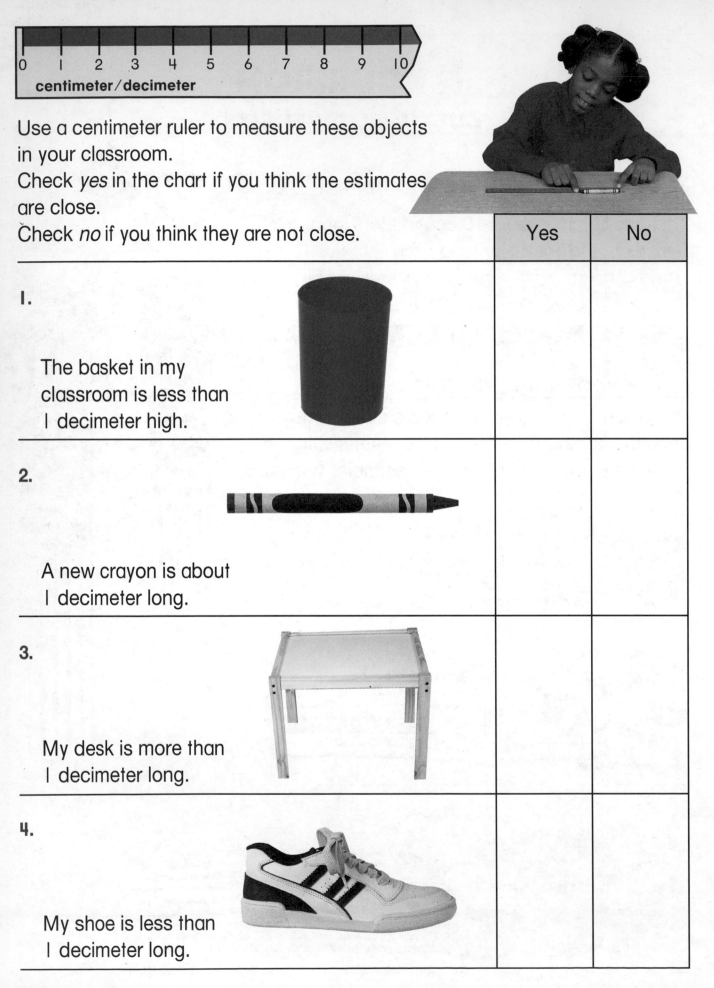

0 1 2 3 4 5 6 7 8 9 10
centimeter/decimeter

Use a centimeter ruler to measure these objects in your classroom.

Check *yes* in the chart if you think the estimates are close.

Check *no* if you think they are not close.

	Yes	No
1. The basket in my classroom is less than 1 decimeter high.		
2. A new crayon is about 1 decimeter long.		
3. My desk is more than 1 decimeter long.		
4. My shoe is less than 1 decimeter long.		

320 (three hundred twenty)

Note to the Family

Your child has been learning multiplication and division readiness skills. This activity sheet gives your child an opportunity to share new skills with you.

EQUAL GROUPS

You will need 12 index cards, 5 cups, and beans or other counters

1. Help your child number three of the cards "2," three "3," three "4," and three "5."

2. Mix the cards thoroughly, and place the stack face down on the table.

3. The first player takes two cards from the stack. The first tells the player how many cups to get, and the second tells how many beans to place in each cup.

4. The player then tells how many equal groups there are, how many are in each group, the total number of beans in the groups, and how he or she figured the total.

5. If all the answers are correct, the player's score is the total number of beans in all the groups. The cards are then placed on the bottom of the stack, and the next player takes a turn.

6. The first player to reach 50 points wins.

Note to the Family

In the next few weeks, your child will be learning about numbers through 1000.

You can help your child at home by encouraging him or her to talk about 3-digit numbers you find, such as house numbers, page numbers in a book, or numbers in articles from newspapers or magazines.

It might be fun to play the following game with your child.

NUMBER SHUFFLEBOARD

You will need a large sheet of paper, a pencil, and one bean or other counter.

1. Using the diagram on this page as a model, draw a game board on a sheet of paper that is large enough to cover a tabletop.

2. Take turns lightly "shuffling," or pushing, the bean with the tip of a pencil so that the bean lands on one of the spaces on the shuffleboard.

3. Ask your child about the number in the space where the bean landed (For example: Which digit is in the ones place? Tens place? Hundreds place?). When it is your turn, encourage your child to ask you similar questions.

4. Extend the game by encouraging your child to write other 3-digit numbers in the shuffleboard spaces. Play the game again, using these new numbers.

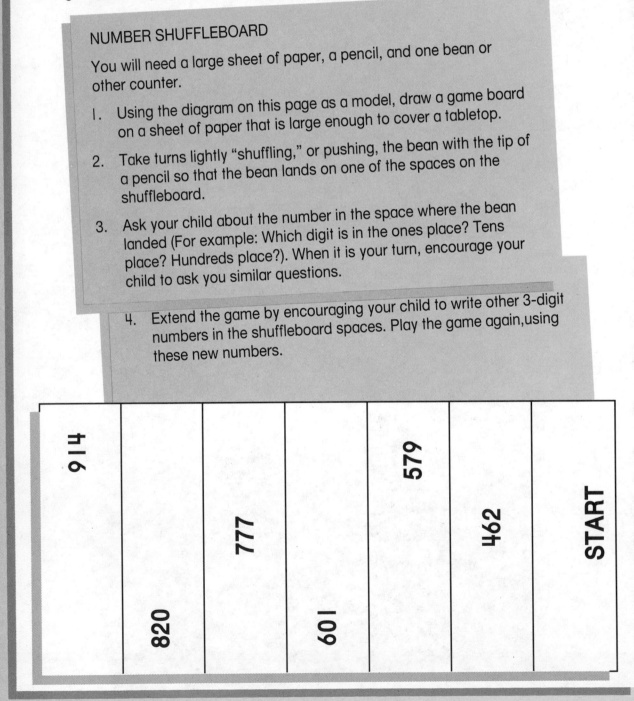

CHAPTER 11

PLACE VALUE THROUGH 1000

Listen to the story.

Erasing Problems the Rubaway Way

(three hundred twenty-three) 323

A box of Rubaway Erasers holds
10 erasers. Each carton holds 10 boxes.

Each square below stands for 1 eraser.
Color a row of 10 squares to show a
box of erasers.
Finish drawing the carton.

1. How many erasers will the carton hold? _____

2. What shape did you draw? _____

Hundreds and Tens

I hundred

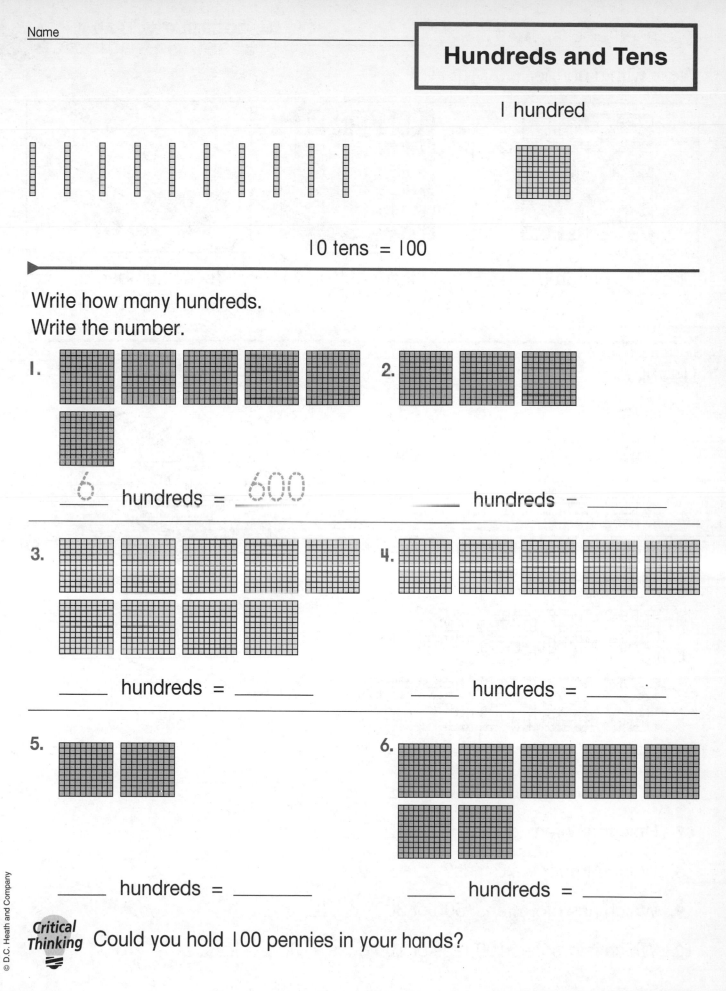

10 tens = 100

Write how many hundreds.
Write the number.

1.

___6___ hundreds = __600__

2.

_____ hundreds – _____

3.

_____ hundreds = _____

4.

_____ hundreds = _____

5.

_____ hundreds = _____

6.

_____ hundreds = _____

Critical Thinking Could you hold 100 pennies in your hands?

You need blocks.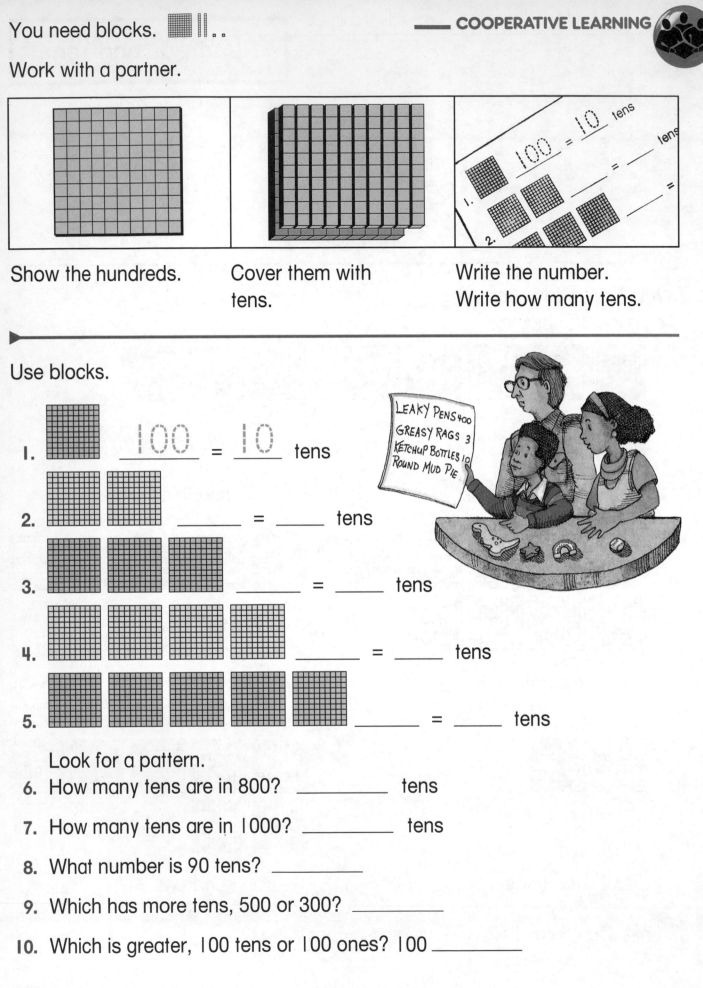

Work with a partner.

Show the hundreds.

Cover them with tens.

Write the number.
Write how many tens.

Use blocks.

LEAKY PENS 400
GREASY RAGS 3
KETCHUP BOTTLES 10
ROUND MUD PIE

1. _100_ = _10_ tens

2. _____ = _____ tens

3. _____ = _____ tens

4. _____ = _____ tens

5. _____ = _____ tens

Look for a pattern.

6. How many tens are in 800? _____ tens

7. How many tens are in 1000? _____ tens

8. What number is 90 tens? _____

9. Which has more tens, 500 or 300? _____

10. Which is greater, 100 tens or 100 ones? 100 _____

Hundreds, Tens, and Ones

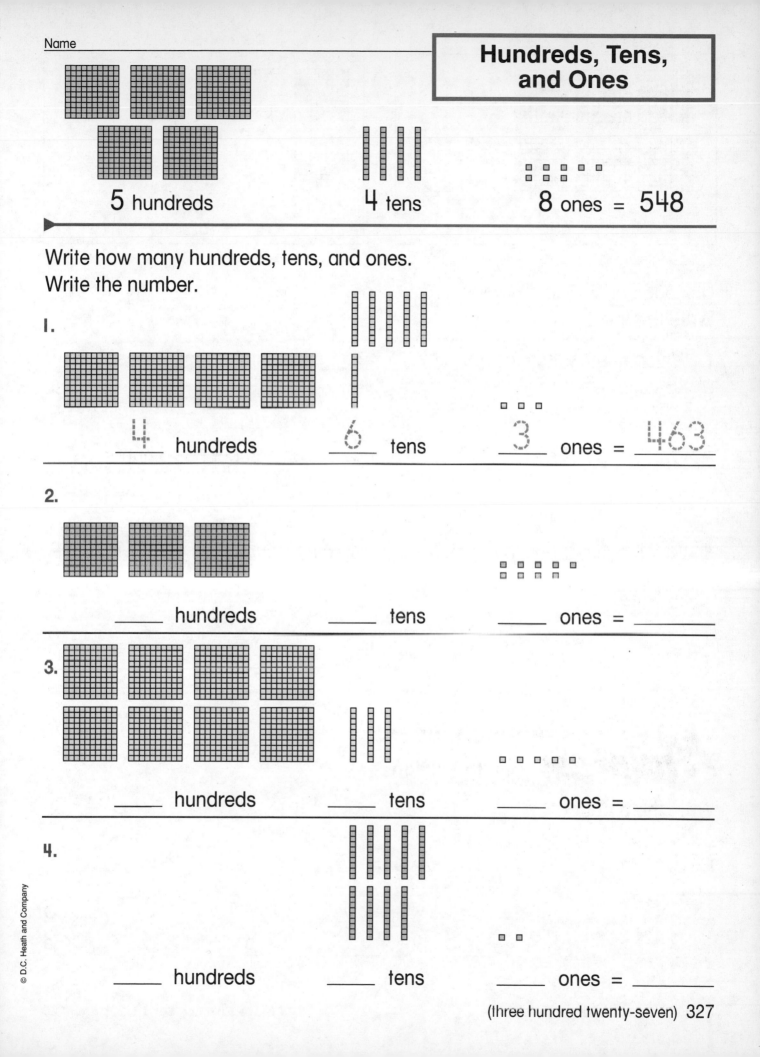

5 hundreds   4 tens   8 ones = 548

Write how many hundreds, tens, and ones.
Write the number.

1.

___4___ hundreds   ___6___ tens   ___3___ ones = ___463___

2.

_____ hundreds   _____ tens   _____ ones = _____

3.

_____ hundreds   _____ tens   _____ ones = _____

4.

_____ hundreds   _____ tens   _____ ones = _____

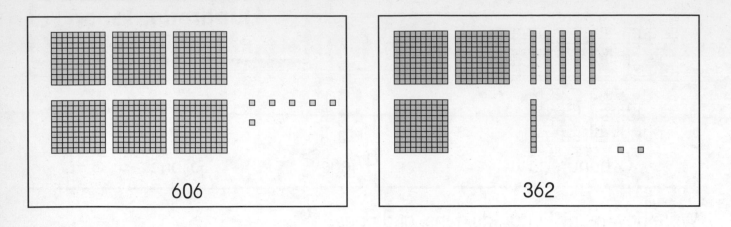

606

362

Use 606 and 362 to answer each question.
Write the number.

1. Which number has 2 ones?

362

2. Which number has 0 tens?

_____

3. Which number has 6 tens?

_____

4. Which number has 3 hundreds?

_____

5. Which number has the same number of hundreds and ones?

_____

6. Which number is greater?

_____

Maintain • **Multiplication**

Write the product.

1. $3 \times 4 =$ _____ $2 \times 5 =$ _____ $4 \times 2 =$ _____

2.
$$\begin{array}{ccccccc} 5 & 4 & 1 & 0 & 2 & 3 & 5 \\ \times 4 & \times 4 & \times 5 & \times 5 & \times 3 & \times 3 & \times 3 \end{array}$$

More Practice Set 11.2, page 420

This is how I draw a picture of these blocks.

I can write the number in 3 different ways.

2 hundreds 2 tens 4 ones
200 + 20 + 4
224

Write the number in 3 different ways.

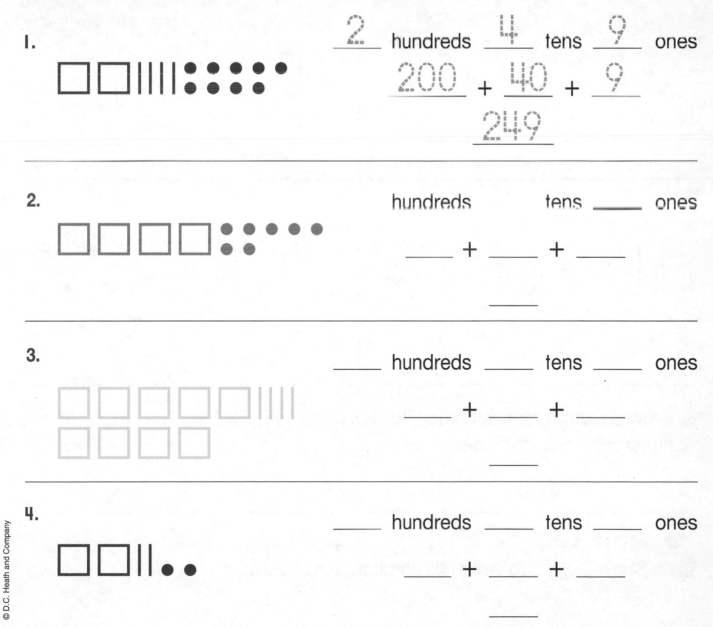

1.

 2 hundreds 4 tens 9 ones

 200 + 40 + 9

 249

2.

____ hundreds ____ tens ____ ones

____ + ____ + ____

____

3.

____ hundreds ____ tens ____ ones

____ + ____ + ____

____

4.

____ hundreds ____ tens ____ ones

____ + ____ + ____

____

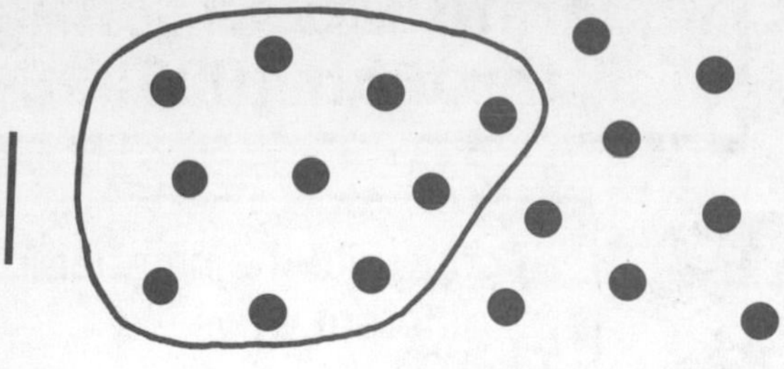

1 ten 18 ones
28

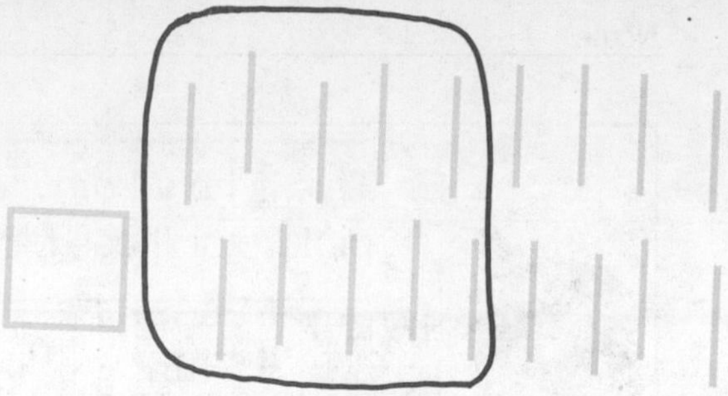

1 hundred 18 tens
280

Loop 10's.
Write the number.

1. _____

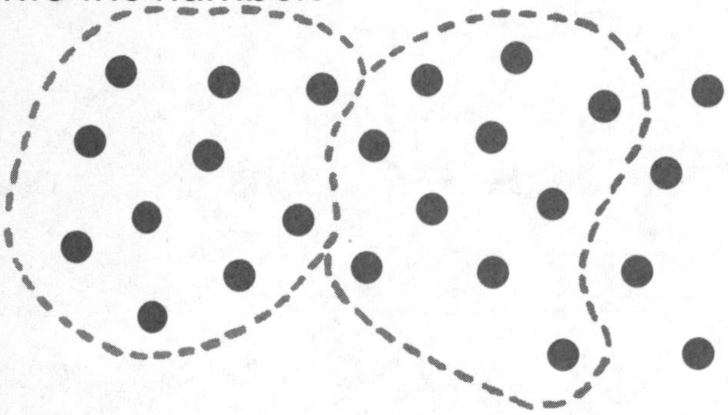

2. _____

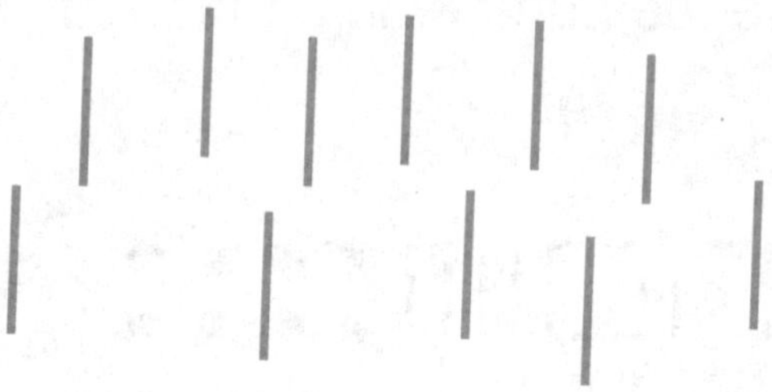

3. _____

4. _____

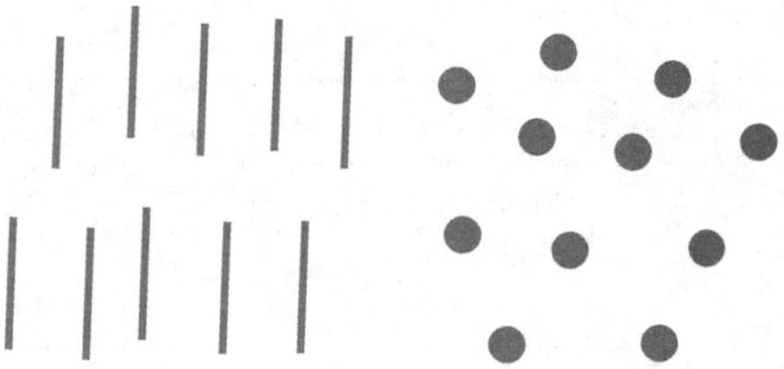

5. Draw a picture for this number, using hundreds, tens, and ones.

153

MATH LOG
Show 2 ways to write this number. ☐ ☐ ☐ | |

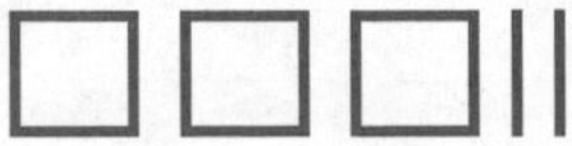

More Practice Set 11.3, page 420

Look at each pair of numbers.
Write < or >.

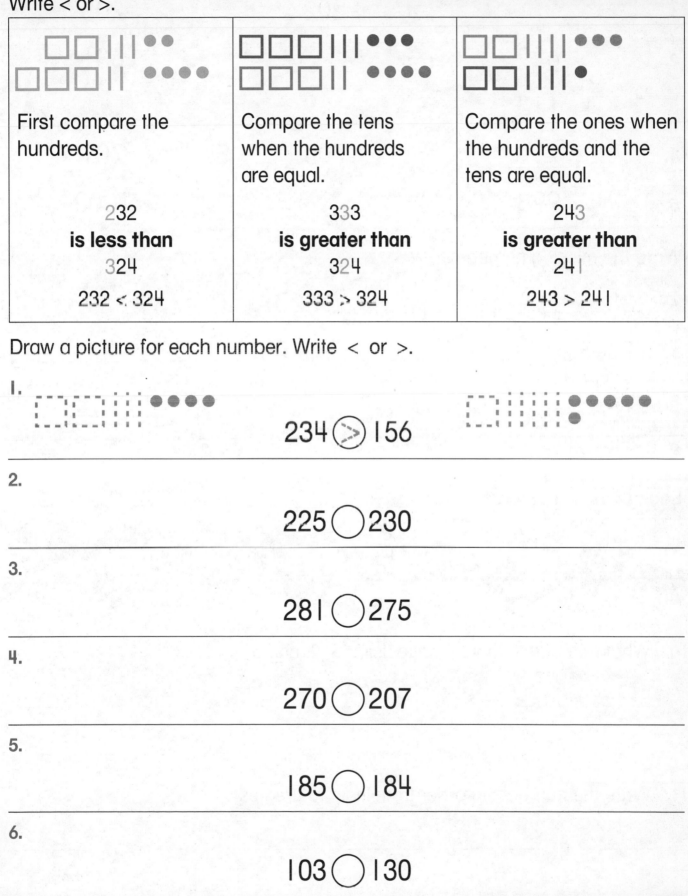

First compare the hundreds.

232
is less than
324

232 < 324

Compare the tens when the hundreds are equal.

333
is greater than
324

333 > 324

Compare the ones when the hundreds and the tens are equal.

243
is greater than
241

243 > 241

Draw a picture for each number. Write < or >.

1. 234 ⊙> 156

2. 225 ◯ 230

3. 281 ◯ 275

4. 270 ◯ 207

5. 185 ◯ 184

6. 103 ◯ 130

Write the missing number.

	Just Before	Between	Just After
1.	_____	202	203
2.	629	_____	631
3.	118	119	_____
4.	_____	700	701
5.	998	_____	1000

Write the missing numbers.

6. 233, _____, _____, _____, 237, _____, _____, 240

7. 101, _____, _____, _____, 105, _____, _____, _____

8. 993, _____, _____, _____, _____, _____, _____, 1000

9. 524, _____, _____, _____, _____, 529, _____, _____

Look at these numbers.

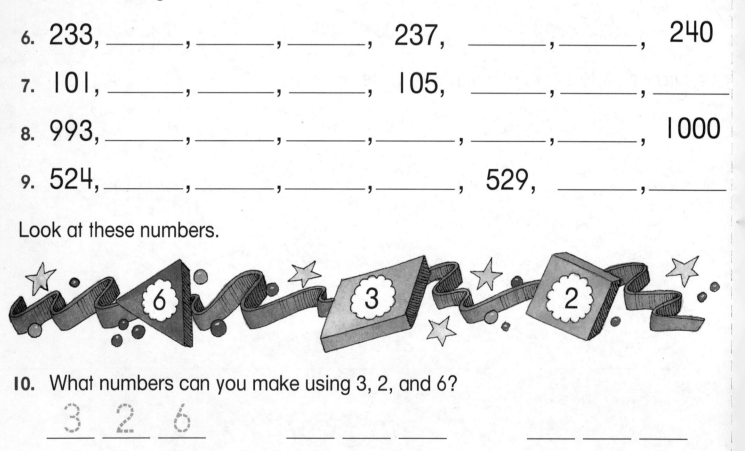

10. What numbers can you make using 3, 2, and 6?

3 2 6

_____ _____ _____   _____ _____ _____   _____ _____ _____

_____ _____ _____   _____ _____ _____   _____ _____ _____

11. Write the numbers in order from least to greatest.

_____, _____, _____, _____, _____, _____

least   greatest

A Cross-Number Puzzle

Complete the puzzle.

Across

1. 500 + 30 + 9

4. 60 tens

5.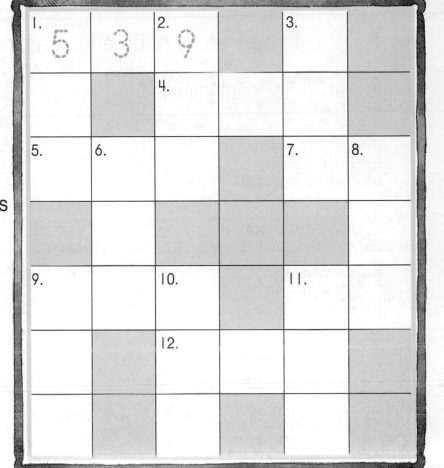

7. ▌▌● ● ●

9. 4 hundreds 9 tens 6 ones

11. fifty

12. ☐ ☐ ▌▌▌ ● ● ● ●
         ● ● ●

Down

1. 50 tens 1 one

2. 900 + 60 + 2

3. 800 + 2

6. ☐ ▌▌▌ ● ● ● ●
         ● ● ●
         ● ● ●

8. 30 tens

9. 4 hundreds 6 tens 2 ones

10. 600 + 20 + 1

11. five hundred seventy-five

(three hundred thirty-three) 333

MID-CHAPTER REVIEW

for pages 325–332

Write how many hundreds, tens, and ones.

1.

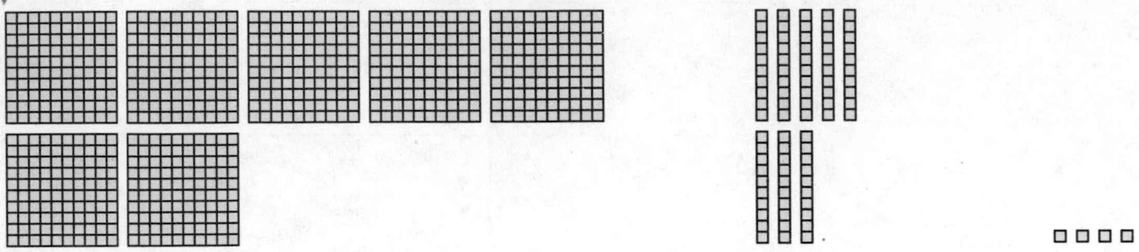

_____ hundreds   _____ tens   _____ ones = _____

2.

_____ hundreds   _____ tens   _____ ones = _____

Write the number in 3 different ways.

3.

_____ hundreds _____ tens _____ ones

_____ + _____ + _____

_____

4.

_____ hundreds _____ tens _____ ones

_____ + _____ + _____

_____

5. Draw a picture for each number.
   Write < or >.

240 ◯ 204

6. Write the missing numbers.

696, _____, _____, _____, _____, _____, 702, _____

334 (three hundred thirty-four)   **Mid-Chapter Review**

Name _____

Work with a partner. Use each kind of eraser only once. Make all the children happy. Write which kind of eraser each child should get.

I need more than 3 erasers.

baseball _____ erasers

I like red the best.

_____ erasers

I want only yellow or blue.

_____ erasers

I want erasers that look like an animal.

_____ erasers

Work with a partner.
What will each person eat?
Use each food only once.
Write the answer.

Chicken Sandwich

Salad

Soup

Hamburger

Egg Sandwich

I want something on a bun.

hamburger

I want something hot.

_____

I do not want a sandwich.

_____

I do not like eggs.

_____

MATH LOG

Make up your own puzzle.
Give it to a friend to solve.

336 (three hundred thirty-six)

Remember, you can use a dollar sign and decimal point to write about money.

Counting Patterns

I dollar and 25 cents

$1.25

Count by $1.00. Write the amounts.

Start with:

1. $1.25, $2.25, $3.25, $4.25, $5.25, $6.25

2. $3.92, $_____ , $_____ , $_____ , $_____ , $_____

Count by 50¢. Write the amounts.

Start with:

3. $0.50, $1.00, $1.50, $2.00, $2.50, $3.00

4. $6.00, $_____ , $_____ , $_____ , $_____ , $_____

Continue the pattern.

5. 745, 755, 765, _____ , _____ , _____ , _____

6. 950, 850, 750, _____ , _____ , _____ , _____

7. 220, 225, 230, _____ , _____ , _____ , _____

8. 896, 897, 898, _____ , _____ , _____ , _____

Problem Solving You may use coins.
Loop the correct answer.

1. Arthur has 5 half-dollars. Amy has $4.00.
   Who has more money?

           Arthur   Amy

2. Dan has 6 half-dollars. Lavinia has $2.50.
   Who has more money?

           Dan   Lavinia

3. Amy started with 50¢. Dan gave her 50¢.
   Then Lavinia gave her 50¢. How much money
   does Amy have now?

       $1.50 $3.50

Write your own numbers for this number story.
Give the number story to a friend to solve.

4. Dan started with _____ ¢. Amy gave

   him _____ ¢. Then Arthur gave him _____ ¢.
   How much money does Dan have now?

   _____

· ·

CHALLENGE •Using Technology

Continue the pattern.
You may use a calculator.

1. 300, 295, 290, _____ , _____ , _____ , _____

2. 131, 242, 353, _____ , _____ , _____ , _____

3. 78, 87, 96, _____ , _____ , _____ , _____

**Estimating by
Skip-Counting**

Work with a partner.
You need beans.

Spread out the beans.

About how many beans are there?
Find out without counting.

1. Cover a group of *about* 10 beans
   with your hand. Slide the handful over.

2. Keep moving handfuls until all
   the beans are moved.

3. Skip count by tens. Write your estimate.

   about _____ beans

**Critical
Thinking** How is estimating different from counting?

Work with a partner.
Get more beans.
Estimate the number of
beans using skip-counting.

Write your estimate.

Try this 3 more times, with
different numbers of beans.

Your Estimate
about _____
about _____
about _____
about _____

CHALLENGE • Division Readiness

You need 18 counters.
Use counters to complete the table.

Number of Counters	15	16	17	18
Number of Equal Sets	3	4		
Number in Each Set			5	6
Left Over				

Name _____

Work with a partner. Read the problem.
Choose the table that will help you. Then fill in
that table until you solve the problem.

1. An eraser machine makes 100 erasers every
   hour. Arthur turns it on at 8:00. At what time

   will there be 400 erasers? _____

Time	8:00	9:00	10:00	11:00				
Erasers	0	100	200					

Time	8:00	9:00	10:00					
Hours	0	1	2					

2. Another machine makes 2 erasers every minute.
   There are 288 erasers already made.
   You need 300 erasers. How many more

   minutes will it take? _____ more minutes

Minutes	60	120					
Hours	1	2					

Minutes	0	1					
Erasers	288	290					

Work with a partner.
Solve each problem.
Make a table to help you.

RUBAWAYERASERS

1. Ten erasers go in each box. You need to pack
80 erasers. How many boxes do you need? _____ boxes

Boxes								
Erasers								

2. Arthur packs 200 erasers every half hour. He
starts at 8:00. He has 700 erasers to pack.

Will he be finished packing by 10:00? _____

Time					
Erasers					

3. Each box has 3 cat erasers and 7 dog
erasers. How many dog erasers are

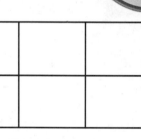

in 5 boxes? _____ dog erasers

Boxes					
Dog Erasers					

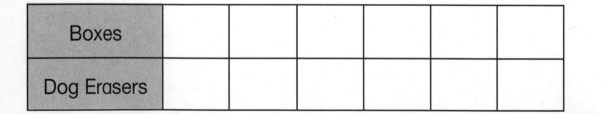

CHAPTER TEST

Use 754 and 505 to answer each question.
Write the number.

1. Which number has 4 ones?

_____

2. Which number has 0 tens?

_____

3. Which number has 5 tens?

_____

4. Which number has 7 hundreds?

_____

5. Which number has the same number of hundreds and ones?

_____

6. Which number is greater?

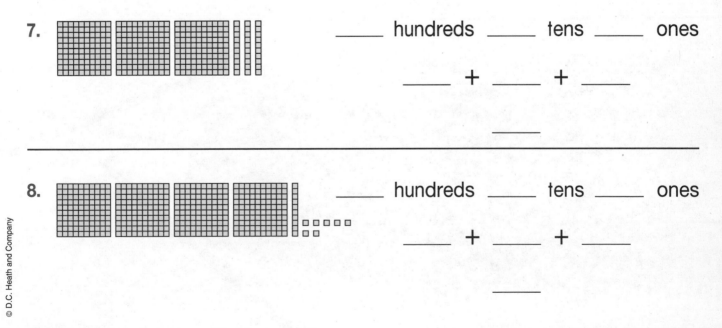

Write the number in three different ways.

7. _____ hundreds _____ tens _____ ones

_____ + _____ + _____

_____

8. _____ hundreds _____ tens _____ ones

_____ + _____ + _____

_____

Chapter Test

Complete. Write < or > in the ◯.

9. 303 ◯ 330
10. 234 ◯ 143
11. 440 ◯ 414
12. 175 ◯ 170
13. 219 ◯ 291
14. 198 ◯ 286

Continue the pattern.

15. 800, 805, 810, _____
16. 552, 551, 550, _____
17. 130, 120, 110, _____
18. 700, 750, 800, _____
19. 641, 741, 841, _____
20. 935, 945, 955, _____

Solve each problem.

21. Marie packs 250 erasers in an empty box. Don puts 10 erasers in the box. How many erasers are in the box now? _____ erasers

22. Carlos counts 300 blue pencils and 300 red pencils. Lana counts 607 blue pencils. Who has counted more pencils, Carlos or Lana?

_____

Excursion
CULTURAL DIVERSITY

You can put 1 bead in only 1 order.

Number of Beads	Number of Ways to Order the Beads
1	1
2	2
3	
4	

You can put 2 beads in 2 different orders.

COOPERATIVE LEARNING

Work with a partner.

1. Use cubes for beads.

   Show the different orders for 3 colors of beads. Write the number of orders in the table above.

Complete the table to solve this problem.

2. You have four beads to make a pattern. In how many different orders can you put them? _____ orders.

You can look at patterns in bead work.

You need crayons.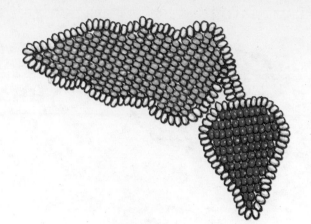

Look at the pattern of red squares.
It matches the red beads in the picture.
The first row has 1 square in it.

1. Write how many squares
   the next 2 rows have.

2. Draw the fourth row in the
   pattern. Write how many
   squares it has.

3. Draw the fifth row in the
   pattern. Write how many
   squares it has.

4. How many squares would
   the seventh row have? ___

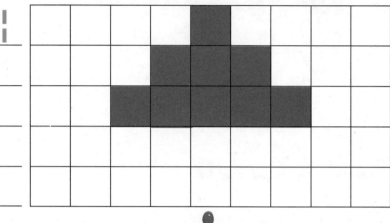

Look at the pattern of green squares.
It matches some of the beads in the picture.

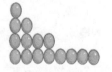

5. Write how many squares are in each row.

6. Draw the fourth row. Write how many squares it has.

7. Draw the fifth row. Write how many squares it has.

Note to the Family

Your child has been learning about numbers through 1000. This activity sheet gives your child an opportunity to share new skills with you.

NUMBER JIGSAW

You need tracing paper, a felt marker, crayons, scissors, cardboard, and glue.

1. Trace the puzzle model onto a sheet of white tracing paper. Using a felt marker, have your child help you write the numbers in each space on the puzzle.

2. Color the numbers greater than 800 yellow.

3. Color the numbers less than 300 orange.

4. Color the numbers greater than 600 but less than 700 blue.

5. Cut out the entire puzzle and glue it onto a piece of cardboard. When the glue is dry, cut out the individual puzzle pieces.

6. Before putting the puzzle back together, give your child a few puzzle pieces and ask her or him to put the pieces in numerical order, from least to greatest. Vary this activity by ordering pieces from greatest to least and by comparing two numbers as greater than or less than each other.

7. Put the puzzle back together.

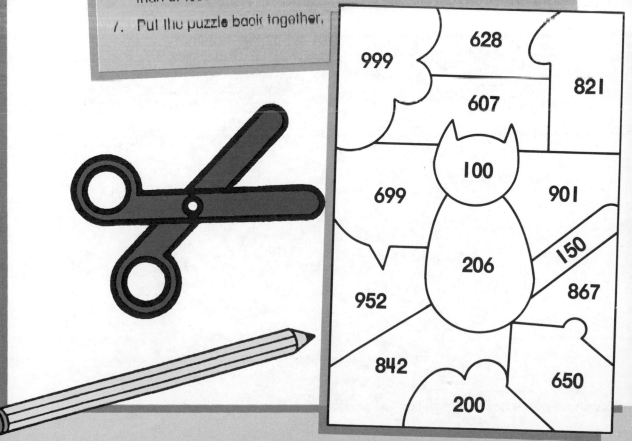

In the next few weeks, your child will be learning about addition and subtraction of 3-digit numbers.

It is important for children to see addition and subtraction used outside of school. Your child can practice these skills by participating in daily activities, such as determining the total cost of a few items purchased at the grocery store or by determining the amount of change that is due from a purchase.

It might be fun to make a number mobile with your child.

NUMBER MOBILE

You will need multi-colored construction paper, scissors, crayons, string, a hole punch or pencil, and a clothes hanger.

1. Have your child cut out 6 different-sized shapes out of different colors of construction paper. If your child wishes, he or she could decorate the shapes in some way, using things such as crayons and stickers.

2. Write these exercises on the shapes.

$$\begin{array}{cc} 400 \\ -400 \end{array} \qquad \begin{array}{cc} 800 \\ -400 \end{array} \qquad \begin{array}{cc} 700 \\ -200 \end{array} \qquad \begin{array}{cc} 100 \\ +600 \end{array} \qquad \begin{array}{cc} 300 \\ +500 \end{array} \qquad \begin{array}{cc} 500 \\ +400 \end{array}$$

3. Mix the shapes up and give them back to your child. Have him or her write the answers (0, 400, 500, 700, 800, 900).

4. Have your child cut 6 different lengths of string and match the lengths of the string to the sizes of the shapes (the largest shape gets the longest piece of string, and so on). Make a hole at the top of each shape. Tie the string to the shapes.

5. Have your child place the shapes in order by the size of their answers, going from least to greatest (the order shown above).

6. Tie each shape on the clothes hanger in that order. (You may need to slide the shapes along the hanger or adjust string lengths to make it balance.)

CHAPTER 12

ADDITION AND SUBTRACTION OF 3-DIGIT NUMBERS

Listen to the story.

Field Day

(three hundred forty-nine) 349

Name _____

About how many people are in the stands?

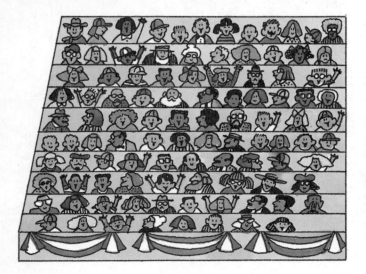

about _____ people

How did you find out?

350 (three hundred fifty)

Add.

Adding Hundreds

1. 3 •••
   +2 ••
   ‾‾‾
   5

   300
   +200
   ‾‾‾‾
   500

2. 4 ••••
   +5 •••••

   400
   +500

3. 6 •••••••
   +1 •

   600
   +100

4. 3 •••
   +5 •••••

   300
   +500

5. 3 •••
   +3 •••

   300
   +300

Critical Thinking How does adding 4 + 5 help you to add 400 + 500?

(three hundred fifty-one) 351

Add.

1. $700 + 230 = \underline{930}$

2. $303 + 600 = \underline{}$

3. $400 + 410 = \underline{}$

4. $206 + 500 = \underline{}$

5. $230 + 300 = \underline{}$

6. $300 + 300 = \underline{}$

7. $400 + 180 = \underline{}$

8. $50 + 500 = \underline{}$

9. $208 + 400 = \underline{}$

10. $140 + 100 = \underline{}$

11. $200 + 100 = \underline{}$

12. $500 + 375 = \underline{}$

13. $422 + 100 = \underline{}$

14. $600 + 116 = \underline{}$

CHALLENGE • Number Sense

Add.

1. $340 + 105 = \underline{}$ $340 + 205 = \underline{}$

2. $340 + 305 = \underline{}$ $107 + 220 = \underline{}$

3. $404 + 150 = \underline{}$ $104 + 560 = \underline{}$

4. $550 + 202 = \underline{}$ $301 + 630 = \underline{}$

5. $110 + 109 = \underline{}$ $530 + 330 = \underline{}$

6. $702 + 207 = \underline{}$ $424 + 420 = \underline{}$

Work with a partner.
Use blocks and number cards.

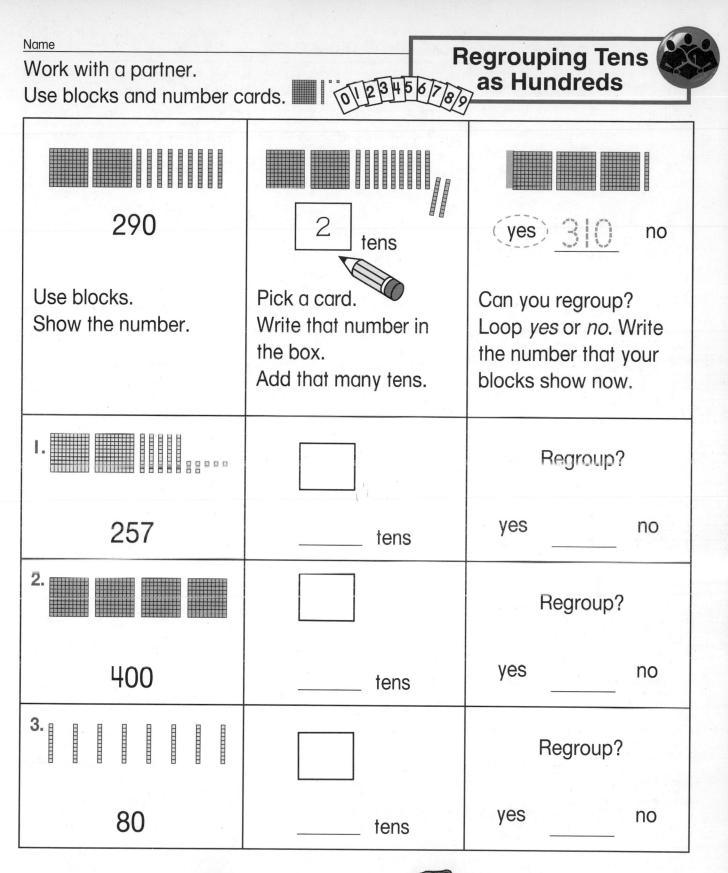

290

Use blocks.
Show the number.

2 tens

Pick a card.
Write that number in the box.
Add that many tens.

yes 310 no

Can you regroup?
Loop *yes* or *no*. Write the number that your blocks show now.

I.

257

_____ tens

Regroup?

yes   no
_____

2.

400

_____ tens

Regroup?

yes   no
_____

3.

80

_____ tens

Regroup?

yes   no
_____

Work with a partner. Use blocks and number cards.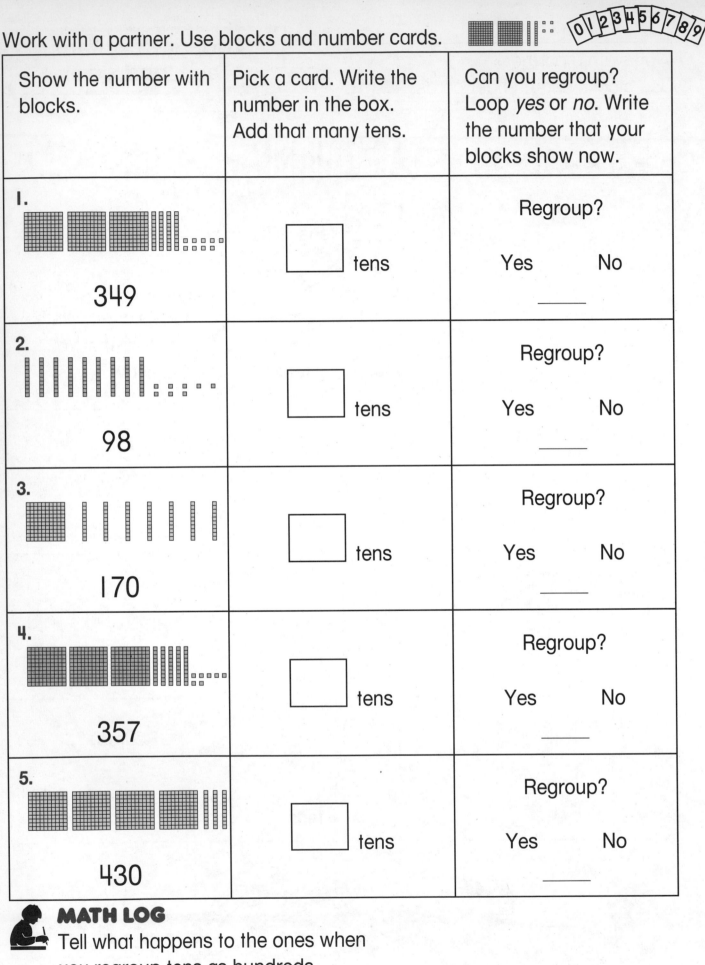

Show the number with blocks.	Pick a card. Write the number in the box. Add that many tens.	Can you regroup? Loop *yes* or *no*. Write the number that your blocks show now.
I. 349	☐ tens	Regroup? Yes No _____
2. 98	☐ tens	Regroup? Yes No _____
3. 170	☐ tens	Regroup? Yes No _____
4. 357	☐ tens	Regroup? Yes No _____
5. 430	☐ tens	Regroup? Yes No _____

MATH LOG
Tell what happens to the ones when you regroup tens as hundreds.

You need blocks.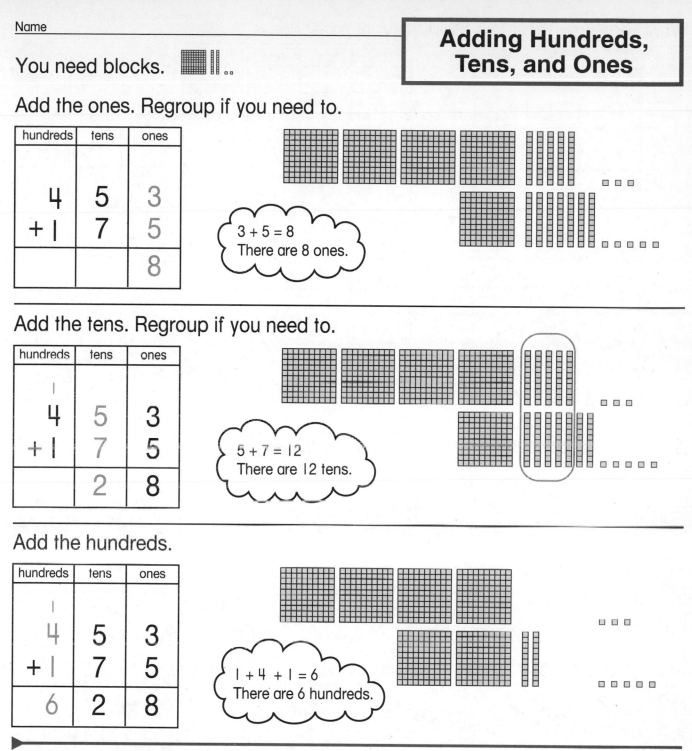

Add the ones. Regroup if you need to.

hundreds	tens	ones
4	5	3
+ 1	7	5
		8

3 + 5 = 8
There are 8 ones.

Add the tens. Regroup if you need to.

hundreds	tens	ones
1		
4	5	3
+ 1	7	5
	2	8

5 + 7 = 12
There are 12 tens.

Add the hundreds.

hundreds	tens	ones
1		
4	5	3
+ 1	7	5
6	2	8

1 + 4 + 1 = 6
There are 6 hundreds.

Use blocks to add. Write the sum.

1.

hundreds	tens	ones
	1	
3	5	4
+ 2	3	7
5	9	1

2.

hundreds	tens	ones
	2	3
+	8	1

3.

hundreds	tens	ones
3	8	3
+ 5	7	2

Write the sum. You may use blocks.

1.

hundreds	tens	ones
5	2	5
+2	8	4

hundreds	tens	ones
4	1	1
+5	8	7

hundreds	tens	ones
3	3	7
+	5	4

2.

hundreds	tens	ones
2	6	8
+2	8	1

hundreds	tens	ones
	5	6
+	8	2

hundreds	tens	ones
6	4	5
+	7	0

3.

hundreds	tens	ones
3	2	8
+	5	5

hundreds	tens	ones
1	6	7
+4	3	2

hundreds	tens	ones
5	5	3
+4	3	8

Maintain • Mixed Practice

Watch the signs!

Complete the number sentences.

1. 8 + 4 = ____   3 × 4 = ____   10 + 2 = ____

2. 10 − 8 = ____   2 × 1 = ____   11 − 9 = ____

3. 5 × 5 = ____   5 − 5 = ____   5 + 5 = ____

4. 13 − 8 = ____   7 + 5 = ____   15 − 6 = ____

Name _____

hundreds	tens	ones
3	5	¹6
+1	8	7
		3

hundreds	tens	ones
3	¹5	6
+1	8	7
	4	3

hundreds	tens	ones
3	¹5	6
+1	8	7
5	4	3

Add the ones. Regroup if you need to.

Add the tens. Regroup if you need to.

Add the hundreds.

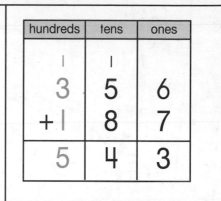

Add.

1.

hundreds	tens	ones
¹4	¹3	8
+2	7	4
7	1	2

hundreds	tens	ones
7	1	5
+2	2	8

hundreds	tens	ones
5	2	6
+1	8	7

2.

666	731	286	947	193
+ 241	+ 28	+ 159	+ 38	+ 39

3.

334	118	654	249	39
+ 78	+ 807	+ 33	+ 42	+65

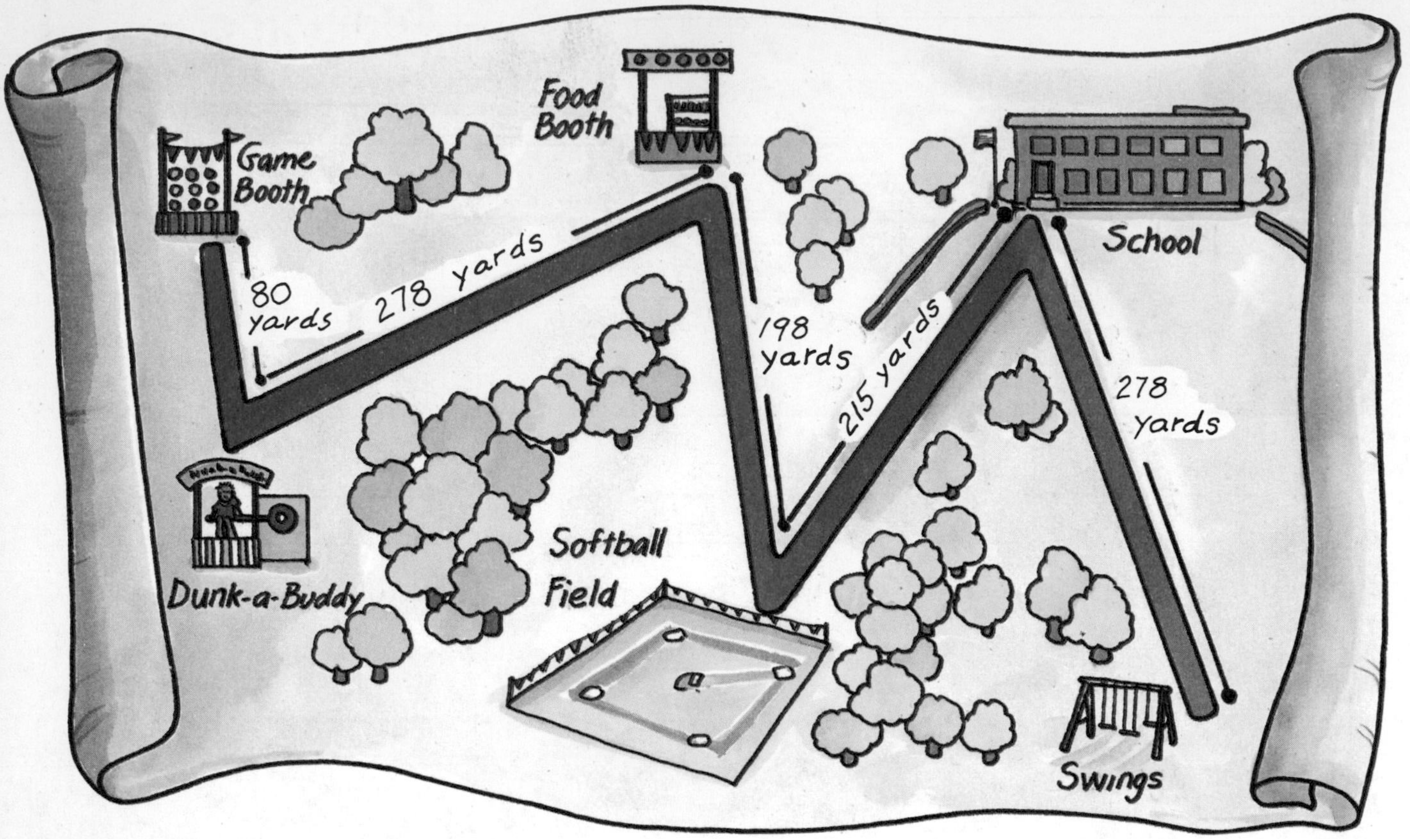

Problem Solving Use the map to solve each problem.

1. How far is it from the game booth to the food

   booth? _____ yards

2. How far is it from the Dunk-A-Buddy to the

   softball field? _____ yards

3. How far is it from the softball field to the swings?

   _____ yards

4. Susanne walked from the softball field to school
   and back. Did she walk more than 500 yards?

   _____

5. Which two things are 413 yards apart?

   _____ and _____

More Practice Set 12.4, page 423

Adding money is like adding plain numbers. Remember to write the dollar sign and decimal point.

$1.83
+$2.46
$4.29

Add.

1.
$1.56	$0.57	$5.28	$3.76	$3.43
+$2.44	+$0.26	+$2.86	+$4.51	+$1.39
$4.00				

2.
$2.77	$5.31	$3.33	$6.44	$1.46
+$6.45	+$4.60	+$4.57	+$3.17	+$8.23

3.
$7.29	$6.47	$6.06	$0.17	$2.49
+$1.00	+$0.18	+$2.82	+$0.93	+$5.04

4.
$3.69	$4.56	$1.63	$2.24	$4.08
+$3.69	+$4.56	+$1.63	+$2.24	+$4.08

Problem Solving

1. Jackie buys 2 slices of pizza at the food booth. Each slice costs $1.25. How much does Jackie

   spend? _____

2. Mr. Martin buys 450 large paper plates for the food booth. He also buys 375 small paper plates. How many paper plates does Mr. Martin buy?

   _____ paper plates

3. Jared has $10.00. Can he buy a T-shirt that costs $5.99 and a baseball cap that costs $2.99?

   _____

4. Jackie and Mike each had 80 raffle tickets to sell. Jackie has 24 tickets left. Mike has 38 tickets left.

   Who sold more tickets? _____

5. Susanne is playing softball. She makes a home run. The bases are 60 feet apart. About how far does

   Susanne run? about _____ feet

6. It is 300 yards around the field. Max starts at one corner and runs 3 times around the field. How far is

   he from where he started? _____ yards

More Practice Set 12.5, page 423

Addition Practice

You need crayons.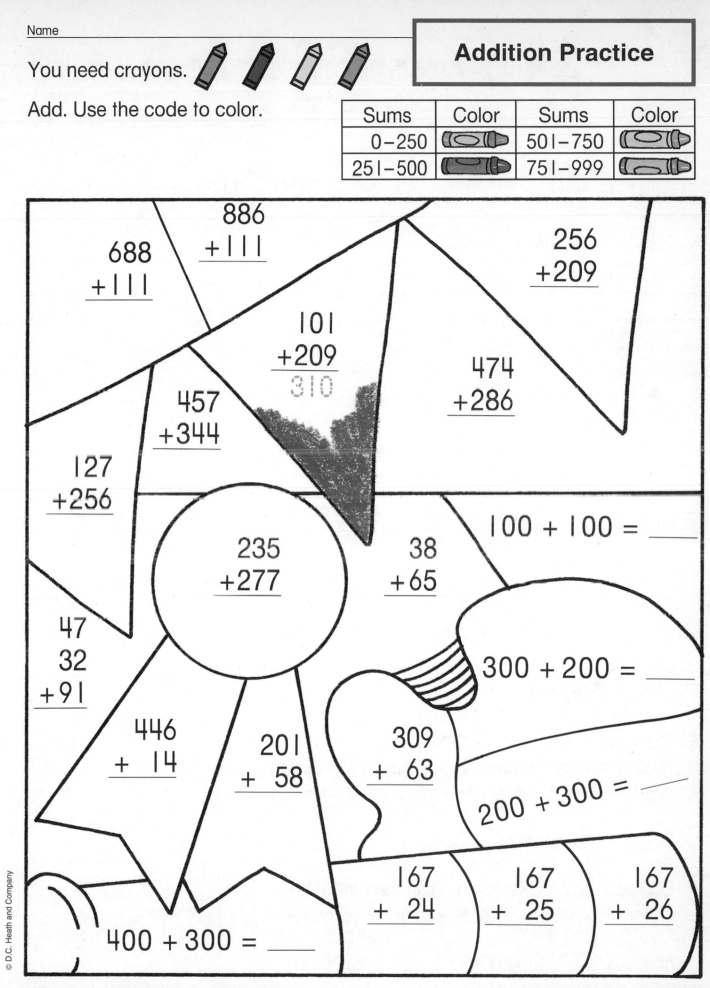

Add. Use the code to color.

Sums	Color	Sums	Color
0–250		501–750	
251–500		751–999	

```
  688      886          256
 +111     +111         +209

            101
           +209
           310           474
    457                 +286
   +344

 127
+256                              100 + 100 = ___

         235      38
        +277     +65

 47
 32                               300 + 200 = ___
+91
    446     201      309
   + 14    + 58     + 63
                                  200 + 300 = ___

                        167   167   167
                       + 24  + 25  + 26
 400 + 300 = ___
```

More Practice Sets 12.6, page 424

(three hundred sixty-one) 361

MID-CHAPTER REVIEW

for pages 351–360

Add.

1. $600 + 200 =$ _____

2. $310 + 500 =$ _____

3. $500 + 100 =$ _____

4. $700 + 205 =$ _____

5.

478	$3.75	$7.61	439	$4.52
+432	+$4.34	+$1.28	+370	+$0.75

6.

$4.88	343	$2.94	77	599
+$0.25	+ 81	+$3.15	+33	+321

7.

356	$6.93	728	$2.66	712
+241	+$2.65	+ 59	+$0.34	+127

Problem Solving

8. The food booth sold 55 tuna sandwiches and 70 cheese sandwiches. It also sold 150 cups of juice. How many sandwiches did the booth sell?

_____ sandwiches

9. On Field Day, 53 children finish the race. Three children finish ahead of Susanne. How many children finish behind her? _____ children

Name _____

Jackie	Susanne	Jared	Mike
$4.00	$8.00	$9.50	$7.50

Edison School Sale

○	**Shorts**	**$6.99**
○	**Sweatshirt**	**$9.50**
○	**Cap**	**$2.50**
○	**T-shirt**	**$4.99**
○	**Mug**	**$3.99**
○	**Flag**	**$1.50**

Work with a partner.
Use the picture to answer each question.

1. Susanne buys a T-shirt and a flag. Does she

   have more than $1.00 left? _____

2. What 2 things can Jackie buy?

   _____ and _____

3. If Mike buys the mug, will he have enough

   money left to buy the shorts? _____

4. Do Jackie and Jared together have enough

   money to buy 2 T-shirts? _____

Ray's Sports Sale! Order Now!

Tennis Balls
3 balls—$2.00

Saucers
Saucer—$1.75

Softballs
softball—$2.25

Ping-Pong Balls
3 balls—$1.10

Hula-Hoops
Hula-Hoop—$1.25

Jump Ropes
jump rope—$0.75

You may use a calculator.

Work with a partner.
Together, you have $9.99 to spend.
Write what you will buy. Fill in the
order form. Write the total amount
you spend.

Sample Form		
Item	How Many	Price
tennis ball	6	$4.00
saucer	2	$3.50

Item	How Many	Price

Total Amount _____

How much of the $9.99 do you have left? _____

364 (three hundred sixty-four)

Subtract.

1. 8 ●●●●●   800 ☐☐☐☐☐
  −2 ●⊗⊗   −200 ☐⊠⊠
  6   600

2. 7 ●●●●●   700 ☐☐☐☐☐
  −5 ●●   −500 ☐☐

3. 6 ●●●●●   600 ☐☐☐☐☐
  −3 ●   −300 ☐

4. 9 ●●●●●   900 ☐☐☐☐☐
  −4 ●●●●   −400 ☐☐☐☐

5. 5 ●●●●●   500 ☐☐☐☐☐
  −2   −200

Critical Thinking How does subtracting 7 − 5 help you to subtract 700 − 500?

Subtract.

□ □ □ □ □ • • •
□ □ □ ⊠

1. 903 – 100 = *803*

2. 640 – 200 = _____

3. 500 – 400 = _____

4. 405 – 200 = _____

5. 330 – 200 = _____

6. 880 – 300 = _____

7. 400 – 100 = _____

8. 550 – 200 = _____

9. 702 – 400 = _____

10. 200 – 100 = _____

11. 390 – 100 = _____

12. 655 – 500 = _____

13. 403 – 300 = _____

14. 616 – 100 = _____

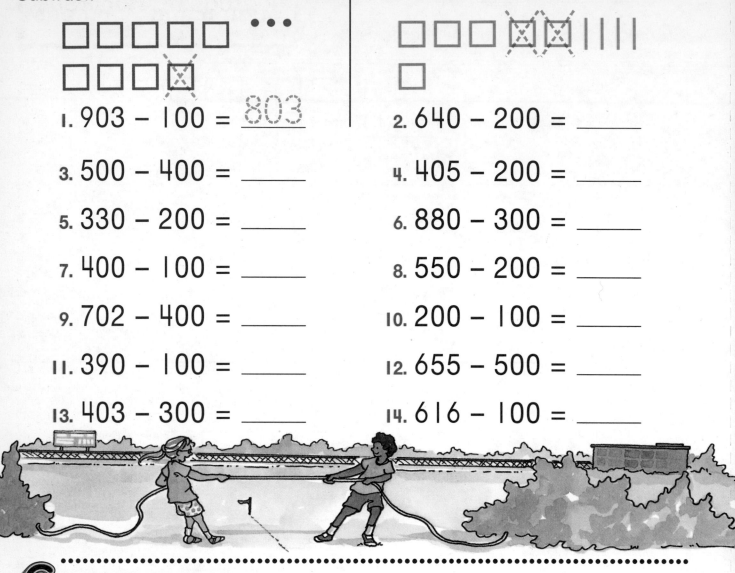

CHALLENGE • Number Sense

Subtract.

1. 439 – 209 = _____   439 – 309 = _____

2. 439 – 409 = _____   679 – 179 = _____

3. 754 – 104 = _____   229 – 120 = _____

4. 562 – 162 = _____   611 – 600 = _____

5. 819 – 109 = _____   947 – 540 = _____

6. 839 – 830 = _____   533 – 433 = _____

366 (three hundred sixty-six)

Name _____

You need blocks and number cards.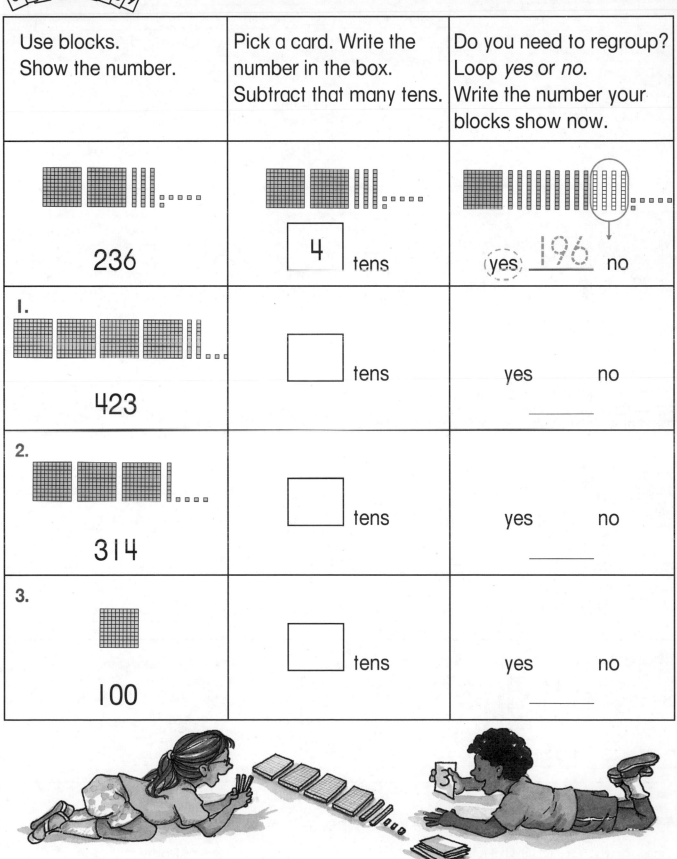

Use blocks. Show the number.	Pick a card. Write the number in the box. Subtract that many tens.	Do you need to regroup? Loop *yes* or *no*. Write the number your blocks show now.
236	**4** tens	(yes) 196 no
1. 423	☐ tens	yes no _____
2. 314	☐ tens	yes no _____
3. 100	☐ tens	yes no _____

Use blocks and number cards.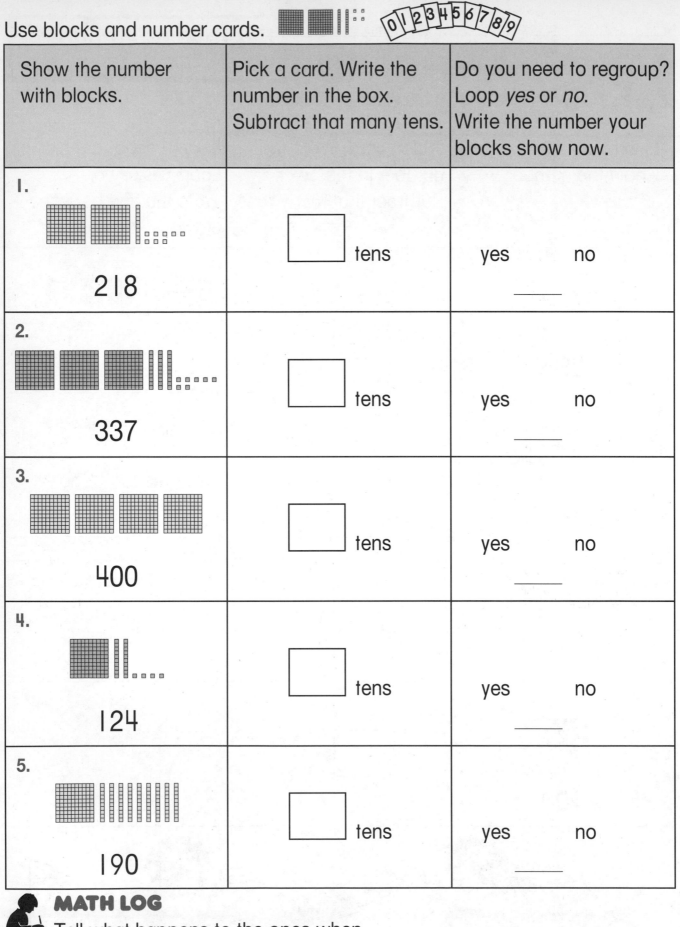

Show the number with blocks.	Pick a card. Write the number in the box. Subtract that many tens.	Do you need to regroup? Loop *yes* or *no*. Write the number your blocks show now.
1. 218	☐ tens	yes no _____
2. 337	☐ tens	yes no _____
3. 400	☐ tens	yes no _____
4. 124	☐ tens	yes no _____
5. 190	☐ tens	yes no _____

MATH LOG

Tell what happens to the ones when you regroup hundreds as tens.

Name _____

You need blocks.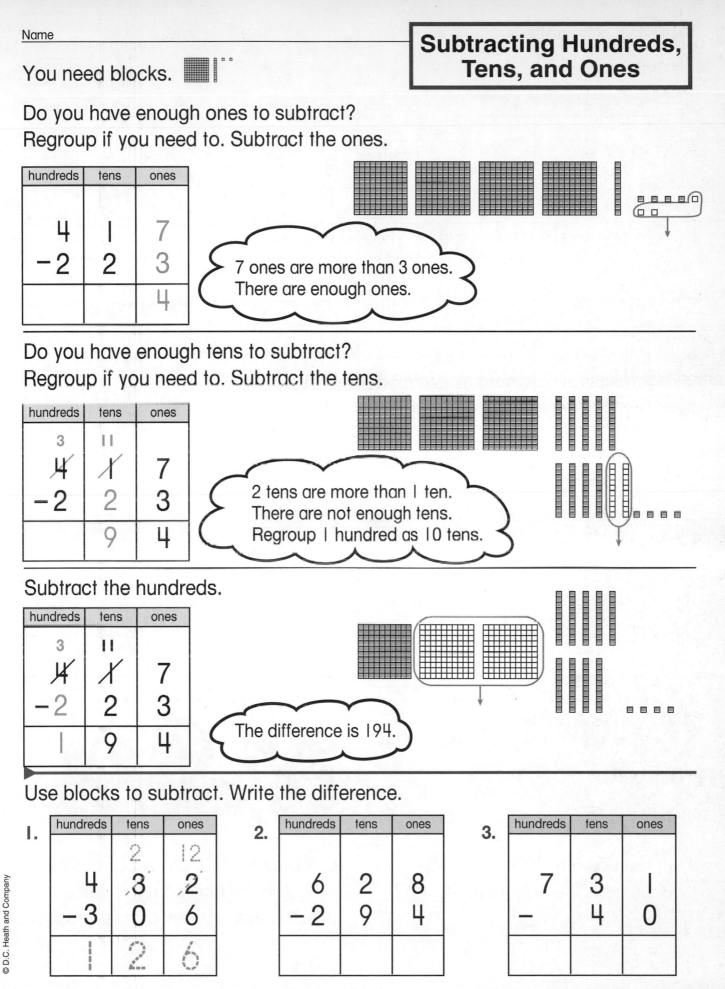

Do you have enough ones to subtract?
Regroup if you need to. Subtract the ones.

hundreds	tens	ones
4	1	7
−2	2	3
		4

7 ones are more than 3 ones.
There are enough ones.

Do you have enough tens to subtract?
Regroup if you need to. Subtract the tens.

hundreds	tens	ones
3	11	
4̸	1̸	7
−2	2	3
	9	4

2 tens are more than 1 ten.
There are not enough tens.
Regroup 1 hundred as 10 tens.

Subtract the hundreds.

hundreds	tens	ones
3	11	
4̸	1̸	7
−2	2	3
1	9	4

The difference is 194.

Use blocks to subtract. Write the difference.

1.

hundreds	tens	ones
	2	12
4	3̸	2̸
−3	0	6
1	2	6

2.

hundreds	tens	ones
6	2	8
−2	9	4

3.

hundreds	tens	ones
7	3	1
−	4	0

Write the difference.
You may use blocks.

1.

hundreds	tens	ones
5 / 6	12 / 2	8
− 3	9	4
2	3	4

hundreds	tens	ones
8	3	2
− 1	1	6

hundreds	tens	ones
9	7	7
− 2	6	9

2.

hundreds	tens	ones
5	3	2
−	4	1

hundreds	tens	ones
7	5	8
−	3	6

hundreds	tens	ones
4	9	2
− 2	7	3

3.

hundreds	tens	ones
2	7	5
− 1	8	4

hundreds	tens	ones
1	4	3
−	7	1

hundreds	tens	ones
5	8	6
− 4	3	2

Maintain • Money Sense

You need coins.

Use coins to solve each problem.

1. Jared has 5 nickels. Mike has 3 dimes. Who has more money?

_____

2. Susanne has 6 dimes. She gives one half of her money to Mike. How much money do they each

have now? _____ ¢

More Practice Set 12.10, page 424

Name _____

Subtraction with Regrouping

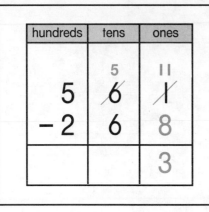
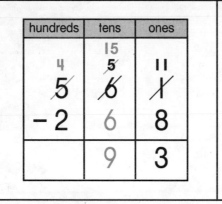
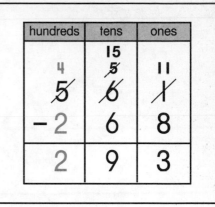

Enough ones? Regroup if you need to. Subtract the ones.

Enough tens? Regroup if you need to. Subtract the tens.

Subtract the hundreds.

Subtract.

1.

hundreds	tens	ones
8	3	2
−3	6	9
4	6	3

hundreds	tens	ones
4	7	5
−2	1	4

hundreds	tens	ones
6	5	9
−1	7	3

2.

$$\begin{array}{r} 9\,4\,2 \\ -8\,4\,5 \\ \hline \end{array}$$
$$\begin{array}{r} 3\,9\,1 \\ -\ \ 6\,4 \\ \hline \end{array}$$
$$\begin{array}{r} 7\,1\,5 \\ -3\,5\,6 \\ \hline \end{array}$$
$$\begin{array}{r} 2\,8\,6 \\ -\ \ 4\,9 \\ \hline \end{array}$$
$$\begin{array}{r} 6\,3\,2 \\ -2\,9\,5 \\ \hline \end{array}$$

3.

$$\begin{array}{r} 3\,7\,8 \\ -2\,9\,9 \\ \hline \end{array}$$
$$\begin{array}{r} 9\,6\,4 \\ -7\,4\,5 \\ \hline \end{array}$$
$$\begin{array}{r} 4\,9\,6 \\ -\ \ 4\,5 \\ \hline \end{array}$$
$$\begin{array}{r} 3\,8\,8 \\ -2\,3\,9 \\ \hline \end{array}$$
$$\begin{array}{r} 8\,5\,3 \\ -\ \ 5\,4 \\ \hline \end{array}$$

Mr. Martin wrote how far the children
ran in one minute.

Max   137 yards
Susanne   153 yards
Jared   168 yards
Mike   174 yards

Problem Solving   Use Mr. Martin's notebook to solve each problem.

1. How many more yards did Susanne run than Max?

_____ yards

2. How many fewer yards did Susanne run than

Jared? _____ yards

3. Who ran 6 more yards than Jared? _____

4. Would it take Susanne more than a minute or
less than a minute to run 100 yards?

_____ than a minute

5. Who would win a race that was 168 yards long?

_____

Name _____

You need blocks. ▦▯

There are not enough
ones to subtract.
But there are no tens
to regroup.
Look at the hundreds.

$$\begin{array}{r} 4\ 0\ 0 \\ -1\ 2\ 8 \\ \hline \end{array}$$

Regroup I hundred
as 10 ones.

$$\begin{array}{r} {\scriptstyle 3\ \ 10} \\ 4\!\!\!/\ \ 0\!\!\!/\ 0 \\ -1\ 2\ 8 \\ \hline \end{array}$$

Regroup I ten
as 10 ones.

$$\begin{array}{r} {\scriptstyle \quad 9} \\ {\scriptstyle 3\ \ 10\ 10} \\ 4\!\!\!/\ \ 0\!\!\!/\ 0\!\!\!/ \\ -1\ 2\ 8 \\ \hline \end{array}$$

Subtract.
Write the number
your blocks show now.

$$\begin{array}{r} {\scriptstyle \quad 9} \\ {\scriptstyle 3\ \ 10\ 10} \\ 4\!\!\!/\ \ 0\!\!\!/\ 0\!\!\!/ \\ -1\ 2\ 8 \\ \hline 2\ 7\ 2 \end{array}$$

▶ ───────────────────────────

Write the difference.

$$\begin{array}{r} {\scriptstyle \quad 9} \\ {\scriptstyle 6\ \ 10\ 13} \\ 7\!\!\!/\ \ 0\!\!\!/\ 3\!\!\!/ \\ -5\ 6\ 5 \\ \hline 1\ 3\ 8 \end{array}$$
$$\begin{array}{r} 6\ 0\ 9 \\ -\ \ 1\ 4 \\ \hline \end{array}$$
$$\begin{array}{r} 5\ 0\ 3 \\ -2\ 0\ 6 \\ \hline \end{array}$$
$$\begin{array}{r} 2\ 9\ 0 \\ -1\ 8\ 9 \\ \hline \end{array}$$
$$\begin{array}{r} 3\ 6\ 4 \\ -2\ 6\ 3 \\ \hline \end{array}$$

Subtract.

1.
$$\begin{array}{r} \overset{9}{} \\ \overset{8\;\cancel{10}15}{\cancel{9}\,0\,5} \\ -\;\;58 \\ \hline 8\,4\,7 \end{array}$$
$$\begin{array}{r} 400 \\ -234 \\ \hline \end{array}$$
$$\begin{array}{r} 206 \\ -165 \\ \hline \end{array}$$
$$\begin{array}{r} 360 \\ -206 \\ \hline \end{array}$$
$$\begin{array}{r} 657 \\ -334 \\ \hline \end{array}$$

2.
$$\begin{array}{r} 458 \\ -\;\;24 \\ \hline \end{array}$$
$$\begin{array}{r} 380 \\ -356 \\ \hline \end{array}$$
$$\begin{array}{r} 500 \\ -\;\;76 \\ \hline \end{array}$$
$$\begin{array}{r} 567 \\ -130 \\ \hline \end{array}$$
$$\begin{array}{r} 329 \\ -\;\;35 \\ \hline \end{array}$$

3.
$$\begin{array}{r} 700 \\ -183 \\ \hline \end{array}$$
$$\begin{array}{r} 359 \\ -\;\;68 \\ \hline \end{array}$$
$$\begin{array}{r} 521 \\ -432 \\ \hline \end{array}$$
$$\begin{array}{r} 830 \\ -542 \\ \hline \end{array}$$
$$\begin{array}{r} 923 \\ -346 \\ \hline \end{array}$$

Problem Solving

4. Mike's mother gives him $6.75 to spend at Field Day. He already has 6 dimes and a nickel in his pocket. How much

   money does Mike have? _____

5. Susanne has 2 one-dollar bills and 4 coins. She has a total of $3.50. What coins does she

   have? _____

6. The Green Team has 30 more points than the Blue Team. In the next race, the Blue Team gets 75 points and the Green Team gets 50 points.

   Which team is ahead now? _____

374 (three hundred seventy-four)

More Practice Set 12.12, page 425

Subtracting money is
like subtracting plain
numbers. Remember to
write the dollar sign
and decimal point.

$$\begin{array}{r} \$9.87 \\ -\$7.58 \\ \hline \$2.29 \end{array}$$

Subtract.

1.
$$\begin{array}{r} \$7.42 \\ -\$3.51 \\ \hline \$3.91 \end{array}$$
$$\begin{array}{r} \$5.28 \\ -\$0.37 \\ \hline \end{array}$$
$$\begin{array}{r} \$6.06 \\ -\$5.04 \\ \hline \end{array}$$
$$\begin{array}{r} \$9.73 \\ -\$4.82 \\ \hline \end{array}$$
$$\begin{array}{r} \$1.18 \\ -\$0.90 \\ \hline \end{array}$$

2.
$$\begin{array}{r} \$8.54 \\ -\$0.84 \\ \hline \end{array}$$
$$\begin{array}{r} \$4.92 \\ -\$3.90 \\ \hline \end{array}$$
$$\begin{array}{r} \$9.32 \\ -\$4.51 \\ \hline \end{array}$$
$$\begin{array}{r} \$8.16 \\ -\$7.17 \\ \hline \end{array}$$
$$\begin{array}{r} \$7.38 \\ -\$6.47 \\ \hline \end{array}$$

3.
$$\begin{array}{r} \$4.66 \\ -\$3.99 \\ \hline \end{array}$$
$$\begin{array}{r} \$1.02 \\ -\$0.91 \\ \hline \end{array}$$
$$\begin{array}{r} \$5.04 \\ -\$4.65 \\ \hline \end{array}$$
$$\begin{array}{r} \$8.88 \\ -\$8.09 \\ \hline \end{array}$$
$$\begin{array}{r} \$4.57 \\ -\$3.60 \\ \hline \end{array}$$

4.
$$\begin{array}{r} \$7.41 \\ -\$4.50 \\ \hline \end{array}$$
$$\begin{array}{r} \$3.92 \\ -\$2.40 \\ \hline \end{array}$$
$$\begin{array}{r} \$1.93 \\ -\$0.94 \\ \hline \end{array}$$
$$\begin{array}{r} \$3.78 \\ -\$2.89 \\ \hline \end{array}$$
$$\begin{array}{r} \$7.68 \\ -\$5.59 \\ \hline \end{array}$$

$8.65
-$2.73
$5.92

I can check **subtraction** with addition.

$5.92
+$2.73
$8.65

Check Mike's homework. If his answer is wrong, show the correct subtraction.

1.

438   284   438   294
-144   +144   --144   +144
284 wrong 428   294   438

2.

$8.28
-$4.17
$4.09

3.

579
- 82
497

4.

$6.13
-$3.29
$2.24

MATH LOG
Think of a way you could check addition.

376 (three hundred seventy-six)   **More Practice Set 12.13, page 426**

Name _____

Add or subtract.
Loop the exercises you can do in your head.

1.
    (400
    +300)
    700

    999
    −999

    376
    +249

    800
    −200

    700
    − 29

2.
    130
    +800

    456
    +379

    148
    − 48

    257
    +257

    932
    − 33

3.
    489
    + 21

    304
    +106

    863
    −109

    762
    −160

    433
    +369

4.
    777
    +108

    949
    −940

    666
    + 11

    988
    −222

    703
    −109

5.
    298
    + 4

    887
    −108

    755
    −455

    877
    −249

    422
    +365

Critical Thinking How did you decide which exercises to loop?

(three hundred seventy-seven) 377

You need a calculator.
Complete the table.

COOPERATIVE LEARNING

> To change 251 to 201, you can subtract 50.

	Enter:	Change to:	How did you do it?
1.	251	201	− 5 0
2.	497	97	☐ ☐ ☐ ☐
3.	125	155	☐ ☐ ☐
4.	918	898	☐ ☐ ☐
5.	299	324	☐ ☐ ☐
6.	638	836	☐ ☐ ☐ ☐

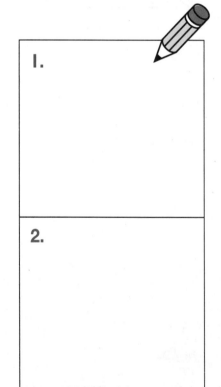

CHALLENGE • Using Technology

Work with a partner. You may use a calculator.
Each letter stands for a number from 0 to 9.
Figure out the missing numbers.
Write them in the table.

1.
```
  3 N 3
+ E 2 2
-------
  7 9 P
```
> 3 + 2 = 5
> So, P = 5

2.
```
  F U N
+ F U R
-------
  P U P
```

CODE:

P	R	E	N	U	F

1.

2.

Use the code to answer the riddle.
Who blows the whistle when puppies play soccer?

THE ◯ ◯ ◯ ◯ ◯ ◯ ◯ ◯
    8 9 2 2 4 8 4 4

More Practice Set 12.14, page 426

Solve each problem.

1. At Field Day, 30 children want to play basketball. Mr. Martin needs to pick 5 children for each team. How many teams can play basketball?

   _____ teams

2. Jared has a dollar bill and 3 dimes. A school banner costs $2.25. How many banners can Jared

   buy? _____ banners

3. Jackie was given some tickets to sell. She sold 75 tickets. She has 25 left. How many tickets was

   Jackie given to sell? _____ tickets

4. Susanne counted 493 pennies and 2 dimes from the wishing well. Is that enough money for Mr.

   Martin to buy a bat that costs $5.00? _____

5. Which team scored more points?

   _____

POINTS		
	MORNING	AFTERNOON
RED TEAM	300	290
ORANGE TEAM	310	320

Solve each problem.

1. Susanne can run around the track in 5 minutes. So can Jared. How many minutes will it take them to

   run around the track together? _____ minutes

2. There are 3 rows of seats at the field. There are 50 seats in each row. All the seats are filled except

   for 5 of them. How many seats are filled? _____ seats

3. Field Day began at 9 o'clock in the morning. It ended at 4 o'clock in the afternoon. How long did it

   last? _____ hours

4. There are 6 pairs of children who run in each three-legged race. How many children run in each

   race? _____ children

5. Jackie sells 37 raffle tickets. The rest of her class sells 775 tickets. What color ribbon do they get?

   _____ ribbon

more than 800   tickets sold

500 — 799

200 — 499

CHAPTER TEST

Add.

1. 109 + 200 = _____

2. 350 + 101 = _____

3. 434 + 400 = _____

4. 707 + 200 = _____

5. 222 + 500 = _____

6. 160 + 100 = _____

7. 134
  +788

8. 119
  +508

9. 476
  + 63

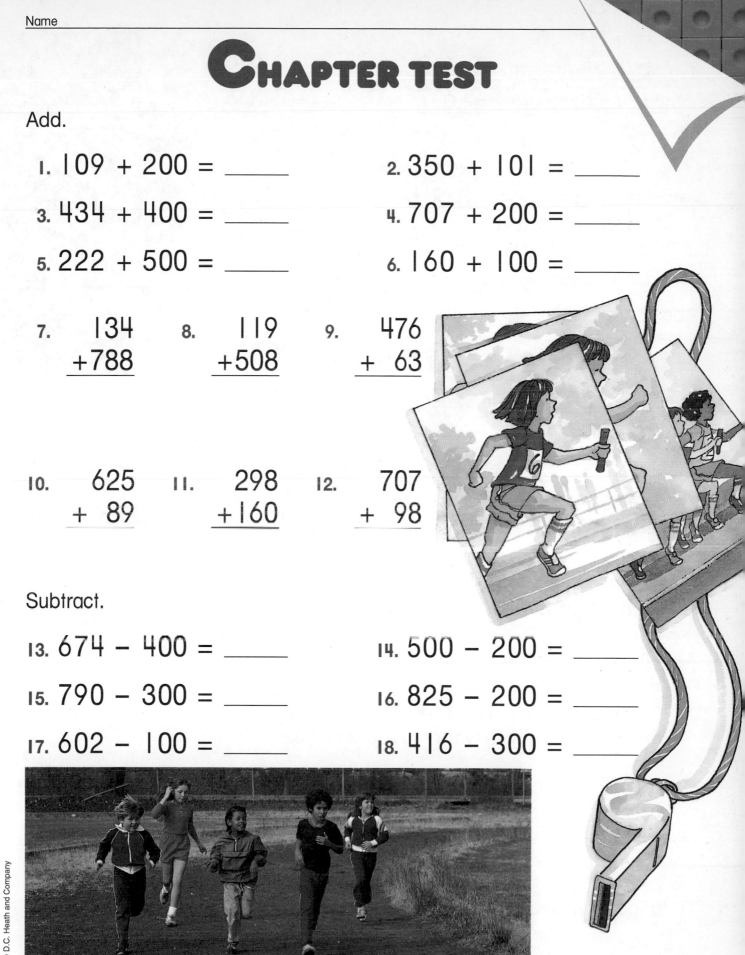

10. 625
   + 89

11. 298
   +160

12. 707
   + 98

Subtract.

13. 674 − 400 = _____

14. 500 − 200 = _____

15. 790 − 300 = _____

16. 825 − 200 = _____

17. 602 − 100 = _____

18. 416 − 300 = _____

Subtract.

19.
$$
\begin{array}{r}
5\ 8\ 4 \\
-\ \ 7\ 9 \\
\hline
\end{array}
$$

20.
$$
\begin{array}{r}
9\ 6\ 3 \\
-\ \ 6\ 7 \\
\hline
\end{array}
$$

21.
$$
\begin{array}{r}
4\ 2\ 9 \\
-2\ 3\ 6 \\
\hline
\end{array}
$$

22.
$$
\begin{array}{r}
6\ 4\ 3 \\
-2\ 9\ 7 \\
\hline
\end{array}
$$

23.
$$
\begin{array}{r}
8\ 2\ 5 \\
-7\ 1\ 8 \\
\hline
\end{array}
$$

24.
$$
\begin{array}{r}
1\ 2\ 7 \\
-\ \ 4\ 9 \\
\hline
\end{array}
$$

Add or subtract.

25.
$$
\begin{array}{r}
\$\ 5.4\ 9 \\
+\$\ 3.3\ 7 \\
\hline
\end{array}
$$

26.
$$
\begin{array}{r}
\$\ 9.9\ 5 \\
-\$\ 6.4\ 7 \\
\hline
\end{array}
$$

27.
$$
\begin{array}{r}
\$\ 1.9\ 3 \\
+\$\ 0.5\ 8 \\
\hline
\end{array}
$$

28.
$$
\begin{array}{r}
\$\ 4.4\ 4 \\
+\$\ 4.6\ 7 \\
\hline
\end{array}
$$

29.
$$
\begin{array}{r}
\$\ 8.5\ 1 \\
-\$\ 0.9\ 4 \\
\hline
\end{array}
$$

30.
$$
\begin{array}{r}
\$\ 5.7\ 2 \\
-\$\ 4.2\ 8 \\
\hline
\end{array}
$$

Solve each problem.

31. There are 940 gallons of water in the Dunk-a-Buddy machine. Some of the water gets splashed out. There are 800 gallons of water left in the machine. How much water was splashed out?

_____ gallons

32. A box of popcorn costs $1.95. Monica and Rod each want a box. How much money will 2 boxes of popcorn cost? _____

CUMULATIVE TEST

Write how many legs.
Write the multiplication sentence.

1.

____ 🦒 each with ____ legs

____ × ____ = ____

2.

____ 🐟 each with ____ legs

____ × ____ = ____

Multiply.

3. 2
   ×5

4. 0
   ×3

5. 6
   ×2

6. 3
   ×5

7. 4
   ×3

8. 3
   ×1

9. 1 × 2 = ____

10. 6 × 0 = ____

11. 4 × 6 = ____

Write the number in three different ways.

12.

____ hundreds ____ tens ____ ones

____ + ____ + ____

____

13.

____ hundreds ____ tens ____ ones

____ + ____ + ____

____

Write < or > in the ◯.

14. 105 ◯ 150

15. 171 ◯ 170

16. 440 ◯ 414

17. 285 ◯ 280

18. 369 ◯ 396

19. 139 ◯ 293

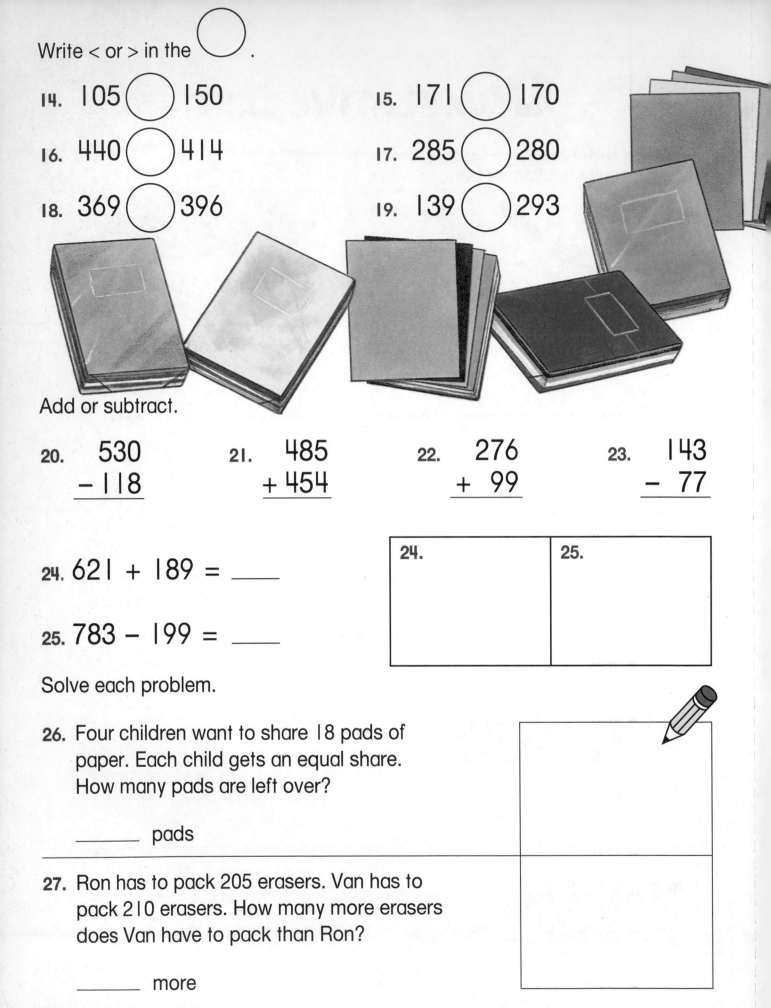

Add or subtract.

20.
$$530$$
$$-118$$

21.
$$485$$
$$+454$$

22.
$$276$$
$$+\ 99$$

23.
$$143$$
$$-\ 77$$

24. 621 + 189 = ____

25. 783 − 199 = ____

24.	25.

Solve each problem.

26. Four children want to share 18 pads of paper. Each child gets an equal share. How many pads are left over?

_____ pads

27. Ron has to pack 205 erasers. Van has to pack 210 erasers. How many more erasers does Van have to pack than Ron?

_____ more

Note to the Family

Your child has been learning about addition and subtraction of 3-digit numbers. This activity sheet gives your child an opportunity to share new skills with you.

3-DIGIT NUMBER RACE

To play, you need 2 different game pieces (for example, buttons) to move along the game board, and a coin.

1. For each turn, the player tosses the coin to determine how many spaces to move along the game board. If the coin lands heads up, the player moves 1 space. If the coin lands tails up, the player moves 2 spaces.

2. Each player must toss the coin and move along the game board to solve the problem in the space on which she or he lands.

3. If the problem in the space on which a player lands has already been solved, he or she moves to the next available space.

4. If a player solves a problem incorrectly, he or she must remain on that space for another turn and try to solve the problem again.

5. If a player lands on a space with special instructions, she or he solves the problem first and then follows the instructions, as indicated.

6. The first player to reach the end wins.

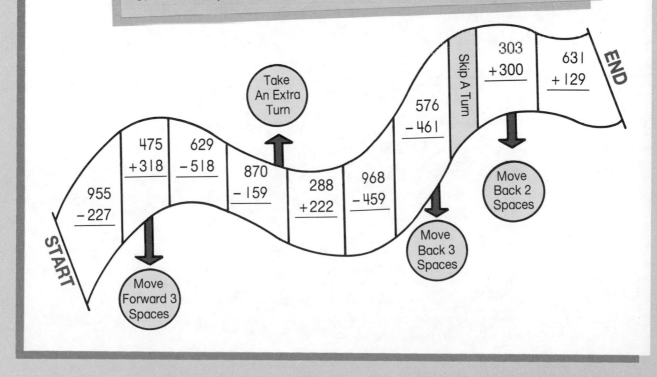

Note to the Family

Now that school is almost over, here are a few games and activities that you can do with your child during summer vacation.

Thank you for your help this year, and keep math alive and fun this summer!

NUMBER SEARCH

While traveling outside of the home or at any time, you and your child can record numbers that are around you. You can specify the number of digits within the numbers that you want to look for. Discuss with your child what the numbers represent. After recording 20 numbers, work with your child to order the numbers from greatest to least or least to greatest.

SHAPE HUNT

You and your child can look for different geometric shapes inside and/or outside of your home. Record in a bar graph or picture graph the different types of shapes and the number of each shape you find.

CREATE-A-SHAPE

Provide 20 toothpicks for your child. Ask your child to make as many triangles as possible with the toothpicks. This activity can be varied by helping your child make as many 4- or 5-sided figures as possible. When the activity is completed, work with your child to create a design by gluing the toothpick shapes onto a sheet of construction paper.

NEIGHBORHOOD BAKE-OFF

Help your child and his or her friends run a neighborhood bake sale. With the help of other parents, involve the children in different baking projects and in the sale of the finished baked goods.

Name _____

MORE PRACTICE

Set 1.1 Use with pages 3–4.

1. Draw more than five 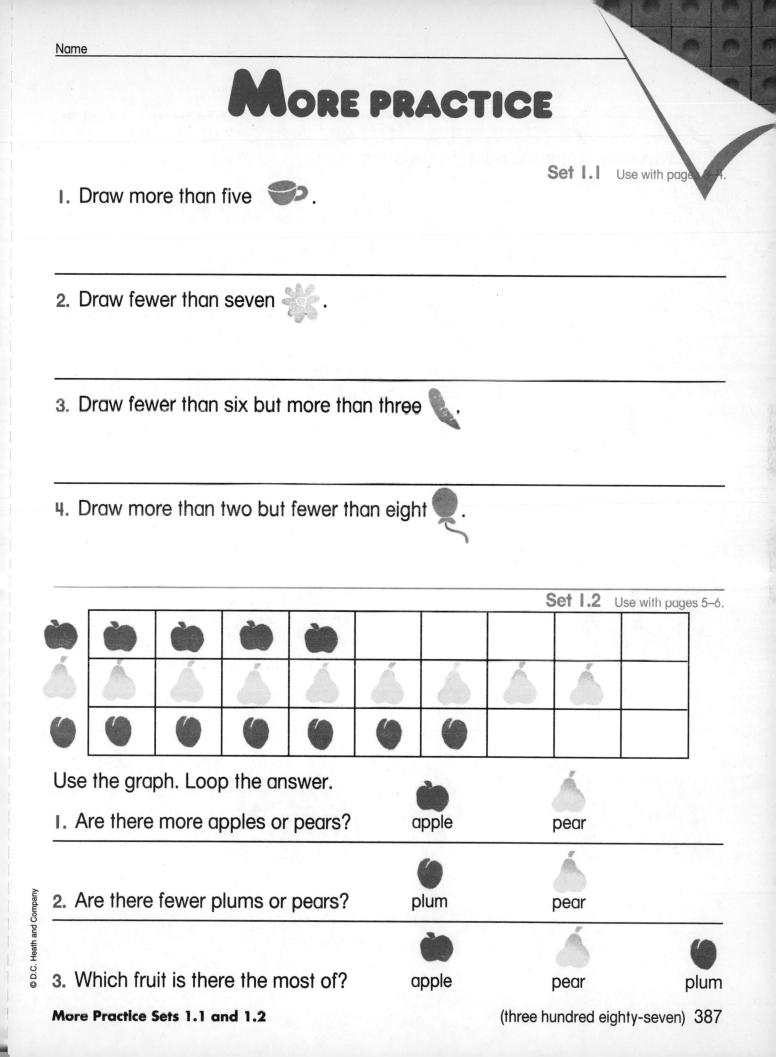 .

_____

2. Draw fewer than seven .

_____

3. Draw fewer than six but more than three .

_____

4. Draw more than two but fewer than eight .

_____

Set 1.2 Use with pages 5–6.

Use the graph. Loop the answer.

1. Are there more apples or pears?   apple   pear

2. Are there fewer plums or pears?   plum   pear

3. Which fruit is there the most of?   apple   pear   plum

More Practice Sets 1.1 and 1.2

(three hundred eighty-seven) 387

© D.C. Heath and Company

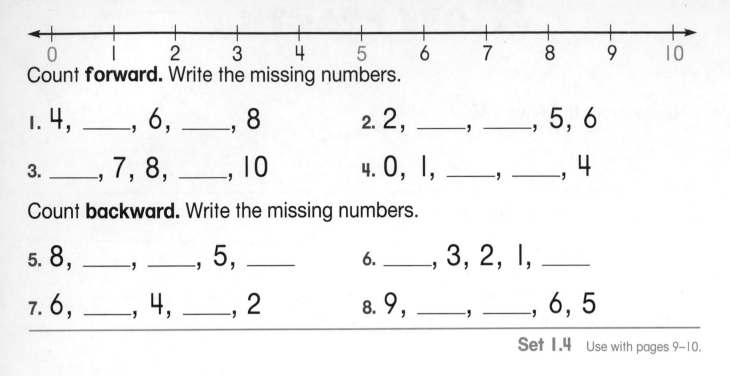

Count **forward.** Write the missing numbers.

1. 4, ____, 6, ____, 8

2. 2, ____, ____, 5, 6

3. ____, 7, 8, ____, 10

4. 0, 1, ____, ____, 4

Count **backward.** Write the missing numbers.

5. 8, ____, ____, 5, ____

6. ____, 3, 2, 1, ____

7. 6, ____, 4, ____, 2

8. 9, ____, ____, 6, 5

Draw more to show the number.
Write how many more.

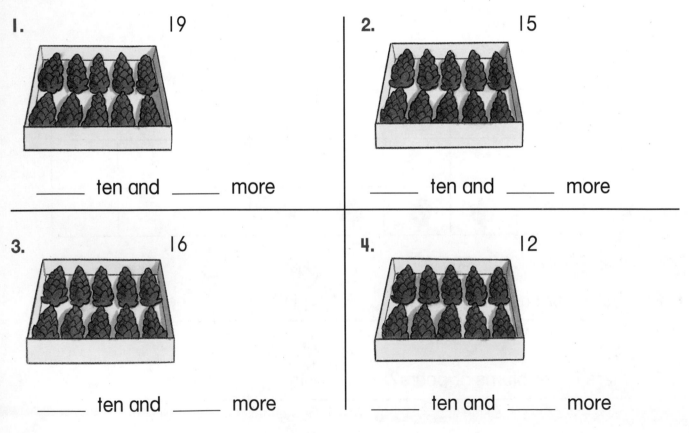

1.   19

____ ten and ____ more

2.   15

____ ten and ____ more

3.   16

____ ten and ____ more

4.   12

____ ten and ____ more

More Practice Sets 1.3 and 1.4

MORE PRACTICE

Write how many.

Loop each number that is greater than 14.

1. [10]

_____

2. [10]

_____

3. [10]

_____

4. [10]

_____

5. [10]

_____

6. [10]

_____

Answer each question.

1. The eagle is on what number? _____

2. What number is between the cloud and 13? _____

3. What number is between the tunnel and 6? _____

4. What 2 numbers are between the cloud and 18? _____ and _____

5. What 2 numbers is the bridge on? _____ and _____

```
0   1   2   3   4   5   6   7   8   9   10   11   12
```

Add. You may use the number line to count on.

1.
```
   4      10      6      7      3      8
 + 6     + 2    + 3    + 4    + 8    + 0
```

2.
```
   8       5      2      5     10      4
 + 2     + 6    + 9    + 5    + 1    + 5
```

3.
```
   9       4      2      7      3      4
 + 3     + 8    + 7    + 5    + 4    + 4
```

Use doubles plus 1 to write the sum.

1.
```
   3
 + 2     { + ___ }
```

2.
```
   4
 + 3     { + ___ }
```

Write the sum. You may use cubes if you like.

3.
```
   2       4      6      1      5      3      5
 + 1     + 5    + 5    + 2    + 4    + 4    + 6
```

MORE PRACTICE

Loop the numbers you add first.
Write the sum.

1.
6	5	4	7	3	5	1
2	3	1	2	0	4	6
+4	+2	+4	+1	+6	+3	+2

2.
4	2	1	4	3	2	8
2	7	5	3	3	3	0
+3	+2	+6	+1	+4	+6	+4

Complete the number sentence.

1. ___ + 9 = 12   11 = ___ + 4   8 + ___ = 8

2. 10 = 4 + ___   5 + ___ = 12   6 + ___ = 11

3. 2 + ___ = 8   ___ + 3 = 10   12 = ___ + 8

4. ___ + 6 = 9   11 = 3 + ___   5 + ___ = 10

5. 12 = 1 + ___   5 + ___ = 10   8 = ___ + 8

Write the sum or difference. You may use cubes.

1. 6 − 3 = _____   7 + 4 = _____   9 − 5 = _____

2. 8 + 3 = _____   9 + 2 = _____   11 − 6 = _____

3.
4	5	10	8	12	5
+4	+7	−3	−6	−5	+4

4.
11	10	6	8	9	11
−8	−6	+3	+2	−2	−4

<----+----+----+----+----+----+----+----+----+----+----+----+---->
  0   1   2   3   4   5   6   7   8   9 10 11 12

Subtract. Use the number line to count back.

1.
9	12	8	10	9	11
− 4	− 8	− 6	− 7	− 8	− 5

2.
12	10	9	11	12	8
− 3	− 5	− 0	− 7	− 6	−8

3.
8	12	11	9	8	10
−4	− 7	− 6	−3	−2	− 6

More Practice Sets 2.12 and 2.14

MORE PRACTICE

You need crayons.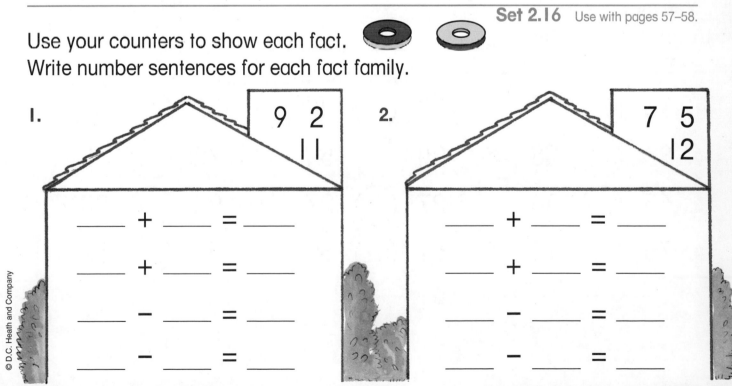

Add or subtract.

3 +4	4 +7	9 − 6	7 − 7	3 +9	11 − 5
10 − 6	10 − 8	10 + 2	12 − 9	8 +4	7 +5

1. Use blue to color the boxes with answers greater than 7.

2. Use red to color the boxes with answers less than 4.

Use your counters to show each fact.
Write number sentences for each fact family.

1.

9 2
11

___ + ___ = ___

___ + ___ = ___

___ − ___ = ___

___ − ___ = ___

2.

7 5
12

___ + ___ = ___

___ + ___ = ___

___ − ___ = ___

___ − ___ = ___

More Practice Sets 2.15 and 2.16

Write the number in 3 different ways.

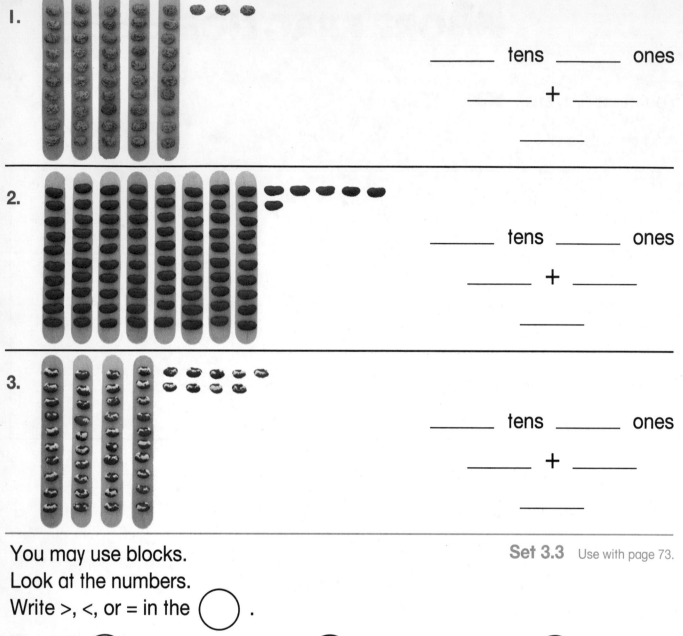

1.

_____ tens _____ ones

_____ + _____

_____

2.

_____ tens _____ ones

_____ + _____

_____

3.

_____ tens _____ ones

_____ + _____

_____

You may use blocks.
Look at the numbers.
Write >, <, or = in the ◯ .

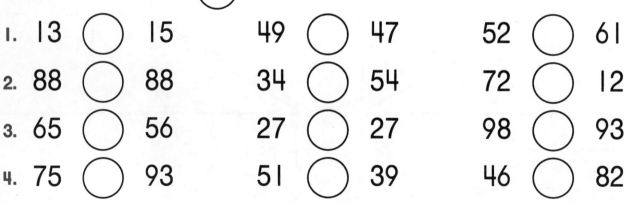

1. 13 ◯ 15   49 ◯ 47   52 ◯ 61

2. 88 ◯ 88   34 ◯ 54   72 ◯ 12

3. 65 ◯ 56   27 ◯ 27   98 ◯ 93

4. 75 ◯ 93   51 ◯ 39   46 ◯ 82

More Practice Sets 3.2 and 3.3

MORE PRACTICE

Write the missing number.

Set 3.5 Use with pages 75-76.

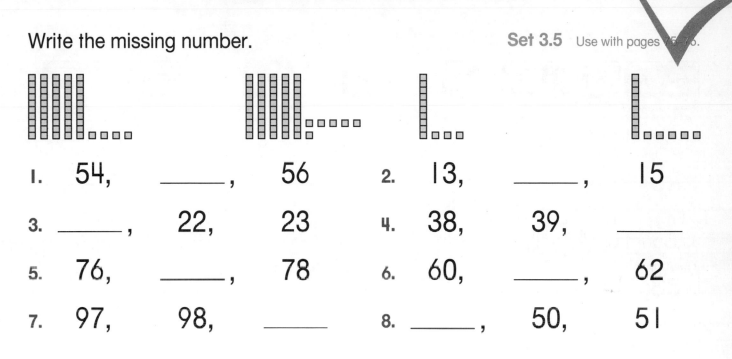

1. 54, _____, 56   2. 13, _____, 15

3. _____, 22, 23   4. 38, 39, _____

5. 76, _____, 78   6. 60, _____, 62

7. 97, 98, _____   8. _____, 50, 51

Set 3.8 Use with pages 81-82.

You need crayons.
Follow the directions.

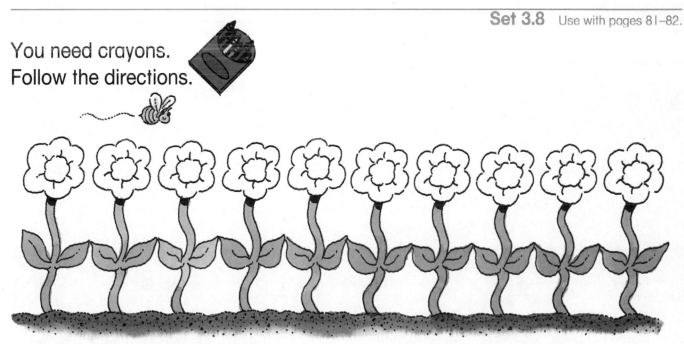

1. Color the fourth flower red.   2. Color the second flower orange.

3. Color the eighth flower yellow.   4. Color the third flower green.

5. Color the tenth flower blue.   6. Color the fifth flower purple.

More Practice Sets 3.5 and 3.8

(three hundred ninety-five) 395

You need a calculator.

Use a calculator to count. Write the missing numbers.

1. Count by 5's.

67,   72, _____, _____, _____, _____, _____

| 6 | 7 | + | 5 | = | = | = | = | = | = |

2. Count by 3's.

45, _____, _____, _____, _____, _____, _____

3. Count back by 4's.

33,   29, _____, _____, _____, _____, _____

4. Count back by 10's

93, _____, _____, _____, _____, _____, _____

Make a ten. Add. You may use counters and a ten frame.

1.

$$\begin{array}{r} 3 \\ +8 \\ \hline \end{array} \qquad \begin{array}{r} 5 \\ +7 \\ \hline \end{array} \qquad \begin{array}{r} 4 \\ +8 \\ \hline \end{array} \qquad \begin{array}{r} 6 \\ +5 \\ \hline \end{array} \qquad \begin{array}{r} 7 \\ +5 \\ \hline \end{array} \qquad \begin{array}{r} 5 \\ +10 \\ \hline \end{array}$$

2.

$$\begin{array}{r} 9 \\ +7 \\ \hline \end{array} \qquad \begin{array}{r} 5 \\ +8 \\ \hline \end{array} \qquad \begin{array}{r} 13 \\ +7 \\ \hline \end{array} \qquad \begin{array}{r} 9 \\ +6 \\ \hline \end{array} \qquad \begin{array}{r} 7 \\ +8 \\ \hline \end{array} \qquad \begin{array}{r} 8 \\ +6 \\ \hline \end{array}$$

3.

$$\begin{array}{r} 14 \\ +6 \\ \hline \end{array} \qquad \begin{array}{r} 15 \\ +5 \\ \hline \end{array} \qquad \begin{array}{r} 4 \\ +9 \\ \hline \end{array} \qquad \begin{array}{r} 5 \\ +9 \\ \hline \end{array} \qquad \begin{array}{r} 8 \\ +9 \\ \hline \end{array} \qquad \begin{array}{r} 16 \\ +4 \\ \hline \end{array}$$

MORE PRACTICE

Write the sum.
You may write a double to help you.

1.
```
    9        8        6        8
  + 8      + 8      + 7      + 7
           ----
            16
```

2.
```
    5        7        9
  + 6      + 9      + 10
```

3.
```
    7        8        6
  + 6      + 9      + 8
```

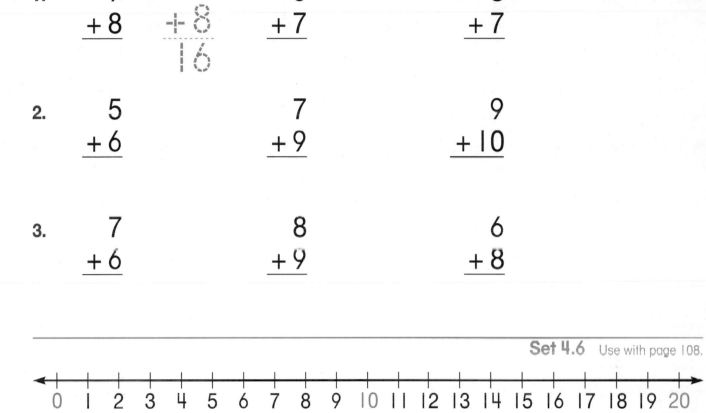

0 1 2 3 4 5 6 7 8 9 10 11 12 13 14 15 16 17 18 19 20

Subtract.
You may use the number line to count on.

1. 15 – 9 = ___   19 – 11 = ___   13 – 7 = ___

2. 20 – 14 = ___   17 – 9 = ___   14 – 6 = ___

3. 13 – 4 = ___   19 – 15 = ___   16 – 12 = ___

4.
```
    18       17       20       16       17       15
  - 15     - 13     - 16     -  8     -  8     -  7
```

More Practice Sets 4.4 and 4.6

You may use counters and a ten frame.
Subtract.

1.
$$17 - 9$$ $$14 - 6$$ $$14 - 5$$ $$13 - 6$$ $$16 - 8$$ $$12 - 9$$

2.
$$12 - 7$$ $$15 - 6$$ $$13 - 5$$ $$14 - 8$$ $$18 - 9$$ $$16 - 6$$

3.
$$11 - 3$$ $$17 - 8$$ $$15 - 7$$ $$12 - 5$$ $$16 - 9$$ $$13 - 8$$

Use your counters to show each fact.
Write number sentences for each fact family.

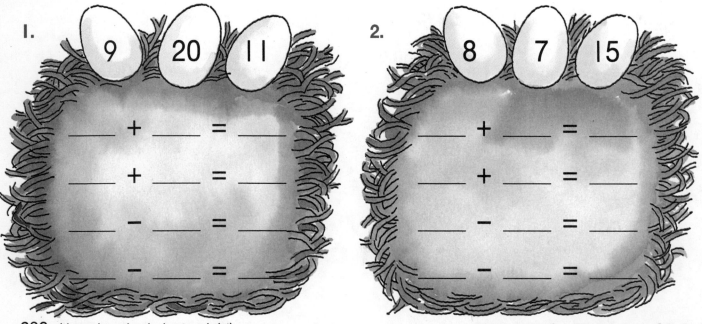

1. 9 20 11

___ + ___ = ___

___ + ___ = ___

___ − ___ = ___

___ − ___ = ___

2. 8 7 15

___ + ___ = ___

___ + ___ = ___

___ − ___ = ___

___ − ___ = ___

398 (three hundred ninety-eight)

More Practice Sets 4.7 and 4.8

MORE PRACTICE

Write addition and subtraction sentences for each number.

$$\boxed{17}$$

$$\boxed{19}$$

1. _____

_____

_____

_____

2. _____

_____

_____

_____

Count by 5's. Write the time 2 ways.

1.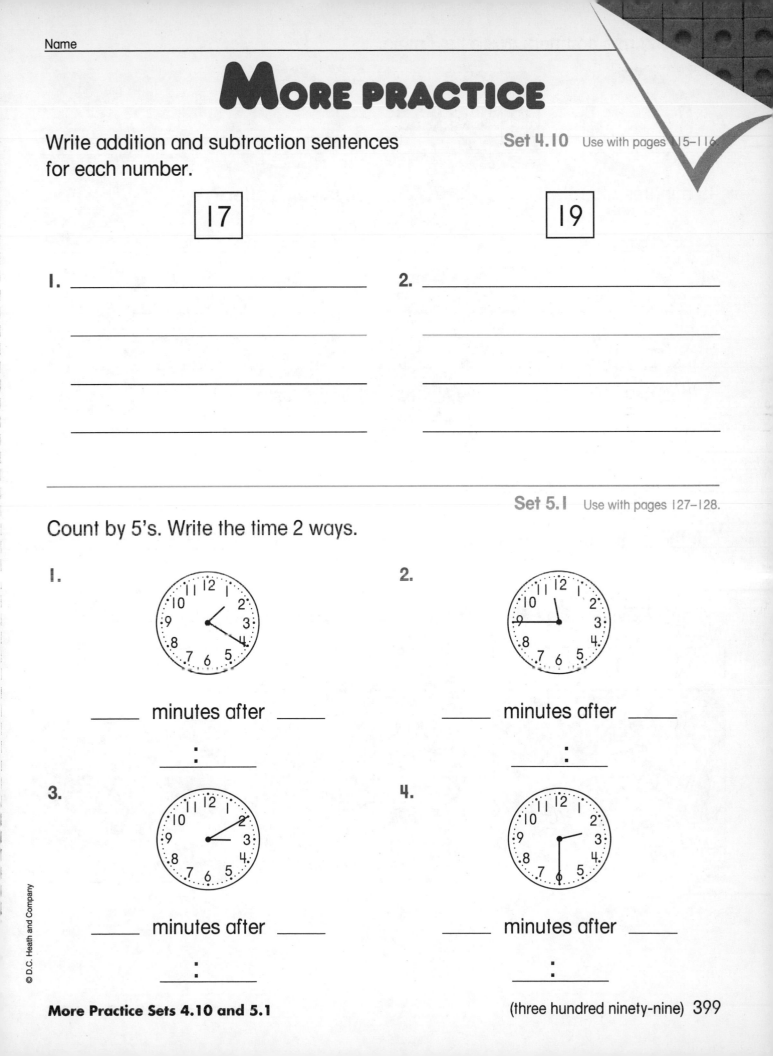

_____ minutes after _____

_____ : _____

2.

_____ minutes after _____

_____ : _____

3.

_____ minutes after _____

_____ : _____

4.

_____ minutes after _____

_____ : _____

Draw the minute hand. Write the time.

1.

45 minutes after 4

___ : ___

2.

30 minutes after 7

___ : ___

3.

half past 10

___ : ___

4.

10 minutes after 3

___ : ___

Look at the pictures of Luis's day.
Write the numbers 1 through 3 to
put the pictures in order.

7 : 00   8 : 00   1 : 00

___   ___   ___

More Practice Sets 5.2 and 5.4

MORE PRACTICE

Write both times.
Write how many hours later.

1.

_____   _____ _____ hours later

2.

_____   _____ _____ hours later

Use these pages of a calendar to answer each question.

1. What month comes just after February? _____

2. What month and date is Groundhog Day? _____

3. What month comes just before February? _____

4. In what month is New Year's Day? _____

Use coins to show each amount.

1. Show 22¢ three ways.

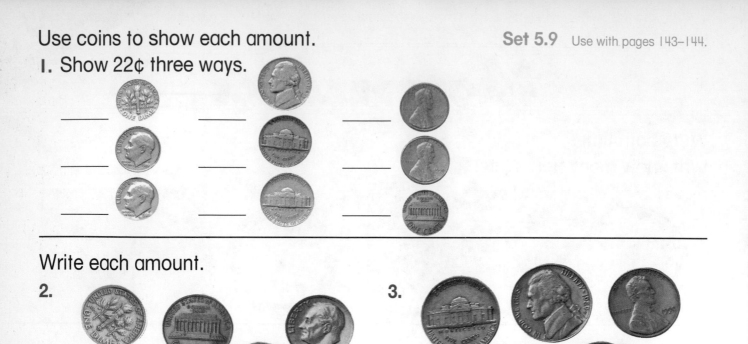

_____   _____   _____

_____   _____   _____

_____   _____   _____

Write each amount.

2.

_____ ¢

3.

_____ ¢

Write the amount.
Can you buy both items?
Estimate. Check *yes* or *no*.

1.

50¢

36¢

_____ ¢   _____ yes   _____ no

2.

67¢

12¢

_____ ¢   _____ yes   _____ no

More Practice Sets 5.9 and 5.11

MORE PRACTICE

Write the amount.
Use a dollar sign and decimal point.

1.

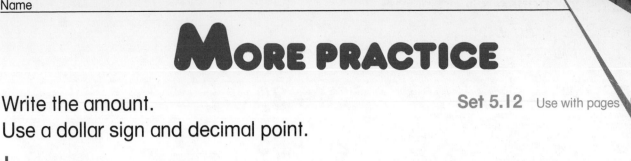

$ _____ . _____

_____

2.

$ _____ . _____

_____

Add. You may use blocks.

1. 2 + 5 = _____   20 + 50 = _____

2. 6 + 3 = _____   60 + 30 = _____

3. 4 + 2 = _____   40 + 20 = _____

4. 2 + 3 = _____   20 + 30 = _____

5. 5 + 3 = _____   50 + 30 = _____

6. 2 + 7 = _____   20 + 70 = _____

7. 4 + 5 = _____   40 + 50 = _____

8. 3 + 4 = _____   30 + 40 = _____

Add. Look for patterns.

1. $30 + 10 =$ _____

   $30 + 20 =$ _____

   $30 + 30 =$ _____

   $30 + 40 =$ _____

2. $20 + 25 =$ _____

   $20 + 30 =$ _____

   $20 + 35 =$ _____

   $20 + 40 =$ _____

3. $30 + 15 =$ _____

   $30 + 25 =$ _____

   $30 + 35 =$ _____

   $30 + 45 =$ _____

4. $25 + 10 =$ _____

   $25 + 15 =$ _____

   $25 + 20 =$ _____

   $25 + 25 =$ _____

Set 6.4 Use with pages 167–168.

You may use blocks and the tens and ones workmat.
Regroup if you can. Write how many.

1.

tens	ones

3 tens   16 ones

_____ tens   _____ ones

_____

2.

tens	ones

5 tens   12 ones

_____ tens   _____ ones

_____

3.   6 tens   10 ones

_____ tens   _____ ones

_____

4.   2 tens   19 ones

_____ tens   _____ ones

_____

More Practice Sets 6.2 and 6.4

MORE PRACTICE

Use blocks and a workmat.

Show the addends with blocks on your workmat.	Can you regroup? Circle *yes* or *no*.	Regroup if needed. Write the sum.
1. 41 + 29 =	yes no	41 + 29 = ____
2. 36 + 23 =	yes no	36 + 23 = ____
3. 37 + 35 =	yes no	37 + 35 = ____
4. 63 + 27 =	yes no	63 + 27 = ____

Add. You may use blocks.

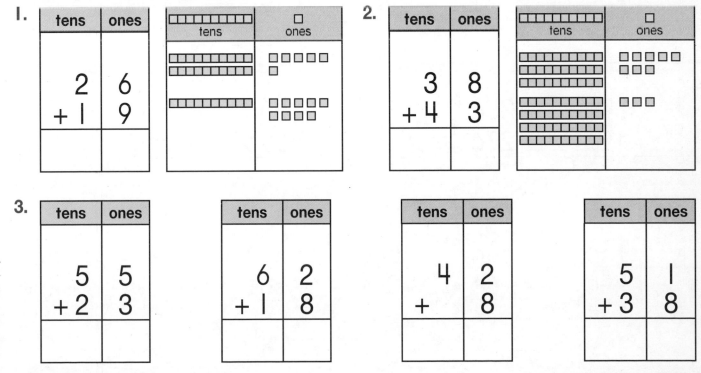

1.

tens	ones
2	6
+ 1	9

2.

tens	ones
3	8
+ 4	3

3.

tens	ones
5	5
+ 2	3

tens	ones
6	2
+ 1	8

tens	ones
4	2
+	8

tens	ones
5	1
+ 3	8

Write the sum.

1.
21	43	28	47	62	32
+37	+49	+38	+22	+ 8	+45

2.
17	56	29	57	73	76
+19	+39	+42	+32	+24	+15

3.
29	18	66	44	87	60
+58	+63	+ 7	+19	+ 5	+28

Add.

1.
53¢	75¢	26¢	44¢	62¢	17¢
+28¢	+ 9¢	+37¢	+16¢	+37¢	+38¢

2.
39¢	25¢	88¢	56¢	33¢	42¢
+15¢	+27¢	+ 6¢	+29¢	+47¢	+36¢

3.
16¢	66¢	54¢	22¢	32¢	67¢
+44¢	+ 6¢	+39¢	+58¢	+53¢	+26¢

More Practice Sets 6.7 and 6.9

MORE PRACTICE

Write the sum.

1.
32	23	18	51	23	40
16	27	14	27	34	27
+25	+15	+43	+17	+42	+15

2.
40	20	31	24	7	5
8	2	15	46	21	13
+22	+19	+36	+ 4	+39	+29

Finish each figure.

1.

square   triangle   rectangle

2.

square   triangle   rectangle

© D.C. Heath and Company

Complete each figure.

1.

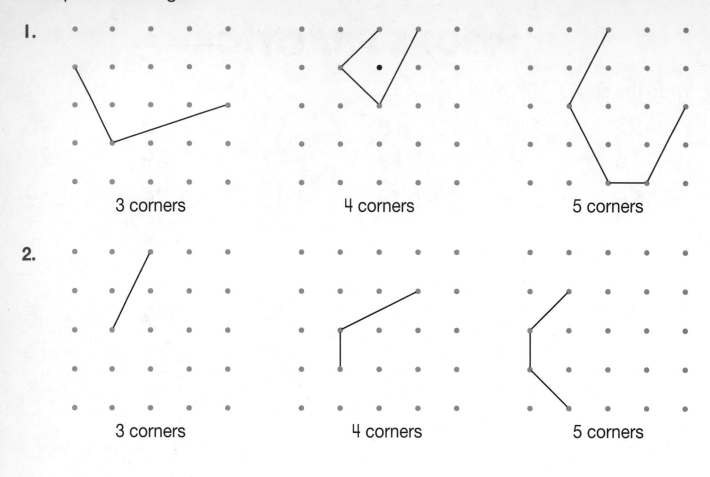

3 corners   4 corners   5 corners

2.

3 corners   4 corners   5 corners

Loop the one that is different.

1.

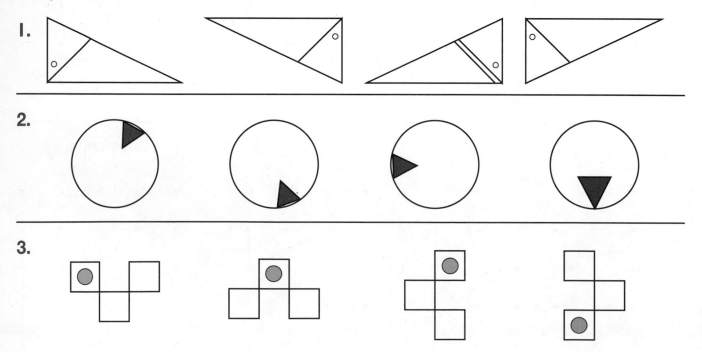

2.

3.

More Practice Sets 7.4 and 7.5

MORE PRACTICE

Draw a line of symmetry for each figure.   **Set 7.6** Use with pages 201–202.

1.

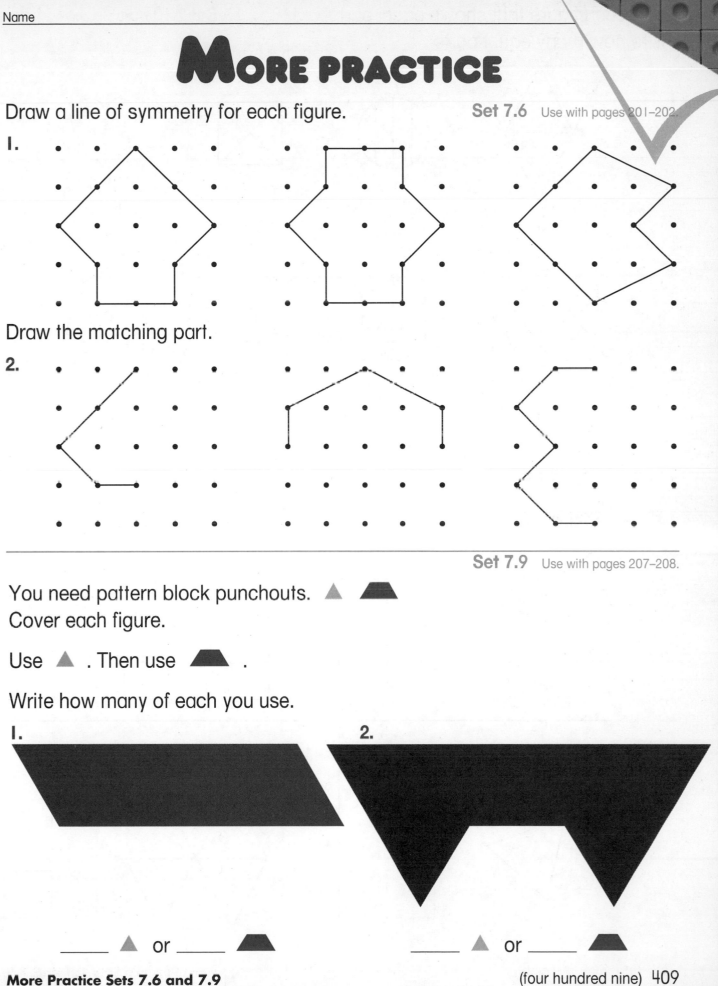

Draw the matching part.

2.

Set 7.9 Use with pages 207–208.

You need pattern block punchouts. ▲ ⬟
Cover each figure.

Use ▲ . Then use ⬟ .

Write how many of each you use.

1.

2.

_____ ▲ or _____ ⬟   _____ ▲ or _____ ⬟

More Practice Sets 7.6 and 7.9

Loop each figure that shows equal parts.
Write how many equal parts.

1.

____ ____   ____ ____   ____ ____   ____ ____

2.

____ ____   ____ ____   ____ ____   ____ ____

Color the figure to show the fraction.
Write the fraction for the shaded part.

1.   one third

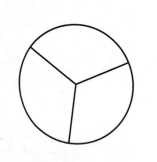

2.   one fourth

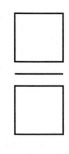

3.   one half

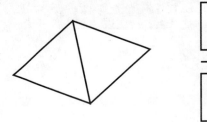

4.   one sixth

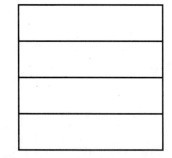
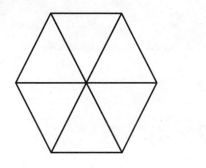

410 (four hundred ten)

More Practice Sets 7.10 and 7.12

MORE PRACTICE

You need crayons.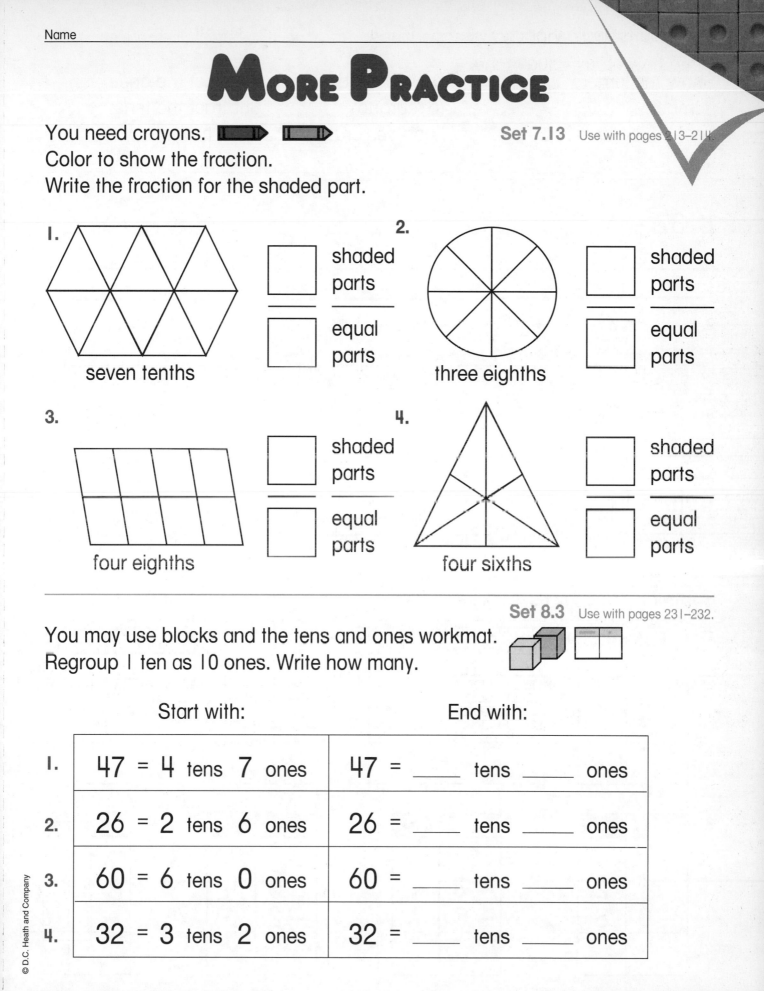
Color to show the fraction.
Write the fraction for the shaded part.

Set 7.13 Use with pages 213–214.

1.

seven tenths

⬜ shaded parts
―――
⬜ equal parts

2.

three eighths

⬜ shaded parts
―――
⬜ equal parts

3.

four eighths

⬜ shaded parts
―――
⬜ equal parts

4.

four sixths

⬜ shaded parts
―――
⬜ equal parts

Set 8.3 Use with pages 231–232.

You may use blocks and the tens and ones workmat.
Regroup 1 ten as 10 ones. Write how many.

	Start with:	End with:
1.	47 = 4 tens 7 ones	47 = ____ tens ____ ones
2.	26 = 2 tens 6 ones	26 = ____ tens ____ ones
3.	60 = 6 tens 0 ones	60 = ____ tens ____ ones
4.	32 = 3 tens 2 ones	32 = ____ tens ____ ones

More Practice Sets 7.13 and 8.3

Use blocks and a workmat.

Show the larger number. Look at the ones.	Do you need to regroup? Loop *yes* or *no*.	Subtract the ones. Subtract the tens. Write how many are left.

1. 37 – 6   yes   no   _____ are left.

2. 76 – 27   yes   no   _____ are left.

3. 85 – 78   yes   no   _____ are left.

4. 49 – 17   yes   no   _____ are left.

Subtract. You may use blocks.

1.

tens	ones
5	3
– 3	7

2.

tens	ones
4	9
– 1	5

3.

tens	ones
6	2
– 0	8

tens	ones
8	4
– 7	7

tens	ones
3	4
– 2	6

tens	ones
5	0
– 1	8

More Practice

Subtract.

1.
$$\begin{array}{r} 71 \\ -19 \\ \hline \end{array}\qquad \begin{array}{r} 50 \\ -35 \\ \hline \end{array}\qquad \begin{array}{r} 88 \\ -22 \\ \hline \end{array}\qquad \begin{array}{r} 67 \\ -\ 7 \\ \hline \end{array}\qquad \begin{array}{r} 43 \\ -16 \\ \hline \end{array}\qquad \begin{array}{r} 95 \\ -48 \\ \hline \end{array}$$

2.
$$\begin{array}{r} 33 \\ -\ 4 \\ \hline \end{array}\qquad \begin{array}{r} 29 \\ -15 \\ \hline \end{array}\qquad \begin{array}{r} 76 \\ -47 \\ \hline \end{array}\qquad \begin{array}{r} 52 \\ -25 \\ \hline \end{array}\qquad \begin{array}{r} 60 \\ -31 \\ \hline \end{array}\qquad \begin{array}{r} 41 \\ -26 \\ \hline \end{array}$$

3.
$$\begin{array}{r} 90 \\ -53 \\ \hline \end{array}\qquad \begin{array}{r} 74 \\ -20 \\ \hline \end{array}\qquad \begin{array}{r} 31 \\ -16 \\ \hline \end{array}\qquad \begin{array}{r} 42 \\ -39 \\ \hline \end{array}\qquad \begin{array}{r} 62 \\ -60 \\ \hline \end{array}\qquad \begin{array}{r} 71 \\ -17 \\ \hline \end{array}$$

Look for a pattern. Write the differences.

1.
$$\begin{array}{r} 44 \\ -23 \\ \hline \end{array}\qquad \begin{array}{r} 45 \\ -24 \\ \hline \end{array}\qquad \begin{array}{r} 46 \\ -25 \\ \hline \end{array}\qquad \begin{array}{r} 47 \\ -26 \\ \hline \end{array}\qquad \begin{array}{r} 48 \\ -27 \\ \hline \end{array}\qquad \begin{array}{r} 49 \\ -28 \\ \hline \end{array}$$

2.
$$\begin{array}{r} 21 \\ -\ 5 \\ \hline \end{array}\qquad \begin{array}{r} 31 \\ -15 \\ \hline \end{array}\qquad \begin{array}{r} 41 \\ -25 \\ \hline \end{array}\qquad \begin{array}{r} 51 \\ -35 \\ \hline \end{array}\qquad \begin{array}{r} 61 \\ -45 \\ \hline \end{array}\qquad \begin{array}{r} 71 \\ -55 \\ \hline \end{array}$$

3.
$$\begin{array}{r} 50 \\ -32 \\ \hline \end{array}\qquad \begin{array}{r} 50 \\ -33 \\ \hline \end{array}\qquad \begin{array}{r} 50 \\ -34 \\ \hline \end{array}\qquad \begin{array}{r} 50 \\ -35 \\ \hline \end{array}\qquad \begin{array}{r} 50 \\ -36 \\ \hline \end{array}\qquad \begin{array}{r} 50 \\ -37 \\ \hline \end{array}$$

Subtract. You may use coins.

1.
$$75¢ - 15¢$$
$$53¢ - 37¢$$
$$80¢ - 42¢$$
$$31¢ - 8¢$$
$$98¢ - 59¢$$
$$44¢ - 26¢$$

2.
$$67¢ - 58¢$$
$$85¢ - 24¢$$
$$72¢ - 33¢$$
$$56¢ - 12¢$$
$$22¢ - 9¢$$
$$94¢ - 47¢$$

3.
$$84¢ - 25¢$$
$$73¢ - 36¢$$
$$50¢ - 29¢$$
$$75¢ - 72¢$$
$$99¢ - 65¢$$
$$60¢ - 53¢$$

Add or Subtract.

1.
$$89 - 73$$
$$76 + 15$$
$$58 + 27$$
$$64 - 33$$
$$49 - 28$$
$$79 + 3$$

2.
$$91 + 8$$
$$69 - 26$$
$$99 - 87$$
$$75 + 16$$
$$62 + 29$$
$$67 - 27$$

3.
$$22 + 33$$
$$45 - 31$$
$$72 + 8$$
$$98 - 6$$
$$48 - 24$$
$$34 + 18$$

MORE PRACTICE

You need an inch ruler. 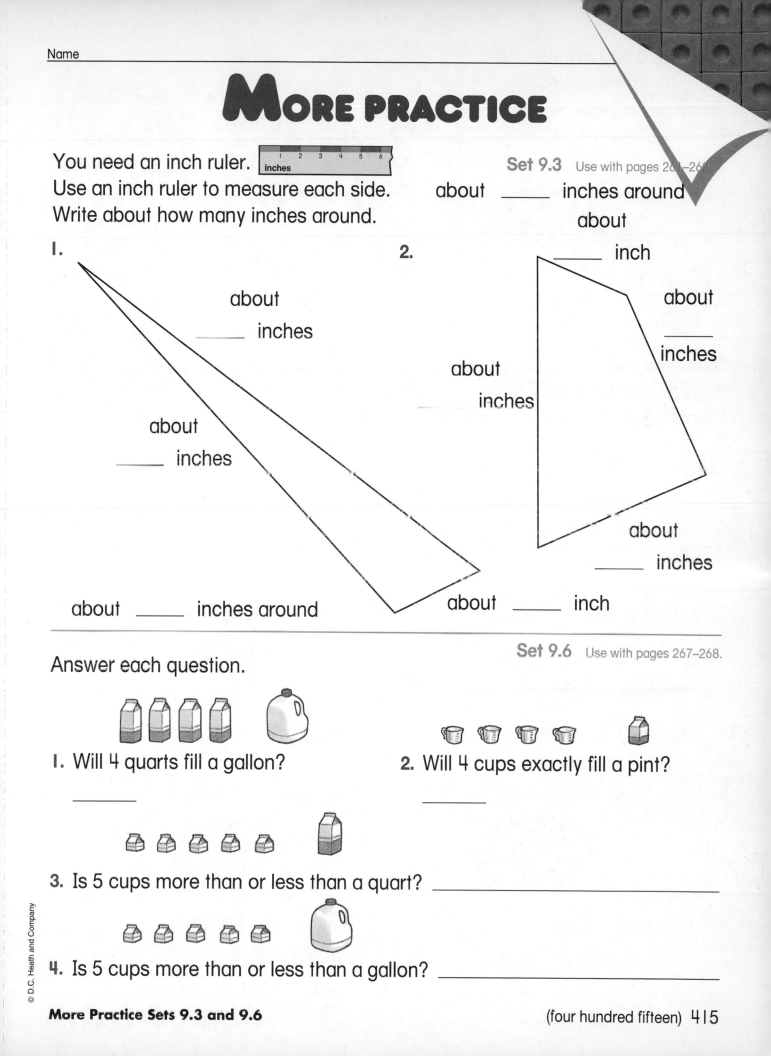 inches 1 2 3 4 5 6

Use an inch ruler to measure each side.
Write about how many inches around.

Set 9.3 Use with pages 261–262.

about _____ inches around

1.

about
_____ inches

about
_____ inches

about _____ inches around

2.

about
_____ inch

about
_____ inches

about
_____ inches

about
_____ inches

about _____ inch

Set 9.6 Use with pages 267–268.

Answer each question.

1. Will 4 quarts fill a gallon?

_____

2. Will 4 cups exactly fill a pint?

_____

3. Is 5 cups more than or less than a quart? _____

4. Is 5 cups more than or less than a gallon? _____

You need a centimeter ruler.
Loop the best estimate.
Then use a centimeter ruler to measure.

Estimate:
about 4 centimeters
about 6 centimeters

Measure:
about _____ centimeters

Estimate:
about 4 centimeters
about 6 centimeters

Measure: about _____ centimeters

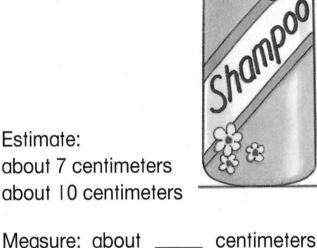

Estimate:
about 7 centimeters
about 10 centimeters

Measure: about _____ centimeters

A base bag is about 1 kilogram.
Loop the best estimate.

1.

less than 1 kilogram
about 1 kilogram
more than 1 kilogram

2.

less than 1 kilogram
about 1 kilogram
more than 1 kilogram

3.

less than 1 kilogram
about 1 kilogram
more than 1 kilogram

4.

less than 1 kilogram
about 1 kilogram
more than 1 kilogram

More Practice Sets 9.9 and 9.11

MORE PRACTICE

Write how many.
Write the product.

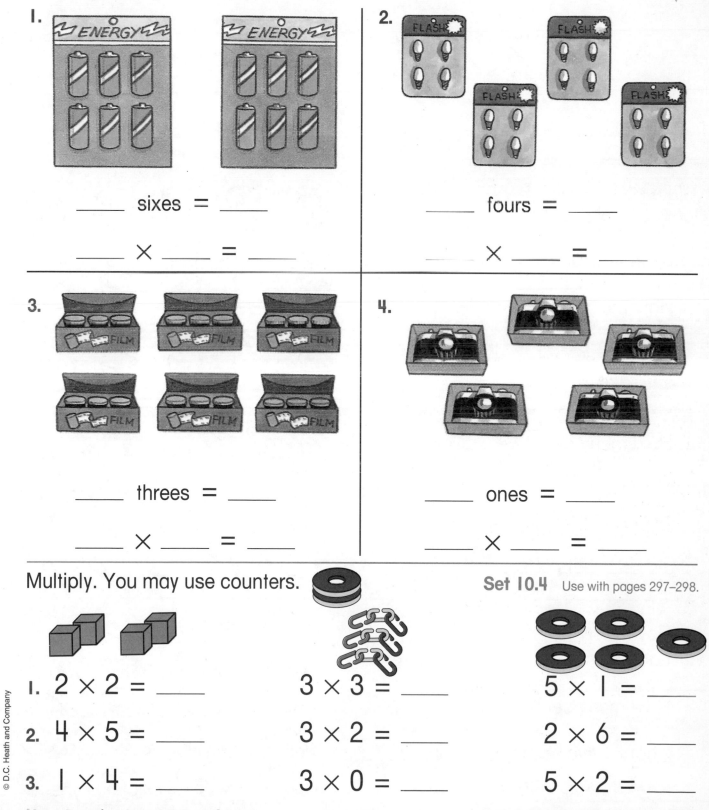

1.

_____ sixes = _____

_____ × _____ = _____

2.

_____ fours = _____

_____ × _____ = _____

3.

_____ threes = _____

_____ × _____ = _____

4.

_____ ones = _____

_____ × _____ = _____

Multiply. You may use counters.

1. $2 \times 2 =$ _____ $3 \times 3 =$ _____ $5 \times 1 =$ _____

2. $4 \times 5 =$ _____ $3 \times 2 =$ _____ $2 \times 6 =$ _____

3. $1 \times 4 =$ _____ $3 \times 0 =$ _____ $5 \times 2 =$ _____

Write the product.

1.
$$\begin{array}{r} 2 \\ \times 6 \\ \hline \end{array}$$
$$\begin{array}{r} 3 \\ \times 2 \\ \hline \end{array}$$
$$\begin{array}{r} 3 \\ \times 3 \\ \hline \end{array}$$
$$\begin{array}{r} 4 \\ \times 5 \\ \hline \end{array}$$
$$\begin{array}{r} 9 \\ \times 2 \\ \hline \end{array}$$
$$\begin{array}{r} 5 \\ \times 3 \\ \hline \end{array}$$

2.
$$\begin{array}{r} 0 \\ \times 9 \\ \hline \end{array}$$
$$\begin{array}{r} 2 \\ \times 5 \\ \hline \end{array}$$
$$\begin{array}{r} 5 \\ \times 5 \\ \hline \end{array}$$
$$\begin{array}{r} 3 \\ \times 4 \\ \hline \end{array}$$
$$\begin{array}{r} 6 \\ \times 3 \\ \hline \end{array}$$
$$\begin{array}{r} 4 \\ \times 4 \\ \hline \end{array}$$

Write how many.

1. How many cups? _____
   Loop sets of 5.

   How many sets? _____

   _____ sets of _____ in _____

2. How many bats? _____
   Loop sets of 3.

   How many sets? _____

   _____ sets of _____ in _____

3. How many balloons? _____
   Loop sets of 4.

   How many sets? _____

   _____ sets of _____ in _____

418 (four hundred eighteen)   **More Practice Sets 10.6 and 10.9**

MORE PRACTICE

You need counters.
Write how many.

1. Use 23 counters.
   Make 4 equal sets.

   How many in each set? _____

   How many left over? _____

2. Use 16 counters.
   Make 5 equal sets.

   How many in each set? _____

   How many left over? _____

3. Use 10 counters.
   Make 2 equal sets.

   How many in each set? _____

   How many left over? _____

4. Use 21 counters.
   Make 4 equal sets.

   How many in each set? _____

   How many left over? _____

Solve each problem.

1. Wally has 16 marbles. He drops
   one half of them on the way
   home. How many marbles does

   Wally drop? _____ marbles

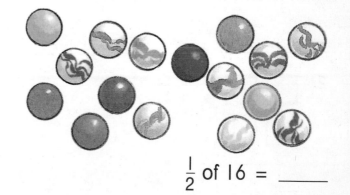

$\frac{1}{2}$ of 16 = _____

---

2. Tessa had 12 raisins.
   She ate one half of them
   with her cereal. How many
   raisins does Tessa have left?

   _____ raisins

$\frac{1}{2}$ of 12 = _____

Write how many hundreds, tens, and ones.
Write the number.

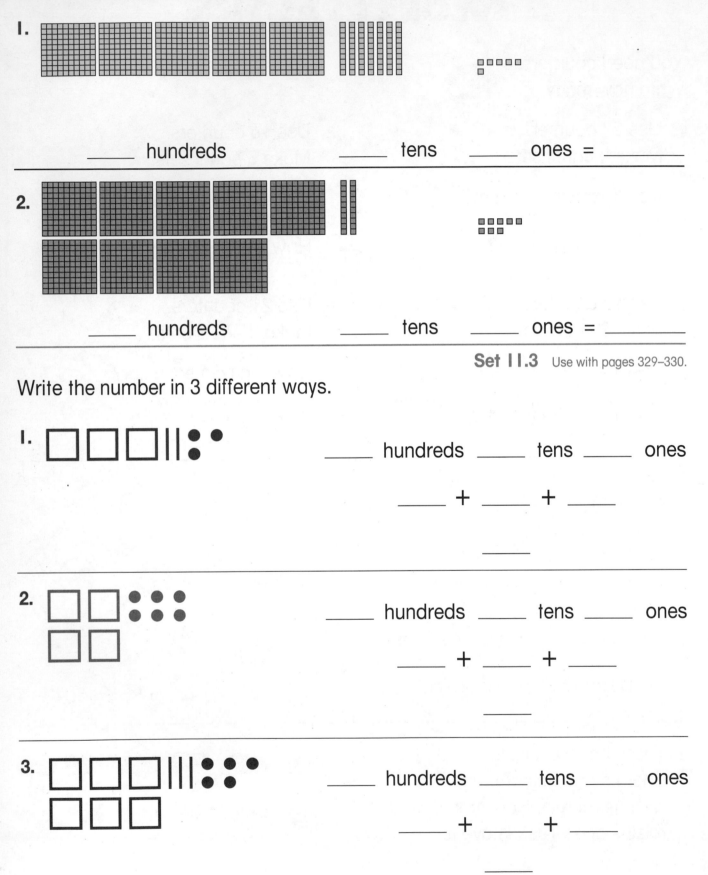

1.

_____ hundreds   _____ tens   _____ ones = _____

2.

_____ hundreds   _____ tens   _____ ones = _____

Write the number in 3 different ways.

1.

_____ hundreds _____ tens _____ ones

_____ + _____ + _____

_____

2.

_____ hundreds _____ tens _____ ones

_____ + _____ + _____

_____

3.

_____ hundreds _____ tens _____ ones

_____ + _____ + _____

_____

MORE PRACTICE

Draw a picture for each number.
Write < or > in each ◯.

1.

436 ◯ 278

2.

123 ◯ 125

3.

291 ◯ 219

4.

354 ◯ 367

Write the missing number.

	Just Before	Between	Just After
1.	599	_____	601
2.	_____	111	112
3.	998	999	_____

Write the missing numbers.

4. 673, _____, _____, _____, 677, _____, _____, 680

5. 399, 400, _____, _____, _____, 404, _____, _____

Count by $1.00. Write the amounts.

Set 11.7 Use with pages 337–338.

1. Start with:

$0.25, $1.25, $___.___, $___.___, $___.___, $___.___

Continue the pattern.

2. 800, 795, 790, _____, _____, _____, _____

3. 240, 260, 280, _____, _____, _____, _____

4. 620, 610, 600, _____, _____, _____, _____

5. 68, 79, 90, _____, _____, _____, _____

Set 12.3 Use with pages 355–356.

Write the sum. You may use blocks.

1.

hundreds	tens	ones
6	6	1
+2	7	5

hundreds	tens	ones
3	5	9
+	2	2

hundreds	tens	ones
7	0	8
+	5	2

2.

hundreds	tens	ones
7	2	6
+	5	4

hundreds	tens	ones
6	1	6
+1	9	2

hundreds	tens	ones
5	4	9
+2	2	5

More Practice Sets 11.7 and 12.3

MORE PRACTICE

Add.

1.
$$\begin{array}{r} 428 \\ + \ 87 \\ \hline \end{array}$$
$$\begin{array}{r} 233 \\ + 719 \\ \hline \end{array}$$
$$\begin{array}{r} 567 \\ + \ 54 \\ \hline \end{array}$$
$$\begin{array}{r} 185 \\ + 205 \\ \hline \end{array}$$
$$\begin{array}{r} 641 \\ + 168 \\ \hline \end{array}$$

2.
$$\begin{array}{r} 352 \\ + 429 \\ \hline \end{array}$$
$$\begin{array}{r} 777 \\ + \ 66 \\ \hline \end{array}$$
$$\begin{array}{r} 290 \\ + 132 \\ \hline \end{array}$$
$$\begin{array}{r} 126 \\ + 431 \\ \hline \end{array}$$
$$\begin{array}{r} 198 \\ + 703 \\ \hline \end{array}$$

3.
$$\begin{array}{r} 815 \\ + \ 49 \\ \hline \end{array}$$
$$\begin{array}{r} 74 \\ +38 \\ \hline \end{array}$$
$$\begin{array}{r} 527 \\ + 172 \\ \hline \end{array}$$
$$\begin{array}{r} 906 \\ + \ 73 \\ \hline \end{array}$$
$$\begin{array}{r} 431 \\ + 169 \\ \hline \end{array}$$

Write the sum.

1.
$$\begin{array}{r} \$2.37 \\ + \ 1.95 \\ \hline \end{array}$$
$$\begin{array}{r} \$0.88 \\ + \ 0.51 \\ \hline \end{array}$$
$$\begin{array}{r} \$5.06 \\ + \ 2.94 \\ \hline \end{array}$$
$$\begin{array}{r} \$3.59 \\ + \ 1.46 \\ \hline \end{array}$$
$$\begin{array}{r} \$4.15 \\ + \ 2.63 \\ \hline \end{array}$$

2.
$$\begin{array}{r} \$6.42 \\ + \ 0.69 \\ \hline \end{array}$$
$$\begin{array}{r} \$1.19 \\ + \ 1.19 \\ \hline \end{array}$$
$$\begin{array}{r} \$7.26 \\ + \ 1.78 \\ \hline \end{array}$$
$$\begin{array}{r} \$0.49 \\ + \ 0.27 \\ \hline \end{array}$$
$$\begin{array}{r} \$2.53 \\ + \ 2.76 \\ \hline \end{array}$$

Add.

1.
$$456 \atop + 139$$
$$508 \atop + 72$$
$$614 \atop + 327$$
$$756 \atop + 158$$
$$718 \atop + 79$$

2.
$$398 \atop + 281$$
$$425 \atop + 65$$
$$79 \atop + 89$$
$$384 \atop + 438$$
$$826 \atop + 75$$

3.
$$500 \atop + 200$$
$$608 \atop + 64$$
$$445 \atop + 25$$
$$781 \atop + 169$$
$$654 \atop + 237$$

Write the difference.
You may use blocks.

1.

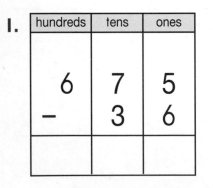

hundreds	tens	ones
6	7	5
–	3	6

hundreds	tens	ones
7	2	1
– 1	5	4

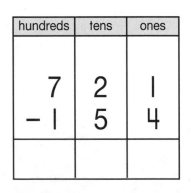

hundreds	tens	ones
9	8	2
– 4	6	7

2.

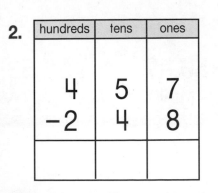

hundreds	tens	ones
4	5	7
–2	4	8

hundreds	tens	ones
3	4	9
– 1	7	2

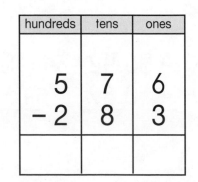

hundreds	tens	ones
5	7	6
– 2	8	3

More Practice Sets 12.6 and 12.10

MORE PRACTICE

Subtract.

1.
```
   562      923      491      687      345
  -275     -617     - 36     -542     -267
```

2.
```
   734      819      947      888      576
  - 85     -698     -379     - 99     -357
```

3.
```
   642      992      726      221      487
  -148     -367     -382     -158     - 45
```

Subtract.

1.
```
   807      600      709      860      900
  - 48     -247     -156     -307     -309
```

2.
```
   609      630      700      902      302
  -527     -427     -346     -506     -248
```

3.
```
   602      940      300      509      800
  -320     -206     -204     -400     -299
```

More Practice Sets 12.11 and 12.12   (four hundred twenty-five) 425

Write the difference.

1. $6.39 $4.07 $3.25 $7.46 $5.02
   – 2.75   – 1.28   – 0.89   – 2.07   – 1.05

2. $8.63 $2.31 $7.89 $4.28 $6.00
   – 0.79   – 1.53   – 3.36   – 2.37   – 0.96

3. $6.14 $4.50 $7.39 $4.08 $8.23
   – 2.82   – 3.99   – 4.65   – 1.92   – 2.99

Add or subtract.
Loop exercises you can do in your head.

1.   200   899   763   500   600
   + 300   –799   + 149   – 39   –200

2.   258   230   436   922   436
   –158   + 700   + 436   – 44   + 279

3.   709   555   788   603   959
   –451   + 11   –333   –208   –956

addend $4 + 3 = 7$

↑ ↑
addends

between 14   15   16

The number 15 is between 14 and 16.

calculator

centimeter   a metric unit of length
100 centimeters equals 1 meter.

centimeter ruler

0 1 2 3 4 5 6 7 8 9 10 11 12 13 14 15 16 17 18 19 20
centimeter/ decimeter

cone

corner
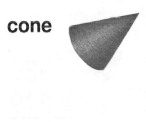

count on   2 . . . 3, 4, 5.

Count on from 2.

cube

cup   a customary unit of capacity
2 cups equal 1 pint.

cylinder

decimal point (.) $5.32

↑
decimal point

decimeter   a metric unit of length
10 centimeters equals 1 decimeter.

0 1 2 3 4 5 6 7 8 9 10 11 12 13 14 15
centimeter/ decimeter

degree Fahrenheit (°F)   the
customary scale of measuring
temperature

 The temperature is 75°F.

difference   12 − 5 = 7

↑
difference

dime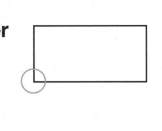

PICTURE GLOSSARY

division sign (÷) $12 \div 4 = 3$

division sign

dollar

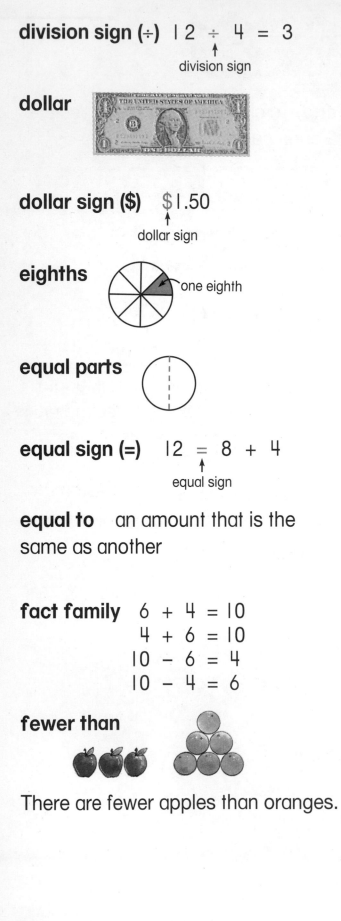

dollar sign ($) $\$1.50$

dollar sign

eighths

one eighth

equal parts

equal sign (=) $12 = 8 + 4$

equal sign

equal to an amount that is the same as another

fact family
$6 + 4 = 10$
$4 + 6 = 10$
$10 - 6 = 4$
$10 - 4 = 6$

fewer than

There are fewer apples than oranges.

foot a customary unit of length 12 inches equal 1 foot.

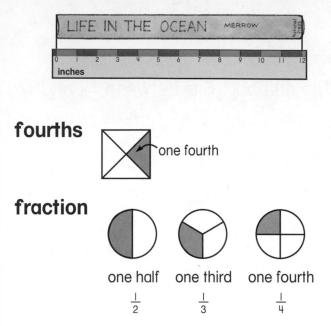

fourths

one fourth

fraction

one half   one third   one fourth

$\frac{1}{2}$ $\frac{1}{3}$ $\frac{1}{4}$

gallon a customary unit of capacity 4 quarts equal 1 gallon.

graph a picture that shows information

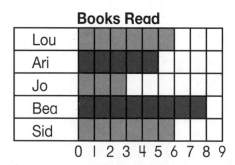

Books Read

Lou		
Ari		
Jo		
Bea		
Sid		

0 1 2 3 4 5 6 7 8 9

greater than (>)

$32 > 23$

The number 32 is greater than 23.

greatest

Ten is the greatest number.

6, 7, 8, 9, **10**

half dollar

half past thirty minutes after the hour

half past 12

halves

one half

hour sixty minutes

hour hand

hour hand

inch a customary unit of length
12 inches equal 1 foot.

inches

inch ruler a ruler marked in inches

inches

just after 14   15   16

The number 15 is just after 14.

just before 14   15   16

The number 14 comes just before 15.

kilogram a metric unit of mass
3 potatoes are about 1 kilogram.

least Three is the least number.

3, 4, 5, 6

less than (<) 23 < 32

The number 23 is less than 32.

line of symmetry

The two parts match.
The dashed line is a line of symmetry.

liter a metric unit of capacity

1 LITER

meter a metric unit of length
100 centimeters equal 1 meter.

meter

minus   to subtract

minute hand   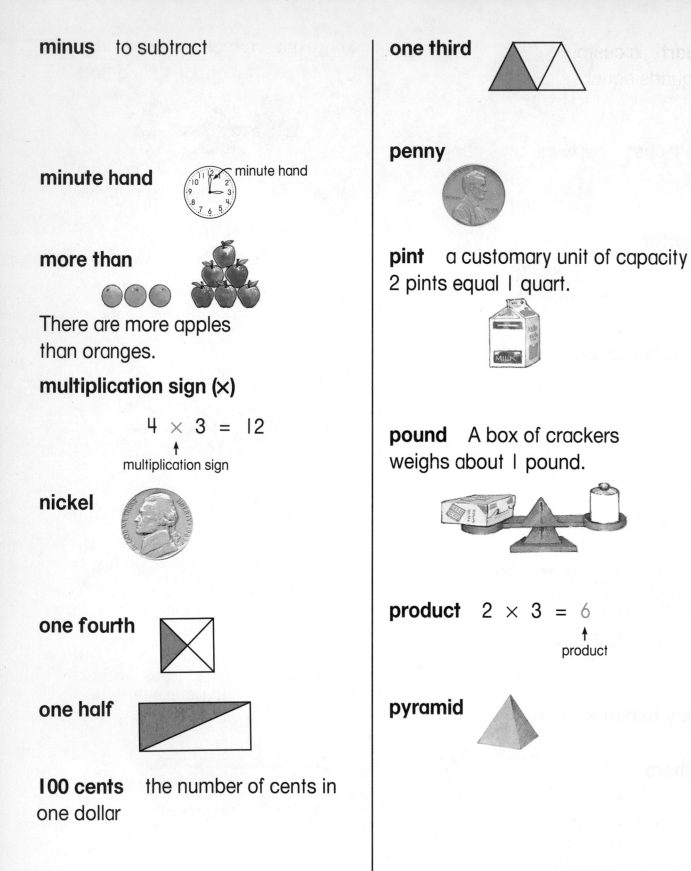minute hand

more than

There are more apples than oranges.

multiplication sign (×)

$$4 \times 3 = 12$$

↑
multiplication sign

nickel

one fourth

one half

100 cents   the number of cents in one dollar

one third

penny

pint   a customary unit of capacity 2 pints equal 1 quart.

pound   A box of crackers weighs about 1 pound.

product $2 \times 3 = 6$

↑
product

pyramid

quart a customary unit of capacity
4 quarts equal 1 gallon.

1 quart

quarter

rectangular prism

side

sixths

one sixth

sixty minutes one hour

sphere

square

sum $4 + 3 = 7$

↑
sum

temperature

cold   warm   hot

thermometer a tool used to
measure temperature

thirds

one third

30 minutes after half past
the hour

30 minutes
after 10

two eighths

two eighths

yard a customary unit of length
3 feet equal 1 yard.

0 feet   1   2   3

yardstick a ruler marked in feet
and yards

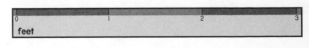

0 feet   1   2   3

CREDITS

The publisher would also like to thank Stride Rite Children's Group, Inc., Boston, MA; Pearle Vision Center, Burlington, MA; Belmont Medical Supply, Belmont, MA; Professional Hearing Center, Brookline, MA; Bread and Circus, Wellesley, MA; Bridge School and Clarke Middle School, Lexington, MA; and Melrose Middle School, Melrose, MA.

Revision Designer Cathy Reynolds
Revision Photo Research Nina Whitney

Illustration Credits

Evelyn Allert: **320, 348.** Maxi Chambliss: **349, 350, 352, 353, 356, 358, 359, 360, 361, 363, 364, 366, 367, 370, 372, 375, 376, 378, 380, 381.** Betsy Day: **190, 192, 194, 195, 225, 230, 234, 235, 237, 239, 241, 243, 244, 245, 247, 248.** Nancy Didion: **159, 160, 162, 163, 164, 165, 166, 167, 172, 173, 174, 175, 177, 178, 179, 180, 181, 182, 183, 184, 185.** Allan Eitzen: **121, 122 (t), 155, 319.** James Graham Hale: **216.** Lydia Halverson: **1, 2, 3, 4, 5, 6, 7, 8, 9, 10, 11, 12, 13, 14, 15, 16, 17, 18, 21, 22.** Josh Hayes: **Calculators.** Meryl Henderson: **223, 255, 256, 257, 258, 259, 260, 261, 262, 263, 264, 265, 266, 267, 268, 269, 270, 271, 273, 274, 275, 276, 277, 278, 280, 281, 282, 283, 284, 286, 383, 384, 391, 392, 397, 399, 400.** Jennifer Hewitson: **122 (b), 156.** Dennis Hockerman: **125, 126, 127, 128, 129, 130, 131, 132, 133, 134, 135, 137, 138, 139, 140, 141, 142, 150, 153, 191, 193, 197, 198, 199, 201, 202, 203, 217, 218.** Susan Jaekel: **67, 68, 69, 70, 71, 72, 73, 74, 75, 77, 79, 80, 81, 82, 83, 85, 88, 93.** Dora Leder: **289, 290, 291, 292, 293, 294, 296, 297, 298, 299, 300, 301, 302, 303, 304, 305, 306, 307, 308, 310, 311, 312, 313, 314, 315, 316, 317, BM.** Kathy McCord: **91, 92, 288, 348.** Cindy Patrick: **387.** Laura Rader: **28, 30, 31, 32, 33, 34, 35, 36, 37, 39, 40, 41, 42, 45, 46, 48, 50, 51, 52, 53, 54, 56, 57, 58, 59, 60, 393.** Marci Dunn Ramsey: **63, 64, 345, 346.** Paul Richer: **BM.** Karen Schmidt: **24, 221, 251, 252.** George Ulrich: **70, 279 (b), 395, 398, 400, 401, BM.** Marsha Winborn: **95, 96, 97, 101, 102, 103, 105, 106, 107, 108, 111, 112, 114, 115, 117, 118, 120.** Lane Yerkes: **324, 326, 329, 332, 333, 335, 336, 337, 338, 341, 342, 343, 345.**

Photo Credits

i: Arie deZanger, © D.C. Heath. **iii:** Kevin Thomas, © D.C. Heath. **v, vi, ix, x:** © Nancy Sheehan. **vii, xiii:** Nancy Sheehan, © D.C. Heath and Company. **14:** Paolo Koch (Photo Researchers). **19:** Mark E. Gibson (The Stock Market). **20:** James Steinberg (Photo Researchers). **23:** Kevin Thomas. **26, 29, 33:** John Lei (Omni-Photo Communications, Inc.). **43, 47:** Michal Heron. **48:** John Lei (Omni-Photo Communications, Inc.). **49:** Michal Heron. **57:** Nancy Sheehan. **62:** l W. Theriot (H. Armstrong Roberts); r Steve Niedorf (The Image Bank). **63:** Stephen Whalen/ Zephyr Pictures. **72, 78, 85, 86:** John Lei (Omni-Photo Communications, Inc.). **87:** Nancy Sheehan.

88: H. Armstrong Roberts. **90, 94:** John Lei (Omni-Photo Communications, Inc.). **98:** l J. Carmichael, Jr. (The Image Bank); r Chris Rogers (The Stock Market). **99:** Michal Heron. **100:** Earl Roberge (Photo Researchers). **104:** l (H. Armstrong Roberts); r Pete Turner (The Image Bank). **110:** t Bill Stanton (The Stock Market). **111:** Nancy Sheehan. **116:** John Lei (Omni-Photo Communications, Inc.). **119:** t Mike Yamashita (Woodfin Camp); c Bill Ross (Woodfin Camp); b Bob Daemmrich. **120:** Nick Koudis (The Stock Market). **127, 131:** Nancy Sheehan. **132:** John Lei (Omni-Photo Communications, Inc.). **136:** Brownie Harris (The Stock Market). **141:** Nancy Sheehan. **143, 144, 145, 146, 147, 148:** John Lei (Omni-Photo Communications, Inc.). **149:** t John Lei (Omni-Photo Communications, Inc.); b Jeffrey W. Myers (The Stock Market). **150, 152, 154:** John Lei (Omni-Photo Communications, Inc.). **155:** The San Diego Musuem of Man. Photo Stephen Whalen/ Zephyr Pictures. **163, 170:** John Lei (Omni-Photo Communications, Inc.). **171:** Nancy Sheehan. **177:** Ken O'Donoghue. **185:** Ernest Manewal (FPG). **186:** l Michal Heron; r John Lei (Omni-Photo Communications, Inc.). **188, 189, 192, 193, 200:** John Lei (Omni-Photo Communications, Inc.). **205:** Nancy Sheehan. **206:** (FPG). **207:** Nancy Sheehan. **213:** Michal Heron. **216:** Karen Halverson Gilborn (Omni-Photo Communications, Inc.). **217, 218, 219, 224, 229:** John Lei (Omni-Photo Communications, Inc.). **236:** l J. Brenneis (FPG); lc, rc, r Norman Owen Tomalin (Bruce Coleman). **242:** l Len Rue, Jr. (Photo Researchers); c Bill Bachman (Photo Researchers); r Yvonne Freund (National Audubon Society/Photo Researchers). **249:** Jim Brandenburg (Woodfin Camp); inset Jim W. Grace (Photo Researchers). **250:** l and r John Lei (Omni-Photo Communications, Inc.); c Coco McCoy (Rainbow). **254:** Michal Heron. **256:** John Lei (Omni-Photo Communications, Inc.). **263:** Nancy Sheehan. **267, 268:** John Lei (Omni-Photo Communications, Inc.). **272:** l Walter Bibikow (The Image Bank). **275:** Nancy Sheehan. **279:** Ken O'Donoghue. **282:** t Adolf Schmidecker (FPG); b Michel Tcherevkoff (The Image Bank). **283:** John Lei (Omni-Photo Communications, Inc.). **284:** t John Lei (Omni-Photo Communications, Inc.); lb George Obremski (The Image Bank); rb G. K. & Vikki Hart (The Image Bank). **291:** John Lei (Omni-Photo Communications, Inc.). **293:** t Michal Heron; b Murray & Associates (The Stock Market). **297:** Bror Karlsson (Omni-Photo Communications, Inc.). **302:** Hamilton Smith (FPG); Tony Freeman (Photo Edit). **303:** Lea (Omni-Photo Communications, Inc.). **309:** Lee Balterman (FPG). **313, 314, 318:** John Lei (Omni-Photo Communications, Inc.). **320:** t Michal Heron; b John Lei (Omni-Photo Communications, Inc.). **321, 337, 338:** John Lei (Omni-Photo Communications, Inc.). **339, 340:** Nancy Sheehan.,© D.C. Heath and Company, **342, 343, 344:** John Lei (Omni-Photo Communications, Inc.). **345:** The San Diego Musum of Man. Photo Stephen Whalen/ Zephyr Pictures. **357:** Grant Faint (The Image Bank). **370:** John Lei (Omni-Photo Communications, Inc.). **377:** MacDonald Photography (The Picture Cube). **381:** Frank Siteman (The Picture Cube). **382:** t Michal Heron; b John Lei (Omni-Photo Communications, Inc.). **394, 402, 403, 422, 427, 428, 429, 430, 431:** John Lei (Omni-Photo Communications, Inc.). **Punchout Photography:** John Lei (Omni-Photo Communications, Inc.).

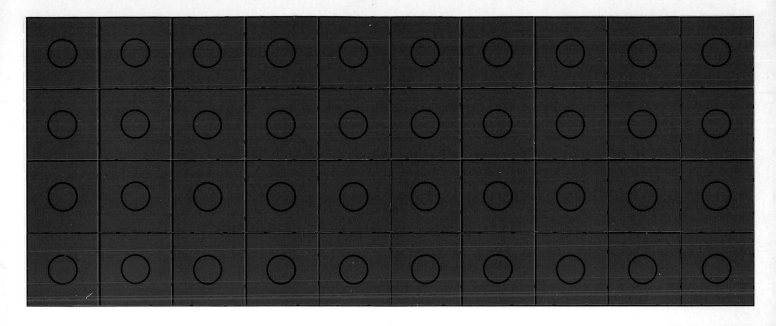

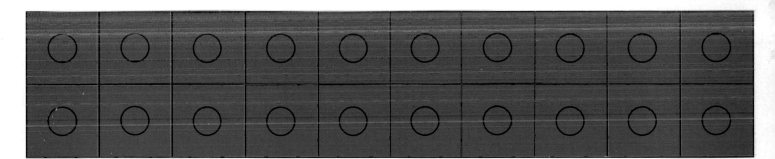

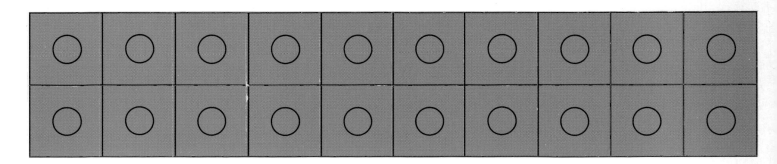

Connecting Cubes

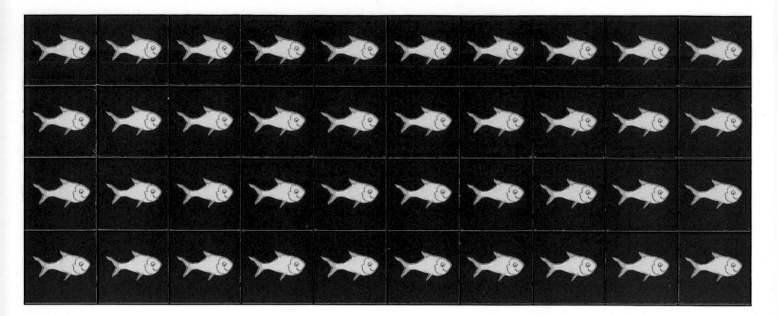

Story Counters

0	1	2	3
4	5	6	7
8	9	10	11
12	13	14	15
16	17	18	19
20	+	+	=
−	<	>	0

Number Cards

Number Cards

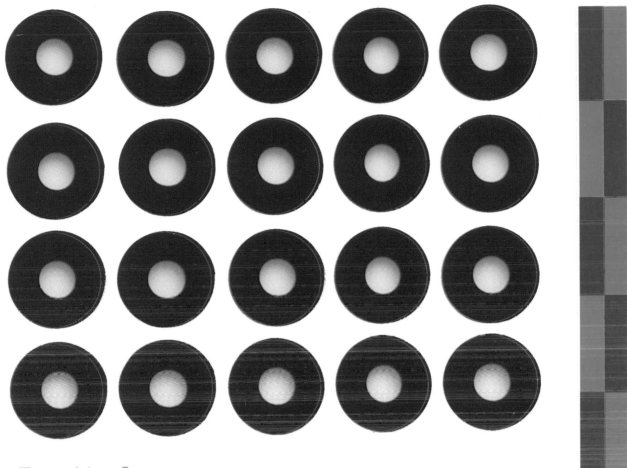

Two-sided Counters

Inch Units

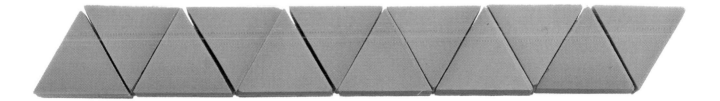

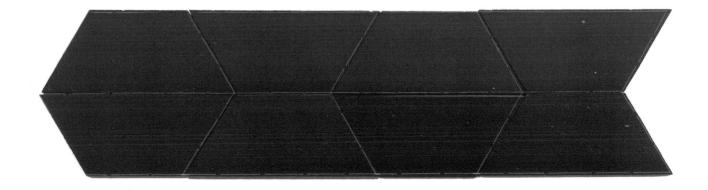

Pattern Blocks

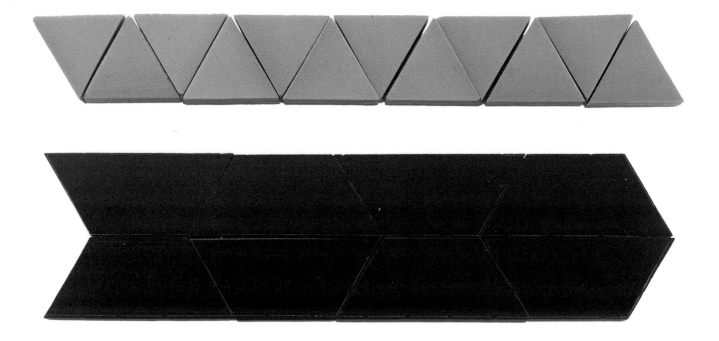

Inch Units

Two-sided Counters

Pattern Blocks

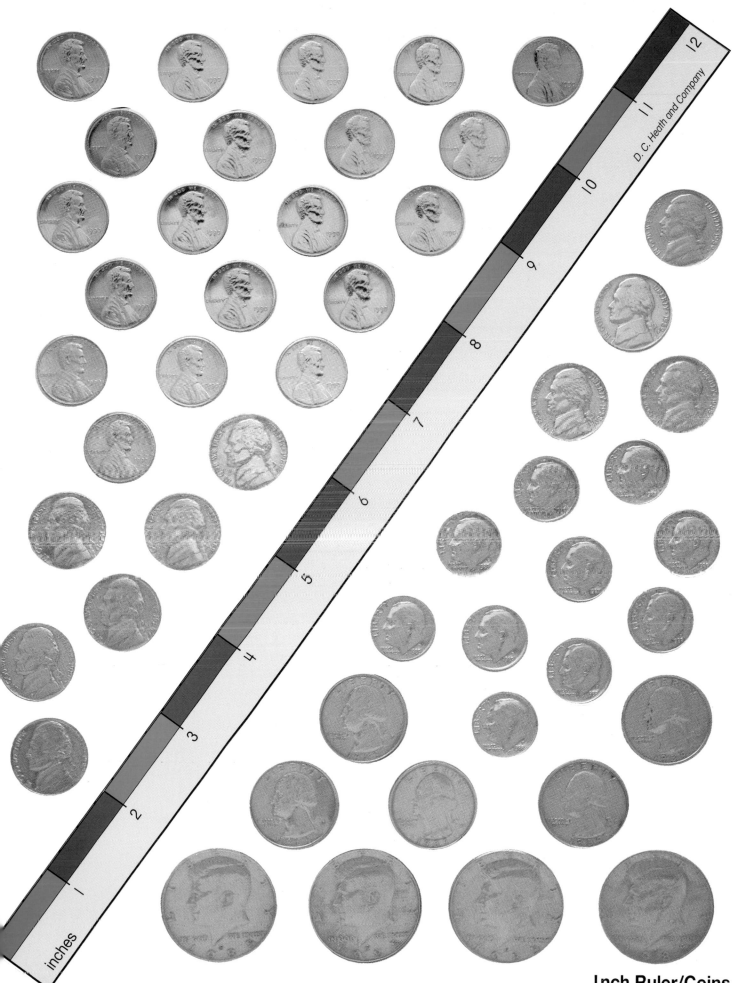

Inch Ruler/Coins

D. C. Heath and Company

inches

Centimeter/Decimeter Ruler/Coins

tens

ones

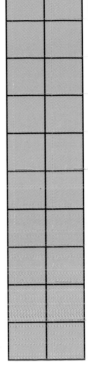

tens

ones

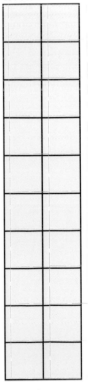

Tens and Ones

Tens and Ones

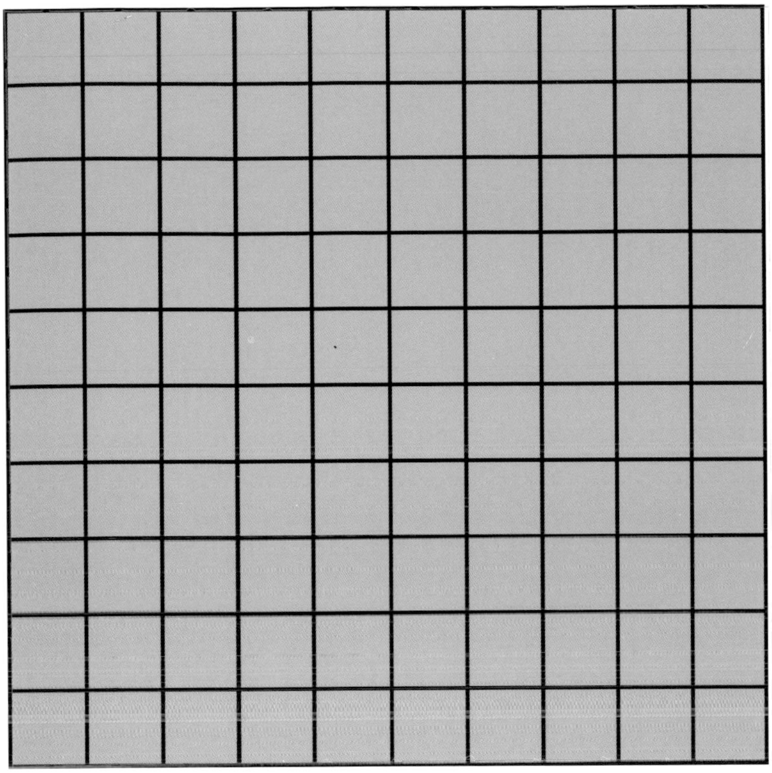

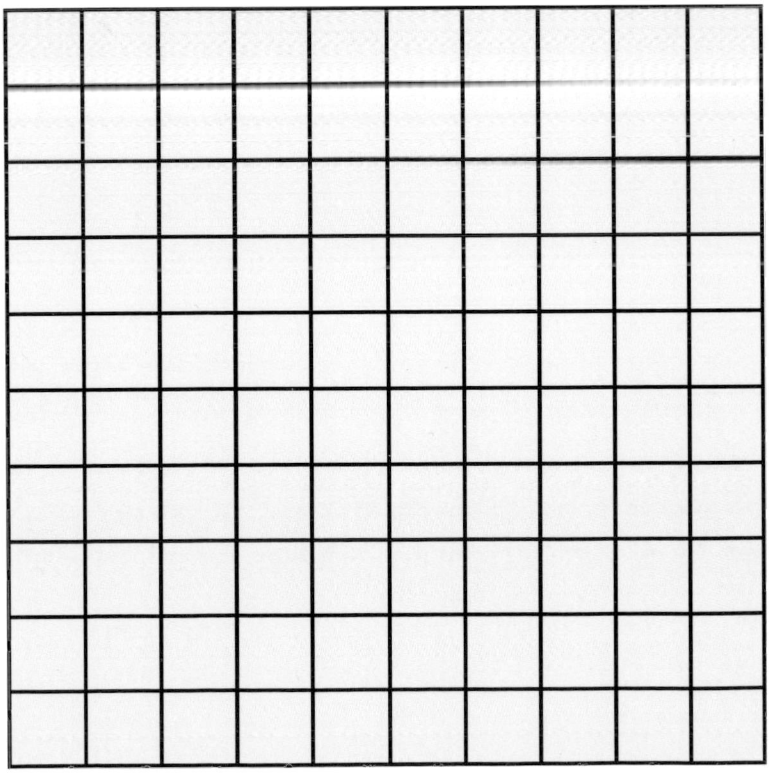

Hundreds

One Dollar Bills

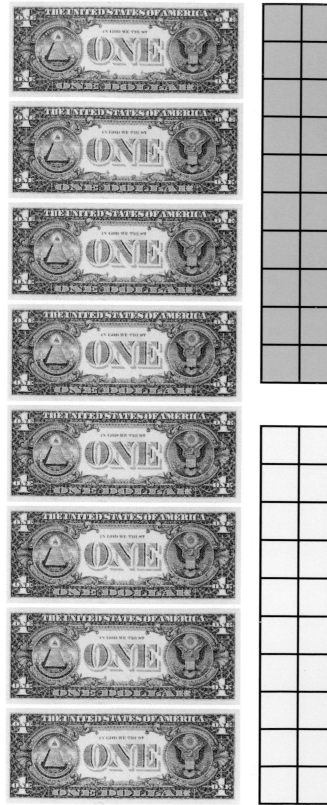

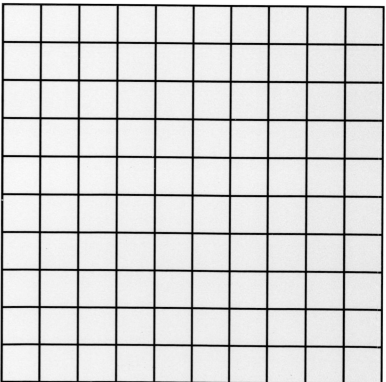

One Dollar Bills

Hundreds

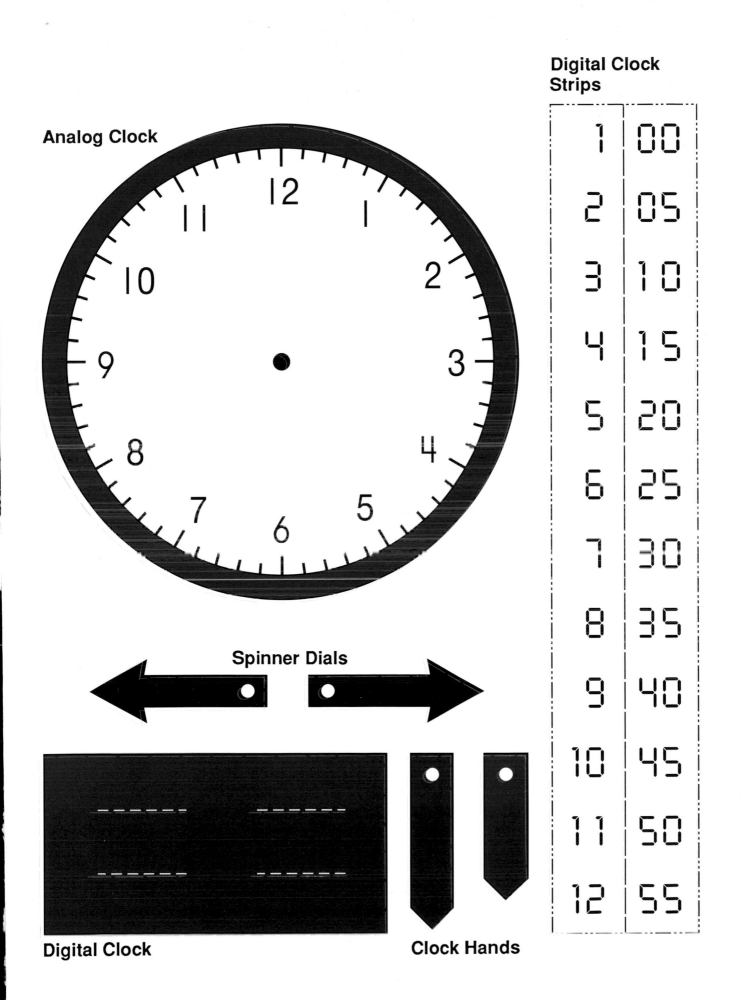

Analog Clock

Digital Clock Strips

1	00
2	05
3	10
4	15
5	20
6	25
7	30
8	35
9	40
10	45
11	50
12	55

Spinner Dials

Digital Clock

Clock Hands

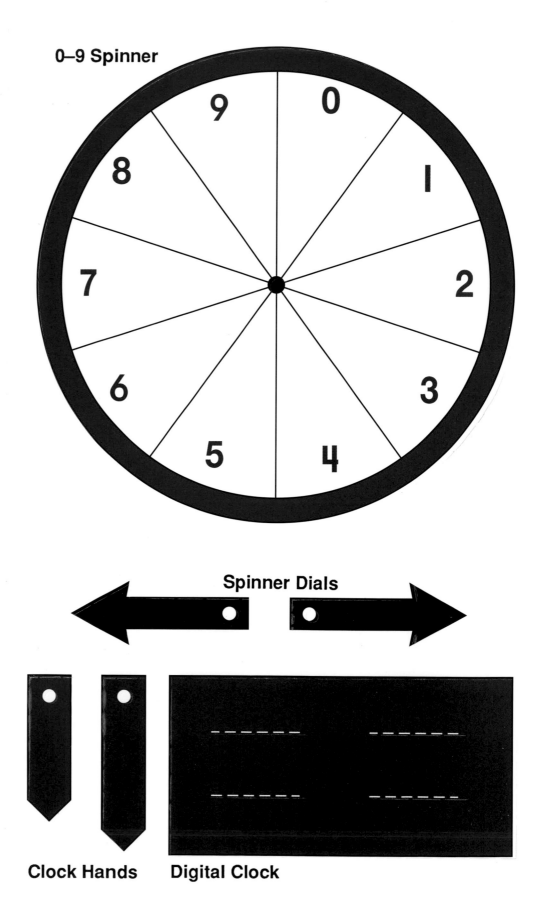

Attribute blocks

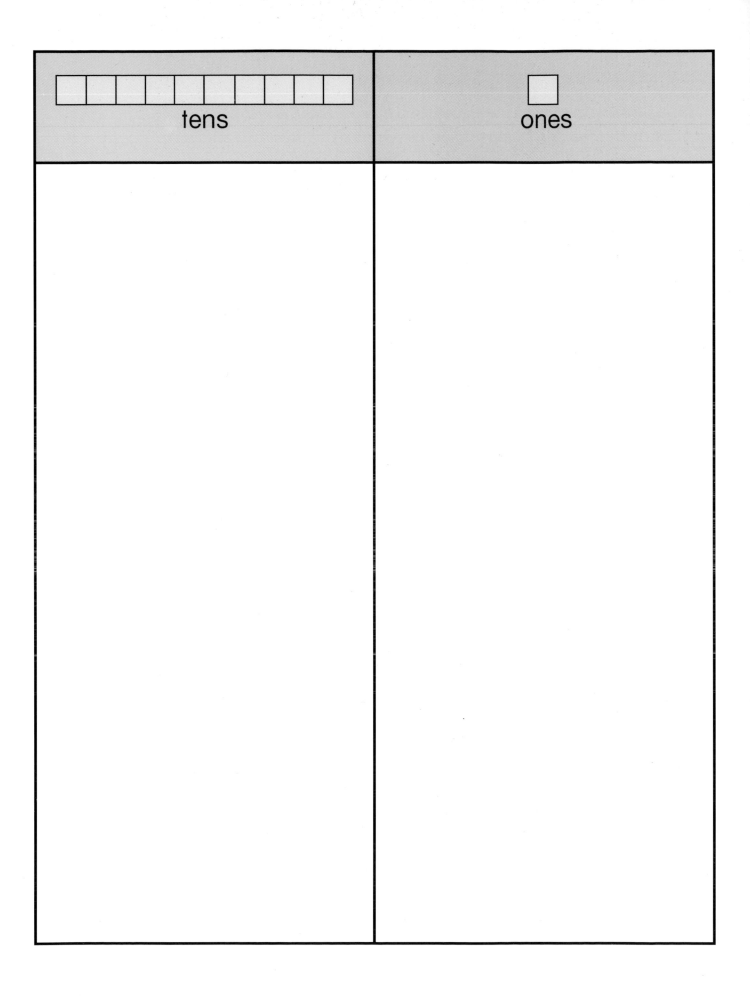

tens	ones

Tens and Ones Workmat

Ten Frame Workmat

Money Workmat

Story Workmat